SHEFFIELD WEDNESDAY FC

THE OFFICIAL HISTORY

JASON DICKINSON

AMBERLEY

First published 2017
This edition published 2018

Amberley Publishing
The Hill, Stroud
Gloucestershire, GL5 4EP

www.amberley-books.com

British Library Cataloguing in Publication Data.
A catalogue record for this book is available from the British Library.

ISBN 978 1 4456 8904 3 (paperback)
ISBN 978 1 4456 1971 2 (ebook)

Origination by Amberley Publishing.
Printed in the UK.

Contents

About the Author

Born in Sheffield in 1969, Jason was first taken to Hillsborough at the age of ten by his father, Ken, the 1979 Boxing Day massacre game against Sheffield United being his first memory. This started an affinity with the club that resulted in frequent visits to Hillsborough until the purchase of his first Kop season ticket for the 1986/87 season, and he is still sat on the Kop today, next to fellow Owls historian Mick Grayson. Back in 1997 came the first purchase of an away season ticket and after initially travelling on the club's ICO coaches, he now shares driving duties with fellow diehards Pete, Stuart and Roger, having missed only a handful of competitive games, home and away, in the last twenty years.

His interest with the history of Sheffield Wednesday was sparked through a rapidly expanding collection of matchday programmes and the first of countless visits to Sheffield City Library were undertaken, to fill the gaps in the programmes' statistics. As his knowledge increased it was co-opted onto the club's programme team in 1994 and he continues to write for the club's official journal to this day. Plans for a post-war 'who's who' on Sheffield Wednesday were first mooted in the late 1990s but it would be many years before that project came to fruition. In 1999 Jason was approached to write *100 Years at Hillsborough*. This 400-page hardback book, published by Hallamshire Press, hit the bookshelves in November 1999 and Jason then took a much-needed breather after managing to write the complete book inside a six-month period.

After several years of research, December 2005 saw the publication of a real labour of love – *Wednesday Boys: A Definitive Who's Who of Sheffield Wednesday 1880–2005*. Co-written with John Brodie, the book featured all 859 players (the figure is now 1,048!) to have appeared for the club at that point in their history, and is without doubt one of the most comprehensive 'who's who' books to have been published on a English league side. Next for Jason was a third book on the Owls plus a non-football publication, as late in 2009 saw *Sheffield Wednesday: On*

This Day and *The Random Book of Christopher* hit the bookshelves, and a year later came *The Sheffield Wednesday Miscellany*. A second collaboration with John Brodie saw the publication of *Sheffield Wednesday: The Complete Record* in 2011 with the extensive book on the club stretching to a mammoth 672 pages. An association with Amberley Publishing then led to the publication of *Sheffield Wednesday: A Pictorial History* in 2014 followed a year later by another labour of love as in *The Origins of Sheffield Wednesday* the history of the cricket club and pre-league football club was covered in greater detail than ever before.

Married to wife Michelle, Jason works as an accountant in the Sheffield suburb of Chapeltown and lives in nearby High Green, with stepchildren Heather and Rick regular visitors along with grandkids Maddi, Sam, Harry and Archie, and not forgetting Australia-residing stepdaughter Kayleigh and her new arrival Dawson. An active member of local environmental group Friends of Charlton Brook, Jason has a great love of nature and wildlife and he loves to travel, the archetypical North American road trip being a particular favourite. The occasional pub quiz night out with friends and all kinds of indie music – from local boys Arctic Monkeys to Of Monsters and Men and from Manic Street Preachers to Kasabian – ensure football doesn't dominate totally.

Acknowledgements

Firstly, thanks must go to Alan Murphy, Kevin Paul and Jenny Stephens at Amberley Publishing, who have ensured the project ran smoothly and helped tremendously with the various stages of producing the finished books. Also thanks are due to Trevor Braithwait and Liam Bashforth at Sheffield Wednesday, while keen census expert Alan Alcott has again been invaluable, providing countless nuggets of new information about the club's players. Also, thanks to Neville Wright (Wednesday Cricket Club) for his assistance with the history of the original cricket club.

The local studies department of the Sheffield Central Library have also played a pivotal role over the last two decades, their source records being an invaluable tool to research the club's fascinating history. Finally, I must thank my wife Michelle, who has spent countless nights in front of the television while I beavered away upstairs in my little office. With regard to the companion volume to this work, I must thank all of the supporters who I interviewed for the fans book and I hope they enjoy the finished article. It's was a pleasure hearing all of the various tales and I hope to have captured some of those stories fittingly.

Jason Dickinson,
August 2017

Chapter 1

It All Started with Cricket
1820–67

'Wednesday, those staunch and almost only supporters of the manly and truly English game of cricket in this town.'
Sheffield Telegraph, May 1840

Without the traditional English summer game of cricket there would certainly not have been Sheffield Wednesday Football Club today. It is now almost 200 years since six 'little mesters' – a Victorian term for 'master or owner' – came together to form Wednesday Cricket Club as the sport started to become popular in the increasingly industrialised and rapidly expanding town of Sheffield. The men in question – to whom all Owls fans of today should be eternally grateful – were William Woolhouse, George Hardesty, William Stratford, Thomas Lindley, George Dawson and John Southern. The club was formed against a background of great social and economic change, with cricket seen by the 'great and good' of Victorian society as a vehicle to move the populist away from old-fashioned, and somewhat barbaric, sports such as dogfighting, bear-baiting and cockfighting. It was seen as such a positive example to the common man that players were even paid by the ruling classes to perform on the green spaces of villages and towns. The fact that these gentlemen were in fact professional sportsmen does not sit easily when you consider the controversy and sheer furore that treated the 'illegal' payment of football players in the 1880s, the criticism no doubt emanating from the same families that paid those early cricket entertainers! Those double standards were also perhaps shown in those early days of cricket, in Sheffield and all over England, as the vast majority of matches played tended to involve a wager of some description, again a practice that was frowned upon by Victorian society many years later, with many 'moral guardians' expressing the opinion that 'filthy lucre' would corrupt the sport of association football. Back in those fledgling cricket days, when there were only four balls per over, matches were played under two distinct formats. The most popular in Sheffield in the early part of the nineteenth century was single-wicket matches where two players, supported by the same fielding and bowling side, tried to simply score as many runs in their two innings before being dismissed. The alternative format, and one more recognisable to modern eyes, was where two sides came together in handicap, sweepstake or challenge matches. Handicap matches involved two teams subscribing to a pool and a joint committee then deciding on their relative merits before adjusting the number of players to compensate – sometimes eleven could be pitted against twelve or thirteen. Sweepstake games would involve several different teams of equal number competing in a knockout tournament with the winning team – clubs tended to put £10–£15 in the pot – sharing what could be quite a considerable bounty. Challenge matches were simply games where money was thrown into the proverbial pot and it was simply 'winner takes all' in a standard 11 versus 11 encounter.

The game of cricket had first been reported in Sheffield in 1802 and it was noted in October 1805 that Hallam beat Stannington by an innings and fifty-two notches – in those days when a run was scored a notch was made in a piece of wood, with cricket followers quite conspicuous to the general public as they could be seen walking to grounds carrying pieces of wood. In the first two decades of the early 1800s, several clubs formed in and around Sheffield with the Monday and Friday clubs all joining the burgeoning cricket scene in the town. Some of the new clubs were named after different days of the week as these corresponded with the half-day holidays that prevailed in specific trades, usually because the vast majority of workers had to work a full day on Saturday. Therefore, when the six men founded Wednesday Cricket Club, they simply decided to call their new side after the half day in their sector – all but one worked in manufacturing – when they could indulge in their new pastime. It is a mistake to say that Wednesday CC only played matches on that day of the week as the club also played on a Saturday; again this is believed to be because the personnel of most cricket sides at the time were employers and not employees, allowing much more flexibility with regard to Saturday working. Unfortunately for historians, the game of cricket was still treated as somewhat of a curiosity in the newspapers of the early nineteenth century, with the actual concept of sports reporting quite some time away. Even if a local scribe wanted to fully cover the cricket scene he was severely limited with regard to space, and this perhaps is a reason why it has proven impossible to find any contemporary evidence to back up Wednesday's formation date of 1820. However, when Wednesday Cricket Club held its Annual General Meeting in 1876, the elected officers informed the members that they were attending the fifty-sixth such meeting, giving some credibility to the formation year. A second vital clue lies in the cricket memoirs, published in the press in 1896, of long-term member Lance Morley, which unequivocally confirms 1820 as the year of birth – the personal records of Henry Stratford (son of founder William) also confirmed a Wednesday game was played in

1820, so it would be reasonable to ascertain the oft-published date to be correct. Within a few years of formation, Wednesday became one of the premier clubs in the town and remained so for the vast majority of the nineteenth century, thanks initially to the following six gentlemen:

William Henry Woolhouse: One of the major cricket figures in the town in the 1820s and 1830s – he was considered the 'father' of the sport in Sheffield, and certainly the 'kingpin' of the early days of WCC. Along with his father-in-law George Steer, he was responsible for building Sheffield's first great cricket enclosure, which opened at Darnall in 1822. Born in Sheffield in 1791, he grew up playing the game and matured into a noted left-handed batsman/bowler. He would make seventeen first-class appearances, including an appearance for an England XI and in what is considered to be the first ever match of Yorkshire County Cricket Club, versus Norfolk in 1833. He was running a table knife manufacturing business on Carver Street when the club was formed and he was certainly a 'larger than life' character, standing over 6 feet tall – a considerable height for an nineteenth-century gentleman. Woolhouse was also a major figure in the new £4,000 Hyde Park Cricket Ground, which stood on the hills around where the modern-day Park Hill flats are situated, which was opened in the late 1820s – the Darnall ground had already fallen into disrepair and staged its last first-class game in 1828. Later in his life, William became a publican but his story ended in most unfortunate circumstances as after travelling to London in the hope of finding a remedy for his troublesome spinal condition, he missed his horse coach back and was forced to find lodgings in the capital. He sadly died in the night, aged just forty-six, and was buried in a paupers grave in All Hallowes churchyard, with no epitaph describing him as a pivotal figure in the development of cricket in general and Wednesday Cricket Club in particular.

William Stratford: Another of the main instigators of the club's formation and its first president. The family of William Stratford – who coincidentally was born in the same year as Woolhouse – were linked to Wednesday Cricket Club, and the subsequent football club, for the whole of the nineteenth century. Silver-plater William served as president on at least two separate occasions – filling the role during the 1850s before his passing in 1859 – while his son, Henry, was a member of the cricket section for over fifty years. He took over his father's business and was also elected president of the cricket club in 1887, while two of his sons, Sydney and Charles, became involved in the 1870s – Sydney serving for a time as secretary of the cricket section while also playing, with Charles mainly linked to the football section, helping win the Wharncliffe Cup in 1879 and also appearing in FA Cup football.

George Edward Dawson: A founder member who was born in Sheffield in 1799. He also ran his own business manufacturing razors from his town centre premises, but was also a professional cricketer from 1827 to 1836, mainly playing for Sheffield CC, and is credited with eight first-class games. In addition to his business and playing cricket, it's also believed he ran the Old White Lion public house, on the Wicker, with his wife Ann. He was twice president of Wednesday CC and was still a serving committee member when he passed away, aged only forty-four, in May 1843.

George Hardesty: Born around 1777/78 in Sheffield, George Hardesty was quite a rarity in nineteenth-century England as he lived to a grand old age, passing away in June 1860 in his eighty-fourth year. He was in his mid-forties when he became involved in the formation of Wednesday CC and was running his Rockingham Street manufacturing business, producing solid silver and silver-plated knives and forks. He was a keen cricketer – noted as still playing in 1838 in an over-sixties game – and served as president of Wednesday in the 1820s, remaining on the committee for many years.

Thomas Lindley and John Southern: Unlike the aforementioned four gentlemen, the lives of both Thomas Lindley and John Southern have required educated assumptions, mainly due to a lack of birth and census records. There is, though, a reasonable degree of certainty that Lindley was born in Sheffield around 1795/96 and worked as a fork manufacturer, seemingly remaining a bachelor all his life – a Thomas Lindley spent many years as a lodger with a Brightside family. His name appeared in cricket club records in the 1840s, while it was briefly reported in April 1857 that Lindley had passed away, aged sixty-one, due to chronic bronchitis, although the two lines in the local press did not allude to his famous role in the creation of Wednesday. The sixth and final founder member, John Southern, is without doubt an unknown quantity as the only gentleman of that name known to have been born in the eighteenth century would have been in his mid-sixties, when a Southern was reported playing for Wednesday CC in the 1830s. The only real source has been trade directories published in the 1820s and 1830s, which list a John Southern working from his Norfolk Row office as an 'agent for the highway'. What is known is that he was elected president in 1830 and was noted on the cricket club committee in 1841. Any further details of his life will in all probability remain a mystery.

The first actual mention of the cricket club in the local press came in June 1826 when the Wednesday Club (with the prefix of Darnall) beat the Friday Club in a two-innings encounter at Darnall – founders Dawson and Woolhouse standing as umpires. A few weeks later the Darnall ground hosted arguably its most famous fixture as a Sheffield & Leicester XI faced the County of Nottingham, with Wednesday player Tom Marsden included in the combined team. Marsden was without doubt the most famous cricketer in the north of England at the time, having made his name in the single-wicket format, and became a national sporting celebrity after scoring 227 – only the second ever double hundred recorded in a first-class game, which was more remarkable when you consider that outfields in those far-off days were most unkempt and sometimes it was virtually impossible to the get the ball to the boundary! He spent over eight hours, during three days, at the crease and after grabbing six wickets was immortalised in verse in a thirteen-stanza poem entitled 'Glorious Tom'. Such was his legendary status that in 1831 the local cricket fraternity presented Tom with a 50-ounce silver cup, manufactured by a Sheffield silversmith, to commemorate his deeds – this fine trophy sits today in the Sheffield Town Hall and 'The Tom Marsden Trophy' is competed for annually, in a 20/20 format, by the reformed cricket club and three invited guests. Wednesday would use the Darnall grounds during their early years before switching to the new Hyde Park enclosure in 1830 – the new ground was so large that ten games of cricket could be played at one time, and it was also a multisport venue with athletics, pony racing, pigeon shooting (not the clay variety) and wrestling all enjoyed. The new addition to the Sheffield sporting scene would record many firsts, with the first recognised Yorkshire CC game being held there in September 1833 and the first Yorkshire versus Lancashire county game in July 1849.

The move to a new ground was no doubt linked to the fact that Woolhouse was now the proprietor of the Hyde Park enclosure, while one of the first games played by Wednesday saw them charge threepence for a game against 'Eleven of the County of York' in October 1830 – at the time the cricket season generally ran from early May to late October with the absence of any other major sport to shoehorn cricket into the summer months. In 1831 the club started to hold regular fortnightly practice sessions while the summer saw a defeat to another 'day of the week' club, the Thursday CC. As the decade progressed, Wednesday ventured further afield, playing against a newly formed Hull team and an XI from Chesterfield. Founding father Dawson appeared in defeat to a Derbyshire team in 1837 while the return game was somewhat controversial as after some dubious decisions from the match umpire, spectators flooded onto the square to protest and the game was suspended. By the time the match was ready to restart, the visiting team, except for two players, had taken their leave and had walked into town. Despite being found by Marsden, they refused to return and Wednesday subsequently claimed the stake money as they led on the first innings.

Incidentally, between the 1820s and 1840s, Sheffield was also home, in the winter months, to the phenomena that was 'cricket on ice'. It was first reported upon in 1826 and perhaps the most notable game came in February 1841 when players, wearing ice skates, competed on a frozen surface at Little London Dam, Heeley. The game duly passed into Sheffield folklore as popular Wednesday player Henry Sampson scored 162 (thought to be the highest ever recorded total in this rather unique format of the game) before fading light put an end to proceedings and all those involved retired to the Union Inn – unsurprisingly owned by another Wednesday man, serving president Henry Bolsover. The diminutive star of the show, Sampson, was a pivotal figure in the history of Sheffield cricket as after he became landlord of the Adelphi Hotel in 1848 it became the hub of cricket activities in the town, with the Wednesday player hosting his club's Annual General Meeting from the 1850s onwards and, notably in 1867, the meeting when Wednesday FC was formed. He was an outstanding player in his own right, playing professionally and also enjoying much success in the single-wicket format, before retiring from his famous public house in 1868 and passing away in March 1885.

In the standard form of the game, Wednesday continued to earn plaudits as the best club in the town with minute books having survived from the mid-nineteenth century showing how stringently officials looked after the club's affairs – entries included a fine for a player who left a ball on the pitch, a ruling that any player late for a 9.30 a.m. start would be fined a shilling and that ball boys (given the grand title of ground staff) received 2s for their labours, although they received just half of their monies if they arrived after 2 p.m. The 1840s saw several players of great distinction appear, including a gentlemen called Thomas Hunt, who was a professional cricketer for fourteen years and it is believed scored the highest ever total in the single-wicket form of the game – 165 against George Chatterton in 1843. He was an outstanding batsman but he came to a gory end when in September 1858 he took the fatal decision to cross the train tracks to catch his train back to his Manchester home. Tragically he became trapped and had both of his legs severed at the calves and a hand shattered as the train literally ran over him. He died a few minutes later. While Hunt had played for Wednesday as his career progressed, another debutant in the decade was Richard Gillott, who would play and be connected to the club for virtually all of his life, first being noted in his late teenage years. He was only in his mid-twenties when he was elected club president in 1848 – he also served in that role in the 1850s and 1860s – and the file grinder by trade constantly topped the batting averages at Wednesday, serving for over three decades.

A controversial game at Dalton Magna CC in June 1842 saw the Wednesday officials accuse the hosts of 'violating the principles of honour, equality and truth' after they disputed a decision from the umpire and refused to continue, being reduced to 14-4, chasing just 63. More importantly, despite the umpire awarding the match to the away club, Dalton refused to pay over the stake money! Later in the year, Wednesday played at Chatsworth and often in those far-off days away trips became an enjoyable social gathering, with cricket just one facet of time taken away from the increasingly polluted town of Sheffield – trips to Balbrough and then regular games against Glossop continued to provide some clean air into the lungs of the good people of Sheffield. In fact, throughout the fledgling cricket team's early years the members never missed a chance to socialise – for many, many years the opening practice game of every summer was followed by a grand dinner with singing, drinking and eating usually stretching into the early hours. Almost twenty-five years after the club's formation, matches were still played on a Wednesday at Hyde Park with the cricketers paying a £12 annual rent for exclusive use on that day – they were also allowed to freely practice on any other day and all members allowed free admission to any games held there. Wednesday would remain at Hyde Park until the mid-1850s while an 1846 representative game at the ground provided a rare insight into the matchday experience for spectators, with an inn inside the ground crammed to the rafters and booths selling cuts of beef and ham. In addition, other vendors offered glasses of porter beer from barrels; in fact watching cricket in those days seemed to involve lots of drinking and eating and it would perhaps be fair to suggest this hasn't changed all these years later!

During the 1850s it is believed that Wednesday actually paid professional player John Berry to wear their colour, although it was by no means an exclusive deal as the Huddersfield-born all-rounder appeared for a variety of clubs before taking up a permanent contract at Accrington Cricket Club. The major talking point, however, of the early part of the 1850s was the steady decline of the Hyde Park enclosure with many in the local cricketing fraternity discussing what could be done to rectify the matter. The outcome of that concern was a public meeting held in January 1854 at the Adelphi Hotel, which proposed the construction of a completely new ground on land owned by the Duke of Norfolk, near to Bramall Lane. Wednesday and all the other major clubs in the town were in attendance and heard from local cricketer Michael Ellison (who later founded Yorkshire County Cricket Club) that the 9-acre plot could be secured on a ninety-nine-year lease, at £5 rent per annum, with the caveat that it could only be used for sporting activities. The idea was accepted after the recommendation of Wednesday president William Stratford, who publicly stated that cricketers had 'nothing to fear' and that the Wednesday club had 'grown tired of suffering the inconvenience of playing first rate matches on grounds totally unsuited to the display of cricket talent'. The Sheffield United Cricket and Bowling Club was formed to oversee the development of the new enclosure and a share subscription opened, all of the major club's in the town taking a stake, in addition to individuals like Wednesday cricketer Richard Gillott, who was top scorer on the day. The new ground was opened on 30 April 1855. The opening day saw the six clubs that had negotiated to use Bramall Lane – Wednesday, Sheffield, Shrewsbury, Milton, Caxton and Broomhall – pick two representative teams, and when the enclosure was completed, it was hailed as inferior to none in England. Wednesday's first game at the new ground, played of course on a Wednesday, came on 9 May 1855 when they also fielded two sides from within the club's membership, the Henry Sampson XI taking the honours. Another club outing, this time to Baslow in August 1855, saw around sixty members enjoy a sunny day in the countryside, although the following summer was a bit of a washout with Wednesday only playing a handful of games. Away from the sporting arena the introduction of new working practices in the early 1850s meant that most employees now ended their working week at 2 p.m. on a

Saturday. Suddenly the populous had additional leisure time and it would prove a catalyst for a new sport, which took its first official breath in the town in 1857 – association football. For the time being the new pastime was of little interest to Wednesday members and they continued playing regularly throughout the summer – it was stated that the officials believed the Wednesday Club to be the oldest provincial club in England, second only maybe to the famous Marylebone Cricket Club (MCC), although the fact that Sheffield's own Hallam Cricket Club was formed earlier seemed to have slipped their minds! As the 1850s progressed the club went from strength to strength with membership almost trebling in 1857 and several members generously paying double their subscriptions so matches could be played further afield. Star performer of the period was local lad William Slinn, who is acknowledged as one of the best fast bowlers of his generation, taking 111 wickets in only nineteen first-class games. He was also a regular for Yorkshire CCC but remained loyal to Wednesday all his career, serving on the committee during the 1850s and appearing in that first game at Bramall Lane. For most of his life he was a professional cricketer and was held in such high regard in the town that his friends and admirers organised a top-class representative game for his benefit in 1863.

As Wednesday entered a new decade the membership numbers continued to grow and the club offered five splendid trophies for such seasonal achievements as best batter and bowler, for both the first and second eleven teams. An economic downturn in Sheffield trade then resulted in a fall in memberships, but Wednesday continued to play games near and far, paying maiden visits to Elsecar, Alfreton and Scarborough. In 1862 Wednesday won a game at Bramall Lane in most fortunate circumstances as the two-wicket win was only achieved because the umpire's watch was a tad slow, as at the correct finish time the match would have ended in a draw! The following year was significant as not only did Michael Ellison form Yorkshire CCC but Wednesday elected Benjamin Chatterton as their new club president, while Thomas Anderson took over as club secretary – four years later both men would play a role in the formation of a new sporting section...

By the mid-1860s the club was booming again and membership numbers were such that Wednesday announced that they had agreed to take two wickets at Bramall Lane on a Wednesday and Saturday, with seasonal subs set at 12s 6d. The club ran three teams for the 1866 season and such was their dominance of the local cricketing scene that they won nine games in a row – a rare feat in any form of sport. The club's fine reputation in Sheffield directly led to a problem: the membership was significant and those subscribers enjoyed both the sporting and social aspect of cricket to such an extent that it is was unfortunate that the season was limited to a few short months. It was at that point that the committee took the momentous decision to form a new section of the Cricket Club. Wednesday Football Club was about to be born.

Chapter 2

Early Years of Wednesday Football Club

Sheffield Wednesday Cricket Club and Football Club

> At a general meeting held on Wednesday last, at the Adelphi Hotel, it was decided to form a football club in connection with the above influential cricket club, with the object of keeping together during the winter season the members of the cricket club. From the great unanimity which prevailed as to the desirability of forming the club, there is every reason to expect that it will take first rank. The office bearers were elected as follows: President, Mr. B. Chatterton; vice-president and treasurer, Mr. F. S. Chambers; hon. secretary, Mr. Jno. Marsh; assistant, Mr. Castleton; Committee: Messers Jno. Rodgers, Jno. Pashley, Wm. Pilch, Wm. Littlehales, Jno. White, C. Stokes, H. Bocking. Above sixty members were enrolled, without any canvas, some of them being the best players of the town.
>
> *Sheffield and Rotherham Independent,*
> Friday 6 September 1867

The above announcement began the next chapter in Wednesday's history as the members of the cricket club agreed a motion to start a football section. The relatively new sport of association football was already starting to make inroads into the town's sporting scene, having first began on an organised basis in 1857 when the world's oldest football club, Sheffield FC, was founded. They were followed by Hallam FC in 1860, who, like Wednesday, were a cricket club that formed a football section, while teams such as Milton, Pitsmoor, Norton, Norfolk and Collegiate were now playing regularly in the town; interest was such that in March 1867 the Sheffield Football Association was formed. The medieval game of football had been played for centuries around the globe in such destinations as China, Greece and Italy, while a 'mob' version was recorded in England as far back as the fifteenth century, with towns and villages involved in games that could take days to complete. It was not until the 1840s that a new regulated version of association football emerged from the public schools of England and this quickly spread countrywide as the various scholars, responsible for formulating those early rules, returned to their hometowns after completing their studies. The game was recorded in Sheffield in the 1830s, 1840s and 1850s but actually it was two Acts of Parliament that provided the biggest boost to the sport – the Factory Acts of 1847 and 1850, which increased the hours of work but put in place regular working patterns and, crucially for football, ensured that work ceased on a Saturday no later than 2 p.m. With Saturday afternoons now at their disposal, the workers started to explore leisure pursuits and the arrival of the exciting game of football quickly captured the imagination – within two decades it grew from just the universities to almost every town and village in England. The new game was fast, exciting, highly competitive, easy to play and involved passion and rivalry that would quickly divide loyalties in work places, public houses, clubs and even families; football was here to stay and quickly became the national sport of England. The town of Sheffield was also expanding rapidly and Victorian society placed great emphasis on fitness, sport and well-being, duly promoting football as a way of achieving all three. Of course, today's product bears little resemblance to those early years with games being played between teams ranging from 11 to 15 a side, hacking, tripping and handling of the ball were all allowed, and the shape of the ball more similar to the modern rugby ball. There were also no formations to speak of with most of the players running around the field following the ball – like you would expect to see in primary school playgrounds today – with injuries commonplace. The only constant was a gentleman guarding the goal and two men who just hung around their opponents' goal in the hope of forcing the ball in – such niceties as throws ins, crossbars, team strips and penalty areas were still years away. Players would often dash straight from their place of employment and play in their work clothes with one side tying handkerchiefs around their arms to distinguish themselves from their opponents. It should also be noted that despite rules being introduced into the game, there was in fact two differing sets, with 'Sheffield Rules' played in the north of England and 'Cambridge Rules' in the south – one difference being the 'rouge' rule, which was introduced by Sheffield in 1861, where drawn games were settled if the ball was put between two rouge posts, which were placed 4 yards either side of the goalposts, which were reduced in width from 8 yards down to 4, and touched down. The rule was borrowed from Eton College but was dropped in 1868, although a version of the rule exists today in Aussie Rules Football. At the end of the 1876/77 season one unified set of rules was adapted by all, and these have remained ever since, with several notable adaptions and additions.

It was against these social, economic and lifestyle changes that the members of Wednesday Cricket Club took the momentous decision, on Wednesday 4 September 1867, of Ben Chatterton becoming the club's first president and John Marsh its secretary and playing captain. While Chatterton was only briefly involved, Marsh became arguably the club's most important 'founding father', leading Wednesday to early success and remaining a mainstay of the team for several seasons. Born around 1843 in Thurlstone, Marsh moved to Sheffield to become an engraver and subsequently became involved with Wednesday Cricket Club, playing regularly during the 1860s, as well as serving on the committee. He later served as secretary but is best known for his seven years at Wednesday FC, leading the club in all their early skirmishes and captaining them to their first trophy. He was known as a fearsome competitor – opponents certainly knew they had been in a game when facing Marsh – and he was a pivotal figure for that fledgling football section. It was a gentleman called John Pashley who rose from his seat to propose that a football section be formed and the brewery traveller – who worked for the Broomspring Lane Brewery Co. – served one season on the football club committee before leaving to concentrate on playing and watching both sports. Just over a month after that Adelphi meeting, Wednesday FC held an inter-club practice match at Highfields and a week later, on 19 October 1867, they played their first game against an another club, winning by three goals and four rouges to a single rouge registered by their opponents, United Mechanics, at Norfolk Park. Games against Milton, Heeley and Dronfield duly took place before Wednesday – sporting their adopted blue and white colours – were invited to compete for the Cromwell Cup, a competition for any clubs aged two years or under. The cup took its name from the manager of the Theatre Royal, Oliver Cromwell, who was linked to one of the competitors, Garrick Club, and had donated the fine trophy for competition. Thanks to information that has only recently be found, it is now known that fourteen players represented Wednesday in their semi-final tie against Exchange, played at the home of the MacKenzie Club, Myrtle Road, on the first Saturday of February 1868:

Marsh, Pring, Whelan, Gillott, Jackson, Wood, Stokes, T. Jenkinson, J. Jenkinson, Goodwin, Broomhead, Hepworth, Wright and Bowler

Included in that team was captain Marsh, the Jenkinson brothers and Charles Stokes, a Sheffield dentist who was not only a founder member of Wednesday FC but was also responsible for the formation of Sheffield United. The conditions on the day were far from ideal with the pitch sodden from overnight rain and a fierce wind causing havoc in the town. Wednesday's opponents went into the game a man short while the blue and whites were at full strength, captained by Marsh. After winning the toss of the coin, Wednesday chose the upper pitch at Myrtle Road and they dominated the first half, helped further when Exchange lost a player to injury. This seemed to dishearten his side and Wednesday won by four goals and two rouges to nil – Gillott 2, J. Jenkinson and Wood scoring – to set up a final against the Garrick Club at Bramall Lane Cricket Ground. Below is the full match report of Wednesday's first cup success, over 149 years ago:

THE CROMWELL CUP – The final match for the above prize was played at Bramall Lane on Saturday. The day, though cold, was very fine for the contest, and upwards of four hundred assembled to witness it. The cup is given by Mr. O. Cromwell, who has now been an established favourite at the Theatre Royal for years, and will be presented to the winning club at the Theatre on the occasion of his benefit. The prize was given to be contended by the four junior clubs in the town, and in drawing for the first event the Wednesday were pitted against the Exchange on the first Saturday of February, which will long be a memorable day, as the one in which rude Boreas took great liberties with chimney pots, slates, tiles and signboards, as the writer has good cause to remember, being in imminent peril from a falling signboard of large dimensions in Waingate. With or against the wind, it mattered not, the Wednesday club scored at both ends. On the following Saturday the contest Garrick v Wellington, came off, and after a severe struggle the Garrick scored a rouge to nothing. This was consequently the struggle for the prize and it was thought by some that Garrick, comprising as it did seven of the best of Hallam, would 'smother' the Wednesday club. A few who felt so certain speculated a trifle of specie [coins] at the rate of three to two. The game began in earnest about three o'clock. Dame Fortune gave the Garrick the wind. Very soon they had the ball down at the low end, and someone sent it direct to the Wednesday's goal. The goal-keeper showed bad judgement by kicking at the ball instead of simply stopping it. He missed his kick, and unfortunately for Garrick it hit the goalpost and rebounded. They played until half-time without scoring, and then reversing the ends, the Wednesday Club had the advantage of the wind. Both sides now went at it with great pluck and determination, and the ball was alternatively at each goal. When time was called neither side had scored. They then agreed to play on, the first score to decide the match. In tossing for choice of goals the Wednesday Club were more fortunate and this time had the wind. The fray recommenced with double vigour. The sides were well balanced, and all went at it ding-dong. J. Marsh, the Wednesday captain, kept putting in his toe with the precision, celerity, and force for which he is so well known. Messers. Denton and Whelan also played well. Jenkinson and Broomhead worked like a pair of horses but what pleased us most was to see A. Wood, a little, slim, diminutive youth, vigorously attack and upset the 'Giant Shang' amidst the applause of the spectators. On the other side Harry Ash particularly distinguished himself by his celerity and good play. J. Donovan also worked extremely hard and frequently got the ball from his opponent but never made any good use of it afterwards, his kicks evidently lacking steam. Not so Shang; when he got to her she had to travel, and a very long way too. Messers. J. Dale and

C. Lee also did good service for the Garrick Club. After playing about ten minutes the Wednesday Club got the ball to the low end, and one of the other side, in making a kick, got too much under. The ball went up almost perpendicularly and in dropping cannoned off someone through the goal. The Wednesday men and their friends, who had assembled in great force, gave vent to their voices, and we have not heard such a shout since the memorable County match v Surrey so unexpectedly won. Some excellent play was shown on both sides but certainly the Garrick showed the most activity and as a whole we think were slightly the better players. A few of the Wednesday men were well adapted for charging, but a trifle slow. This butting we would have done away with, as it gives the heavy man an undue advantage over the slender, unless the latter has corresponding quickness to compensate. Altogether the match was tolerably free from the unpleasant wrangling which too frequently occurs in football contests. Wednesday: J. Marsh, J. Denton, J. Jenkinson, C. Stokes, A. Wood, R. Gillott, S. Wright, J. Whelan, W. Jackson, T. Goodwin, J. Broomhead, W. Hepworth, W. Wright, J. Pashley

On the evening of 16 March 1868, Marsh received the trophy from Cromwell at his theatre, and the success meant the football section had enjoyed a glorious first season, with membership having grown so rapidly that Wednesday even ran a second team in that debut campaign – it was perhaps not a surprise, considering the standing and popularity of Wednesday Cricket Club, that Wednesday FC made such a 'big splash' in that first campaign. The popularity of Wednesday Club as a whole was also cemented when the club ran their first 'Athletics Sports Day' at Bramall Lane Cricket Ground. Such events were popular in towns across England and around 2,000 attended the day to see such events as the 120-yards dash, the 300-yards steeplechase, a 1-mile walk and even a sack race. This annual event grew into the biggest and most popular in Sheffield, earning the club much needed additional income, and was held for almost twenty years.

During the remainder of the decade, Wednesday evolved from a football club run by cricketers to a football team run by players and spectators of the new game. Most of those 'founding fathers' left the committee in the summer of 1868 to concentrate their leisure time on their first love – cricket. Wednesday FC held its first Annual General Meeting at the Adelphi Hotel – now ran by new committee member Ralph Armfield – although a complete lack of football coverage in the local press meant that no results have survived from that second season. Despite the rapid growth of the game, the town of Sheffield was not overly endowed with football clubs during the first few seasons of Wednesday's existence, exemplified in the 1869/70 campaign when eighteen games were arranged but against only five clubs – for an unknown reason, Wednesday did not face either Sheffield or Hallam for many years. The names of William and Charles Clegg started to appear around this time while a regular on the scoresheet for Wednesday was William Littlehales, a pivotal individual who served on the club's committee for several years before taking over as honorary secretary in 1874, serving until ill health caused his resignation in 1883. It was also common in the 1870s for players to literally switch sides on a weekly basis, due to all being strictly amateur, with the concept of being 'cup-tied' not being introduced until later in the decade. Until that time, Wednesday played a staple diet of friendly games, although as the decade progressed the club did start to venture outside of the town, visiting such exotic destinations as Chesterfield and Derby. Regulars at the time included 'little' Frank Butler, 'Barnsley Tom' Cawthorn and committeemen John Hollingsworth and George Sampson – the latter being the son of Henry, who was a player and supporter of the cricket club for over forty years. Wednesday even introduced third team fixtures at the start of the 1870/71 season while at first team level only one solitary defeat was recorded, Wednesday winning six consecutive games without conceding a goal during the campaign. New club president Henry Hawksley was in the Wednesday side for the 4-0 win at Derby in January 1871, with the travelling party not arriving back until the early hours – those first few years of football were often more a social event than a sporting one and it was only in 1872 that the post-match practice of the winners drinking a gallon of beer and the losers half as much ended. Player of the season, George Sampson, was described by a local journalist as a 'veritable giant' while new clubs continued to take their first breath – this was greatly aided by a conscious decision by Victorian society to increase the number of green spaces and public parks, with the Public Parks Act of 1871 having a significant effect on the areas available for the purpose of leisure activities. New opponents for Wednesday included Attercliffe Christ Church, while the scarcity of resources available in those early days was maybe shown in October 1871 when the Myrtle Road game against MacKenzie was abandoned in the first half when the ball burst and neither side was able to source a replacement. The strength of Wednesday was shown in December 1871 when seven club men – Marsh, Sampson, Wood, Carr, Hollingsworth, Charles Clegg and William Clegg – were in the Sheffield FA side that faced London in the first ever representative game.

During the 1872/73 season, Wednesday started to regularly use Bramall Lane, while at the end of the campaign their first goalscoring hero, Bob Gregory, made his debut. The town of Sheffield was also a pioneer when Bramall Lane hosted a charity game in aid of the town's Cherry Tree Orphanage. In fact, Sheffield was hugely influential in the development of association football as several innovations and rules originated in the town, including goalkeepers, corner kicks, corner flags, throw-ins, goal kicks, indirect free-kicks, cup ties, half-time, trophies, neutral referees, cup-tied players, extra-time and even the heading of the ball. The season ended on the first day of March while the following season saw Wednesday recorded as losing only two games, to Rotherham and Broomhall, with some big victories including 5-0 against Exchange Brewery and 6-0 against Derbyshire. The February 1874 game at Shirecliffe Lane against Fir Vale was significant as

William Stacey captained Wednesday for the first time; he had joined the club's committee in 1873 and in the summer officially replaced Marsh in the role after his predecessor moved away from Sheffield to take over the Crystal Palace public house back in the place of his birth. The other change behind the scenes was the appointment of 'dyed in the wool' Wednesdayite Charlie Hill to the role of vice-president. A great enthusiast of both cricket and football, Hill said at the club's 1878 Sports Day dinner that he was 'born, christened and married on a Wednesday' and was a hugely popular figure at all the club's various social gatherings, his droll and outlandish speeches being his forte. He served the cricket section for almost thirty years and spent six years in his new position at the football club. The brother of Stacey, Fred, also joined the club's committee and the siblings would appear regularly over the years, with Fred being Wednesday's first long-term goalkeeper. Older brother William, who was a headmaster at Darnall National School for twenty-five years, was a key figure, both on and off the field, as Wednesday grew to be the dominant club in the town by the late 1870s.

The 1874/75 season opened with a win at Attercliffe while their visit to Thurlstone Crystal Palace in October 1874 saw a reacquaintance with the popular Marsh, who had just formed the new club, and it was fittingly Wednesday who provided their first opposition – a carriage load of Marsh's friends travelled from Midland Station to attend the game, before all parties retired to the Crystal Palace for a 'meat tea' and copious amounts of ale. The season ended in late March but the final game was somewhat farcical as when the teams kicked off, visitors Fir Vale had only five men and when it became apparent that no more were coming to their aid, the game was stopped with a practice match taking place in the remaining time. Meanwhile the club's athletics day was still the best in town with around 5,000 attending the Easter Monday event in 1875, having been charged sixpence for admission and a further sixpence for a place in the enclosure (ladies admission was free). The day included a bicycle race and the usual athletics disciplines with competitors travelling from far and wide to take part, no doubt attracted by the generous prizes on offer thanks to kind donations from Wednesday members and items bought by the club themselves. One competitor of note was local footballer and sprinter Billy Mosforth, who would arguably become Wednesday's greatest player of the pre-league era and one of the best English players of his generation. Nicknamed 'the little wonder', the diminutive Mosforth – he stood only 5 foot 3 inches tall – was an outstanding winger, possessing amazing dribbling ability and a deadly finish. He lit up Sheffield football for over a decade and won the first of nine caps for England at the tender age of nineteen. His first appearance for Wednesday was in 1875 and he would later appear in Sheffield United's first game before a knee injury forced his retirement in the late 1880s. The following season saw several new opponents and these included a first meeting with Nottingham Forest, who were soundly beaten 5-0 away and 9-1 at Bramall Lane in the return match; Francis

'Little Frank' Butler with a hat-trick. Butler was a real Victorian character as he would usually hang around the opposition's goal, idly chatting to his opponent, before battle commenced when the ball came near, Butler usually forcing the ball into the net with his opponent usually going into the goal along with it. The bow-legged Butler was once described as the 'most extraordinary little player and when once seen will never be forgotten'. He played many of his games for the club alongside his younger sibling, Tom. The season was also notable for the first appearance of Jack Hunter, plus the fact that Wednesday travelled outside of England for the first time, facing Clydesdale in Glasgow in the final game of the season. The sheer appetite of the Scottish public for football was clearly shown when a huge crowd (by 1876 standards) of around 17,000 attended, won 2-0 by the home side in what was quite an experience for the parochial team from Yorkshire. The campaign was not without controversy though as during the 3-0 win at Derby Derwent the match was constantly stopped due to spectator encroachment and when the home umpire waved away two Wednesday appeals, two of the away side walked off the pitch in protest. Without doubt the most problematic game though was the return meeting with Thurlstone Crystal Palace, who arrived three players short of their full complement. Only forty-five minutes was played due to the terrible state of the pitch and the match ball burst twice!

The close season of 1876 saw one of the club's major administrative figures of the nineteenth century, John Holmes, join the club's committee and there was cup-tie football back on the menu when the Sheffield FA announced it was offering a splendid £50 silver trophy for competition. The local FA were following in the steps of the Football Association, who introduced their English Cup five years earlier, while their new competition still remains today the second oldest cup tournament in existence – playing under the banner of the Sheffield & Hallamshire Senior Cup. With Wednesday boasting a membership of 230 and now established as one of the most popular clubs in the town, they were tipped to lift the trophy and duly played in the inaugural game, beating Parkwood Springs 3-1. A month later Wednesday met Hallam FC for the first time with a Scots attacker called James Lang appearing for Wednesday. Lang is widely regarded as the first Scottish footballer to cross the border to play football as a professional, although in those days the game was strictly amateur, with any form of payment severely frowned upon. He had impressed the Wednesday hierarchy with his display for Glasgow in a meeting with the Sheffield FA, and soon arrived in Sheffield after being given a job at the knife manufacturing business of club official Walter Fearnehough. However, his employment was just a thin veil to cover his real intentions for being in Sheffield, as 'Reddie' spent most of his day reading the newspapers and drinking tea. Back on the field of play, Wednesday progressed further in the new Challenge Cup to set up a semi-final meeting with Exchange at Bramall Lane, in February 1877. The quarter-final tie against Attercliffe was significant as it is the first recorded instance of a referee being in charge of a Wednesday fixture; what we would today recognise as a referee first appeared around 1874 and it was not until 1891 that the FA deemed that the official should be fully in charge of events on the field, the old style umpires being 'downgraded' to linesmen. Meanwhile the semi-finals of the Challenge Cup were held at Bramall Lane with the rising popularity of the game shown with an attendance of 6,000, the highest so far seen for a football match in the town. The two favourites, Wednesday and Heeley, progressed to set up a final tie back at the same venue. The increasing rivalry between the clubs added extra spice to the tie but in front of another record crowd of 8,000, it was Heeley who looked likely to win the inaugural final as they raced into a three-goal half-time lead. Wednesday, who included three sets of brothers, were missing star man Mosforth but rallied spectacularly in the second half, both Butler brothers scoring, to eventually grab an equaliser through William Clegg. Near the end a Heeley player also handled a Wednesday shot on the line but there were no penalty kicks in those days, so the game went into 'sudden death' extra-time, after the teams had met in the middle of the pitch to discuss their options. The 'golden goal' was duly grabbed by Wednesday in the second half of the extra-time, as Tommy Bishop broke away and crossed for Bill Skinner to fire home and win the cup. The fine trophy was presented to Wednesday captain Stacey at the post-match gala dinner with all the winning players receiving 'swell' silver medals in the shape of a Maltese Cross, which would have been the first tangible item any of the men would have received since they started playing the new sport of football. A few weeks later they were also presented with commemorative pocket knives by John Holmes at the club's tenth anniversary dinner. Victory in the tournament instantly installed Wednesday as 'top dogs' in the town and they would retain the trophy just under a year later, goals from Francis Butler and Bishop defeating Attercliffe in the blue-ribbon event of the Sheffield football calendar. The 1877/78 season also saw Wednesday welcome a Scottish side for the first time, losing 2-1 to Glasgow Rangers. The club's popularity was shown in January 1878 when two 'senior' games were played on the same afternoon with one side beating Hallam in the Sheffield Cup and a slightly weaker XI losing 4-1 in Nottingham against the 'Foresters'. By the start of the following campaign the Wednesday Club boasted 300 members in their football section while Wednesday provided the vast majority of the players for the innovative 'football by electric light' game, which was staged at Bramall Lane and was the first football match to be played under artificial light, several decades before floodlights became a regular sight on the skylines of towns and cities. Wednesday actually experienced a poor start to the 1878/79 season, winning only once in their first seven games, and relinquished their grip on the Sheffield Cup in game eight as they were beaten at Hallam; it should be noted that Bob Gregory, who scored twice for the home side, would later become Wednesday's greatest scorer of their early years as he netted freely in the late 1870s and early 1880s, spearheading the club's first forays in the English Cup and appearing in several sides that won local honours. He was described as one of the 'most sterling forwards of his day' and was a real handful, difficult to knock off the ball and a great dribbler, being awarded a benefit game in 1883 such was his service. A few days after the cup exit, the first game in a new competition, the Wharncliffe Charity Cup, was played at Bramall Lane. The new silver trophy had been donated by the Earl of Wharncliffe to be competed for by clubs of the 'town and district' with all proceeds, after expenses, donated to worthy local charitable institutions. The competition was invitation only with four teams entering in the first tournament. The money from the aforementioned first game was used to relieve suffering in the town, via the Lord Mayor's Relief Fund. The new competition would be the only real bright spot for Wednesday in a disappointing campaign, and they did not even have to play their semi-final as opponents Attercliffe failed to appear for the tie, claiming they had not received enough notice to fulfil the fixture, with the Sheffield FA subsequently awarding the game to Wednesday. The scene was set for another Wednesday versus Heeley final but even though Heeley were favourites, it was Wednesday who scored first, the opposing 'keeper clearing a ball only to see it rebound off the legs of Woodcock and back into the goal. The slice of luck was a huge fillip to an out of form side, which included brothers Edwin and Tom Buttery, and Woodcock would complete a hat-trick as his side won 3-2 to swiftly re-establish themselves as 'top dogs'.

For the first time in their relatively short history, the following season saw rumours of discontent among the club's followers as their side suffered a very inconsistent campaign, which included a 7-0 defeat at Derby and a new record home loss – 6-0 against Staveley. The main reason was that many of their experienced players had failed to commit to the club for the new season and even though Lang had returned from a spell back in Scotland, this was shown when they lost a Sheffield Cup tie to an Exchange Brewery team that included ex-Wednesday men Winterbottom, Tom Buttery and Anthony. Wednesday gained revenge over Hallam by progressing in the Wharncliffe Charity Cup and it would be that tournament that would again keep the season alive, Wednesday overcoming Spital Chesterfield to set up a repeat of the 1879 final against Heeley. Before the final, Wednesday welcomed renowned Scottish side Vale of Leven, with the visitors winning 3-0 in a match remembered for the broken arm suffered by William Clegg, which brought his playing career to a premature end. It was also possibly the first ever instance of a substitute being used as the visitors kindly allowed Wednesday to replace the stricken Clegg. The final of the Wharncliffe Cup, simply referred to as the 'Charity Cup' by Sheffield's football fraternity, was played several weeks earlier than the inaugural season, with a mid-January 1880 date allocated, as the town's top two sides again locked horns. Unfortunately, Wednesday's run of cup success finally came to an end as, despite a second-half equaliser from Hawley, it was the 'Heeleyites' who took the honours, securing a late winner to slightly realign the power base of Sheffield football. The club's first foray into the FA Cup dominated the 1880/81 season, while the first win of the season was recorded on the first

Saturday of October, 4-2 against Heeley at Bramall Lane, with new captain Gregory netting. The campaign had opened a week earlier with a goalless encounter at Attercliffe, which proved significant as the fine display of Jack Hudson, for the home side, resulted in him quickly being recruited to the Wednesday ranks. Six goals were subsequently shared with Staveley and Wednesday would only play one first team game throughout the season at Sheaf House, having signed a deal with the Bramall Lane ground committee to rent the cricket ground, along with Sheffield FC, for the campaign. Wednesday had significantly strengthened their ranks for the advent of FA Cup football and this was shown as Wednesday bulldozed their way to the final of the Sheffield Cup, scoring twenty-six goals in four ties to set up a clash with Ecclesfield. That remarkable cup-tie form continued in the final as they raced away to record an 8-1 victory, with captain Gregory claiming five goals – Mosforth and Gregory were given a huge ovation by the Wednesdayites in a 3,000 crowd. The Sheffield Cup was the only local trophy on offer in that season as the Charity Cup was withdrawn after various problems linked to the 'Zulu' games played in the town. These were fundraising novelty matches that courted huge controversy when it was alleged that some of the strictly amateur players had been paid a percentage of the gate money. The Charity Cup committee thought it had no option but to withdraw the trophy after Wednesday had beaten Heeley in a replayed semi-final tie only for their opponents to be reinstated – both teams had suffered player suspensions in the first game due to the Zulu controversy, and it proved impossible to complete the competition. The season finished with a heavy defeat at Blackburn Rovers – in Wednesday's first ever fixture in April – but it had been a highly successful season, wrestling the crown of Sheffield's best side back off their fierce rivals Heeley. Away from FA Cup football, the 1881/82 season was a mixed one for Wednesday, crashing out of the Sheffield Cup at Heeley, although the Wharncliffe Cup was this time played to a conclusion, with Wednesday comprehensively beating Heeley 5-0 at Bramall Lane.

The 1882/83 campaign would be the busiest so far in Wednesday's short history with the football season now starting in late September, a date that within five years would move to the first available date in the month as football grew and grew in popularity. The season opened with the Newbould brothers, Fred and Herbert, in a Wednesday side that won at Attercliffe before a heavy loss at Darwen – the away side were severely weakened when the Sheffield FA called up several of their 'star' players for a representative fixture. A bad start to the season continued with a 6-1 defeat at Aston Villa, where the club was first referred to as the 'Blades' in a press report, before an 8-0 win in Leeds against a village side called Oulton got their Sheffield Cup campaign off to a great start. Wednesday would dominate the local football scene in this season, winning both of the trophies available, beating surprise finalists Pyebank 4-0 in the Wharncliffe Cup – the club maintaining their record of reaching every final since the tournament was introduced. A week later the Sheffield Cup was won in a replay, the first tie having ended 2-2, when new club Lockwood Brothers pushing Wednesday all the way before a winner from Mosforth clinched a cup double. There was no doubt that Wednesday were the most popular and successful club in the town but over the next four years they slipped from that position of power and influence to the brink of closure, the thorny subject of professionalism being the main reason behind their decline. There was no sign of the troubles ahead in the early weeks of the 1883/84 campaign with a six-game winning start including a long trip to face Redcar, in the Sheffield Cup, and a much shorter journey to play Deepcar. A few weeks later – on 13 November 1883 – president Hawksley announced that the football and cricket sections would be split financially, although they would remain as one sporting institution. Fortunes on the football field then took a nosedive as Wednesday crashed out of the Sheffield Cup before scoring somewhat of an own goal when increasing admission prices for the meeting with Darwen – supporters voting with their feet at the decision, only a hundred paying in a crowd of only around 700. Just over two weeks later Wednesday were then beaten in the Wharncliffe Cup by little-fancied Park Grange, with even the local press commenting about how 'good old Wednesday' had lost again. A handful of morale-boosting wins wrapped up the campaign but twelve months later the club's fortunes had failed to improve with the Lockwood Brothers again proving their nemesis in the Sheffield Cup, while old rivals Heeley handed Wednesday their heaviest defeat in 'competitive' local cup football when they embarrassed them 4-0 in the final of the Wharncliffe Cup. Away from parochial matters, Wednesday recorded some excellent wins, such as 5-0 at Nottingham Forest and 6-0 against Blackburn Olympic, but also suffered a couple of disastrous days with an 8-1 mauling at Preston North End preceded by a 12-0 disaster at Blackburn Olympic, the only consolation being that a weakened team, due to Sheffield FA call-ups, travelled over the Pennines for the latter. The spectre of professionalism was also shadowing the club, although all at Wednesday – officials, players and fans – were determined that they remain amateur. This opinion was strengthened after a particularly distasteful encounter with Bolton Wanderers in January 1885, when the Lancashire visitors showed a 'win at all costs' attitude and literally bullied the home players into submission (through fear of being injured), with their players jeered off the pitch at the end of the game after a prime example of the 'evils' of professional sport. Forty-eight hours later the name of Haydn Morley first appeared in a Wednesday team, while on a snowy afternoon in February visitors Preston gave a masterclass and showed Sheffield football fans a positive side to professionalism. Whatever the rights and wrongs of professionalism, the meetings with Bolton and Preston did reveal one inescapable fact: Wednesday had suddenly fallen behind their Lancashire neighbours and was no longer a force nationally, or even in their own town. If that season had been a sobering experience for Wednesday fans accustomed to success, then the 1885/86 campaign was bordering on disastrous as the club, at times, even struggled to field a full complement of players, such as when they arrived for a first game at Port Vale with only nine men. The only solace, in the first half of the season, came in the Sheffield Cup where Wednesday advanced to a last-four clash with Heeley. Their cup hopes floundered in a replay defeat to their great rivals, although the season did have a 'silver lining' as Heeley was again the club's opponent in the final of the Wharncliffe Cup, goals from Mosforth and Davy sealing a 2-0 victory. Wednesday and Heeley also met in the first, and what proved only, final of the newly introduced Mayor's Relief Charity Cup – a tournament for the best four teams in Sheffield with a handsome new silver trophy having been donated by an anonymous benefactor. It was the Heeleyites, though, who picked up their second trophy of the season, winning 2-1 in the final at Sheaf House – the rivalry between the two clubs was perhaps no more shown than in the Sheffield Cup semi-final replay meeting when the game was suspended near the end when fans of both sides started to brawl in the corner of the ground and supporters from both teams raced across the pitch. The summer of 1886 saw Wednesday hold its last Athletics Days, after eighteen years, but an administrational error then put the club's very future in the melting pot as Wednesday failed to submit their entry for the 1886/87 FA Cup competition on time. The mistake could not have been made at a worse time after two seasons of relative struggle, and meant the club's reputation, nationwide and locally, was further damaged. The campaign would prove to be arguably the most important of those early years as local side Lockwood Brothers took advantage of Wednesday's absence by reaching the last sixteen of the FA Cup, greatly helped by several Wednesday men, who switched allegiance to ensure a strong Sheffield XI was represented in the 'English Cup'. It was now becoming a belief among the best players in Sheffield that a professional side from the town would be competitive against any team in the land, and near the end of the season a side called Sheffield Rovers was formed, arranging two games and applying, and being accepted, into the FA Cup for the following season. While the debate in Sheffield surrounding professionalism continued – Wednesday officials remained steadfastly against the notion – the town's best-supported club had to be content with a diet of club matches and local cup ties. Some heavy defeats were suffered along the way – a club record 16-0 loss at Halliwell, where Wednesday arrived with only nine men in January 1887 being particularly damaging to Wednesday's diminishing reputation. Even the local press commented that the club should 'wake up or your long established good name will sink into oblivion'. Despite lifting the Sheffield Cup again, it was crisis time and the whole issue came to a head in April 1887 when at a meeting of Sheffield Rovers, Wednesday stalwart Cawley asked that the 'old club' be given one last chance to agree to the payment of players. As the meeting was packed with Wednesday members, they signed a requisition for a special meeting to be held, which duly took place on 22 April 1887 at the Garrick Hotel. The members who gathered at that pivotal meeting heard a report from a special committee, which had been established by Wednesday FC to look into the matter of the club turning professional. Their findings changed the history of Sheffield Wednesday forever and arguably saved the club from extinction:

> The special committee, having sat twice, sent out a circular to 20 of the most prominent players of the town, who are also members of the club (the circular stated that the committee had a scheme in view to form a very strong and representative club team in the ensuing season, and questions to the terms of which players would join were asked). The committee recommend the registration of professionals to the meeting and that a certain amount be paid to each registered player per match.

The recommendation was voted through with 'wages' set at 5s for home games and 7s 6d for away fixtures. It was certainly a pivotal moment, and the appointment of Holmes as president and purchase of Olive Grove ensured Wednesday was well equipped for the new challenge – Sheffield was also still growing in the late 1880s, driven by steel and cutlery, with the population now 300,000, so there was no lack of numbers to support Wednesday's new professional status.

The club's new status ensured the 1887/88 fixture list contained a significantly better standard of opposition, with the likes of Aston Villa, West Bromwich Albion, Derby County and Burnley all faced in what could be considered a transitional season. The decision to turn professional instantly ensured the club could call upon the vast majority of the town's best players – a second professional club, Sheffield United, was still two years from being formed – and Wednesday quickly regained their crown as Sheffield's best team, completing a Sheffield cup double by beating Rotherham Town and Ecclesfield in the finals of the Wharncliffe and Sheffield cups respectively. It was also noticeable that several local sides were beaten by six goals or more with a 7-0 Wharncliffe cup romp over former 'equals' Heeley perhaps showing a considerable shift in power due to the onset of professionalism, Wednesday registering a considerable profit in what had been a highly successful first campaign. Soon after the season came to a close, the Football League was formed. Wednesday later applied for membership but was refused as it was thought more than ten members would be unworkable. The instant success of the new league format dominated the football headlines in 1888/89, leaving the remaining professional clubs with a diet of high-profile friendly games and local cup football. The new season would be the busiest in the club's short history as Wednesday played forty-nine times at first team level, hitting double figures against Park

Grange, Ecclesfield, Sheffield and Doncaster Rovers, although the only cup football experienced, other than the English Cup, was four games in the Gainsborough News Charity Cup, where Wednesday reached the final and defeated Burton Swifts 4-1. This was because Wednesday had withdrawn from the Sheffield FA in July 1888, after claiming that the governing body had called up their players, for representative fixtures, on far too many occasions and the club commented that, although they bore no malice, they did not see any benefit in employing professional players only to find themselves short of senior players. There was therefore no opportunity to defend the Sheffield and Wharncliffe cups and those competitions were effectively confined to the history books, in relation to the club's first XI, when in the following summer the club entered their first league, the Football Alliance League. The formation of the new competition – initially called the Northern Counties League – was credited to Wednesday supremo Holmes as a direct consequence of the club's unsuccessful second application to join the Football League. Despite the media making Wednesday 'odds on' to be accepted, the voting left them in fifth place when the four clubs applying for re-election went to ballot. Despite Holmes pointing out that Yorkshire did not yet have a league representative, and owned their own ground, the Football League closed ranks and agreed to the status quo continuing. Six days later, at the same Douglas Hotel in Manchester, Wednesday invited several clubs, including Nottingham Forest, Newton Heath (Manchester United) and Sunderland, to the table and the outcome was the formation of the new rival to the Football League, with Holmes elected president. Prior to their opening league fixture, Olive Grove hosted three public trial matches, including first team versus reserves and forwards versus backs, and this ensured the players were well prepared for the onset of the 1889/90 season, which commenced at home to Bootle in the Alliance League. Around 2,000 attended that first league fixture and were delighted as a brace from Ingram secured a 2-1 success:

Smith, Thompson, Hazelwood, Dungworth, Betts, Brayshaw, Winterbottom, Ingram, Mumford, Cawley, Woolhouse

A victory in the first away fixture at Birmingham St George put Wednesday among the early leaders and after beating Newton Heath 3-1 at Olive Grove on the final day of November 1889, the club went top of the league; it was a position they did not relinquish. The aforementioned success over Newton Heath was the second match of an eight-game winning run in the Alliance, which started with a 9-1 trouncing of Long Eaton Rangers. A victory at Nottingham Forest left the club in prime position to lift the title and despite the poor run of only one win in five games that followed, Wednesday was duly crowned champions after beating Sunderland Abion

4-1 in their final home game, Wednesday winning all but one of their eleven home fixtures, scoring forty-eight times.

Alliance League (Top 4)	P	W	D	L	F	A	Pts
WEDNESDAY	22	15	2	5	70	39	32
Bootle	22	13	2	7	66	39	28
Sunderland Albion	22	12	2	8	44	28	28*
Grimsby Town	22	12	2	8	47	26	26

*awarded two points despite losing at Birmingham St George

App/Goals – Smith 22, Betts 22/2, Dungworth 22, Cawley 21/11, Ingram 21/20, Mumford 19/7, Brayshaw 18, Winterbottom 18/5, Waller 16, Bennett 15/12, Thompson 15, Woolhouse 15/5, Morley 6, W. Hiller 3/2, Gill 2, Hazelwood 2, White 2/1, Cutts 1, Drabble 1, Parkin 1

It had been the most successful season in the club's history but surprisingly Wednesday then did not apply for membership to the Football League – it was ironic that the common consensus in the game was that if the club had attended the AGM they would in all probability have been elected in; one could say it was a missed opportunity. The advent of league football meant average home attendances were just short of the 4,000 mark and that average increased by almost 30 per cent during the 1890/91 season despite Wednesday going from prince to pauper, finishing bottom of the league with only four wins. Inexplicably, Wednesday lost five of their opening six fixtures despite scoring twelve times, and after dropping into last position in late October 1890, they never hauled themselves away from trouble, a 4-2 last day victory over Sunderland Albion bringing them level with second bottom Bootle but three goals short of overhauling them on goal average – it was unique that the top two clubs from the previous season ended the campaign as the bottom two clubs. Around the same time, Wednesday welcomed four different Glasgow clubs – Partick Thistle, Battlefield, Rangers and Celtic – to Olive Grove for friendly matches and despite twenty-two league fixtures, Wednesday also played thirty-one club matches, including a game against FA Cup finalists Notts County, which attracted a five-figure crowd to Olive Grove. That poor league form during the season also saw the first real regular instance of fans airing their forthright opinions in the local press, many slating the club for constantly changing the forward line and even one supporter swearing he would not go to Olive Grove again until the goalkeeper had been dropped. Expectations had perhaps been raised due to the success of the previous season and thankfully Wednesday enjoyed a much-improved third season in the Alliance League, registering a final position of fourth, five points behind champions Nottingham Forest. Incidentally, in the preceding summer the club did not apply for membership to the Football League as they were effectively under an embargo after being found 'guilty' by the league of poaching Blackburn Rovers player Tom Brandon. The league did not even recognise Wednesday and their member clubs were also told they could not even play them in a friendly game – the league was eventually censured by the Football Association while Wednesday president Holmes indignantly commented that 'the league reserved to themselves the right to carry off the men of any team but they denied the privilege of returning the compliment'.

The club's woes during the 1890/91 campaign were firmly blamed by the so-called collapse of local talent. Mickey Bennett failed to repeat his goalscoring feats and, sadly, popular captain Fred Thompson started to suffer from a severe illness that would lead to his premature death at just twenty-eight years of age. To strengthen their ranks, several Scotsmen arrived in the town, including Bob Brown, Gavin Thompson and the aforementioned Brandon. With the new men in the side, which also included a home debut for Fred Spiksley, a bumper 10,000 Olive Grove attendance welcomed in the new season and the 4-2 win over Grimsby Town ensured a positive start to the 1891/92 campaign with popular attacker Harry 'Toddles' Woolhouse grabbing a hat-trick. The start of the season also saw the club's reserve side – rebranded as Wednesday Wanderers – enter their first league, joining the likes of old first team foes Heeley in the Sheffield & District League. In the Alliance League, Wednesday scored the first penalty kick in their history in the 3-2 defeat at Bootle, and five straight wins at Olive Grove and a 4-0 win at Ardwick (Manchester City) pushed them into second place. The club remained in contention for a second championship until the final few weeks of the season, with a surprise 4-3 loss at Burton Swifts being particularly damaging to those hopes. Accruing only a point from visits to Lincoln and Grimsby ended the club's challenge and those away trips looked set to be the last Alliance games of the season after final-day opponents Birmingham St George's sent a telegram that they were penniless and could not afford to travel. With the possible loss of income from the game, Wednesday sent over the travel expenses, although that was where the charity stopped as a 4-0 win completed their competitive season. There were, however, still ten games left to play, with a 9-1 romp over Partick Thistle and 6-3 victory over St Mirren the standout results. What proved to be Wednesday's final game as a non-league club took place on the final day of April 1892 when Derby County played out a goalless game at Olive Grove, watched by 2,000 supporters – it was the end of an era.

Chapter 3

4,682 League Games (and Counting)

By Wisdom and Courage

The story of Sheffield Wednesday and the Football League started back on Friday 13 May 1892 when Wednesday fans, and Sheffield United fans as their fledgling club had also applied, gathered in Sheffield town centre to hear news of the club's application for membership. Several vacancies had become available as the league was introducing a Second Division while the First Division was also increasing. Unlike previous applications, this time Wednesday was fully expected to gain membership and their confidence was no more shown than when club treasurer Arthur Dixon was asked about their prospects and he retorted, with a twinkle in his eye, 'Oh, we are certain to get in.' His confidence was not misplaced and the news duly came through: 'Wednesday in the First Division, United in the Second.' The local pubs were packed with supporters of both Sheffield teams awaiting the news and one single telegram meant the town of Sheffield now had two Football League clubs, joining Nottingham (County and Forest), Birmingham (Aston Villa and Small Heath) and Manchester (Newton Heath and Ardwick). Wednesday received the maximum ten votes and was joined by Football Alliance champions Nottingham Forest in the top division, with the likes of Northwich Victoria, Lincoln City, Darwen, Grimsby Town and Bootle all voted into the second tier.

The Olive Grove Years

The fixtures were duly released and Wednesday was handed an opening day trip to Notts County on Saturday 3 September 1892. During preseason the club strengthened their playing personnel, signing Alec Brady from Glasgow Celtic, Harry Davis from defunct club Birmingham St George's and winger Walter Dunlop from local football. The fixture was switched to the Castle Cricket Ground – County's home in March,

April and September every year when Nottingham County Cricket Club utilised Trent Bridge – and the ground's capacity was severely tested on that day, 125 years ago, with the mass of people so great, including over a thousand Wednesdayites who made the journey, that the pitchside barriers were broken down and fans spilled onto the pitch, delaying the kick-off by thirty-five minutes. When the teams finally entered the arena they were both at full strength with Wednesday represented by the following:

Allan, T. Brandon, Mumford, H. Brandon, Betts, Hall, Dunlop, Brown, Davis, Brady, Spiksley

Three of the away team were making their debuts for Wednesday, although one, Dunlop, would never play first team football again. At six minutes to 4 o'clock, Oswald kicked off for County and Wednesday's story in league football officially started. A blustery wind ensured the game was somewhat scrappy but it was quickly clear that Wednesday was far superior in the forward positions and after eleven minutes, Captain Tom Brandon entered the club's history books – a corner fell at his feet and his long-range effort sailed goalwards, cannoning into the net off two or three players. Cue scenes of celebrations from the travelling fans. The interval was reached with no further score while two mounted policemen arrived at the ground, ensuring that the estimated 10,000 spectators stayed off the playing surface. Early in the second half, Spiksley had a goal disallowed for offside and Wednesday were only really troubled when a desperate home side utilised six forwards in the final ten minutes. However, they couldn't get past Wednesday's solid back line and the whistle blew with the away side deserved winners on that historic day. Around 12,000 packed into Olive Grove for the first league home game against Accrington seven days later, and they were delighted as their favourites continued their great start by registering a 5-2 success. In fact, the new boys enjoyed a great beginning to life in the league, beating reigning champions Sunderland in October and taking their goal tally to an impressive forty-seven when beating West Bromwich Albion 6-0 in the opening game of 1893. The win over the Throstles maintained Wednesday's position of third, just five points behind leaders Preston North End, and there seemed a distinct possibility that a tilt at the championship was on the cards. Sadly though, that remarkable start to life in the league then inexplicably changed as the club did not win any of their next ten fixtures, including seven straight defeats, to plummet down the table and find themselves in danger of facing the lottery of the 'test matches' – an olden-day version of today's play-offs with the bottom three teams in the First Division playing the top three in the Second Division to either retain, or gain, membership of the top section. The task for Wednesday was simple: beat Notts County at Olive Grove in their final game, which in turn would condemn the visitors to that fate. Wednesday abandoned their usual blue and white stripes for the fixture, switching to a white kit to avoid a clash with County's black-and-white striped jersey. The change of colours brought a change of luck as Wednesday recovered from an early deficit for Harry Brandon to fire in the winning goal amid huge cheers, with just twelve minutes remaining, securing a 3-2 win and guaranteed survival.

The 1893/94 campaign was almost a mirror image of that debut campaign as a dreadful start gave way to greatly improved form after Christmas, Wednesday recording six of their nine wins in the new year. The fixture list could not have handed the club a more attractive opening game than champions Sunderland travelling to Olive Grove. The team captaincy moved from the departed Tom Brandon to his relation Harry, while Wednesday again had several new faces on show, including Ambrose Langley and Jim Jamieson. What followed was a thrilling encounter that finished 2-2, before a trio of defeats pushed the club towards the foot of the table. A 5-1 loss at Blackburn Rovers was quickly redressed thanks to a 4-2 success on a gloriously sunny afternoon at Olive Grove but it was a rare high spot in a taxing start to the club's second season in the Football League – the lowest point being an 8-1 thrashing at Everton, although Brady entered the record books in October 1893 when he became the first Wednesday man to score a hat-trick in the Football League, achieving the feat against Derby County. Incredibly, by the end of December, Wednesday had played all but seven of their thirty fixtures – fulfilling eight in the final month of the year – and this perhaps showed that despite the roaring success of league soccer the English Cup was still king, with the league programme tailored to ensure maximum exposure for the competition. For the second season running Spiksley finished top scorer as he repeated his sixteen-goal tally of the previous season, netting three times during a late season run of four straight wins that ensured Wednesday finished in the identical position to twelve months earlier – twelfth. That late season form did, however, have a story behind it as in mid-January club officials called a meeting with the players to discuss the club's perilous situation and how the 'test matches' must be avoided. The outcome was that President Holmes announced that the directors were willing to give the players £50, to share among themselves, if they managed to win the five games needed; the task was completed with a game to spare after a 1-0 success at Burnley on Good Friday. During those early years of league football, clubs supplemented their fixture lists with a variety of minor competitions and club matches, the 1893/94 season seeing Wednesday visit Gainsborough Trinity, Scottish club Queens Park and Barnsley St Peters, plus also welcoming Glasgow Battlefield. They also played eight ties in the United Counties League – a competition where all the matches were treated as first team fixtures by the competitors, namely Wednesday, Sheffield United, Nottingham Forest, Derby County and Notts County. In total Wednesday played fifty-three games in that season, consisting of thirty league fixtures, four FA Cup ties and nineteen minor and sundry club matches. As the decade progressed these minor games would start to diminish with only two friendlies played in the 1899/00 season, one of which was a game against their neighbours United after the fixture list inexplicably failed to arrange any Boxing Day matches. The club's third season in the league proved the most successful so far, although it was yet another 'boom and bust' campaign with eleven wins secured in the opening nineteen fixtures before the new-year slump brought eight defeats in the final eleven. The close season saw Wednesday sign several players who would become great heroes to the Olive Grove faithful, men such as Tommy Crawshaw, Bob Ferrier and Archie Brash, and several of the newcomers were in the team that lost 3-1 at Goodison Park on the opening day of the season. Four consecutive wins pushed Wednesday up to third, two points behind runaway early leaders Everton, and in early January a quick-fire 'Liverpool double' saw Everton and Liverpool beaten at Olive Grove – after beating the Toffeemen, Wednesday received a one-line telegram from Everton's championship rivals Sunderland which read 'hearty congratulations, Sunderland committee'. A few weeks later Wednesday was 'doubled' by the Wearside club, who again won the league title, and the season finished like a damp squib as Wednesday lost their last three games, conceding thirteen times including a 6-0 beating at West Bromwich Albion on the final day. One of those defeats was a 4-2 home reverse to Stoke FC but it was the original Olive Grove meeting that grabbed the headlines, following its abandonment due to crowd disorder. The referee, Mr Lewis from Blackburn, had first experienced the ire of supporters two weeks earlier when his display in the game against Sunderland left Wednesday fans hooting with derision at many of his decisions (of which several were clearly incorrect). He was greeted with audible groans when he departed the field at full-time. I am sure the Olive Grove regulars would have groaned again when they realised he was in charge of the next Saturday fixture against Stoke, and he continued to anger the fans, giving a Brash goal offside when he was palpably not. As the second half wore on his decisions became ever more erratic and at one point he stopped play and went to the fans at the Sheffield end of the ground, evidently remonstrating with several individuals. Play was restarted with a drop ball but there were several more sarcastic jeers before a fan, in the Heeley end, threw a grass sod at the referee, which just missed him. This was after seventy-five minutes and the official duly walked off the pitch and abandoned the game – the club was reported to the Football Association by Mr Lewis and Wednesday was perhaps fortunate to escape a ground closure after they were 'severely censured' at a subsequent Football League meeting.

Before the First World War, the cricket and football season did not tend to overlap, with the Football League always starting on the earliest date in September. This usually meant that the first round of league games were often played on a Monday or Tuesday evening and this was the case in September 1895 when Wednesday travelled to Everton for a 5.45 p.m. kick-off. A goal from newcomer Lawrie Bell – who decided to sign for Wednesday instead of Everton – helped put his new side two goals ahead at the break but the match finished all square. Of course, the 1895/96 campaign would be dominated by the club's FA Cup success but in the bread and butter of the league, Wednesday enjoyed a trouble-free season, deviating little from the mid-table positions. Wednesday was now an established league club and the experienced gained in those first three seasons meant that it was 'as you were' for the playing personnel, with the exception of the aforementioned Bell, although crowd favourites Betts and Woolhouse both retired. Wednesday won all their games in October 1895, a run that began with a thrilling 5-3 Olive Grove win against old advisors West Bromwich Albion. They completed a quick-fire double three weeks later as a last-ditch strike from Bell secured a 3-2 success and Wednesday would end the campaign in eighth place, with Spiksley, again, leading scorer. After the FA Cup triumph, hopes were high that Wednesday could finally launch a challenge for the league championship and they did register their highest finish so far – sixth – although they were a considerable sixteen points behind champions Aston Villa. Unsurprisingly, the incomparable Spiksley finished top scorer for the fifth consecutive season, while Olive Grove crowds fluctuated from a season's best 12,000, against Preston North End, down to around 1,000 for the rematch of the 1896 cup final against Wolverhampton Wanderers – unfortunately for all of the league clubs the 1896/97 campaign was remembered for rain, rain and rain, which tended to reach a crescendo on a Saturday afternoon, the aforementioned Wolves game being afflicted by such inclement weather. Incidentally, in that game was an example of a nineteenth-century penalty kick, which was a different animal than today. There was not a penalty spot until 1902 and before that date the penalty taker could place the ball anywhere on the 12-yard penalty line, which ran across the whole width of the pitch – there was not an 18-yard box either with a penalty given for a foul or handball anywhere inside the 12-yard line. All players, other than the penalty taker and goalkeeper, had to stand a further 6 yards behind the line while the goalkeeper was allowed 'carte blanche' to advance off his line by up to 6 yards – this happened in the Wolves game when Langley's second-half penalty was saved by visiting 'keeper Tennant after he'd raced off his line. The season also saw a greatly deserved benefit game for Spiksley, with a splendid crowd of around 8,000 watching his game against famous amateurs Corinthians.

What proved to be the club's penultimate season at Olive Grove ended with Wednesday having improved their final league position again, this time finishing fifth – a certain other team from Sheffield, who shall remain nameless, winning their only title. The fine season actually started with three straight defeats, new signing William Dryburgh starting all three, while rain again dogged the fixtures with the wet stuff falling heavily during the opening-day loss at Villa Park. The second home game against Liverpool was finally met with sunshine and Wednesday thrilled the home crowd by recovering from a 2-0 deficit to register a 4-2 win, while the 4-0 home debacle against Stoke was best remembered for the dismissal of crowd favourite Spiksley by Lincoln referee West. Fred had previously come across the biased officiating of the staunch Lincoln City man while playing for Gainsborough Trinity, with many clubs having complained about the official when he acted as linesman in Lincoln City games. He seemed determined to quieten his detractors, dismissing Spiksley for seemingly not retreating at a free-kick, even though he was the required distance away from the ball. It would, however, be another season to remember for the 'Olive Grove Flyer' as Spiksley was ever present and finished top scorer, yet again, with his tally of seventeen league goals leaving him second in the First Division scoring chart. Wednesday also staged a benefit game for another stalwart, Harry Brandon, with Notts County providing the opposition at Olive Grove. After becoming an established member of England's top division, the 1898/99 campaign proved a shock to fans and players as the club struggled from the opening game, a 4-0 reverse at Liverpool. Despite that defeat, there was no sign of the struggles ahead as after five games they had moved to second – a position equalled only once before, in the second week of their league history. The month of October saw home wins over Bury and Wolverhampton Wanderers while Brandon left for neighbours Chesterfield. The next month's home game against Aston Villa was memorable for two reasons as the club handed out polling cards to gauge the fans' opinions about a possible new ground. The game will forever be remembered, though, due to being abandoned after seventy-nine and a half minutes with the remainder played almost four months later! The tale began with the late arrival of the referee and, combined with a gloomy overcast afternoon, this meant that with fifteen minutes remaining, it was becoming increasingly difficult to make out the players. Within a few minutes the referee called a halt with both clubs fully expecting the whole match to be replayed at a later date. However, the Football League committee had other ideas and bizarrely they ordered only the remaining ten and a half minutes to be played – the abridged game taking place in March 1899 with Richards completing a 4-1 win for Wednesday before a benefit game was played for Davis. Following that uncompleted game, the club's season suddenly took a nosedive with a winless run of six games sending Wednesday spiralling towards the wrong end of the division, although they still had a comfortable cushion over the last two stragglers. The uncertainty regarding Olive Grove had certainly had an effect, with the club's impending homelessness also casting a dark cloud over Wednesday's entire future as a Football League side. Incredibly, Wednesday failed to win or score away from home until late December and it would be that poor away record that would hang like a millstone around their neck for the entire season, Wednesday only recording six draws on their travels. A terrible afternoon at the Baseball Ground in January 1899 was the start of a dramatic decline as everything that could go wrong did go wrong: within six minutes of the start, Wednesday lost Spiksley to injury and before long they were down to nine men as Ferrier pulled up injured. What followed was a 9-0 beating with County's Steve Bloomer gorging on his injury-hit opponents to score six times – after the game the majority of the players decided to return to their training base in Matlock instead of returning to Sheffield to 'face the music'. The subsequent trio of defeats that followed pushed Wednesday into the bottom two places for the first time before the rot was stopped with a goalless encounter at Wolves, a game where Langley was separated from his teammates and kicked and punched by the home fans for the perceived rough treatment handed out to their players during the fixture. Many of the senior players were now getting frustrated with the club's struggles as chances were being created but not taken – new centre-forward Pryce made his debut in the 2-1 home reverse to Sunderland but did not prove a long-term solution. A series of missed penalties did not help either and it was probably not best for team morale when a frustrated fan sent in a team photograph, from which he had cut out all of the players' eyes, with the words 'The Blind XI'. In the end, all attempts to save themselves proved futile with Wednesday finishing the season in last place, winning only eight games – they also had no chance to redeem themselves as the 'test matches' had been abolished in 1898. Even the last game played at Olive Grove could not bring any joy – Newcastle United winning 3-1 – with the loss of Brady for almost the entire season, in addition to star man Spiksley's injury problems, proving crucial. It was indeed a time of worry for Wednesdayites with relegation confirmed and a risky move out of the town centre on the horizon – all this while neighbours United followed up their league win of 1898 with FA Cup success a year later. There was genuine concern that Sheffield could become a 'one-club' city if Wednesday didn't recover from their woes quickly.

A Move to the Countryside and the First Golden Age

With the club's new Owlerton ground still being prepared, late August saw several pre-season public trial matches staged at the Niagara Grounds with new signing centre-forward Harry Millar appearing for the stripes, alongside the returning Archie Brash, in the first game. There was a worry that not many Wednesday fans would travel so far out of town but around 2,000 did, including the Lord Mayor (who did happen to be Charles Clegg). That reasonable attendance for the stripes versus whites encounter gave a fair indication that the move to Owlerton would not be the disaster many had predicted and this was emphatically shown on the opening day of the season when a splendid 12,000 crowd attended the game against a Chesterfield side newly elected into the Football League. Charles Clegg was again prominent – officially kicking off the game – and despite the visitors scoring the first goal, it was Wednesday who powered to a morale-boosting 5-1 success. It was perhaps fitting that Spiksley, who had defined the club's time at Olive Grove, was the first man to score for the 'Blades' at their new home. The great start to the campaign continued as Wednesday won eleven of their opening thirteen games to top the division, with Spiksley, again, becoming the first player to score a treble at Owlerton in the November

1899 rout of Luton Town. Wednesday did not taste defeat until the return game with Chesterfield on 30 December, and would lose only five times to lift the Second Division title by two points from Bolton Wanderers. A Good Friday win at Grimsby Town, where hundreds followed the club from Sheffield, brought promotion close and it was secured twenty-four hours later when a hat-trick from 'Jocky' Wright helped Wednesday beat Burslem Port Vale at Olive Grove. Unlike the previous season, Wednesday scored freely, ending the campaign with eighty-four goals from only thirty-four games, with a virtually new forward line all contributing, Millar netting twenty-five times to top the league list. During the run in, Wednesday broke their transfer record by paying neighbours Barnsley £200 for exciting winger Harry Davis while the Easter Tuesday win over Lincoln City clinched the championship shield. By winning all seventeen home games they became the fourth club to achieve the feat and one of only six, the last being Brentford in 1929/30. Twelve months after the despair of relegation and loss of their home, Wednesday's fortunes were on a real high and the club transfer record was equalled when a player was captured who would become Wednesday's greatest – Andrew Wilson. Another new arrival was left-winger 'Jock' Malloch, although his signing was because the club knew Spiksley would be out of action for several months due to ligament damage. The summer also saw Wednesday, who had become a limited liability company in 1899, release their first set of financial statements. The new season began with four goals shared at Manchester City, Millar scoring twice, although within a few weeks his time in the first team at Wednesday came to an abrupt halt – he was suspended without pay for missing training and soon moved on. Thankfully Wednesday had a ready-made replacement in Wilson and the new recruit ended his debut season as top scorer, netting thirteen. The club's 100 per cent home record at their new home was ended by Preston North End in October 1900 while, incredibly to a modern perspective, the next home league engagement was postponed by the Football League as opponents Wolves had arranged a 'prestige' friendly against the Corinthians – football was a more innocent and gentlemanly sport back in those days! Wednesday relied on an excellent home record to stay out of trouble as their first season back in the top flight matched the 1898/99 relegation campaign as they failed to win a game on their travels – their last First Division away win was back in March 1898 and the run was not broken until a victory at Liverpool in October 1901. This great disparity between home and away records was not just specific to Wednesday as for the first fifty years of league soccer it tended to be that only the very best sides did not struggle away from their home comforts. The 1900/01 campaign also gave a rare glimpse into pre-match training, which involved a brisk walk in the 'bracing air' of Ecclesfield followed by lunch. It was then time for a 'good rest' before the players returned for the game – trainer Frith did work the players harder on non-matchdays but today's training regimes would have been totally alien to all parties.

Wednesday ended their first season back in a satisfactory eighth position, with the signing of goalie Jack Lyall and emergence of Sheffield-born inside-forward Harry Chapman crucial factors in the success that would follow.

Fans hoped their side would improve even further but the campaign proved somewhat of a disappointment with Wednesday slipping down a place to finish ninth. Surprisingly Wednesday did not capture any major names in the summer of 1901 and there were actually murmurs of discontent among the club's shareholders in the spring of 1902, who subsequently called a special meeting to air their dissatisfaction at how the club was being run. Between the meeting being called and it actually taking place, Wednesday deflected some of the criticism by winning three consecutive away games for the first time in the First Division, although several salient points were made to the club that the chairman of the supporters club 'hoped the Wednesday directors present would take on board'. They also expressed an opinion that an assistant should be appointed to secretary Arthur Dickinson and that a full-time coach should be employed, who could mould the team into a title winning side – the shareholders believed the club had underachieved since coming into the Football League and were perhaps understandably frustrated, the success of neighbours United no doubt fuelling that dissatisfaction. Before the season had kicked off, Wednesday was one of the clubs to vote unsuccessfully for an expansion of the Football League to forty teams, although they did successfully gain entrance into the strong Midland League for their reserves, an opening-day 13-1 win over Derby County reserves giving them an astonishing start. Season highlights included a five-goal haul at home to Bolton Wanderers, victory at reigning champions Liverpool and a stunning 2-1 win at eventual champions Sunderland. During the campaign 'keeper Lyall made his senior debut although one player, William Gosling, departed after being found guilty of being 'drunk and disorderly' on a public highway and then suspended and released after failing to turn up for a reserve fixture. All in all the season had been a topsy-turvy campaign with Chapman and Wilson joint top scorers and Langley playing in every competitive fixture. In sharp contrast to the previous summer, and perhaps partly in response to the earlier criticism, Wednesday went quickly into the transfer market with all three signings – Jimmy Stewart, Harry Burton and George Simpson – becoming regular first team players, although they only initially appeared briefly. Off the field, Wednesday showed a perhaps more professional outlook by appointing their first groundsman – Chapeltown resident William Tolly – while famous Sheffield programme seller Billy Whitham was handed the club's selling rights, Wednesday charging him £21. There were also changes on the field of play with a new 6-yard rectangular box replacing the old 6-yard semi-circle and a new penalty area introduced – measuring 44 yards wide and 18 yards deep. A penalty spot also appeared – 12 yards from the goal – with all the changes still visible on a modern-day pitch.

An opening-day win over Sheffield United kicked off the new campaign – Wednesday winning their first three fixtures – and in early October a Spiksley hat-trick clinched a win at Notts County to send the club top of the First Division table for the first time. The club's form at the start of the season came as a surprise to Wednesday fans as their side showed a real defensive solidity, with the famous 'three Ls' backline of Lyall-Layton-Langley forming a considerable barrier. No club would concede fewer goals (thirty-six) and despite not being prolific scorers (fifty-four), this meant Wednesday was finally a force to be reckoned with, spending only one week outside of the top six places. By the dawn of the new year Wednesday sat fifth – an almost unheard of six away wins contributing greatly – while club minutes showed they rejected a claim from a Walsall Town Swifts player who asked for compensation after he had broken his false teeth during a reserve game at Owlerton! Back-to-back home wins then propelled them into second and they remained in the divisional top two for the remainder of the season, battling with Sunderland for the championship. When the top combatants met at Roker Park in March 1903, the Wearside club had not lost since Wednesday beat them in November 1902 and the game was seen as crucial to the eventual destination of the title. A fiercely competitive match ensued and it was Wednesday who grabbed the ever-so-vital two points, with Wilson's fine shot after fifty-five minutes proving decisive. The game though was marred by the actions of the home fans, who during the match pelted the referee with oranges and orange peel, the official stopping play at one point before consulting his assistants and deciding to continue. After the final whistle the man in the middle was smuggled past the angry mob that gathered outside Roker but the away players and officials were not so lucky, being pelted with stones and various missiles as their horse-drawn waggonette was chased away from the ground. It was remarkable that there were no serious injuries and after the incident was reported to the FA, Sunderland had their ground closed for two weeks, a decision that no doubt did little to help their pursuit of Wednesday. That race for the championship actually went to the final fixture as after going top in mid-March, Wednesday remained there and were actually in Devon when the fate of the title was decided. Wednesday had completed their fixtures and were playing Notts County at Home Park, Plymouth, in a game for the impressive 25-guinea Plymouth Bowl. Wednesday won the friendly but it was events hundreds of miles away that were uppermost in the minds as Sunderland travelled to fierce rivals Newcastle in the knowledge that victory would secure them the title. Back in Sheffield, around 5,000 attended the Midland League fixture against Worksop Town – the reserves scored 192 goals in the season, winning the league, Wharncliffe Charity Cup and Sheffield Challenge Cup – and waited for the news from Tyneside, and there was great celebrations in Yorkshire and Devon when the score was posted – Newcastle United 1 Sunderland 0. The club's forward, Wilson, later commented that the party were 'having tea at our hotel when someone dashed in and said that Newcastle had beaten Sunderland by a single goal. We thought that it was a joke at first but soon telegrams of congratulations started coming in, and we found that we were league champions'. After being crowned, Wednesday were presented with the Plymouth Bowl at the town's Theatre Royal and were 'heartily congratulated' on their league success; the Wednesday players were also presented with impressive gold medals before returning to Sheffield a few days later. On arriving back in Yorkshire on 29 April, the team was met by the Sheffield Recreation Band, who played 'See the Conquering Hero Comes' as the train arrived. There were also hundreds of fans waiting to greet them – who had been given special dispensation to leave work for a few minutes – and the party proceeded along Sheaf Street and then up Commercial Street and High Street to the acclaim of the large crowds that lined the way. Dinner at the Carlton Restaurant followed and then to the Empire Theatre where they received the Championship Trophy, to huge applause, and a special flag to mark their success. In those days players did not receive medals but Wednesday solved that glaring omission by commissioning their own medals as keepsakes for the men who had won the Football League title for the first time.

FIRST DIVISION	P	W	D	L	F	A	Pts
WEDNESDAY	34	19	4	11	54	36	42
Aston Villa	34	19	3	12	61	40	41
Sunderland	34	16	9	9	51	36	41

Appearances (goals):
Langley 34 (5), Ruddlesdin 34 (2), Wilson 34 (12), T. Crawshaw 33, Ferrier 33, Malloch 33 (1), Lyall 33, Spiksley 32 (8), Chapman 32 (12), Layton 29, Davis 26 (13), Thackeray 5, Beech 3, V. Simpson 3, Hounsfield 2, Marrison 1 (1), Stubbs 1, P. Crawshaw 1, Moralee 1, Barron 1, Ryalls 1, G. Simpson 1, Stewart 1

Unsurprisingly, Wednesday changed their squad little in the summer of 1903 with only Spiksley missing from the 1903 title success, a serious injury suffered in pre-season meaning the star winger had played his last game for Wednesday. The summer saw a celebration dinner held at the Masonic Hall and Wednesday were granted permission for a summer fayre to be held at Owlerton, with the proviso that the elephants should be kept off the pitch! Wednesday started the season like champions, winning their opening three fixtures, and the first half of the season was dominated with a Sheffield tussle for the top spot, United leading the division until early into the new year before fading badly. Wednesday's form though was imperious and the players that excelled in the previous season upped their game even more to ensure the title remained at Owlerton. The defensive display was again outstanding with only twenty-eight goals conceded; Wednesday did not concede a penalty kick all season, suggesting the defence was firm but fair. Wednesday did not lose at home and half a dozen away wins ensured the trophy was retained. A series of consecutive wins in January and February took the club to the top of the table – a home success over title rivals Manchester City being crucial – and opened up such a gap that losses at Notts County and Everton in early April did not dislodge them from their pedestal. A crucial Sheffield derby win steadied the ship but fans and players were stunned by a 4-0 beating at Newcastle, a result that allowed Manchester City to sneak back ahead, although Wednesday still had a game in hand. A week later, Aston Villa were beaten 4-2 at Owlerton and all eyes were then on Manchester City as they finished their programme with a midweek trip to Everton. They simply had to win to stand any chance of denying Wednesday the title and it proved beyond them as Taylor scored the game's only goal to clinch a 1-0 win for the Goodison Park club and confirmed that Wednesday became the third club to retain the title. The final game, at Derby County, was therefore academic but Wednesday showed their title-winning class by ending the season with a win, the ever-present Chapman opening the scoring in a 2-0 success. As in the previous season, the league had been won by virtually the same eleven individuals, with Simpson replacing the stricken Spiksley on the left wing and Burton taking over from Langley. It was another glorious season and a third divisional title in just four short years since moving to Owlerton.

FIRST DIVISION	P	W	D	L	F	A	Pts
WEDNESDAY	34	20	7	7	48	28	47
Manchester City	34	19	6	9	71	45	44
Everton	34	19	5	10	59	32	43

Appearances (goals):
Chapman 34 (16), Layton 34, Lyall 33, T. Crawshaw 32 (2), Davis 32 (5), Ferrier 31, Ruddlesdin 30, Wilson 29 (11), Burton 26, G. Simpson 25 (6), Malloch 24 (2), Stewart 10 (1), Langley 8 (1), V. Simpson 7 (2), Hemmingfield 6 (1), Bartlett 4, Beech 4, Eyre 1, Hoyland 1, Jarvis 1, Moralee 1, Ryalls 1

There was again little activity to report in the summer of 1904 with Wednesday retaining the 'status quo' as they tried to become the first side to win a hat-trick of championships. The club's tremendous run of success was also shown off the field as record profits and turnover were recorded – £2,024 and £9,758 respectively. Supporters would have been full of optimism for the new campaign and they were duly stunned, like the majority of the football world, when Wednesday started the season like the proverbial steam train, winning their first seven league fixtures to lead the First Division by two points. It was old foes Sunderland who ended the remarkable start at Roker Park and there was a further shock in store a week later when Woolwich Arsenal became the first team to win at Owlerton since December 1902. Unfortunately the back-to-back defeats were not a blip as Wednesday slipped down the table to finish in a disappointing ninth. The aforementioned defeats to Sunderland and Arsenal were followed by another reverse before a remarkable home match with Everton summed up the entire season with the 5-5 scoreline – ten-man Wednesday recovering from a 5-1 deficit to level in the last minute – showing that the 'Blades' had started scoring freely but were simply failing to keep the goals out at the opposite end. The title wins had been based on a rock-solid and settled defence but neither showed on a regular basis during the 1904/05 campaign, leading to that unexpected mid-table finish. Lady Luck was also absent on several occasions – the biggest blow being an injury-hit season for key man Chapman – with the defeat at Woolwich Arsenal being a case in point as Wednesday were missing the injured Ruddlesdin before captain Crawshaw was taken ill at the team hotel and confined to bed. To complete the pre-match problems, winger Simpson managed to badly injure his head in the dressing rooms and it was therefore no surprise that the Gunners completed the double.

So Close Again Before a Title Slips Away

After the relative disappointment of the club's failed attempt to record a treble of championships, Wednesday enjoyed a much-improved 1905/06 season, finishing in a laudable third place, just seven points behind champions Liverpool. In the summer it was decided to extend the top division to twenty clubs, while in the off season Wednesday said goodbye to stalwart defender Langley and there was sadness at the passing of director John Mastin, whose construction company was heavily involved in the building of both Olive Grove and Owlerton. Wednesday enjoyed a great start, hitting the top of the table after a draw at home to Newcastle United extended the unbeaten start to seven matches. A first ever win at Woolwich Arsenal ensured Wednesday retained pole position but a disappointing reverse against Blackburn Rovers – the visitors scoring early and holding on with ten men after their centre-half suffered a broken leg – and a loss at old foes Sunderland saw a slide down to fourth. The Boxing Day home encounter with Wolverhampton Wanderers saw inside-left Stewart, who had taken the place of Malloch halfway through the previous campaign, enter the record books by becoming the first player to net four times at Owlerton. A six-game winless run early in the new year meant there was no title challenge but Wednesday did remain a top-six side for the remainder of the season to post an excellent finish. The outstanding Stewart netted twenty-two league and cup goals (becoming the first Wednesday player to net twenty top-flight goals in a season) and

Wilson weighed in with seventeen. Defensively, Bill Bartlett had effectively replaced the aging Ruddlesdin, although Lyall and Layton remained from the 'Three Ls' back line – Ferrier also failed to make an appearance and subsequently retired. The side was in a transitional period with the purchase of Tom Brittleton proving an important addition to the changing first eleven. Four wins in their final six games had clinched the high finish, although Wednesday fans were again in hot water after a stormy home game against Preston North End in January 1906. The bad-tempered game, which was not helped by a poor display from Leicester referee Mr Bailey, had ended all square, with tackles flying in from all directions, and it was a surprise that the game ended with a full complement of players. The game just needed a spark to ignite the flame and that proved to be visiting director Mr Houghton, who abused the home fans as he walked to the dressing room. It was said that the North End players then acted in a 'vulgar' way from the dressing room window, which resulted in stones and various missiles being thrown and the Preston players attacked by an angry mob as they travelled back to their team hotel. The visitors reported the incident to the FA but it was not exactly the outcome that Mr Houghton had expected as he was suspended for a month, due to his behaviour, and each Preston player fined £1. The Sheffield commission also ordered Owlerton to be closed for two weeks, despite Wednesday being absolved of any blame. The closure was nothing more than a token gesture though as Wednesday did not have a home game scheduled, the only sign of the trouble being posters plastered around the ground for the home win over Woolwich Arsenal, which doubled as a benefit game for Ruddlesdin and Chapman. The 1906/07 season was dominated by FA Cup success but in the league it was a different story as the club dropped into the bottom half for the first time since being promoted back into the top division. There was no sign of this early in the season though, as Wednesday made a great start, climbing up to second place in early December and giving genuine hope of another title. However, Wednesday's form then slumped, the run in the FA Cup seemingly being the main contributory factor, with an 8-1 mauling at Aston Villa taking place just forty-eight hours after a cup victory had been secured – Harry Davis later commented that if it had not been for Lyall's brilliance then the score could have been 38-1. Suffice to say it was somewhat of a one-sided game, although the away side did take the lead, Davis again recounting that his initial penalty was saved by the home goalie but the pitch was so muddy that he momentarily could not complete the clearance, allowing Davis another shot. He succeeded only in miskicking the ball but it still apologetically tricked over the line and stopped in the mud. As the season reached its conclusion, goals and points dried up – Wednesday scored only seven times in the final ten games – but Wilson still grabbed seventeen league goals to top the club's goals chart. Wednesday also broke their transfer record in March 1907 by paying £500 to Kilmarnock for attacker James Maxwell, who was later killed in the First World War. The FA Cup win re-established Wednesday as one of the leading sides in English football and the addition of Frank Bradshaw to the first team ranks resulted in another tilt at the title in 1907/08. The now almost expected great start included six wins in the first eight games as Wednesday took their customary early season seat at the top of the table. This time though there was no slump with the November meeting between second placed Wednesday and runaway leaders Manchester United drawing not only the biggest league gate so far at Owlerton – 43,143 – but also the largest for a league fixture in Sheffield. Second-half goals from Bartlett and Stewart closed the gap on the Mancunians to four points but the win only put a temporary halt on their progress, United eventually winning the league by an impressive nine points. Wednesday pushed them all the way but failure to win any of their final three games ruined their chances of adding a runners-up finish to their honours. There were many high spots with the club's goal tally of seventy-three being a Wednesday record in the First Division – the remarkably consistent Wilson scoring nineteen – while on New Year's Eve, visitors Woolwich Arsenal were vanquished 6-0 with Bradshaw firing home a hat-trick. The campaign also saw the club's north-east scout, future manager Bob Brown, secure the services of both Jimmy Spoors and 'keeper Teddy Davison, both of whom would give great service to the club. The summer of 1908 was dominated by the contractual dispute with star forward Stewart, the attacker refusing to sign a new deal twelve months after he had done the same thing. A club record £1,000 fee eventually resulted in a move to Newcastle United. The major departure was that of Captain Crawshaw and stalwarts Ruddlesdin and Davis both left. The club also sold the disappointing Maxwell, while English McConnell was signed and trainer Paul Frith departed with Charlie Parramore taking his place. To complete a busy summer recess, the Owlerton pitch was dug up and relaid to solve a dandelion problem, and Bob Brown was appointed assistant to club secretary Dickinson. Despite all the changes, Wednesday continued to score freely in the 1908/09 campaign and remained in the top six for the entire season, although, like the previous one, they were never really in the hunt for the championship as Newcastle United walked away with the title. A Wilson goal kicked off the season with a draw at Leicester Fosse but the club had an annoying habit of letting two-goal leads slip in the early weeks as they did at both Chelsea and Blackburn Rovers – drawing both games – although they did collect both points at home to Bury, conceding a two-goal advantage again only to grab a last-minute winner. For the second year running, Woolwich Arsenal was the club's final opponents of the calendar year and again they travelled to Sheffield and conceded six goals, with Wilson this time helping himself to three. Wednesday did manage to keep on the coat-tails of the leaders but a five-game winless run ended any hopes of the title, with a 5-2 home reverse against Sunderland the club's biggest defeat at their new ground. There was also a big shock in store for Wednesdayites as stalwarts Simpson and Burton left for West Bromwich Albion for a joint fee of £850 as the club again shuffled its playing pack in the hope of gaining a winning hand.

There were again wholesale changes to the playing personnel before the next campaign but they did not have the desired effect as a dreadful start saw Wednesday in bottom spot after a six-game winless start, a rare occurrence for Wednesday in the early years of the twentieth century. What was even rarer was that the first three home games were lost, with fans taken aback at the sudden collapse of their usually good home record. When their home form returned, Preston North End were beaten to register the first two-point haul while a hat-trick from newcomer Frank Rollinson helped to beat Newcastle United in the following home engagement. By the onset of winter, the club had pulled themselves out of danger and remained stuck in mid-table from early March until the season's end. New signings George Robertson and James Murray both scored in the 2-1 home win over Bradford City while the 5-0 loss at Aston Villa will always be remembered for the bizarre behaviour of Wednesday man English McConnell. The Irishman had refused to sign a new contract in the preceding summer despite being offered the maximum wage, but did eventually resign, although it was several weeks before he broke back into the first team. It is not known if the events at Villa Park were connected, but after Villa scored their third goal it was noticeable that McConnell was standing well away from play, on the touchline opposite the centre circle. From that point onwards he seemed to take no further part in the game and was seen standing in the middle of the pitch, arms folded, as opposition players ran past him. His behaviour left the home fans astonished as he strolled around the pitch making no discernible effort to get the ball. There was no reasonable explanation for his actions but it would be his last season at Wednesday. Thankfully it was Wednesday's football that was the talking point of the club's final away trip of the season, as fellow mid-table outfit Nottingham Forest were beaten by six clear goals at the City Ground, setting a record-winning margin in an away league game for Wednesday, which still stands today. Whereas during the 1909/10 season the team changed frequently, the following campaign saw Wednesday revert back to a more settled line-up, which is always a key element of success. With many of the old guard now having departed, the season saw seven players appear in thirty or more league games – Brittleton, Davison, Kirkman, Robertson, Spoors, Weir and Wilson – and that contributed greatly to a much-improved finish. Men to leave included Layton, and the departure of the outstanding Bradshaw to non-league Northampton Town was more connected to his injury record than his ability on the pitch. Despite his departure, Wednesday could still field a highly competitive line-up, although they lost on the opening day, Chapman netting in a 3-1 setback at Tottenham Hotspur. As the new side started to gel results were inconsistent, with a lack of a proven centre-forward the main stumbling block to Wednesday climbing away from lower mid-table. Several men were tried in the No. 9 shirt, but it would not be until February 1911 that the arrival of one man solved the conundrum. His name was David McLean and he proved to be the club's first four-figure signing, Preston North End receiving £1,000 for his transfer. Also joining around the same time were two more fellow Scots, defender Jimmy Campbell and winger Marr Paterson, and all three played together for the first time in a derby win at Bramall Lane in February 1911. Of the three new boys both Campbell and McLean proved fine captures, their arrival greatly contributing to just one loss in the final thirteen games of the season, pushing Wednesday from sixteenth up to a final finishing position of sixth. Although McLean scored only twice in that terrific finish, his overall play was outstanding and it would be his goals that ensured Wednesday launched back-to-back title challenges in the next two seasons. Before the 1911/12 campaign began, the club changed first team trainer – Ted Kinnear replacing Parramore – and hopes were high after the club's first foreign tour, in May 1911 to Scandinavia, had greatly enhanced team spirit and had bonded a team together that, on paper, looked like possible champions – it was not just Wednesday fans who were confident of a challenge, as many pundits agreed. It was therefore a huge shock when after five games the club sat bottom of the league with one point! The first win came at home to Tottenham Hotspur but there was no dramatic climb up the table as, despite scoring regularly, chances were still being missed and victory was often followed by defeat. However, a tremendous run of form at Owlerton would power a run of results that by early March had taken Wednesday all the way to second place, just three points behind leaders Blackburn Rovers. That home run consisted of eight consecutive wins and twenty-nine goals with the Boxing Day 1911 clash with Sunderland setting a new league record win for Wednesday as McLean netted four and his side ran in eight goals without reply, including seven before half-time. Despite a surprise loss at Oldham Athletic, the division's form team remained in their new lofty position, although the great run seemed to have taken its toll on the players as a heavy defeat at Bradford City (where Davison was brilliant despite letting in five goals) realistically dashed hopes of a late charge for the title. Even so, Wednesday had enjoyed a remarkable run and despite finishing eight points shy of the top spot, in fifth, hopes for the following season soared once again as Wednesday had the First Division top scorer in their ranks, McLean's haul of twenty-five ensuring he not only topped the divisional scoring charts but also setting a new club record for a top-flight season, eclipsing the twenty scored by Stewart six years earlier.

The 1912/13 season proved memorable for several reasons as not only did Wednesday go agonisingly close to a third league title but the gift of a wooden owl subsequently led to a, somewhat reluctant, change of club nickname from the Blades to the Owls. It was also a season when Wednesday fell to their all-time worst league defeat – a shocking 10-0 reverse at Aston Villa in October 1912. Before that black day in Birmingham, Wednesday had said goodbye to long-serving attacker Chapman, with his departure meaning that only Wilson remained from those back-to-back titles. A McLean brace ensured the new season started with a home success over champions Blackburn Rovers. Three more wins left Wednesday in third place before travelling to Villa Park on that fateful Saturday in October. As the goals started to fly into the visitors' net, rumours circulated back in Sheffield that Davison had left the field with a broken leg, but Villa simply scored every time they went forward, building up a six-goal half-time advantage in a game where the scoreline bore no reflection on the general play. It was said that Wednesday contributed to their own downfall by constantly attacking throughout the ninety minutes and if the missing McLean had been present then the final result could have been markedly different. Regardless of the reasons for the collapse, it was vital that Wednesday recovered quickly from the debacle and this they did quickly, beating Sheffield United in a charity game on the Monday that followed before a Wright header was enough to beat Liverpool. The victory over the Liverpudlians was the first in a run of four consecutive home wins, which Wednesday achieved without conceding a goal and coincided with the placing of a wooden owl statue under the North Stand roof. The owl had been given to the club by player George Robertson and despite Wednesday insisting they were called the Blades, their comments fell on deaf ears as the name stuck. Back in the league, McLean continued to score and his side continued to move back up the table, hitting the front after a quite remarkable New Year's Day game at Hillsborough (the ground name now being in common usage after the club's directors met to decide the matter) against Derby County. Thousands of Rams fans followed their team to Sheffield and they were in fine voice as their favourites took a seemingly unassailable 3-0 lead. They still led with fifteen minutes remaining but Wednesdayites then roared their approval as a tremendous comeback ensured the game ended all square – the point feeling more like two after a remarkable match. With ten games remaining, Wednesday were top in what was becoming a three-horse race for the title, Sunderland and Aston Villa being the Owls' rivals. A terrific run of five straight wins then lifted the club to the brink of glory with just four games remaining. A week later Wednesday recovered from two goals down to earn a vital point at Manchester City, the dropped point allowing Sunderland to nip back in front. Unfortunately the title effectively slipped from Wednesday's grasp on Easter Monday as a slow start against visitors Newcastle United allowed the Geordies to score twice, and despite a second-half rally, the game ended 2-1 to the away side – a huge blow with the club now relying on others if the championship was to be procured. A win over West Bromwich Albion in the final home game proved merely academic as Sunderland won nine of their last ten to take the plaudits with fifty-four points, five more than Wednesday. Despite missing out on the ultimate prize, McLean again broke records as his total of thirty-eight league and cup goals set a new club mark for Wednesday, while his thirty league goals left him top of the First Division scorers' chart. It had been a remarkable season and surely the title would return to Hillsborough in 1914.

One event, though, would derail any chances of a third title as the summer of 1913 was dominated by the impasse reached with McLean. Wednesday had offered the Scot the maximum £5 weekly wage – plus a benefit match with a £350 guarantee – but he wanted a three-year contract, something almost unheard of over a hundred years ago when the clubs were king and players only signed one-year deals, only finding out if they'd been retained or released every May. Wednesday countered with a two-year deal and a £400 benefit game but it was again 'no deal' and astonishingly he returned to Scotland to play his football at minnows Forfar Athletic – back in those days players could not sign elsewhere without their club's consent, hence why the prolific marksman was not snapped up by England's finest clubs. In response to his departure, the Owls brought in Swindon Town attacker Jack Burkinshaw, joining his brother Laurie, while an old face returned with Langley recruited as assistant secretary. New goalkeeper George Streets started the new season in goal after a pre-season injury to Davison, and Wednesday got off to a winning start, a 1-0 win at Bolton Wanderers. The loss of McLean certainly meant a tilt at the title was unlikely but Wednesday coped well without their talisman and sat in a comfortable mid-table position, going into the Christmas programme of fixture, the highlight being a 2-1 home win over champions Sunderland and victory at Manchester City where there was such a large number of Wednesday fans in the crowd that it was asked if 'any club is so considerably supported away from home'. However, one win in seven games – including a new record home loss of 6-2 versus Burnley – saw the club drop perilously to the fringes of the relegation zone. It was perhaps no coincidence that the following week saw Wednesday and their wayward centre-forward 'kiss and make up' with McLean returning, although, somewhat bizarrely, Wednesday had to pay his club £250 to get him back! He was quickly into the scoring groove, netting in a 2-1 win at Anfield, and his nine goals in the final fifteen games ensured Wednesday just avoided the drop into the Second Division, finishing third from bottom but a comfortable four points from relegated Preston North End. The return of McLean therefore offered a chance for the Owls to start afresh in what was the final Football League season before the start of the First World War. The build-up to that 1914/15 campaign was dominated by the worsening political situation in mainland Europe and before the season started Wednesday lost key defender Campbell to the war draft. There was, unsurprisingly, a lot of uncertainty with regard to sport in general, so it was therefore unexpected when Wednesday decided to smash their transfer record to sign Scottish International Jimmy Blair for a £1,975 fee. Unfortunately the new man could not make his debut in the opening day 3-1 home win over Middlesbrough as just after signing he crashed his motorbike and was out injured for several weeks – the club quickly introduced a no cycles or motorcycles rule, threatening that wages would not be paid if a player was injured. After Britain entered the war in August 1914, all top-flight players unselfishly agreed to take a pay cut with the money paid into a fund to be used to fund the payroll of the league's smaller clubs, who faced financial hardship – club captain Brittleton, speaking on behalf of the players, commented that they had agreed wholeheartedly and unanimously to the proposal, which was also adopted by all Wednesday's staff. Away from the troubles abroad, Wednesday made a great start to the season with McLean grabbing all of the headlines as he scored a hat-trick in consecutive home games, which included a remarkable five-minute treble in the 6-0 romp over Bradford Park Avenue. The wins continued and when Bolton Wanderers were thrashed 7-0 (uniquely seven different men scoring) in early March 1915, they went top of the league with only ten games remaining. Disastrously though, Wednesday's form then suddenly stuttered and like in several previous seasons they finished the campaign badly and blew any chance of securing that elusive third title. They won only two of those final ten games and in one of the tightest ever races for the title, eventually finished down in seventh, three points behind champions Everton. The top scorer was again McLean with twenty-two league goals, and remarkably Wednesday only used sixteen players in the season, an almost unbelievable record that will never be beaten. It had been a frustrating and ultimately disappointing end to a highly promising season but matters elsewhere came to the fore with the Football League subsequently closing down until 1919.

Relegation, Rebuild and Promotion

When the horror of war had been confined to the history books, Wednesday made plans for the new season but were again hit by some of the problems experienced in the summer of 1913 with McLean (again) and record purchase Blair refusing to sign contracts. McLean did eventually put pen to paper but didn't stay for much longer, being sold to Bradford Park Avenue after appearing in the first three games. The issue with Blair was somewhat more complicated, involving his benefit and the possibility of gaining employment to supplement his £8 per week maximum wage, with the short-term situation being that Blair returned to Scotland, signing for Alloa Athletic. The club could certainly have done without all the disruption before a season that was full of uncertainty as every club contained squads that had not played competitive football for four years and they simply had no idea how their respective 'old guards' would perform. Sadly for Wednesday, the answer to that question was 'badly' as they would endure a torturous season, with their reliance on too many of their pre-war players resulting in the second worst season in their history, finishing thirteen points adrift at the bottom of the First Division with only seven victories and twenty-three points – their tally of twenty-six defeats set an unwelcome club record. A club record forty-one players were also used, including a string of centre-forwards that all failed to find the net consistently. As is often the case, Lady Luck also deserted Wednesday with Kirkman contracting malaria and new signing Gilmour being so badly hurt in the reserves that he never made a senior appearance; injuries also befell several other senior players, to increase the club's woes. As the season progressed Wednesday became more and more desperate with a plethora of players being signed, an astonishing twenty-four making their debuts, the vast majority failing to show any real quality or longevity. As the situation become more desperate the directors were heavily criticised for constantly changing the team, in addition to not signing any 'star' players, and in one last effort to stave off relegation they entered the transfer market in spectacular fashion to sign Blackpool's outstanding centre half George Wilson and Fulham centre-forward Johnny McIntyre, a club record fee of £2,500 prising the former away from the Lancashire coast. It was, however, expecting a small miracle for the new boys to lift the club out of danger and this proved the case, relegation being confirmed after defeat at Aston Villa with four games remaining. Wednesday posted a financial loss for a sixth consecutive season and it was clear that a major overhaul, on and off the pitch, was needed to reclaim their top-flight place. The first act was the decision to release a club record twenty-one players, while the next was a fundamental change in the structure as secretary Dickinson stepped down from his role after a stormy Annual General Meeting, with his former assistant Bob Brown appointed as the club's first secretary-manager, the subtle difference being that Brown would have sole responsibility for picking the matchday side as opposed to the old system where Dickinson and his board of directors would be responsible. Changes also took place on the coaching staff with trainer William Barr departing after just one season to be replaced by former Burnley player Jerry Jackson. It was a fresh start, although their Second Division campaign could not have been more underwhelming as three 0-0 stalemates kicked off the new era. A goal from McIntrye stopped the goal drought and the centre-forward would prove that he was the man Wednesday would have found very useful twelve months earlier as he duly scored a treble in the home win over Coventry City, and ended the season with an impressive twenty-seven goals in forty-one league appearances. The problem for the Owls was that if their clinical centre-forward did not net, then the team usually did not score, and it was this lack of goals from elsewhere that led to Wednesday finding themselves on the edge of the relegation zone after a disastrous run of results from mid-October 1920 to mid-January 1921, which consisted of just one win in fifteen. The paucity of points dragged Wednesday down from eighth to twentieth and included a 4-0 beating at West Ham, where home forward Syd Puddefoot bagged all of his side's goals, while the final game of the winless stretch came at Port Vale where bizarrely the referee had to clear the half-time marching band off the pitch after he suddenly realised he had played three minutes short! The same game saw the debut of new attacker Sam Taylor, and it would be his nine goals that helped Wednesday to string together a fine run of results, which included ten wins before the season's end, and post a final position of tenth in only their second season of second-tier football. The season also saw the departure of the previous season's 'contract rebel' Blair, who was sold to Cardiff City for a record fee, while a new shareholders' association was formed with 200 joining at the December 1920 initial meeting. The much-improved campaign was reflected in a profit of over £8,000 while Brown entered the transfer market to sign several new men, including James Armstrong, Emil Thompson and Archie Ratcliffe. The winning formula would prove elusive though as the vast majority of the 1921/22 season was spent firmly entrenched in mid-table with yet more player problems surfacing. This time is was McIntrye who was placed on the transfer list by Wednesday in December after an undisclosed problem between club and player, and, much to the chagrin of Owls fans, he was sold to Blackburn Rovers for a large fee – it was one step forward and two back as far as Wednesdayites were concerned. A few weeks later there was sad news when 'A' team player (Wednesday had joined the newly formed Yorkshire Midweek League in the summer) George Pennington died of pneumonia. The arrival of Bury centre-forward Jimmy Trotter would prove highly significant for the club's long-term success – he would play less than a dozen senior games in the next three seasons before coming to the fore. In the end, Wednesday finished in the same positon as the previous campaign, with a few less relegation scares along the way, but if Brown's prophecy, when he joined, of requiring three seasons to get Wednesday out of the division was to come true, there needed to be clear signs that a promotion push was imminent. For once Wednesday did not encounter any problems with any players and also had three forwards – Binks, Smailes and Taylor – who ended the 1922/23 season with double-figure goals. Despite this the new season was again one of frustration, although a splendid 4-2 win at Barnsley in December 1922 pushed Wednesday into the divisional top six and raised hopes. A six-game winless spell then dashed those hopes; this was ended with a 2-0 home victory over Bury, which included one of the greatest goals scored at Hillsborough, described as

> Following a corner to Bury, the ball was returned and Binks getting possession beat Gallagher and started on a dazzling run three-fourths of the length of the field. With Gallagher following, the Wednesday centre-forward went swiftly ahead, eluding first McCrae and then Heap, and finally when Richardson came out to meet him, driving the ball past the goalkeeper into the net, a feat that was greeted with wildly enthusiastic appreciation from the crowd.

As the season progressed, Brown continued to trade regularly as he tried to add consistency to a side that was not without individual talent, and in the spring of 1923 he struck gold as he signed three players who would form the backbone of the success that did eventually follow, namely full backs Ernie Blenkinsop and Billy Felton, plus Worksop Town goalkeeper

Jack Brown. Although it was not known at the time, this flurry of arrivals was perhaps the most important moment, so far, of Brown's tenure. A final position of eighth place was eventually secured – five points off the promotion places – and the Owls supremo must have been happy with his squad as there was only minimal transfer activity in the close season with most being outgoings, including Wally Dickinson, who was, rather bluntly, described as being 'a clever player but slow'. The summer also saw Wednesday's reserve team move from the Midland League into the stronger Central League, and it was shown that the club's support was still strong with 25,000 attending the opening game of the new season, a goalless encounter with Bradford City. Two days later came an extraordinary game at Port Vale where two Wednesday players, Felton and Williams, missed the 1.48 p.m. train. Therefore Wednesday arrived at Vale Park with only nine men, with travelling reserve Petrie filling one of the gaps. It was club trainer Jerry Jackson who stepped into the breach and so became the oldest player to represent Sheffield Wednesday – it is now believed he was fifty years old when he made his cameo appearance. It was actually his only game in league football – he was a professional at Burnley before the First World War but failed to make a senior appearance – and he retired from proceedings with ten minutes remaining of the first half as the pace of the game told. Wednesday, unsurprisingly, lost 2-0 with the two tardy players fined £5 each by the Football League management committee. During those early weeks of the season, Wednesday was unbeaten at home but failed to pick up a point away, and it was this inconsistency that led to a flurry of letters in the local press, berating the club on various issues and suggesting that several of the players were unhappy and would soon be moving to pastures new. Such was the media coverage that the club took the unique stop of releasing a statement:

> The directors of Wednesday F.C. have made full enquiry into matters affecting the club and find that there were some minor matters which have caused friction, these have now been satisfactorily dealt with, and, it is believed, will not recur. The directors desire to express their strong condemnation of the paragraphs suggesting the probability of George Wilson and Fred Kean leaving the club, as there is no foundation for such suggestions, which can only cause mischief.

Wednesday may have quashed rumours of unrest but the team continued to struggle before a swap deal saw Smailes move to Bristol City and William Walker travel in the opposite direction, triggering a much better run of form, Walker netting twice as Nelson were beaten 5-0. An excellent run of form then pushed Wednesday into the divisional top six, the improved results including a 6-0 thrashing of Crystal Palace and a Boxing Day home win over Coventry City, which was played on a snowy pitch with the goalposts painted blue by the groundsman. The victories helped push Wednesday into mid-table but the Christmas period was again tinged with tragedy as reserve team player Tom Armitage – brother of former Owls attacker Len – was badly injured in a Wharncliffe Charity Cup tie. He was taken to Sheffield Royal Infirmary where an emergency operation was performed, but he passed away, aged only twenty-four. The Wednesday players wore black armbands in the next home game. Results continued to be inconsistent with a surge up the table quickly followed by a slide back down. The considerable difference between the club's home and away form would eventually define the season as on their travels the Owls won only once, while at Hillsborough Wednesday's colours were only lowered once, by Oldham Athletic in March 1924 on the occasion of the club's 1000th game in the Football League. The final standings showed Wednesday in eighth place, slightly worse off than twelve months earlier, but it seemed that promotion was now getting closer and closer. The following season though proved a big disappointment as Wednesday not only failed to challenge for promotion but ended down in fourteenth place, the worst finish under Brown. The summer had been filled with optimism as Wednesday brought in several players, including key man Billy Marsden, while the likes of Walker, Prior and Brelsford left. There was also another change in backroom staff with both Chris Craig and George Utley joining. A debut goal from Marsden was enough to secure an opening-day win at Crystal Palace – the Lord Mayor of London officially opened the home side's newly constructed Selhurst Park enclosure, although it was only partly built due to industrial action! The success proved a false dawn as, despite George Ayres grabbing a treble in a win over Stockport County, Wednesday never really threatened the top six, rising as high as seventh after a home game against Portsmouth in December 1924, which was remarkable for the feat of Jimmy Trotter, who became the first Wednesday player to score five times in a league fixture – netting after five, twelve, sixty-two, seventy-five and eighty-eight minutes. The Pompey chairman visited the home dressing room after the game to congratulate Trotter. The Christmas Day 6-2 defeat to Blackpool set a new unwanted record of heaviest home defeat (which remained so until 1992), although one of the instigators of the win, Tangerines captain Matt Barrass, would join Wednesday later in the season. Incidentally, a few weeks earlier, on 5 September 1924 to be precise, a link with the past was broken when the Wednesday Cricket Club was officially wound up by long-time member Lance Morley, with the 1868 Cromwell Cup given to Wednesday FC and the 1831 Marsden Cricket Trophy gifted to the Weston Park Museum. The aforementioned scoring deeds of Trotter, who was now linking up with another signing, Harold Hill, did suggest that Brown was now close to that long-awaited promotion, although results in the second half of the campaign did suggest otherwise; four consecutive games were lost without scoring but the long-suffering fans were given a present to take into the summer months as Hull City were beaten 5-0. Before that finale, many supporters were asking why the club was no nearer to promotion than in 1920 and again criticised

Wednesday for constantly changing the side. There was certainly a mood of general disappointment among the Wednesdayites but a new season brings renewed hope and the ever-optimistic fans expressed yet again that it would be their year.

It was clear that Brown was happy with the side now at his disposal and made only minor additions to the squad, signing prolific Crystal Palace centre-forward George Whitworth, although the newcomer would never play a senior game. There were, however, numerous departures, several being players who had failed to make a lasting impression, but one was a shock as captain Wilson moved into regional football at Barrow, the club captaincy moving to Frank Froggatt, who had broken into the side in 1924/25. There was also one change off the pitch that proved crucial, as Chris Craig was promoted from reserve team trainer to being responsible for the senior side. The new campaign opened with a comfortable win over Fulham and it quickly became apparent that Brown had found that winning formula as Wednesday moved into the top echelons of the Second Division table and remained there for the duration, finally winning back their long-lost top-flight place. From that opening-day victory the club scored freely with prolific marksman Trotter grabbing all the headlines, scoring four in the home game with Preston before getting another five in the 6-2 win over Stockport County – his first three came in only four minutes and is the fastest Wednesday hat-trick. With new captain Froggatt imperious at the back and both Marsden and Blenkinsop showing the form that would win them England honours, Wednesday hit top spot in late November – the recalled Hill bagging a hat-trick to help beat Chelsea – and they remained in the top promotion positions for virtually the remainder of the season. There were a few blips along the way, including a 5-1 loss at a Mark Hooper-inspired Darlington, before a crucial point was secured at promotion rivals Chelsea in the penultimate away game of the season, Jack Brown brilliantly saving a late penalty, leaving his side three points from promotion. Promotion was secured at Southampton thanks to a Trotter brace, and the loyal band of fans that travelled to the south coast celebrated widely. The championship was sealed a week later, being won by three points from Derby County, while Trotter took his league tally to a club record thirty-seven goals with his seasonal total of thirty-eight matching McLean's remarkable total in 1912/13. It had been a dream season for all concerned, which included twenty-seven wins, and finally vindicated the transfer policy of Brown as he slowly built a team that brought the smile back to the faces of those of the blue and white persuasion.

Consolidation, the Great Escape and a Second Golden Period

After celebrating promotion with a gala dinner at the Royal Victoria Hotel, the next task was to stay up, but Wednesday fans need not have worried as incredibly Trotter would replicate exactly his record of 1925/26 by scoring thirty-seven times to finish the season as England's top division's leading goal getter – the third and last time this has been achieved by an Owls player. What was perhaps more incredible was that Wednesday failed to finish in the top half of the table, despite Trotter setting a new Owls record with thirty-nine league and cup goals, as Wednesday failed to win away from home while conversely registering fifteen home wins. In early December, Wednesday climbed as high as sixth place but a defence which conceded ninety-two goals generally struggled to deal with the higher-quality attacker on show and the club soon slipped down to an eventual finishing position of sixteenth, a comfortable nine points clear of relegation. Most of the recorded wins were by the odd goal but Wednesday's back line was particularly porous away from home, conceding six at Arsenal, seven at Leicester and eight at Derby. The home game against Manchester United saw the strange sight of home full-back Felton running the line after the appointed official failed to appear, while the campaign ended with some silverware as Barnsley were beaten 4-1 to lift the Sheffield & Hallamshire County Cup for the first time, at the seventh attempt. Overall it had been a satisfactory return to the top division while in retrospect the most important events occurred after the Christmas period as first Hooper arrived from Darlington, followed soon after by Brentford centre-forward Jack Allen and then Port Vale inside forward Alf Strange; all three would have a major impact on the history of Sheffield Wednesday. For the second season running the club posted a profit – income being reported at just under £29,000 – and Wednesday looked set to 'kick on' from their satisfactory return, especially after Brown swooped to sign Tottenham inside forward Jimmy Seed. However, what followed was a huge shock as Wednesday lost 4-0 at Everton on the opening day and after conceding just twenty-five seconds into their first home game, lost that one as well, 2-0 to Manchester United. Defeat quickly followed defeat and although Wednesday was scoring regularly, they simply could not keep their opponents out and slumped to the bottom of the league. Incidentally in September 1927, Wednesday refused the BBC permission to radio broadcast their home game against Newcastle United, an example of how club's generally frowned upon the media as many believed live coverage would significantly affect attendances. During the autumn, promotion-winning captain Froggatt departed while the move to sign centre-forward Ted Harper smacked of desperation, although he became the only Owl to score a hat-trick on his league debut, scoring three in a 6-4 win at Derby County. His impact was relatively brief though, and even the arrival of winger Ellis Rimmer failed to stop the rot as Wednesday seemingly careered back into the Second Division. With ten games to play, Wednesday were seven points adrift at the bottom with a small miracle needed even to drag them into a position where they could launch a realistic attempt at escaping. Wednesday fans had virtually given up hope at this point as only just over 12,000 watched a morale-boosting 4-0 win over Liverpool. An away point followed before a busy Easter period where home and away meetings with Tottenham Hotspur would prove vital to Wednesday's survival hopes. Inspired by Seed, Wednesday recorded a quick double and a tremendous win at Sunderland suddenly gave them real hope – still bottom but now just a point from safety. Crucially, Wednesday still had a game in hand at Highbury, but all looked lost until virtually the final second when Seed headed home to earn a draw. Wednesday went up to nineteenth, ahead on goal average from the three teams now below them. This set up one of the most dramatic relegation dogfights of all time as only two points separated Liverpool in twelfth from bottom club Manchester United, with Wednesday knowing that only a point was needed against Aston Villa to clinch safety. Almost 37,000 were inside Hillsborough to watch the drama and the ground erupted when just two minutes into the second period Allen fired home. When Trotter netted a second, the 'great escape' had been completed as an unbeaten run of seven wins and three draws had pushed them up to fourteenth with Spurs and Middlesbrough going down. When the final whistle went in Sheffield, fans swarmed onto the pitch, calling loudly for the players, and there were huge cheers when captain Seed led his men back out into the stand. It had been a quite remarkable achievement and it is difficult not to draw parallels with the Leicester City side of 2014/15 as, like Wednesday, they survived when all seemed lost and then enjoyed a quite remarkable following season, which ended with the title in their possession. Exactly the same would be achieved by Wednesday as the confidence gained was taken into the 1928/29 campaign and eight months later they were celebrating their third league championship, with a certain Leicester City finishing a point behind. Free-scoring winger Hooper had finished top scorer in 1927/28 with twenty-one goals and he continued to score freely, although Allen proved deadlier to net thirty-three times in only thirty-five league appearances. The season kicked off with an always welcome home success over Arsenal (the Londoners running out of the tunnel with numbers on their shirts, the first instance of this occurring in league soccer) while a run of six wins in seven games, which included back-to-back trebles from Allen, took Wednesday top in late November 1928 – in hindsight it could be said that the title was clinched earlier in the month when the Owls travelled to Leicester City and 'keeper Jack Brown badly injured his left shoulder after just ten minutes. For the remainder of the game he could only punch with his right arm but Wednesday showed tremendous grit to secure a vital 1-1 scoreline. A change of position for Allen, from inside forward to centre-forward, proved an inspirational decision from Brown and Allen could not stop scoring to spearhead the title challenge. Remarkably, when one considers the small margin by which the league was won, they remained at the summit for the duration of the season despite recording consecutive wins only once from January onwards. An unbeaten home record was the backbone of their success with only three away wins recorded – from December the club failed to win away and lost six of their seven final away engagements. Luckily for the Owls, they were not alone in their relatively poor away form and this ensured the race for title went to the last Saturday. The only change to the side from the previous campaign was that of inside forward Harry Gregg, while the Leach-Marsden-Strange back line was outstanding, Rimmer and Hooper were in fine form on the wings, Brown solid in the goal, the aforementioned Allen banging in the goals and Blenkinsop and Walker tremendous at full back. One man, though, who was a truly key figure was the inspirational Seed, who manager Brown once told 'If you are not fit Jimmy, just throw your shirt on the pitch', a comment that emphasised his worth. A 6-0 win over West Ham United in the penultimate home game meant Wednesday had set a new club record points tally in the top division and, more importantly, sent them five points clear and meant a win at Newcastle United would clinch the title. Conceding an early penalty was not the perfect start and, although Wednesday pulled a goal back in the second period, they lost 2-1. It was then Burnley at Hillsborough and you could hear a pin drop when the Clarets opened the scoring after seventy minutes. However, the home fans then showed their mettle as instead of despondency pervading the ground, they roared their team on and just over ten minutes later Allen headed home. The ground erupted and Wednesday spent the last nine minutes encamped in the visitors' half, trying in vain to score the goal that would guarantee the title. It was not to be though and players and fans waited nervously for news of their rivals' fortunes. It was known that Aston Villa were losing heavily at Manchester City, so it was Yorkshire neighbours Huddersfield Town who could win the title for Wednesday as they hosted Leicester. The news did eventually come through that the sides had drawn and Wednesday were champions! It was left to captain Seed to address the fans:

> There is no doubt that we owe a very great deal to the splendid support we have received from you this season. I can hardly speak; I am almost overcome by the splendid fight our chaps have made. Believe me; your vocal support had a lot to do with us getting the equaliser today. Your help was a telling factor last season; but I do not think you have ever made a bigger effort for us than just before we got our equalising goal.

It had a been a remarkable season – the reserves also won the Central League for the first time – with tremendous team spirit, several outstanding players and the great management of Brown all combining to secure the silverware.

FIRST DIVISION	P	W	D	L	F	A	Pts
WEDNESDAY	42	21	10	11	86	62	52
Leicester City	42	21	9	12	96	67	51
Aston Villa	42	23	4	15	98	81	50

Appearances (goals):
Brown 42, Hooper 42 (15), Marsden 42 (1), Strange 42 (5), Walker 41, Blenkinsop 39 (1), Seed 39 (8), Leach 36, Allen 35 (33), Rimmer 34 (7), Gregg 30 (7), Harper 6 (5), Trotter 6 (1), Whitehouse 6 (1), Wilkinson 6, Kean 4, Felton 3, Wilson 3 (1), Burridge 2, Hargreaves 2 (1), Hatfield 1, Hill 1

The following summer was notable as on 3 August 1929 the club officially changed their name with the board of trade from The Wednesday to Sheffield Wednesday Football Club Ltd. Wednesday also signed highly rated inside forward Harry Burgess and the new man would be the catalyst for another remarkable season, which not only saw the title retained by a record ten points, but also 105 league goals scored with Burgess netting nineteen, although Allen topped the scoring charts again with thirty-three. Eleven away wins was the significant difference from the 1929 title win, with this Wednesday side – surely the greatest in the club's history – utterly dominant after going top following the final round of fixtures in 1929. Highlight of the first half of the campaign included a 7-2 win over Manchester United, although in early September Arsenal became the first team to win at Hillsborough since February 1928. Wednesday kept the chasing pack at arm's-length until late April when they faced crucial games against their nearest rivals, Derby County, on consecutive days. Unfortunately Wednesday had to play the vast majority of the away fixture with only ten men after Marsden was forced to retire, and they were eventually beaten 4-1, narrowing the lead to three points. Over 41,000 were inside Hillsborough for the return game and Wednesday knew a win would retain the championship. From the kick-off it was obvious that the Owls were determined to 'finish the job' and by half-time led 2-0 through goals from Allen and new man Walter Millership. A remarkable scoring sequence then wrapped up the championship as by the hour mark it was 6-0, goals being added from Allen (two), Rimmer and Hooper to overwhelm the only club that could realistically deny Wednesday the ultimate prize. Wednesday subsequently netted their 100th league goal in a 4-2 win at Sunderland, before a Hooper hat-trick in the 5-1 win over Manchester City helped his side finish the season in style. At the end of the City game, the Wednesday players – who were lauded as the fittest team in the league due to the sterling work of their trainer, Craig – were presented with the trophy and their winners' medals by Football League President John McKenna to mark the end of a truly remarkable season.

FIRST DIVISION	P	W	D	L	F	A	Pts
WEDNESDAY	42	26	8	8	105	57	60
Derby County	42	21	8	13	90	82	50
Manchester City	42	19	9	14	91	81	47

<u>Appearances (goals)</u>:
Hooper 42 (18), Allen 41 (33), Brown 41, Strange 41 (3), Leach 40 (2), Rimmer 40 (15), Blenkinsop 39, Burgess 39 (19), Marsden 37 (3), Walker 34, Seed 32 (9), Wilson 9, Millership 6 (1), Gregg 5, Smith 4, Whitehouse 4, Beeson 2, Burridge 2, Jones 1, MacKay 1, Mellors 1, Wilkinson 1

In hindsight, one event in the following summer proved a huge blow to the club's chances of recording a hat-trick of league titles as, after being injured on England duty, star man Marsden was forced to retire. Several players were also sold, although none had played a significant role, while the arrival of Manchester United centre-forward Jack Ball did seem unnecessary after the scoring exploits of Allen. New man Ball did quickly displace Allen though, duly flourished on the outstanding service provided by his new teammates and scored twenty-seven times to top the scoring charts. Wednesday would again break the 100 league goal barrier and amassed a highly credible fifty-two points. Unfortunately this was the season of the legendary Arsenal side that ranaway with the league, amassing new records for both points and goals for a champion club. Wednesday recovered from a mixed start to hit top form in November with Ball (twice) and Hooper scoring hat-tricks in big wins against Sunderland (7-2), Leicester City (5-2) and Blackpool (7-1), but the game they needed to win, at home to runaway leaders Arsenal, went against them as the Gunners won 2-1 in Sheffield. This rounded off a bad week for Wednesday as the players wore black armbands in remembrance of Arthur Dickinson. Four weeks later, Wednesday recorded their highest ever league win – 9-1 versus Birmingham City – and remained near to the top to post a third-place finish. There were also several ins and outs during the campaign with Gregg the most high-profile departure, while the likes of Jack Breedon, George Stephenson, Ted Catlin and Tommy Davison arrived. The Owls also played in the Charity Shield for the first time, losing 2-1 to Arsenal at Stamford Bridge. The following close season saw the departure of Seed and Allen but Wednesday still remained highly competitive after making a tremendous start by winning their first four games and scoring twenty goals, Stephenson getting four in a remarkable opening-day 6-1 win at Blackburn Rovers. They did, unsurprisingly, top the table in those early weeks but needed a late charge to secure third place again, just six points behind champions Everton. Ball was again top scorer with twenty-three while it should be noted that Hooper's incredible ever-present run ceased at 182 games after he missed the final away game of the 1931/32 campaign at Manchester City. Also, as they had to deal with several years earlier, Wednesday were forced to dampen speculation that they were to lose many of their star players due to increasingly poor attendances – the economic depression of the early 1930s was certainly having an effect with average crowds dropping under 20,000 in 1930/31 and then under 17,000 for the next four seasons. It was the *London Press* that reported that the club had 'invited offers for any of their players' and 'negotiations could be opened for the transfer of any one, or several, of their playing staff'. Wednesday again felt that a public statement was necessary in which they stated they were 'not in any financial difficulty but on the contrary were in an enviably strong position in that regard'. Despite quashing those rumours, fans were somewhat apprehensive about the new season with doubts being raised about how an aging Owls team could maintain their position as one of England's leading clubs. Brown, though, allayed those fears, expressing his full confidence in his squad and promised not to change his tactic of 'pursuing a forward policy'. Wednesday's legendary manager was proven correct again as his side, including newcomer Ronnie Starling, recovered from a poor start to remain in the divisional top three from late November until the end of the season. The Owls' climb up the table started in early October and reached a crescendo on 2 January 1933 when Arsenal, who again were seemingly running away with the league, visited for a game that Wednesday simply had to win. The fixture fired the imagination of Wednesdayites to such an extent that a new record figure for a home league fixture was set (65,345) and the vast majority went home delighted after a 3-2 win. Incidentally, in that game, Ball claimed one of his goals from the penalty spot and by the season's end had netted ten times from there, from fourteen attempts, to set a club record that would stand for almost fifty years. Wednesday maintained their title challenge for several more weeks and in late March were within two points of the Gunners with a game in hand, but crucially then lost Leach to a twenty-eight-day suspension after he was sent off in a win against Wolverhampton Wanderers. The loss of a key member of the back line clearly disrupted Wednesday, with several players being tried unsuccessfully as his replacement, and with new signing George Bratley in the side, a defeat at Newcastle United dashed hopes. Wednesday only won once during Leach's absence and that effectively ended a title challenge that had seemed so likely to succeed just a few weeks earlier. Despite being second from late February, Wednesday eventually had to be content with third place, three points behind Aston Villa, who crucially won 2-0 at Hillsborough in the penultimate home game. In the final analysis, it had been another season where a poor finish denied Wednesday the chance of a fifth title, although the opportunity had on this occasion slipped away over several matches, as opposed to a dramatic late collapse.

After such a near miss, the question for Brown was how to add that extra bit of quality, and in which position, to drag the club over the finishing line in those final few weeks of a season. Sadly, he would not be around at the end of the 1933/34 campaign as in October the club was rocked when he tendered his resignation due to poor health, with assistant Joe McClelland put in temporary charge. Several names were linked with the vacant position, including ex-players Brough Fletcher and Andrew Wilson, but Wednesday had their eyes firmly set on only one man – Jimmy Seed. However, after they failed to persuade Seed to return, their attention turned to St Johnstone manager Thomas Muirhead, the Owls announcing his appointment in November 1933. However, the club had 'jumped the gun' and a few days later the deal fell through altogether. In the end it was Billy Walker who took over, with the rudderless ship having almost sunken to the bottom of the division. It had been a disastrous season so far but the new man at the helm did spark a revival, winning his first four games and embarking on a sixteen-game unbeaten run in league and cup. In the end Wednesday had to be content with a mid-table finish after a season of changes in both playing and managerial personnel; one of Walker's first acts was to swap Ball for Manchester United's Neil Dewar, while he courted criticism when crowd darling Blenkinsop was sold to rivals Liverpool. There was also sad news when long-serving trainer Chris Craig passed away after a brief illness – it had been a bad season in so many ways.

The first full season in charge for Walker almost began in tragedy as the club's annual outing, to Filey in August 1934, courted with disaster as the charabanc transporting the players almost got stuck on the railway lines at a crossing. The oncoming train just missed the party, although the railway crossing gates were smashed beyond repair – it was a lucky escape. After that pre-season scare, Walker announced that Starling would be the club's new captain – George Irwin had taken over from the late Craig – and Wednesday made a great start, winning the first two league fixtures to top the table. It would not last though and by the onset of autumn, Walker's new-look side had slipped down into mid-table – the likes of Jack Palethorpe and Jack Surtess were added to the squad. It was also noted in October 1934 that there was now no reason for players to be lonely or walk the streets at night as a new social club had been opened at the ground with billiards, table tennis, whist, darts, quoits, skittles and refreshments all available to club personnel. Whether the new social amenities helped team spirit is not known but Wednesday did enjoy a fine run to the end of the 1934 calendar year and by early January 1935 had climbed to fourth, triggering optimism that a rather unexpected title challenge could materialise. The fact that Wednesday failed to stop Arsenal's march to a hat-trick of league titles was perhaps mainly due to the club's progress in the FA Cup, which of course ended in glory at Wembley. It was not that Wednesday fell away – they stayed in the top four from mid-February onwards and ended in third place – but it would be fair to say that the cup run did provide a quite substantial distraction and a plethora of late-season draws ensured a finish nine points behind the Gunners. It had, however, been a great season with Wednesday, after the blip of 1933/34, remaining unbeaten at home – the last time a Wednesday side has achieved that feat.

Fall from Grace: Relegation and Revival

Thankfully, there was none of the drama of the previous pre-season when 100 players, officials, staff and friends visited Trentham Gardens (in Staffordshire) for the club's annual outing in August 1935. Cheques were presented to all eleven players of the cup-winning side, plus the two reserves (Walker and Cooper), while medals were also presented to Walker & Irwin. It was going to be difficult for Walker to top his first full season in charge but he seemed content with the players at his disposal, despite the departure of another player from that 1930 championship team, Alf Strange, who was surprisingly allowed to join Bradford Park Avenue. Other departures included Law, Brolly and Breedon, none of whom had made much of an impact at senior level. The club announced plans for a new share issue with 700 £10 shares to be released, hoping to settle a mortgage of £3,300 and debentures of £3,700. It was perhaps noticeable that none of the extra funds were to be made available for player purchases and questions were soon being asked when a good start gave way to a poor run of results that plunged the club down the table. As early as September 1935, Walker commented after back-to-back defeats that 'we are certainly not getting panicky. They were two off days but the side did well enough in the previous games and there is no reason to think they will fail the club this season. However if it is necessary to get other players, we shall'. Soon after, Wednesday won the Charity Shield, beating Arsenal at Highbury, but it was clear that all was not well behind the scenes, exemplified by the shock sale of FA Cup hero Palethorpe to Aston Villa, leaving the club with only one centre-forward. He was very reluctant to leave – publically stating that he did not want to go – but depart he did, with Wednesday slipping further down the league as the months passed. The club's predicament reached crisis point on Easter Monday following a 5-0 beating at Middlesbrough, as Wednesday dropped into the two relegation positions with only five games left. The real possibility of relegation for the FA Cup winners loomed large on the horizon but a 3-0 win at Stoke City steadied the ship and Wednesday just survived. As soon as the season ended the inquest began, the club's lack of power in the half-back positions – the days of Strange-Leach-Marsden being a distant memory – pinpointed as the main reason for the rapid decline, with the team losing confidence due to that deficiency. It was also stated that if Starling did not perform then Wednesday did not and it was clear that Walker had a lot of work to do in the close season. It was a busy summer in the transfer market with two new goalkeepers signed,

Roy Smith and Derwick Goodfellow, but several of the other newcomers, like Allenby Driver and James McCambridge, were simply not of the sufficient quality and Wednesday would endure a desperate season. A hat-trick from Dewar helped Wednesday win their second home game 6-4 versus Everton, but it would be another two months before another was secured, by which time Wednesday had slipped down into the lower reaches. Problems piled up with three players, Grosvenor, McCambridge and Rhodes, all transfer listed over an unknown issue. Injuries also bit deeply into a squad that already looked paper thin. One bright spot was the emergence of inside forward George Drury, who was compared to early twentieth-century winger Harry Davis, while fellow attacker Jackie Robinson was continuing to flourish in his first full season. However, by early January, Walker had tried six different men in the No. 9 shirt (the figure would increase to ten by the seasons' end) and Wednesday fans were apoplectic when their club turned down a huge bid from Arsenal for Robinson only to instead sell Starling to Aston Villa. As the club's league position gradually worsened, Walker even employed the services of the sports psychologist – a real novelty in pre-war British football – and in March 1937 held a 'heart to heart' talk with the players. However, nothing altered the club's fortunes and at the end of the campaign Dewar was top scorer with a paltry ten goals with his side rock bottom of the division. They did, mathematically, take the fight to the last day at Huddersfield Town, although their fate was effectively sealed a week earlier when Manchester City won 5-1 at Maine Road. The Owls finished the season four points from safety with fans disgruntled as the club seemingly put financial profit ahead of playing success – Wednesday had posted their worst financial results at the end of the 1935/36 season but actually recorded a considerable profit in the relegation campaign with the strategy of buying low and selling high coming to fruition. It would be a long summer as Wednesday found themselves back in the second tier after a, largely successful, eleven-year stay in the top flight.

Any Owls fans who hoped for better news in the summer of 1937 were sadly disappointed as not only did Wednesday sell top-scorer Dewar, but one of his direct replacements was a centre-forward, Sid Chedgzoy, from non-league club Runcorn. Wednesday also had a new trainer – Sam Powell, being promoted from assistant – but the club's other new centre-forward, Harry Ware, only scored once in the opening eight games of the season as Wednesday experienced a terrible start back in the Second Division. The new man's lack of goals led to the capture of Bury centre-forward Ernie Matthews but despite a brace on his debut, he also would not prove to be a long-term solution. Confidence was clearly lacking while Wednesday were even fined 2 guineas by the Football Association after being found guilty of fielding an unregistered player – Bob Curry at Aston Villa. A reminder of happy days departed the club when 'keeper Brown moved to Hartlepool United, while the home game against Stockport County had the despairing home fans 'tearing their hair out' as Wednesday squandered a 3-0 lead to draw. The situation would get a lot worse though as a week later Wednesday lost 4-1 at Barnsley and went bottom of the Second Division, their lowest ever placing in league football up until that point. It was obvious that something had to give and it was manager Walker who tendered his resignation. Ironically, Wednesday soared to a 4-0 win over Luton Town immediately after his departure and caretaker boss Eric Taylor remained in charge until early into the new year, when Jimmy McMullan took the reins. While searching for a new manager, Taylor had steered the Owls away from immediate danger but McMullan then oversaw a poor set of results that put Wednesday back in serious trouble, dropping into the bottom two in late March 1938. During this run, the club was the subject of heavy criticism when another key player, outstanding inside forward Drury, was sold to Arsenal, with the club's shareholders even threatening to arrange a protest meeting to show their distinct displeasure – this was akin to mutiny back in those days! Wednesday deflected some of the flack by buying internationals Charlie Napier and Bill Fallon, although it was the capture of Doug Hunt that finally solved the club's dearth of goals. The new attacker hit the winner in the 2-1 home victory over Coventry City (where it was said the Hillsborough roar of old lifted Wednesday) and then grabbed the only goal as a win at fellow strugglers Nottingham Forest pulled his new club out of the relegation places. A brace from newcomer Len Massarella then helped Wednesday record a third straight victory. They were not safe yet though and after winning their final home game went into the last day trip to Tottenham just one point clear of Barnsley. The Tykes were facing Nottingham Forest at Oakwell and Wednesday knew the issue would go to goal average if those two sides drew and the Owls lost at White Hart Lane. Thankfully there was no need for calculations as an early goal from Fallon and second from Hunt ensured the drop into regional football was avoided. Everybody concerned was glad to see the back of the season and for once, Wednesday surprised their fans by starting much better than was expected to top the early league tables. McMullan's new-look side included headline grabbing capture David Russell, and it clearly showed that team spirit had been rekindled as Wednesday were behind three times at Tottenham in the first away game, only to register a draw. The crowds were also returning with over 32,000 watching a win over Tranmere Rovers that put the Owls top. After three awful seasons, Wednesday would remain in contention for promotion for the entire season, which eventually became a straight fight with Sheffield United. The month of October saw Napier score a hat-trick at Southampton but still end up on the losing side, while November saw Doug Hunt create club history when he became the only Sheffield Wednesday player to score a double hat-trick in a competitive fixture, netting after seventeen, twenty-five, thirty-nine, forty-four , sixty-five and eight-seven minutes against Norwich City. A week later he bagged another treble at Luton Town, and it would be his goal tally of twenty-four in the league that meant Wednesday completed their fixtures second in the table. Unfortunately this did not mean promotion as the Blades still had a game to play and the red half of the city would celebrate a return to the First Division after United beat Spurs 6-1 a few days later. Despite falling at the last hurdle, pride had been returned to Owls fans and there was great enthusiasm for the 1939/40 campaign.

Post-war Readjustment and Back in the Top Flight

Of course, the advent of the war meant that league football consisted of only three games before the entire competition was mothballed until returning in 1946/47. The 1939/40 season fixtures were repeated with Wednesday, now managed by Eric Taylor, opening the season with a 4-1 loss at Luton Town. The effect of the war was shown with only two players in that first line-up, Robinson and Goodfellow, having represented the club before the conflict; the nine debutants included Hugh Swift, Joe Cockroft, Redfern Froggatt and Charlie Tomlinson. In the close season the traditionalists among the Owls' following were happy to see the stripes replace the hooped shirt worn in 1945/46. Eric England was appointed assistant to Taylor and Powell and Slynn returned to their pre-war roles as trainer and assistant. Like all of the clubs, the new season was very much a campaign of uncertainly but sadly Wednesday would struggle yet again, just like they had in the first season after the First World War. Thankfully, the season was not quite as disastrous as that one but Wednesday would be fighting against relegation from virtually the first whistle. To compound matters, fans were stunned when Jackie Robinson was sold and it would be literally a very long season as the atrocious winter of 1946 meant that football did not finish until June. As the season progressed, newcomers included attackers George Hunt and Jimmy Dailey with the latter scoring seven times in his first eight games to keep Wednesday just off the bottom rung of the league ladder. Over 41,000 were inside Hillsborough for the Boxing Day defeat to Bury – the biggest home gate of 1946/47 – while the club decided to advertise for a team manager before changing their minds and appointing a trainer-coach instead, William Knox. Over the next few weeks, games were either postponed or played on snowbound pitches, and it was not until spring that football returned to some sort of normality. Wednesday introduced new men Jackie Marriott and Doug Witcomb into their side but the struggles continued with safety only guaranteed in the final home game when Tommy Ward fired home the winner against Manchester City. Owls chairman William Fearnehough admitted it had been the worst season in Wednesday's history – the final position of twentieth was the lowest ever finish – but would not comment further when quizzed what might have actually caused the season of struggle, and more importantly how it was to be corrected. That unanswered question may have been the reason behind a shareholders' association being formed in the summer of 1947, with the intent of challenging for four vacant seats on the board of directors. Unbeknown to fans, though, was that Wednesday had spent the summer trying to sign a high-profile player and was willing to break the transfer record to achieve that aim. However, attempts at signing Jack Stamps and then Walter Ardron both failed and it was not until October 1947 that they got their man, paying Bury £12,000 for Eddie Quigley. The highlight of the opening weeks was a five-goal haul for Dailey against Barnsley, while overall it was a surprisingly positive start and after a fruitful Christmas period Wednesday were in the promotion race, sitting fourth. After a winless run, Wednesday suddenly hit form and six consecutive wins put them a point behind second placed Newcastle United, with five games remaining. Fans were also flocking back to the old ground, as they were countrywide, as a post-war boom in attendances continued unabated, with over 51,000 watching the Easter Monday win over Doncaster Rovers and the seasonal average of almost 36,000 broke club records. In the final analysis a huge crowd at St James' Park, Newcastle, witnessed the game that decided who would accompany Birmingham City into the First Division. The two rivals met with only three games to play and interest in the game was such that fans started arriving at the ground at 9 a.m. and the gates were closed over an hour before the start with 66,480 crammed inside. The game was tied precariously at 2-2 with just a few minutes remaining but disaster then struck for Wednesday as home forward Houghton scored twice, taking his side to the two points and eventual promotion; Wednesday ended the season in a credible fourth place.

After a much-improved season, Taylor decided there was no reason to tinker with his playing personnel with only the departure of Hunt and Ward, although fourteen-year-old Albert Quixall left school to join the club's ground staff. The first goal of the 1948/49 campaign came against Wednesday – Tottenham scoring after ninety seconds – but Wednesday enjoyed another encouraging campaign, although the promotion push failed dramatically after winning only one of their final eight games, slipping down to finish eighth. Wednesday was also cursed with bad luck as in December they equalled the British transfer record when paying £20,000 for Eddie Kilshaw, only for their new capture to snap his cruciate ligament and end his playing days after just nineteen games. At the club's Annual General Meeting it was revealed there had a been a sizeable deficit of £17,000 on transfers, the club commenting that 'it was found impossible to strengthen all the known weaknesses, determined efforts will again be made during the coming season to bring the team up to the required strength'. None of the aforementioned recruiting took place until the 1949/50 campaign had commenced but it was clearly not a priority as the team made a terrific start after overcoming the blow of losing two men with broken legs on the opening day – Dennis Woodhead in the first team and goalie Albert Morton in the reserves. Goals came from several sources, Quigley hitting a treble inside five minutes, just a minute longer than Trotter's record, and finished the win over Chesterfield with four goals. Clarrie Jordan also grabbed four versus Hull City, while four weeks later the only goal of the game at Preston was scored after just twelve seconds by Tomlinson – the quickest scored by Wednesday. The Owls also sold Quigley for a British record fee, but suffered only three defeats in the first half of the campaign, finishing the calendar year sat in second after a thirteen-game unbeaten run. Although form dipped somewhat in the new year, they remained in the promotion mix, but there was sad news when trainer Knox died suddenly. It was third time lucky in attempts to replace Quigley as Gerry Henry arrived from Bradford Park Avenue, with Hugh McJarrow also signing; the new men played their part as the season reached a dramatic conclusion, a late-season 'promotion wobble' from Wednesday meaning they finished third when most of their rivals had completed their fixtures – Sheffield United won their final four league games to sneak past Wednesday into second. However, the Blades had finished their fixtures and, in a mirror image of the situation in 1939, it was Wednesday who still had a game to play, at home to champions Tottenham. The race for promotion was so tight that the difference would be a fraction of a percent, but all Wednesday knew was that a win or a 0-0 draw would be enough to pip United and Southampton. In the end, the goal average margin was a mere 0.008 as 50,853 nervously watched Wednesday and Spurs play out a 0-0. At the final whistle thousands swarmed onto the pitch and the police had to break up a fight in front of the south stand so the players could return to the dressing rooms. Wednesday had hidden their 'best' corner flags and goal nets under the stand so any souvenir hunters would avail themselves of 'reserve' items; five of the six touchline flags duly found new homes. The club had, somewhat presumptuously, erected a platform in the director's box and the players appeared, to a huge ovation, before chairman Fearnehough addressed the crowd. It was then the turn of Captain Swift to say a few words, expressing the team's pleasure at being promoted. After six attempts, the Owls were back in the 'big time', but it was just the beginning of a topsy-turvy decade.

Down, Up, Down, Up, Down and Up Again

As seemed to be club policy in those early years after the war, there were almost no incomings into Hillsborough in the summer months as Taylor prepared for life back in the higher league. A heavy defeat at Chelsea and then a resounding 2-1 home success over champions Portsmouth opened the season but it would be a long campaign as sixteen away defeats put enormous pressure on home form. That record at Hillsborough was reasonable and at least kept Wednesday in with a chance of avoiding the drop on the final Saturday of the season. Prior to that 'red letter day', Wednesday had been involved in two sensational transfer stories as they tried to stave off relegation. The first rocked Sheffield football to its foundations when Sheffield United accepted a British transfer record fee of

£32,500 for arguably their greatest ever player, Jimmy Hagan. The Blades fans were furious that their club had accepted the bid and it was only Hagan who blocked the move – Wednesday had, unbeknown to their supporters, also tried to sign Nat Lofthouse from Bolton Wanderers! A few weeks later they did break the British record, paying £35,000 for inside forward Jackie Sewell. It was a desperate, and expensive, last-ditch attempt to preserve top-flight status and Sewell did net six times in ten games before the end of the season. Two of those came in the final game against Everton at Hillsborough, when the Owls knew that they had to win by at least six clear goals to have any chance of sending Chelsea down instead. Incredibly they did win 6-0 but the Londoners won 4-0, sending Wednesday back from whence they had come, this time by a goal average of 0.044. It was just the start of a period in the club's history commonly referred to as the 'yo-yo years' as they bounced up and down between the top two divisions. They would come straight back up in 1952 with the goals of Sewell and the remarkable season enjoyed by Derek Dooley, who netted forty-six times in only thirty league games. Dooley's scoring record was phenomenal as he grabbed five hat-tricks, which included a five and two four-goal hauls, plus by netting in nine consecutive games he set an unsurpassed club record. The season had actually started disappointingly and it was only when Taylor called up Dooley that goals and wins started to flow. All of his five goals against Notts County came in the second half – another club record – and it was fitting that he scored the final goal of the season, and Wednesday's 100th in the league, in the final day home draw against West Ham United, the title and promotion having been secured a week earlier at Coventry City. Attendances at Hillsborough, despite Wednesday being in the lower division, actually topped the huge average of 1950/51 (the Dooley factor being the main reason) with the Boxing Day game against Nottingham Forest attracting over 61,000. That average would rise to the highest in Wednesday history in 1952/53 (42,539) and it would be a bittersweet season, which saw Wednesday start brightly and occupy a mid-table position before tragedy struck on a February afternoon as chairman Fearnehough died and then talisman forward Dooley broke his leg in a game at Preston North End. What followed shocked the football world as Dooley contracted gas gangrene and despite the doctor's best efforts, he became gravely ill; the medics had no choice but to amputate his right leg, saving his life. Before that fateful day, Wednesday had enjoyed a comfortable season and sat firmly in mid-table, Dooley having scored sixteen times. Perhaps understandably, the team's form dipped after that Preston game and Wednesday supporters were somewhat fraught after they lost a 3-1 lead at Aston Villa, in the final away game, to lose 4-3 and blow their first opportunity to save themselves. This meant the issue went to final game of the season at home to Sunderland, with a win required. Thankfully, Wednesday started confidently and with Sewell in fine form they recorded a comprehensive 4-0 win to end a turbulent season on a high, with thoughts still with Dooley. The bumper crowds were reflected in a record turnover figure in the club's accounts and some of the profit on the season was utilised to bring in centre-forward Jack Shaw. The new season followed almost an identical path to the previous campaign, with Wednesday enjoying a creditable first half before slipping down the division to finish nineteenth, although they were never in any danger of relegation. A return visit to Deepdale again proved disastrous as not only did McIntosh break his arm but Wednesday lost 6-0, stand-in goalie Curtis saving two penalties. In November, Wednesday played their first match in the UK under floodlights, wearing special silk shirts with blue sleeves for the friendly game at Derby County. With the club progressing in the FA Cup, league form suffered, Wednesday losing three in a row after being knocked out, but a 4-2 victory against Sunderland all but guaranteed safety.

Owls' fans hoped that after two seasons of consolidation, Wednesday would progress towards a top-half finish, although the major story of the summer was the installation of floodlights at Hillsborough. However, a few weeks into the season it had become apparent that the side was lacking two major qualities – defensive solidity and the ability to hold on to an advantage. Wednesday conceded fifteen goals in their first five games and dropped to the bottom of the league after leaking four goals at home to Manchester City in early November 1954. Wednesday did not win again until 19 March 1955, the terrible run including the club's 2000th league game, a 2-1 home loss to Sunderland. Earlier in the season around 40,000 had packed Hillsborough to see the state visit of the newly crowned Elizabeth II and this would be one of the biggest crowds of the campaign as the fans voted with their feet at the club's poor form – Wednesday's average attendance had fallen to just over 27,000, the loss of Dooley and relegation being the obvious contributory factors. The biggest gate of the season was actually for Dooley when 55,000 attended his benefit game. Unsurprisingly, there was no escape this time as despite bringing in both Peter Baker and Don McEvoy to shore up the back line, they finished rock bottom and were relegated on Good Friday, with five games remaining. Only eight wins were recorded all season, 100 goals conceded and they finished thirteen points from the safety line. The search for a replacement for Dooley finally ended when Taylor secured the services of centre-forward Roy Shiner from Huddersfield Town. It was a very busy summer as Walter Bingley, Gerry Young, Don Gibson and Albert Broadbent all arrived, with Wednesday totally revamping their side in an attempt to bounce straight back. Four of the new men were in the first line-up of the new season but it was Sewell and Quixall who scored jointly five times to give the Owls a perfect start. As the new boys settled in, Wednesday's form was inconsistent and it was not until Christmas Eve, after beating Stoke City 4-0, that they went top of the division. Before Wednesday reached the summit, Sewell and Woodhead departed but with Shiner in terrific form, Wednesday ended the season with 101 league goals, the new attacker netting thirty-three. It was in mid-March that promotion started to look

likely, the Owls opening up a five-point advantage at the top after beating
Barnsley in the first home league match under floodlights. That lead was
extended and Wednesday knew a win, with three games remaining, at
home to mid-table Fulham would secure an immediate return to the top
flight. The plan did not quite work, however, as the Londoners led 2-0 at
the break before Wednesday stormed back with a goal from Shiner and
then a penalty from Finney, with just nine minutes left, drawing their side
level with the Hillsborough crowd roaring their approval. Another goal
would be enough but as Wednesday flooded forward they were caught on
the break and it was Fulham who grabbed the winner – promotion was
put back on ice. Wednesday's next chance came at Bury and this time there
was no doubt, winning 5-2 to seal promotion and the championship. All
that was left was the final game of the season where the president of the
Football League was on hand to present the Championship Shield and
Wednesday, who had fielded the same side for thirteen of the final fourteen
games, delighted the 32,129 crowd with a 5-3 win over Lincoln City. Late
in the game a few home fans also cheered at the result coming in from
Tottenham where city rivals United simply had to win to have any chance
of avoiding relegation – they drew 1-1 and ensured the clubs swapped
places, thirty-four years before the opposite occurred. For the third time in
the decade, Wednesday had returned to the First Division and fans hoped
that this time they would stick around. Those hopes, though, would not
be fulfilled as Wednesday experienced another down on the rollercoaster
of the yo-yo years, as although they comfortably retained their status in
1956/57, the proverbial axe fell in 1958 with a third relegation in seven
years. The Owls, with Jack Marshall now ensconced as trainer-coach,
made a great start to the 1956/57 season. It would be a tremendous home
record that ensured a final position of fourteenth as sixteen losses on their
travels meant the season could be nothing more than one of consolidation.
There were very few changes to the squad after the promotion in 1956
but although Wednesday had no problems scoring – netting eighty-two –
it was a different story at the back where eighty-eight goals were leaked.
It was clear that defensive reinforcements were required. Those new men
did not materialise though, in one of the quietest summers for years, and
there was genuine worry that another season of struggle was imminent.
A good start was again needed but Wednesday were suddenly hit with
a flu epidemic that saw the opening game, at home to Manchester City,
postponed with several players and staff showing severe symptoms – back
in the 1950s flu could easily turn to pneumonia, which was a serious
danger to life. Wednesday were also allowed to call off their midweek
visit to Newcastle United and when the season did eventually start,
they could only field a depleted side. The patched-up team lost 2-1 and
Wednesday quickly slumped to the wrong end of the table. A crazy month
of December showed their problems as Wednesday scored fifteen times
in five games but managed to secure a solitary point as the porous back

line leaked twenty-six, including four in the draw with Preston North End on the club's last Christmas Day fixture. The festive period ended with Wednesday firmly in last place, the position of goalkeeper becoming a major issue as several men were tried, including Charlie Pllu, Brian Ryalls and veteran Dave McIntosh, before Taylor made arguably his greatest ever signing as Ron Springett arrived to emphatically plug the gap. His arrival had an instant effect as Springett kept two clean sheets in his first three games and saw the goals against column dramatically slow down. It could be argued that if the new 'keeper had arrived a month earlier then the Owls could have escaped relegation, as they did take the issue until the final day of the season, although their survival was dependent upon other teams slipping up. Just over 25,000 watched their side beat Wolves 2-1 at Hillsborough but with their two relegation rivals, Sunderland and Leicester City, winning it was academic, another spell back in the Second Division the club's fate.

It had become abundantly clear that a solution was needed to end this inconsistency and they did indeed make a quite revolutionary change, deciding to split the traditional secretary-manager role in two. Therefore, Rochdale manager Harry Catterick arrived as the first Wednesday team manager, Taylor becoming solely an administrator. It was not known publically though that Catterick was not the club's first choice for the role, with Tottenham manager Bill Nicholson – who led his side to the 'double' in 1961 – interviewed but, for an unknown reason, not appointed. The change in the club's backroom structure was perhaps a reason why there was again no transfer activity before the 1958/59 season began, the club understandably confident that a first-choice side of Springett, Curtis, Megson, McAnearney, Swan, Kay, Wilkinson, Shiner, Froggatt and Finney would be highly competitive. This did indeed prove the case and Catterick was perhaps fortunate to take over when many of those aforementioned players were reaching their 'peak years'. Despite that, the new manager soon moulded a team that would end the season with a club record 106 league goals and bring another divisional honour to Hillsborough. A remarkable start to the season saw the club win eleven of their opening thirteen games, the only draw being 3-3 at Sunderland where Eric and Derek Wilkinson became the only twins to appear in a senior fixture for Wednesday. That start also included a 6-0 home win over Sunderland, which proved to be the final appearance for 'golden boy' Albert Quixall as a few days later he departed for Manchester United for a British record £45,000. His departure did not impact greatly on the club's form as he'd only started four games and Froggatt quickly filled the void as Wednesday continued to score freely and lead the division. As the season reached its conclusion it effectively became a straight fight between Wednesday and Fulham for the title and it was the Cottagers who sneaked back into first place on Good Friday, winning 6-2 at Craven Cottage. The teams subsequently drew back in Sheffield on Easter Monday but the Owls reclaimed the summit and went into the midweek home game with Liverpool in the knowledge that a win would secure promotion. As is often the case in these situations, the game was tension filled and low on chances but the one goal that did hit the net was for the Owls as Froggatt side-footed home from a right-wing centre from Finney after sixty-five minutes. Celebrations followed in the dressing rooms and in the stands, with a fourth promotion in the decade secure, the match winner commenting, as he sipped on champagne, 'It was worth waiting for. But it was a relief when I saw the ball slip past Younger.' Despite those celebrations, Wednesday was not mathematically promoted but rivals Sheffield United needed to win each of their last six games by at least 4-0, and for Wednesday to lose all of theirs in the same manner, so the celebrations were perhaps understandable. The race for the Championship Shield went to the penultimate Saturday as after a midweek loss for Fulham, Wednesday knew a home win over Barnsley would clinch the title. The Tykes also went into the game needing a win to have any chance of avoiding relegation, but the teams were met with heavy rain, which kept the attendance down to a season low of only 17,917. Those that did brave the inclement conditions witnessed a totally one-sided game, which Wednesday won 5-0 to emphatically seal the title.

A First Division Force and Bribes Scandal Hits Hard

After several years of false dawns, the 1959/60 campaign finally saw Wednesday become a force again in the top division. The club was actually criticised by many for not making any major signings but Catterick was clearly happy with his squad and that faith was rewarded as Wednesday enjoyed their best season in England's top division for a quarter of a century, finishing fifth, just six points behind champions Burnley, after an unlikely title challenge only fell away in the dying embers of the season – the Owls sat third with five games remaining. The campaign had started with a rare win at Highbury, but early results were decidedly mixed with Wednesday in the lower mid-table before an incredible burst of goalscoring, which began with a 3-1 win at Leeds United, followed by a 7-0 thrashing of West Ham United, who at the time were top of the league. Wednesday, including new signing Bobby Craig, then grabbed four at Chelsea and put five past Arsenal as they jumped up several places to the fringes of the top six. The goals did dry up somewhat but the wins continued and it was only a run of one win in their final five games that scuppered hopes of a fifth league title and becoming the first club to win the title immediately after promotion. Catterick's first season in charge in the top division had been a great success and he would follow that with an even better campaign in 1960/61 as Wednesday became the only challengers to the great Tottenham 'double' side; it was unfortunate that arguably the club's best side since the war peaked at the same time as Tottenham as their points total of fifty-eight would have been enough to win the championship in the season before and season afterwards. In the end, Wednesday had to settle for the runners-up spot, eight points behind Spurs, after a terrific campaign that included just seven defeats. Unsurprisingly, there was no criticism from fans after Wednesday again brought no new players into the club in the summer of 1960, and Catterick's faith in his squad again came to fruition as Wednesday were unbeaten for the first twelve games – the best start since 1899/00 – to sit four points behind Spurs, who had dropped only a point. A first defeat was eventually suffered at Wolves before one of the most memorable games ever staged at Hillsborough as the unbeaten leaders rolled into town. It was highly likely that Wednesday would have set a record attendance for a league fixture on that day if it was not for the small fact that the ground was only three-sided, as the old North Stand had been demolished and the current Cantilever structure being built. Despite there being no accommodation on the North side, over 56,000 packed in, with the gates closed before kick-off, and were treated to a hard-fought encounter that was won in the sixty-eighth minute when Fantham pounced on a loose ball in the area to fire home and clinch a 2-1 win – it was said that the roar for both Owls goals could be heard at Bramall Lane where United fans were watching a reserve game. Unfortunately, it was a case of 'After the Lord Mayor's Show' following that win as Wednesday lost three consecutive games, although they did remain second. A nerve-shredding 5-4 home win over Blackburn Rovers followed (Wednesday were 5-1 ahead at half-time) before the festive period was dominated by the terrible accident that resulted in young professional Dougie McMillan having his leg amputated at the scene when the Wednesday team coach careered off the road, in icy conditions, near Huntington, on their way home from a Boxing Day draw at Highbury. The vast majority of the passengers only suffered cuts and bruises, although Swan did suffer a double fracture of his shoulder, but it was the tragic career-ending injury of McMillan that grabbed the headlines, just a few short years after Dooley underwent the same life-saving medical procedure. Five days later, McMillan phoned his teammates from his hospital bed to wish them good luck and the team duly dedicated the 2-0 success over Birmingham City to him. The first two months of 1961 was a wonderful time for Wednesdayites as not only did their side produce some terrific football but also recorded some striking wins, commencing with a remarkable 6-1 victory at Fulham where Mullery put the ball into his own net after just thirty seconds. Wednesday also grabbed five against Preston and four at Burnley, and five wins in a row catapulted the club back into the title chase – before the Easter programme they were just three points behind Spurs. Sadly the club's Achilles heel of finishing seasons badly came back to haunt them again as they won only one of their final seven games, including a 2-1 loss at White Hart Lane, which clinched the title for Tottenham. The last four games saw caretaker boss Taylor in charge after Catterick tendered his resignation and it proved a disappointing end to the season, despite Wednesday posting their highest finish since 1930. Despite finishing the season without a manager, the reserves' winning of the Central League, for only the second time, suggested Wednesday also boasted strength in depth and there was no reason for fans to worry that Catterick's departure would adversely affect the club's fortunes, certainly in the short term. The 1960s would be characterised by several great starts and new manager Vic Buckingham oversaw a five-game start that included four wins, which put his new charges top of the league. There was no new blood in the ranks, the club relying on the players that had enjoyed three excellent back-to-back seasons, and Wednesday spent most of the season in and around the top six positions. A loss of form in the spring, though, suggested all was not well behind the scenes and led to a remarkable outburst from Buckingham, his comments after a defeat at Nottingham Forest hitting the front page of the *Sheffield Telegraph*:

> It's just not good enough. As a team they have not got the skill, and in the long run hard work will never make up for that defect. Their recent displays have been a disgrace to a great club; completely unworthy of Sheffield Wednesday who are an organisation deserving of the highest standard and class that football can offer. The displays have been a let-down in every respect. As team manager I never shirk my own responsibilities and the team's performances rightly reflect just as badly on myself. I am the man who picks the team and thereby I am also to blame. At a time when Sheffield Wednesday should be setting the pace for the game's honours, they are slipping, and unless the slide is halted I can see nothing but a tough battle against relegation next season instead of a stirring fight for the top spots.

It was an unprecedented critique of his players, with the supremo laying part of the blame at Wednesday's new wage structure, which gave players an extra £10 appearance bonus on top of their basic weekly wage, suggesting the league's £4 win and £2 draw bonuses be scrapped and clubs allowed to set their own wage structure, as it was on the Continent. It's not known how the Owls players reacted to his comments but one would assume the criticism was taken on board in a positive manner as the last four games of the season were won to move Wednesday up to a final finishing position of sixth. Fantham, Kay and Megson were ever present with the first named finishing top scorer with eighteen goals. At the season's end, the club announced the departure of stalwart Froggatt, while the biggest capture of the summer was that of centre-forward David Layne. The first appearance of any commercial activity was also noted as a development fund prize draw was launched, the net proceeds going directly to the development of Hillsborough for the benefit of the supporters. Wednesday also boasted a new kit, consisting of much narrower stripes than ever before, but the season would be dominated by one of the worst winters in Britain since records began, which took its icy grip in late December, Wednesday playing only once in the first two months of 1963. The fixture pile-up suffered by all somewhat skewed the league tables, with Wednesday winning five consecutive games in the new year but only moving slightly up the table. Before the weather hit the schedule, Wednesday had experienced a terrible run of twelve matches without a win, which dropped them from seventh down to fifteenth, but overall enjoyed a good season, a uncharacteristic great finish ensuring sixth place again, although a considerable number of points behind Catterick's Everton, a fact not unnoticed by Wednesday followers. The overwhelming positive taken from the campaign though was the outstanding top-flight debut of Layne, who scored twenty-nine goals in thirty-nine games, reminding fans of another brave and strong deadly centre-forward that graced Hillsborough almost ten years earlier. The 1963/64 season again saw Layne terrorise the First Division defences, scoring twenty-three goals in thirty-five appearances, as Wednesday recovered from a bad start to surge up the table to finish sixth again, although this time just eight points behind champions Liverpool. The only notable new arrival was Mark Pearson but the season would only be remembered for a newspaper exclusive, published in April 1964, which had a devastating effect on the club. What became known as the 'bribes scandal' involved several Football League players. Unfortunately for Wednesday the three highest-profile players involved were Layne, Swan and ex-Owl Kay. The players were immediately suspended by the club, Taylor making an impassioned speech at the game against Spurs, which was played on the day following the revelations, asking for the fans to 'be patient with the club in its time of trouble'. It would be over a year before the fate of the conspirators became known – jail sentences and life bans following – with the December 1962 2-0 loss at Ipswich Town being the game where Layne and Swan made their wagers. For Wednesday, the scandal was nothing short of disastrous as they not only lost an outstanding defender but also their deadliest top-flight scorer since the days of Allen and Ball; it could be argued that it was not until the arrival of David Hirst that Wednesday found his replacement. Another season of promise had given way to uncertainty and disappointment as just before the scandal hit Wednesday also said goodbye to team manager Buckingham with Taylor again taking temporary charge.

Centenary Celebrations Before Decline Sets In

The new man at the helm was Alan Brown and he had the job of restoring the good name of the club and trying to equal or better those five consecutive top-six finishes. It would not be an easy task with the loss of Swan and Layne but the new man did secure a reasonable top-ten finish, the switching of John Hickton from defence to attack proving an inspired decision from youth coach Dooley, Hickton netting ten times in a forward partnership with the ever-reliable Fantham as Wednesday finished a couple of points outside of the top six. Another change of home jersey – the stripes being dropped for an all-blue shirt with white sleeves – heralded the start of Brown's second campaign and it would, ironically, be remembered for the club's all-white away kit, which took them all the way to the cup final. Back in the bread and butter of the league, Brown presided over a campaign that was mainly spent in the bottom half of the division, Wednesday dropping as low at nineteenth before ending the season two places higher but only three points away from relegated Northampton Town. The season saw the introduction of substitutes and it was David Ford who entered club history as the first man to take the field in that capacity – versus Sunderland in October 1965. Also newsworthy was the £35,000 fee paid to Chelsea for the services of Jim McCalliog, Wednesday surprising their fans by dishing out what was a record fee for a teenager. The disappointing season in the league was, of course, overshadowed by the cup run while the summer that followed was dominated by the World Cup with Hillsborough staging four games, thanks greatly to the sterling work of Taylor. The ground now had its first 'electronic' scoreboard, installed at the back of the Kop, which, at a cost of £12,800 contained sixty-four characters at £200 each, and over £200,000 was spent to make other improvements, which included a new gymnasium and a restaurant, built on stilts at the back of the South Stand. Minnows Switzerland were adopted by the Wednesday faithful – cow bells were a regular sound on matchdays – and excellent crowds watched them beaten by West Germany, Spain and Argentina before the Germans returned to comprehensively beat Uruguay 4-0 in a quarter-final tie. The city also arranged a multitude of cultural events while the tournament was being played, which included golf matches at Hillsborough Golf Club, a Swiss night at an ice rink, and exhibitions showing the city's cutlery and stainless steel heritage, although the 'golden ticket' was surely the half-hour guided tour of the Park Hill flats development!

The Owls appearance at Wembley and success for England in the World Cup ensured that Wednesday, and football in general, experienced a real boom in attendance figures, the Owls seeing a rise of almost a third in 1966/67 to an average of 30,629. Wednesday also made a great start, topping the table after six games before falling away to experience a season firmly entrenched in mid-table. One of the most notable events occurred at Southampton in October 1966 when, with two minutes remaining, the referee awarded the away side a penalty kick. It was the first spot kick awarded to Wednesday since Boxing Day 1964, an unbelievable eighty-two games earlier, which Peter Eustace duly dispatched. On the transfer front, Wednesday brought in prolific scorer John Ritchie with fans particularly grateful for the deal as whenever Wednesday faced the Potteries club it always seemed that Ritchie scored. Despite finishing down in mid-table, Hillsborough fans were treated to some spectacular home displays with Chelsea beaten 6-1, Sunderland hit for five and Burnley beaten 7-0, Jack Whitham becoming the first Owls player to score as a substitute. There were also big changes behind the scenes as Brown made multiple alterations to his staff as he looked for more consistency: trainer-coach David Smith departed, along with former players Logan, Swift and Bannister, while Jack Marshall returned, in addition to Lawrie McMenemy. Before commencing their centenary season, a unique swap deal took place that saw Ron Springett swap clubs with his Queen's Park Rangers custodian brother Peter to ensure the Springett name would appear on Wednesday team sheets for three decades. The opening-day success at West Ham United was significant as when Fantham fired home it brought his Owls total to 149 goals, passing the post-war record set by Froggatt – he would add seventeen more to set a record that still stands today, second only to Wilson. It was perhaps appropriate that when Wednesday celebrated their 100th birthday the team was actually atop the First Division table and duly won the next game against Fulham 4-2, which was designated as a celebration match, Wednesday distributing special pin badges and cutting admission prices by 50 per cent, although this was done without any publicity beforehand, presumably to reward the diehards who would routinely attend a fairly unglamorous midweek home fixture. Everything seemed rosy in the garden, despite fielding a relatively young side, with the club top of the division, attendances increasing again and hopes high that Brown had finally found the solution to the infuriating inconsistency that had kept the club out of the chase for league honours since earlier in the decade. It would be fair to say that the club's team manager did solve that inconsistency but unfortunately it was achieved with a series of defeats, Wednesday experiencing a run of eight losses in nine games, as they plunged down the table. Their form was so poor that Wednesday only won twice after the December 1967 success over West Ham United and the alarming slump ran all the way to the end of the season as Wednesday just stayed up, by two points, from relegated Sheffield United – the three points gleaned off their city rivals proving vital. The season also saw the departure of Brown, who moved back to Sunderland, with his assistant Marshall taking temporary charge before being appointed full time. It was becoming clear that Wednesday's playing personnel had diminished in both size and quality and with the reserves also struggling at the wrong end of their division, it was a big job ahead for Marshall if the decline was to be stopped before it gathered further momentum. Those worries continued into the close season when several players asked to leave and Wednesday failed, despite efforts, to add to their threadbare squad. When the season started though, those concerns disappeared into the background as another tremendous beginning somewhat papered over the cracks, including arguably the greatest game ever played at the ground – an incredible 5-4 win over reigning European Champions Manchester United. With Whitham taking over the scoring responsibility from Fantham, the squad performed admirably to maintain a comfortable top-ten position well into the new year, although Whitham had been lost to injury in late October. Sadly, it was then a case of déjà vu for Wednesday supporters as the terrible post-Christmas slump of the previous campaign was repeated with only one victory accrued from 21 December 1968 until the end of the season. The dreadful run of results peaked with a shocking 5-0 home loss to Arsenal, which saw the team booed off the pitch by increasingly frustrated and disappointed Wednesdayites. Wednesday then decided that enough was enough – manager Marshall departing – and with Tom McAnearney in a caretaker role, Wednesday limped to the finishing line, their excellent early season form ensuring a respectable finish of fifteenth. Despite Wednesday not having a manager, they still hit the headlines in May 1969 when teenager Tommy Craig arrived from Aberdeen, Wednesday not only breaking their own transfer record by paying £100,000 for his signature but also setting a new British record for a teenager. The surprise arrival did bring a late season boost to the Wednesday fans but, despite Craig proving to be an excellent player, the following season would be tortuous as Wednesday struggled from the first game, after a summer which saw Ritchie return to Stoke City before Danny Williams was appointed manager. Hopes of a good season took a further nosedive when McCalliog was sold to Wolves, with Wednesdayites legitimately asking who was left at the club to score the goals. The previous season's regulars included the departed McCalliog, 'keeper Springett and defenders Vic Mobley (who soon departed also) and Gerry Young. So when Scottish minnows Airdrie won a preseason match at Hillsborough, Wednesday supporters must have had a sense of foreboding. Defeats in their first three league engagements did little to raise any hopes and despite the subsequent arrival of Willie Lawson, Jackie Sinclair and Tony Coleman, the club spent all season in the lower reaches of the table. A brief flurry in late February/early March, consisting of three straight wins, did raise hopes that the drop could be avoided before five consecutive defeats left the club's First Division tenure hanging by a thread. By this time, Fantham had also departed and stalwart Megson announced his retirement. It was clear to all that hardly any of the players who had made the club one of the best in the country in the early 1960s had been replaced with similar quality and this situation had left Wednesday with two games to save themselves. The first opportunity, at Manchester United, did produce some fight of old as despite Best and Charlton putting the home side 2-0 ahead, Wednesday hit back, with Coleman and Whitham scoring to gain a precious point. The result left the Owls with a golden chance to escape as they faced Manchester City at Hillsborough knowing a win would be enough to lift them off the foot of the table and squeeze above Crystal Palace on goal average. The visitors certainly had one eye on their forthcoming final in the European Cup Winners Cup and many people believed that they would take the game fairly easy to ensure no injuries were sustained in advance of that final – key men Bell and Lee were rested. Wednesday fans rallied around their club in their hour of need with 45,258 attending – the biggest crowd of the season – but Wednesday had already lost nine times at Hillsborough and the reason was clear as City dominated the opening exchanges and Wednesday started badly. History suggests that an incident in the twenty-third minute relegated the Owls as a poor tackle from Prophett curtailed the night for Summerbee, substitute Ian Bowyer taking his place. Many of the City players were somewhat aggrieved by the tackle and seemed to double their efforts to go in front through Bowyer before a long-range shot from Coleman levelled matters after sixty-five minutes. Unfortunately, the team just could not raise their game and when Bowyer headed home in the final minute, it was all over. Many fans booed the team off at the final whistle and a local press reporter best summed up the game, and perhaps even the whole campaign, by commenting that Wednesday were 'indifferent at the back, hapless in midfield and impotent in attack'. It would be a long road back.

No Quick Return Before a Slide Down the Divisions

Preparation for life in the lower tier started with several backroom changes as ex-players Albert Broadbent and Tom McAnearney departed and Dave Ewing was appointed to a senior trainer/coach role – it was a quick return to S6 for Ewing as he was the man who carried off the injured Summerbee in that fateful game against City. On the playing front, the signings of Sammy Todd and John Sissons seemed excellent business but it was obvious where the club's deficiency lay, as with Whitham sold to Liverpool, the Owls were again lacking a goalscorer. The emerging Mick Prendergast would partly solve that problem – he finished the season with sixteen league goals – but the club never showed any sign of launching a promotion challenge, spending most the season in the wrong half of the table, eventually finishing fifteenth. The highs were far outweighed by the lows with a shocking 5-1 home defeat to Luton Town leaving the home fans apoplectic at how far their club had fallen in such a short time. One of the last players on their books who could be classed as being of First Division quality, Wilf Smith, was sold – he became the most expensive full-back in the British game – and despite his direct replacement, Peter Rodrigues, being of a good standard, it was yet another case of replacing a player with an inferior one. With Wednesday stagnating, the departure of Williams was no real surprise, a flu epidemic having further impeded the Owls a few weeks earlier, the club unsuccessfully asking the Football League to postpone their match at Birmingham City in mid-December. The Boxing Day game at Hull City was memorable only for the fact that Wednesday led 4-1 with only seven minutes to play but still only managed to come home with a single point. The new manager would certainly prove a popular choice as Derek Dooley stepped into the breach, but he was inheriting a Wednesday side lacking any real quality, with the exception of Craig, although he did take the club on a mini-unbeaten run at Hillsborough, which proved sufficient to allay relegation fears. The season finished with a 3-0 beating at Carlisle United and players, fans and officials were just glad to see the back of a hugely disappointing season, which saw a rebel shareholders' association formed, the club report a large loss in its annual accounts (income fell by almost half) and, perhaps even more of concern, average home crowds plummet to just over 16,000, the club's lowest figure for almost fifty years. The first job for the new boss was to revamp his playing personnel and to that end he secured the signatures of John Holsgrove before both Brian Joicey and Dave Clements arrived a few weeks into the 1971/72 campaign. With the club again on the receiving end of huge criticism from the shareholders' association, they must have prayed for a good start but sadly the opposite occurred, a 5-1 home reverse to Bristol City the worst result in a six-game winless start, which dumped the Owls firmly last. The aforementioned captures from Coventry City did, though, have the desired effect, Joicey quickly becoming a popular figure among Wednesday fans as the club registered some notable wins, including a 3-0 victory at Orient in November 1971 – the biggest away league victory for almost three years. As Wednesday entered the busy Christmas period, they sat tenth in the league, but a poor run then scuppered any hopes of a promotion challenge, Wednesday not winning again until February 1972. Hat-tricks for both Sissons and Joicey featured in the remaining games of the season with the former's treble being somewhat unique as he ended the game on the losing side as Wednesday lost 5-3 at Burnley. Wednesday also took the decision to take their squad away for a five-day break in Majorca, although a defeat at Bristol City on their return suggested all that was achieved was impressive tans. The only other incident of note was the goalkeeping crisis that engulfed the club in late March when both senior goalies, Springett and Grummitt, were unavailable for the trip to Fulham. In a real 'Roy of the Rovers' story, Wednesday were forced to call up nineteen-year-old amateur Trevor Pearson after the Football League refused permission for them to sign a loanee. The youngster had never played league soccer, and never did again after four games for Wednesday, and commented when being asked to fill the breach: 'I was stunned. First he (Dooley) asked me if I was fit to play. I thought there must be a reserve match or something. I nearly fell over when he said he wanted me at Fulham. Good job I was in the ambulance room.' It was certainly a season to remember for Pearson but for Wednesday it was another of disappointment.

The summer of 1972 was a busy one with new arrivals including mercurial winger Willie Henderson and old faces Eustace, Swan and Layne. One departure was a shock to Wednesday fans as the popular Graham Pugh was sold to Huddersfield Town while Steve Downes also departed. A new contract was also given to Dooley and there was a genuine feeling of optimism among the fans, who were delighted to see their side run out on the opening day resplendent in their new striped home shirt. A highly encouraging crowd of over 23,000 were in attendance for that first game and the vast majority went home delighted after a 3-0 success. Over the next few weeks, Dooley's new-look side provided some great entertainment for the long-suffering fans, and with Joicey and Sunley combining well up front and Craig and Henderson in fine form, the club led the Second Division table until well into

October. Over 30,000 then saw Burnley win at Hillsborough, knocking Wednesday off the top spot, but although a promotion challenge was never a realistic possibility – Burnley and Queens Park Rangers ran away with the two promotion places – the club remained in the divisional top ten for the whole season. The first abandoned game at Hillsborough, in peacetime football, against Bristol City, did not help their chase of the leading pack, although Dooley remained bullish after his side knocked Burnley off the top of the division thanks to a single goal win at Turf Moor in March 1973. The Owls' boss commented 'We could yet do it, Burnley are dropping points while we are on song. We still have hope and obviously have a little more after this win. We won't give up until it is mathematically impossible for us. We have got six points from the last three matches and if we win the next two or three, we will be pushing the leaders.' Unfortunately, a fortnight later the Wednesday supremo admitted his side 'were awful' after a defeat at Nottingham Forest. They were quickly back to winning ways a week later against Orient, a match notable for another goalkeeping injury crisis, which resulted in the debut of Peter Fox, who aged just fifteen years, eight months and twenty-six days became Wednesday's youngest player. Overall, it was a vastly improved campaign and it was certainly unfortunate that their position at 4.45 p.m. on the final day of the season was their lowest of the whole campaign, three defeats in their final five games seeing them slip down to tenth. Although not prolific, the team recorded their highest number of goals in the league for eight seasons (fifty-nine), Joicey, Sunley and Craig all reaching double figures. Hope was now tangible that a return to the top flight could be just around the corner.

The start to the following season was somewhat beset by injuries and suspensions, although the club did lose Colin Prophett to Norwich City. It was perhaps not unconnected that the success of the previous campaign seemed to have been based on a much higher wage bill, resulting in the Owls posting a sizable loss. Wednesday was clearly not in rude health from a financial perspective, and the subsequent poor start to the 1973/74 season added additional pressure with Wednesday collecting a large fee when key defender Dave Clements left for Everton. Problems mounted in October as a mystery stomach bug swept through the club, decimating the first team squad. A thirteen-game winless run saw a slump from mid-table to the fringes of the relegation places; the only highlight during that barren run was a hard-fought home draw with leaders Middlesbrough, although it was worrying that less than 12,000 attended. Behind the scenes there were also several changes with new chairman Sheppard presiding over a marathon board meeting, which discussed such topics as the virus, coaching, tactics, management, injuries and team spirit. An emergency board meeting was then called just before Christmas, and the outcome was the dismissal of Dooley to all-round condemnation due to the Christmas Eve date, with Gerry Young handed the reins on a temporary basis. Under their caretaker boss, performances did improve, Wednesday staying unbeaten in his first five games, although four were drawn. By early March the club was still firmly in the final relegation places; new manager Steve Burtenshaw had taken over in January, despite Ron Atkinson and Brian Clough both having supposedly applied for the job. Wednesday fans must have then watched in almost disbelief as their previously shot-shy side proceeded to register a 5-1 win at Notts County, followed by a 5-0 home success over Cardiff City. A third straight win duly lifted them to the dizzy heights of seventeenth before another poor set of results ended with an embarrassing day at Middlesbrough where the home side proceeded to run in eight goals with reply, taking the fight for survival to the last game. A win over Bolton Wanderers at Hillsborough would be enough and, just like four years earlier, the biggest crowd of the season clicked through the turnstiles to give vocal backing to the team when it was most needed. The visitors had nothing to play for but the fans endured a nerve-racking afternoon, the game still evenly poised at 0-0 with just four minutes to go. Then Craig got the ball on the left wing and centred into the penalty area where, from 6 yards out, Captain Ken Knighton gleefully lashed the ball home and took the adulation of the celebrating Kop. At the final whistle fans swarmed onto the pitch with the hero of the day chaired off by the jubilant supporters. Post-match comments included promises to the fans that the side would be much better the following season but sadly that optimism proved to be misplaced; Wednesday suffered the bleakest season in their 150 years, recording their lowest ever points tally and slipping into the Third Division for the first time. The increasingly precarious financial position was shown by a 25 per cent rise in season ticket prices, which was met with great dismay and led to only just over 3,000 buying season passes – another new low. The club's business in the transfer market did not court any optimism either and when Wednesday lined up for the opening game they had four players suspended, Knighton and Prendergast injured, manager Burtenshaw having no choice but to hand debuts to Hugh Dowd and trialist Fred McIver. Against this backdrop Wednesday did well to only lose by 2-1 at Oldham Athletic but fans were unimpressed a week later when the side played poorly in a home stalemate with Bristol Rovers. Through those early weeks of the 1974/75 campaign, the Owls did show signs of resilience, gaining some praiseworthy away points. It was, however, blatantly obvious that Wednesday simply did not possess a goalscorer – Prendergast missed virtually the whole season due to injury – and by late November they had slipped to twenty-first. It was at this point that Wednesday secured the services of Eric McMordie on loan from Middlesbrough, and his six goals in nine appearances lifted spirits considerably as three wins followed, plus a crazy 4-4 Hillsborough draw with Manchester United, which made the headlines due to several outbreaks of crowd disorder, the worst witnessed at the ground so far as hooliganism started to become a blight on the game. A huge crowd of 35,067 attended the fixture – the biggest since 1971 – but it would only be a taste of the 'good old days' as on the pitch fortunes deteriorated quickly after McMordie decided against moving permanently to Wednesday. Incredibly, after winning 1-0 at Southampton in the final game of 1974, Wednesday did not win again, a terrible run of seventeen games that included only two goals. Wednesday slumped to bottom place in January and never moved, being officially relegated at Nottingham Forest on April Fool's Day 1975; the defeat at the City Ground was one of five consecutive 1-0 losses, which again showed how the lack of a goalscorer had been decisive. Wednesday was in such dire straits that the *Sheffield Star* newspaper even launched a 'Save our Owls' campaign. Almost unbelievably the club did not score a goal at home for fourteen hours and twenty-five minutes, until Joicey netted in the final minute against Oxford United. By this time only the truly committed were making the pilgrimage to Hillsborough, a post-war low crowd of 7,444 attending that particular game; the match also showed how fans were thankful for any small mercies as a gleeful supporter commented at the final whistle, 'I was glad I was there to see that goal. I shall tell my grandchildren in years to come that I was there for that one.' The club's fans though continued their incredible loyalty to Wednesday, Hull City officials even commenting, at the final game of the season, how numerous and vocal the Wednesdayites were who had travelled to give the last rights to a horrendous season. The campaign was perhaps best summarised by a local reporter, who suggested that watching Wednesday was like seeing a constant rerun of a really bad film that you had seen too many times already but somehow could not stop watching again.

It was perhaps understandable that most fans thought the club's fortunes could not sink any lower as Wednesday prepared for their first season in the third tier. Those supporters were in for a nasty shock though, as Wednesday seemingly spiralled ever downward as several higher-earning players were released, the backroom staff culled and another huge loss announced; the aggregate deficit since relegation in 1970 was now approaching £500,000, a considerable and greatly worrying amount in the mid-1970s. It was clear that Wednesday were simply haemorrhaging money and a revival on the pitch would not occur until the club was on a more firm financial footing. It was therefore not a surprise that Wednesday endured another season of struggle with Burtenshaw paying the price in September, Len Ashurst taking over, and a new chairman, Bert McGee, also taking the reins. It was the two aforementioned key appointments that would lead to better times but in the interim the 1975/76 season was a desperate struggle until the very last game, Wednesday failing to record an away win all season and spending the vast majority of the campaign in the relegation places. The season also saw another serious outbreak of flu, which caused two games in February, at home to Chesterfield and away at Shrewsbury Town, to be postponed and the ground completely closed down for several days. By this time, only Ashurst and his assistant Tony Toms remained as full-time employees after more cost-cutting, and the future looked bleak on the pitch after a particularly damaging defeat to Chesterfield sent them down to twenty-third place to leave Fourth Division soccer looming large. Thankfully, Wednesday then suddenly turned around their Hillsborough form and four consecutive home victories, all by a nail-biting 1-0, made sure their fate went to the very last game – a home meeting with Southend United, which was played after the regular season had been completed after being postponed due to a FA Cup semi-final at Hillsborough. The Owls needed a point to ensure safety while Southend had to win and the club's biggest gate of the season – the fans turning out in big numbers yet again to aid the old club in their time of yet more trouble – turned out on a Thursday evening to watch the events unfold. Chairman McGee knew what was at stake, commenting, 'We are still in the trenches. There will be 11 good men out on the pitch fighting for this club; that I promise the supporters.'

It was not an understatement to say that the whole future of the club was almost dependent upon one game and Wednesday started like a team possessed. After constant pressure the ground erupted as Prendergast bounced on a loose ball to put his side in front. Wednesday were effectively saved six minutes later when Eric Potts fired home a spectacular volley and although the visitors did pull a goal back, there was only going to be one ultimate outcome. Wednesday saved themselves, although they still finished in their lowest ever position – twentieth in Division Three. After that brush with relegation, Wednesday fans were treated to a season that did not involve a fight for survival as, with Rodger Wylde in fine goalscoring form, the team posted a top-ten finish. As soon as the previous season had ended, Ashurst released nine players while one significant arrival was that of midfielder Jeff Johnson. Preseason action was limited to three games in the new Shipp Cup competition and Wednesday gained an unmeasurable amount of confidence by winning the trophy, a small but significant stride. Wednesday enjoyed a hugely encouraging start to the season and after winning 1-0 at Reading in October 1976, they reached as high as third in the table. The victory at Elm Park was also significant as Johnson's terrific 25-yard goal secured Wednesday their first away win since December 1974, thirty-five games ago. There was also good news off the field as Wednesday started to reduce their losses and announced a new £400,000 share issue, which, it was hoped, would clear the club's debts. This involved the issuing of A, B and C shares and after being voted through at a special general meeting, it did indeed provide a much-needed financial shot in the arm. Those improving finances even allowed a move into the transfer market, paying fees for Tommy Tynan and Paul Bradshaw. During the remainder of the season the club had a few brushes with the top six positions, and although a promotion challenge never came to fruition, it was still a season of progress on and off the pitch. There was actually genuine optimism among Wednesdayites before the 1977/78 season commenced, but eight league games later that feeling had totally evaporated with the team winless and bottom of the division. At this point Jack Charlton entered, although the former World Cup winner did not immediately bring a sudden upturn in results and it was not until a home win over Exeter City, in mid-January 1978, that Wednesday lifted themselves out of the relegation places. As winter turned to spring, Wednesday moved up the table, aided by the signing of Brian Hornsby, and delighted their fans by losing only one of their final twelve games.

The Revival under Big Jack Before Howard Completes the Job

The 1978/79 season was actually no improvement on the previous one, Wednesday again finishing in fourteenth. But the campaign contained none of previous relegation worries as a hard-to-beat side registered nineteen draws and seventeen clean sheets – one of the stalemates being Wednesday's 3,000th league game at Mansfield Town in September 1978. Top of the goals list was Hornsby while it would be fair to say that the league was somewhat overshadowed by the club's magnificent FA Cup battles with Arsenal. Before and during the season, Charlton had added some notable players to his squad, Ray Blackhall, Mike Pickering and Terry Curran all arriving – the latter for a club record equalling £100,000 fee, emphatically confirming the club's money troubles were now behind them. One departure was the popular Tynan, but the season would be seen as one of consolidation before the subsequent promotion push of 1979/80. More transfer activity in the summer months significantly strengthened the first team squad, Andy McCulloch, Ian Mellor and Jeff King all becoming regulars in a Third Division team that would face four of their local neighbours in league battles, with only Doncaster Rovers not invited to the party. Eight derby games in the season certainly added significant spice with Wednesday enjoying a great start in the first of those fixtures, new boys McCulloch and Mellor among the scorers in a 3-0 success at Barnsley. The Tykes returned the favour, winning 2-0 at Hillsborough, in November, while defeat was suffered at Chesterfield, plus the almost expected win at Rotherham United. The local battles, though, were nothing but a sideshow to the main event and before the Christmas programme started, Wednesday sat sixth in the table and certainly in the frame for promotion. The subsequent Boxing Day win over Sheffield United boosted those chances further and Wednesday slowly moved up the league rankings to reach the top three in late February, a McCulloch hat-trick helping to beat the Millers 5-0 to reach those lofty heights. A tremendous fifteen-game unbeaten run from 19 January to 7 April 1980 would be the bedrock of the promotion challenge and some great attacking football resulted in crowds flooding back to Hillsborough, the seasonal average being the highest since 1969/70. Wednesday finished the season as top divisional scorers with eighty-one goals, eleven coming from the penalty spot, Mark Smith duly breaking the 1930s mark of Ball. The fight for promotion effectively came down to a Tuesday night visit to promotion rivals Blackburn Rovers, accompanied by a travelling army estimated at anywhere from 10,000 to 15,000. A win for Wednesday would take them within touching distance and when Ian Mellor dived to head in Ray Blackhall's cross with only eight minutes left, it sealed a significant victory. The promotion bandwagon duly travelled to Exeter with thousands of Owls fans making the long trip down the M5. It was fitting the promotion issue would be decided at the Devon club as it was the venue for Charlton's first game in charge of Wednesday. Tension filled the air, especially when Smith missed from the penalty spot, but news quickly filtered through that the only club that could catch them, Chesterfield, were losing at Millwall and celebrations started. Wednesday lost 1-0 but it mattered little as confirmation of defeat for the Spireites meant promotion was secured, fans spilling onto the playing surface to join the players in celebration. 'Big Jack' commented that 'It seems daft to get promoted after losing. I'm not worried about the Second Division, We've got a good set of young players – and the best fans in the world.' The final game of the season was significant as the crowd of almost 33,000 was only bettered by two games in the whole of England and showed that the dark days of the 1970s were firmly in the past. At the final whistle thousands poured onto the pitch and it was fifteen minutes before all the players emerged – minus shirts, socks, boots and shorts! The final word on the season came from Charlton as he pledged 'First Division in two years'; it was a bullish promise that almost came true.

The backbone of Charlton's team for the higher league would come from that triumphant promotion side, with Bolder in goal, Blackhall and Grant at full-back, Pickering and Smith at centre-half and offensive players such as McCulloch, Hornsby, Mellor, King, Johnson and the incomparable Curran, who had finished the previous campaign with twenty-two goals, a tally not scored by a Wednesday winger since the days of Rimmer and Hooper, and was so idolised by supporters that they formed a fan club in his honour and bought his 'Singing the Blues' record in their droves. The side showed their qualities by making an excellent start to the season and took their unbeaten home run to over twelve months before losing to Notts County. Before surrendering that terrific Hillsborough record, Wednesday were comfortably in the top ten and still harboured hopes of recording back-to-back promotions, much earlier than 'Big Jack' had vowed. The only notable signing during the season was that of Yugoslavian Ante Mirocevic, with Wednesday breaking their transfer record to secure the services of the club's first truly foreign player. The biggest news story of the season, though, did not reflect well on the club's supporters as a sizable minority rioted at Oldham Athletic in September 1980, after favourite Curran was sent off. There was a delay of almost half an hour before the game could restart, and nine days later the club was in the FA Dock and subsequently told to close their terracing for the next four home fixtures with the next four away trips also being made all-ticket with none available to Wednesday fans; the club also had to pay compensation to each home side of £3,000 due to lost revenue. The ruling actually increased revenue for the Owls due to higher seating prices – not a benefit the FA had intended – while at the first of the away 'ban' games, Captain Mick Pickering commented that 'They'll get where water won't' after a huge roar greeted the Owls' goals in a 3-2 win at Swansea. The club had recorded a record profit during the promotion campaign and the Wednesday squad was even treated to a mid-season break in Majorca, which no doubt aided a great run that took the club into the promotion places by early March 1981. They couldn't sustain that challenge though and losses in their last four games did mean their final position of tenth – the club's lowest position of the season – was somewhat unrepresentative of what had been a tremendous season. Two summer signings would ensure the Owls were agonisingly close to promotion twelve months later as flame-haired midfielder Gary Megson and forward Gary Bannister gave the side a new dynamic, the former missing only two games all season and the latter being ever present, scoring twenty-two league goals. Wednesday started the season like the proverbial train, taking maximum points from their first four games, and was comfortably in the divisional top six before an icy winter decimated the fixture list, Wednesday losing 2-1 at Chelsea on 6 December 1981 but not playing again for six weeks. Promotion seemed to fade away in the early part of the new year but a great spell of six wins in seven games then pushed the club into the top three with their destiny in their own hands. The arrival of Aston Villa midfielder Gary Shelton boosted that promotion push and with just three games remaining Wednesday sat third, just ahead of rivals Leicester City and Norwich City. A controversial draw at Rotherham followed – Charlton being incensed after the awarding of a dubious penalty kick – but those hopes then suffered a mortal blow as Wednesday crashed to a 3-1 loss at Bolton Wanderers, despite having led through an early Curran goal, with Charlton admitting his side were 'rubbish'. The defeat meant the season was effectively over and they had to settle for fourth place with the club they beat on the last day, Norwich City, pipping them to the third promotion spot. It was also unfortunate that the 1981/82 season saw the introduction of the three points for a win ruling as this did Wednesday no favours – under the old system they would have been promoted alongside Luton Town and Watford.

After narrowly missing promotion two years running, manager Charlton decided he needed to add some experience to his side, signing Mick Lyons and Ian Bailey, while several of the team that won promotion in 1980 departed, the highest profile, and certainly most controversial, move being that of Curran to neighbours United! If one was being critical of the 1982/83 season, it would be that after two promotion challenging seasons, Wednesday somewhat fell away, although they did finish sixth in the division. Another great start saw them atop the table – a 3-1 home win over Bolton Wanderers being notable for the fastest ever goal scored at Hillsborough, thirteen seconds by John Pearson. They remained at the top until a terrible run of only one win in thirteen. A late revival ensured a reasonable finish, seven points from the promotion places, but it spelt the end for Charlton as he decided he could take the club no further. New incumbent Howard Wilkinson brought Peter Eustace and Alan Smith into the club and was immediately busy in the transfer market, a multitude of players arriving and leaving, with the former including England U-21 goalie Iain Hesford, Lawrie Madden and Imre Varadi. The new goalie would be kept out by new loan signing Martin Hodge as Wednesday, playing a more direct, fast and all-action style of play, made a flying start to the season. A free-scoring Wednesday side literally steamrollered a succession of opponents to take a place at the top of the division and in the process set a new club record of fifteen league games unbeaten from the start of a season, the final game of the run being a memorable 4-2 home success over a Newcastle United side including Waddle, Beardsley and Keegan. That tremendous run ended at Crystal Palace but Wednesday quickly bounced back, winning a crucial game at promotion rivals Manchester City, and they would never drop out of the top two all season, amassing seventy-two goals – Gary Bannister repeating his goal haul of twenty-two from the previous two campaigns – and recording a club record points haul of eighty-eight points, a figure only beaten in 2012. Wednesday only lost once at Hillsborough and it was at their home ground that promotion was sealed on 28 April 1984 when Mel Sterland scored the penalty to ensure a 1-0 victory over Crystal Palace. Wilkinson's style of play may not have gained favour with the purists but Owls fans were delighted with their side, marshalled brilliantly by ever-present captain Lyons and with 'player of the year' Shelton linking up with Megson in the heart of midfield. Goals also came from Varadi, the likes of Madden, Smith, Shirtliff, Cunningham and the aforementioned Sterland making up the rest of the regulars that steered Wednesday to the promised land. Lyons commented, prophetically, about Wilkinson that,

> Of all the bosses I have played under I think he will get more success than any of them and it wouldn't surprise me if, in future, he becomes manager of England. He knows his stuff and he is completely dedicated to it. Football is his life – I don't think he regards it as work.

Wednesday did miss out on the title but after winning on the final day at Cardiff City thousands of Owls fans serenaded their team with 'we're proud of you' – a fitting end to a glorious campaign. The big question in the summer of 1984 was how Wednesday was going to cope back in the First Division but hopes were hit when both Bannister and Megson departed. However, Wilkinson quickly recruited Lee Chapman, Brian Marwood and Andy Blair and the Owls enjoyed another terrific start, beating Nottingham Forest 3-1 on the opening day and climbing as high as second in October 1984 after a Varadi treble in a 5-0 win over Leicester City. Arguably the most memorable league result of the entire decade came in September when goals from Sterland and Shelton took the Owls to a victory at Liverpool. As the season progressed, Wednesday's league form did suffer somewhat as they advanced in both domestic cup competitions, but the record £250,000 buy of Simon Stainrod helped a late season revival that lifted the club to fourth position and brought the possibility of UEFA Cup football closer. In the end four losses in their last five outings left Wednesday in eighth place, with qualification for European football made irrelevant due to a five-year ban imposed on English clubs after Heysel. It was unfortunate that twelve months later they did indeed finish inside the top six, which ordinarily would have secured European football, after another terrific campaign, which commenced in the close season with the loss of top scorer Varadi to West Bromwich Albion, Wednesday receiving a club record £285,000 fee for his services. His replacement, ironically from Varadi's new club, was bustling attacker Garry Thompson, who cost a record fee of £450,000. Other newcomers in the season included former England winger Mark Chamberlain and Glynn Snodin, although Stainrod departed. The club's all-action style remained the same and fellow top-flight sides seemed incapable of combating Wilkinson's tactics as Wednesday finished the season fifth on seventy-three points, eight more than their first season back. Memorable afternoons included the arrival of Ron Atkinson's unbeaten Manchester United side, which was won by a late Chapman goal in front of over 48,000. A hat-trick by former non-league striker Carl Shutt – in a 5-1 win over Birmingham City – also grabbed the headlines while the final game of the season, a win over Ipswich Town, marked the end of fans being soaked on the Kop, a new roof being constructed for the beginning of the next season. It had been another season of progress. The summer that followed perhaps showed the first signs that the club was not really willing to pay the 'big money' being splashed by other First Division clubs, Wilkinson being thwarted in several attempts to add to his squad, which was a man down after Thompson departed. One signing though was significant as Barnsley striker David Hirst joined, making a typically dramatic entrance to his new home by scoring with his first touch after entering the fray as a substitute in a 2-2 draw with Everton in front of the new-roofed Kop. The Owls made another good start to the season, reaching as high as fourth after putting six goals past Oxford United. Three weeks after that big win fans inside Hillsborough witnessed a unique event as a long punt from Coventry City 'keeper Steve Ogrizovic bounced once before looping over a startled Hodge in the home goal. The Owls continued to compete at the top end of the division until the Christmas period, when two defeats triggered a poor run of ten games without a win, which dumped the team down into lower mid-table. It would be fair to say that Wednesday's run in the FA Cup did have a negative effect in the league and it was perhaps no surprise that a week after being knocked out they returned to winning ways, Hirst again grabbing the headlines with a stunning last-minute volley to beat Manchester United. The last few weeks of the season were a mixed bag, although Wednesday did find their scoring boots again as Queens Park Rangers were hit for seven. The club ended the season down in thirteenth place – Chapman top scorer with twenty-two league and cup goals – but it had been an inconsistent campaign with Wilkinson certainly aware of his team's shortcomings. He again attempted to bolster his squad in the close season but became increasingly frustrated as numerous targets all went elsewhere, the club's strict budget becoming a major stumbling block. New men did arrive, such as Gary Owen, Steve McCall and Mark Procter, while Colin West and Tony Galvin also checked in after the season had kicked off, but none of the players significantly improved the side and Wednesday found themselves bottom of the new streamlined twenty-one-club First Division by mid-October. The arrival of Nigel Pearson, from Shrewsbury Town, and emergence of Kevin Pressman promised hope for the future (his debut had come at Southampton after Hodge's remarkable run of 173 consecutive games had come to an end) and thankfully the Owls did improve, a three-game winning spell over the Christmas period lifting them seven places in the league standings in just six days. Generally though the campaign proved a big disappointment, although there was small solace in April 1988 when the Owls reached the final of the Mercantile Credit Festival, an eleven-a-side tournament staged at Wembley as part of the celebrations linked to the centenary of the Football League. Without doubt the game of the season came on the final day of April 1988 when the Owls raced into a 3-0 lead against Arsenal; the spectacular opening goal after three minutes was described as:

> Mel Sterland charged seventy yards down the right with the ball and ignoring an obvious short centre, cut in to hammer a narrow angle shot into the roof of the visitor's net.

It was a tremendous goal from the popular player, although a last-minute equaliser did take the shine off the final score. The last day of season saw newly crowned champions Liverpool hit five past the Owls at Hillsborough and Wednesdayites went into the summer break somewhat disgruntled and in lesser numbers with the Owls' average home crowd dropping below 20,000 for the first time in a top-flight season since the great economic depression of the early 1930s; those figures should, however, be put in context as the mid to late 1980s saw the poorest gates in English football since the Second World War, with a combination of crowd trouble, sterile football and dilapidated stadiums all playing significant roles in pushing matchday crowds downwards.

After two seasons of relative mediocrity, the patience of Wilkinson finally expired early in the following season as he resigned. His departure was not unexpected to the vast majority of Wednesday fans as the strength of the club's wafer-thin squad was shown when Sterland started the new season in attack, remaining there for several weeks and netting six times. The club's paucity in front of goal was such that he ended the season as second top scorer, despite leaving for Rangers in February 1989! Those early goals ensured Wednesday kept their proverbial heads above water but the season would be one of the most eventual and tragic in their history, off the field events being dominated by the terrible scenes at the FA Cup semi-final between Liverpool and Nottingham Forest, which left ninety-six fans dead, and had a seismic impact on English and world football. The replacement for Wilkinson was his former assistant Eustace, who was in caretaker charge when Wednesday visited Southampton in October 1988; the game was notable as the home side fielded the three Wallace brothers, Ray, Rodney and Danny, in the their side, the first time this had happened in post-war league soccer. A goal from David Reeves clinched a 2-1 win but the reign of Eustace would be nothing short of disastrous as he won only one league game in just 109 days at the helm. When searching for Wilkinson's replacement, the Owls were rebuffed by several high-profile managers, including Ray Harford, Graham Turner and Jim Smith, so Wednesday fans were shocked when Ron Atkinson walked through the doors of Hillsborough to take charge. It was clear that the club's purse strings were being loosened as two weeks after his arrival, Wednesday's transfer record was broken when Carlton Palmer signed. Further 'wheeler dealing' ensured Wednesday just avoided relegation, a 1-0 victory over Middlesbrough in the penultimate home game being sufficient to preserve their status.

Shock Relegation Followed by a Third Golden Period

It had been the most traumatic season in Wednesday's history and fans could only look forward to better days on the field, under the tutelage of Atkinson. The new boss was involved in several ins and outs during the summer, Dalian Atkinson being the most high-profile arrival, although Peter Shirtliff also returned for a second spell. With both Atkinson's at the club, Owls fans were full of hope for the new season and were therefore stunned when Wednesday scored only twice in their first eleven games and slumped to the bottom of the league. All was not lost though as the purchase of three players – John Sheridan, Phil King and Roland Nilsson – had a huge impact on the short- and long-term future of Sheffield Wednesday. Both King and Sheridan made their debut in a 1-0 win at Nottingham Forest and the latter became an instant hero when his wonder goal against Sheffield United, in the short-lived Full Members Cup, sealed a 3-2 win. The crowd of over 30,000 was the highest recorded in the competition outside of Wembley. When Nilsson joined the ranks, Wednesday fans started to see some of the most entertaining football witnessed at the ground since the 1960s, from a purist's point of view, and a surge up the table resulted in the side being on the cusp of the top ten in March 1990. During the club's history, a few late season collapses have cost league titles and promotions but what happened at the end of the 1989/90 season was arguably the most unexpected and dramatic fall from grace of them all. Wednesday still had an eye on a high finish when goals from Atkinson and Hirst failed to stop Tottenham winning 4-2 at Hillsborough in an entertaining game illuminated by the performance of Paul Gascoigne. Defeats followed and it was then five in a row after Wednesday did everything but score in a 1-0 loss at Queens Park Rangers. Suddenly pressure was being applied from the quickly improving Luton Town, who were now just three points in arrears with two games remaining. Thousands of Wednesdayites subsequently followed their side to Selhurst Park, the temporary home of Charlton Athletic, and celebrations began at the full-time whistle when two goals from Hirst sealed a win and the PA system announced that their rivals had only drawn. Unfortunately the score was proven to be incorrect as a late winner meant the issue went to the final day, with Wednesday at home to Nottingham Forest and Luton at Derby County. The Owls only needed a point but fans were left listening to their transistor radios as the side froze on the day and were three goals down with just a few minutes remaining. A rumour then started – given credence when the score was changed on the old scoreboard in front of the North Stand – that Derby had equalised and Wednesday were safe! However, it was Groundhog Day for Owls fans as just like a week earlier, the news was again incorrect and in fact Luton had won and Wednesday were agonisingly relegated. On the same day, Sheffield United effectively took the Owls' place in the top flight but perhaps uniquely there was no depression among the Wednesday rank and file with the only emotion being disbelief that a team full of such quality had been relegated. The manager and players both vowed to right the wrong and those supporters were repaid as Wednesday enjoyed a glorious 1990/91 campaign, not only winning the League Cup but also earning promotion, as well as playing some quite superb football along the way. The major departure in the close season was that of Dalian Atkinson, who moved to Spanish football with the club receiving a £1.7 million fee, which was easily a club record receipt. The money was spent wisely with Paul Williams brought in to partner Hirst and experienced midfielder Danny Wilson signed. There was huge optimism for the new season and it was not misplaced as a sparkling opening-day win at Ipswich Town was followed by an unforgettable day for Hirst as he became the first man to score four times in a league fixture for Wednesday since the days of Derek Dooley. It would be a golden season for Hirst – he'd net thirty-two times – as Wednesday did not taste defeat until their thirteenth game of the season and remained in the promotion frame for the entire season. Wednesday only topped the division for one Saturday, in October 1990, but as progress was being made in cup competitions they juggled their expanding fixture list to show great consistency and after moving into third place in late December 1990, they never relinquished that spot over the final twenty-three games of the season. A slight stumble over the Easter programme – Oxford United the only team to win at Hillsborough – allowed main rivals Notts County to edger closer but there was never any real doubt, a brace from Hirst and a goal from Trevor Francis sealing the 3-1 Hillsborough win over Bristol City, watched by almost 32,000, which clinched an instant return to the top flight. Atkinson's commented that 'winning promotion was like having a prison sentence quashed' while Phil King praised the support: 'I think we were lifted by the atmosphere. The crowd were brilliant.' To complete a wonderful season, the reserve team lifted the Central League title for the first time in thirty years and even the youngsters reached the final of the FA Youth Cup, for the first and only time, before losing over two legs to Millwall. Boss Atkinson had also signed a new contract and everything seemed rosy in the Wednesdayites garden, if only for a few weeks...

Just before Wednesday were due to parade the League Cup through the streets of Sheffield, Wednesdayites were shocked with the news that Atkinson was set to leave for his boyhood club, Aston Villa. Emergency talks were immediately held between the manager and new chairman Dave Richards and there were celebrations among the waiting fans when it was announced that Ron was staying. The civic reception duly took place but within a few days he did leave, much to the anger of supporters, with Francis appointed to a player-manager role. He quickly smashed the club's transfer record, paying £1.2 million for England goalkeeper Chris Woods, just a few days after Paul Warhurst arrived. There had been high hopes that Atkinson's team would be able to compete adequately in the First Division but this proved to be pessimistic as Wednesday enjoyed a remarkable season that saw them even launch a late challenge for the title. The return of Atkinson on the opening day made for an electric Hillsborough atmosphere, although the former boss had the last laugh as his Villa side recovered from two goals down to win 3-2. Some of the football played by Wednesday was outstanding and they would rack up seventy-five points and record some memorable wins, a tremendous 3-2 success over Manchester United perhaps being the pick of the crop. A first-half hat-trick from Carlton Palmer in a 4-1 win over QPR was certainly the most unexpected, as was a shocking 6-1 home loss to Leeds United and a bizarre game at Highbury where Arsenal scored six times in the last twenty minutes. In the end it could be said conceding a Sheffield double to the Blades cost Wednesday the title but third place was still a remarkable achievement – qualification for the UEFA Cup being clinched at Crystal Palace on the penultimate day. Average attendances at Hillsborough just fell short of the 30,000 mark and fans were thrilled in the summer when Chris Waddle arrived. Although Wednesday would not challenge for the title in 1992/93, they would, in the opinion of many, produce the best football seen from a Wednesday side in post-war soccer, the mercurial talents of Waddle seeing the winger become the only Owls player to be voted the Football Writers 'Player of the Year'. Four appearances at Wembley did, of course, have a detrimental effect on league form with Wednesday ending the season in seventh place with a seven-game winning run, between late December and late February, contributing greatly to that final position. Defender-cum-striker Warhurst also became the first man since Froggatt in 1958 to net in six consecutive games, such was his astonishing impact after being switched up front by Francis. The season was, of course, the inaugural one of the new FA Premier League, with fledgling satellite company BskyB winning the television rights – the English game would never be the same. After that breathtaking, and ultimately trophy-less, season Wednesday were tipped by many as favourites for the second Premier League title and this was strengthened further with the arrival of £2.75-million record signings Des Walker and Andy Sinton – the club certainly had the squad to compete at the very top. A new £1-million kit deal with Puma, record season ticket sales and a team packed with international players meant the 1993/94 campaign was anticipated by Owls fans like no other. There was therefore a lot of perplexed supporters as Wednesday scored only once in the first four games, accruing just a solitary point! It was not until late October that the 'true' Wednesday side emerged from its shell and by the end of the year had climbed into the top ten, eventually finishing seventh for the second consecutive season. A definite highlight was a December 5-0 win over West Ham United, which included an astonishing individual display from Waddle. In hindsight though, the 1993/94 season would be pivotal in the modern history of Sheffield Wednesday as several of Atkinson's side departed, such as Harkes, Shirtliff and Williams, while when the season ended Palmer, King, Worthington and Nilsson all moved on. That wonderful side of the early 1990s was suddenly breaking up with the likes of Ian Taylor, Peter Atherton, Ian Nolan and Dan Petrescu brought in by Francis as replacements. In addition, Pearson and Hirst were beset with injury problems and it needed the December signing of Guy Whittingham to effectively save Wednesday from relegation. A late season slump, including a club record 7-1 home loss to Nottingham Forest, made fans somewhat restless and there were rumours of discontent behind the scenes, inflamed by a national newspaper story, which alleged that several players were unhappy with the tactics employed by Francis. The story blew over fairly quickly but any possible problems proved irrelevant as on the day of the FA Cup final, Wednesday announced they had parted company with Francis.

Pleat, Wilson, Italians and Relegation

After protracted negotiations, David Pleat moved into the hot seat but fortunes would not immediately improve with Wednesday struggling against relegation for the entire 1995/96 season. New signings included Marc Degryse and Mark Pembridge while Wednesday subsequently paid £4.5 million for highly rated Yugoslavian duo Darko Kovacevic and Dejan Stefanovic, neither of who provided any long-term benefit, although the former would eventually be sold for a club record £4.6 million. Despite the arrival of the expensive forward, Wednesday's main problem was a lack of goals – Hirst finishing top scorer with fourteen of the club's forty-eight league goals – although that was not the case when Leeds United was beaten 6-2. It was one of only a few highlights as Wednesday arrived at the final day knowing that, although relegation was unlikely – it needed several results to go against them – it would be a tense afternoon. In the first half everything seemed to be conspiring against Wednesday but by the time Newsome headed home a last-minute leveller Wednesday had long since been safe, with hope of a better season to come. In fairness to Pleat he did engineer a significant revival in the 1996/97 campaign as after two disappointing seasons, Wednesday came extremely close to securing European football. Before the season started, Hillsborough hosted games in the European Championship, with Denmark, Portugal, Croatia and Turkey all playing at the ground, the abiding memory being the sight of thousands of Danes, bedecked totally in red, swaying from side to side on the cavernous Kop. Wednesday started the new season with only three players remaining from Atkinson's team and Sheridan also soon departed. However, Pleat's new-look side started exceptionally well and surprised their own supporters by winning the first four games to top the Premier League for the only time. The emergence of teenager Ritchie Humphreys proved a major bonus for Pleat and, although Wednesday lost their fifth game at home to Chelsea, they would remain unbeaten at Hillsborough for the remainder of the season, a laudable record that underpinned a challenge for a top-six place. Despite the bright start a stormy AGM saw the club fiercely criticised for their transfer policy, although this was somewhat nullified when Italian Benito Carbone arrived for a new £3-million club record fee. A poor run of form continued before the Owls embarked on a quite remarkable mid-season run of games that saw defeat suffered only once in twenty-one league and cup games. This included several notable wins, the 3-2 win at Southampton being significant as it was the first time since 1963 that the Owls had recovered from a 2-0 deficit to win. With Wednesday riding high in the Premier League, the long-term prospects of the club also received a huge shot in the arm when it was announced that City of London investment company, Charterhouse Development Capital Funds, was to take a 20 per cent share in the club with Wednesday receiving £17 million. Wednesday pledged to spend the new found wealth on players, reduce bank borrowing, and improvements to the training ground and catering facilities at Hillsborough. With increased financial backing, another European adventure would have been ideal but sadly it was not to be as Pleat's side simply ran out of steam at the end of the season, crashing to a trio of losses. By the time Liverpool rolled into town for the final game, hopes of UEFA Cup qualification had ended, although a sellout 38,943 Hillsborough crowd perhaps showed that it had been a season of which there had been much to admire.

Despite the financial investment of spring 1997, there was little transfer activity in the following close season with only Patrick Blondeau added to the squad. That changed though just before the season kicked off when the mercurial talent of Italian winger Paolo Di Canio arrived from Glasgow Celtic, Wednesday paying a club record £4.5 million for his services, £1.5-million-rated Regi Blinker swapping clubs as part of the deal. It was his Italian compatriot Carbone, though, who stole the early headlines, scoring a stunning overhead kick in the opening-day loss at Newcastle before netting twice, but being red-carded, in a 7-2 thrashing at Blackburn Rovers. Di Canio duly scored his first goal in Wednesday colours in a draw at Wimbledon but there was an early indication of the disciplinary problems ahead when he was fined £1,000 by the FA after baring his buttocks after scoring! A Carbone penalty brought the first win of the season at home to Leicester City, but the terrible start continued with a 5-2 home defeat to Derby rubbing further salt into the wounds; it was also the end of an era when Hirst moved to Southampton. That run of poor results reached a nadir at Old Trafford where the six goals scored by Manchester United marked the end of Pleat's reign with Wednesday rock bottom. Incredibly a week later, with Peter Shreeves in caretaker charge, Wednesday scored five first-half goals – Booth getting a hat-trick – in a romp over Bolton Wanderers. Those three points took the club off the bottom rung and ensured the new manager had a little bit of breathing space. The subsequent appointment of Atkinson, for a second time, split opinion among the supporters – many unwilling to forgive the nature of his departure in 1991 – but a trio of wins quickly changed the minds of many. Almost 35,000 watched his first game back in the hot seat – a 2-0 win over Arsenal – and if any manager could harness the skills of the club's two Italian players, it was suggested that Atkinson could be that man – Di Canio actually commented at the time about Atkinson that 'he has charisma, he has presence, he speaks the players' language and, when he talks, it makes good sense. He brings the best out of you. He is a motivator. He is like an Italian manager.' In his first away game, a goal from Paolo Di Canio would long be remembered by the travelling Owls fans:

> With six minutes left, Carbone swung a pass towards his Italian countryman. Benali teed it up and Di Canio danced past Jones the goalkeeper. 'Shoot, pass, do something' the Wednesday bench bellowed. Di Canio dribbled round Jones again instead, then Benali, then scored. Arrogant stuff – and Atkinson loved it.

It would be those four wins that in hindsight kept Wednesday in the Premier League as despite rising as high as tenth, the season did tail off somewhat, a last-minute goal on the final day pushing the club down to sixteenth. Despite that disappointing finish, Atkinson had succeeded in ensuring survival, in addition to bringing in the likes of Niclas Alexandersson, Emerson Thome and Andy Hinchcliffe, so there was general surprise when Wednesday announced that he would not been awarded a new contract. It was six weeks before a new boss was appointed as after missing out on Rangers manager Walter Smith they turned to former player Danny Wilson. One of his first signings was Wim Jonk and overall Wilson's first season at the helm could certainly be classed as a success as the Owls finished in a comfortable mid-table position, despite the dramatic loss of star man Di Canio in September after his infamous push on referee Paul Alcock in the 1-0 home win over Arsenal. In the league, Wednesday occasionally flirted with the lower end of the division and it would be a lack of goals that again prevented progress, winger Carbone finishing top scorer with just eight. In September of 1999, the club celebrated 100 years at their home but by the time of the designated celebration match, against Everton, had been reached the Owls were rock bottom and in a disastrous season never climbed out of the relegation places, fans having to suffer a season that included a 8-0 defeat at Newcastle United and only eight wins. In hindsight it would be the transfer policy in the summer of 1999 that spelt the death knell for the season, and proved a financial millstone around the club's neck for over a decade to come, as the captures of Phil O'Donnell, Simon Donnelly, Phil Scott, Gerald Sibon and Gilles De Bilde proved desperately poor value for money, big fees, big wages and long-term contracts being offered as Wednesday arguably pushed the boat out too far from a financial point of view. Of the 'famous five', two signings hardly played at all (Scott and O'Donnell) due to horrendous injury problems while Donnelly was only a bit-part player, again due to fitness issues. Belgian De Bilde only netted fifteen times while the only player to emerge with any credit was lanky striker Sibon, who did remain a first team player during three and a half years at Wednesday. It was not just on the pitch that problems mounted as chairman Richards departed for the Premier League top job and it was new incumbent Culley who relieved Wilson of his duties in March 2000 after a desperate loss at bottom club Watford. It was Peter Shreeves who again took the caretaker role and he did extend hopes of avoiding the drop until the last away game of the season, Wednesday going down after leading 3-1 at Highbury only for Arsenal to score twice in as many minutes to force a draw.

Managerial Merry-go-round and Relegation Struggles Before Sturrock Reawakens the Giant

The new manager would be Paul Jewell and Wednesday marketed their 2000/01 season tickets under the banner of a return ticket to the Premier

League. They did almost leave the division but unfortunately it was at the wrong end after another season of trouble and strife. It's likely that Jewell did not appreciate what he was walking into when he agreed to join as the season started in dramatic fashion with Pressman red-carded in a record thirteen seconds on the opening day at Wolves. Rookie goalie Chris Stringer performed heroics as the Owls gained a praiseworthy point but a club record eight consecutive defeats quickly followed and a place at the bottom of the table. With finances tight and many players on high wages and injured, there was very little movement for Jewell in the transfer market and he had to be content with a handful of loan signings. He did manage to steer the Owls away from the foot of the division but it did not last long and he departed in mid-February 2001 after a shocking 4-1 loss at Wimbledon left the club back in the wooden spoon position. The financial deal with Charterhouse also came to an end, the company cutting ties with Wednesday early in 2001, Sheffield businessman Dave Allen becoming the club's majority shareholder. The first three seasons of the naughties would follow a similar pattern with bad starts followed by managerial changes, followed by escapes from relegation, in addition to many changes at boardroom level. Both Shreeves and Yorath managed to keep the Owls out of the third tier, in 2001 and 2002 respectively, but the latter departed just a few weeks after Wednesday played their 4,000th game in the league – a 1-1 draw at Coventry City in September 2002. The new man at the helm was former club 'keeper Chris Turner but he could not halt the decline as Wednesday were relegated in April 2003 after they was unable able to get the win required at Brighton. It was somewhat ironic that after being relegated, the team recorded the club's highest ever goal tally away from home in a league fixture, netting seven at Burnley in a crazy match – the saying 'too little too late' seemed apt for the situation. Hopes that dropping down a division would mean Wednesday would be more competitive also proved unfounded as despite a promising start they ended the season in sixteenth place. It was a truly depressing and desperate time for Wednesdayites but, as is often the case with football, better days were not far away, with Turner the man to spark the revival, although he wasn't in charge when his 2004 summer transfer deals came to fruition. That first season back in the third tier of the English game opened with a 3-2 win at Swindon Town, mainly remembered by fans that travelled to Wiltshire for the boiling hot weather that greeted the new season. Wednesday jumped up to second after a home success over Tranmere Rovers, but that was as good as it got as a terrible mid-season run resulted in a tumble down the league, with goals and wins conspicuous by their absence. The arrival of Middlesbrough youngster Chris Brunt provided hope for the future while the end of the 2003/04 campaign saw a mass clear-out, with thirteen, including Bromby, Quinn and Pressman, released. It was who came through the Hillsborough doors though that would have a significant impact as Lee Bullen, Lee Peacock,

David Lucas, Paul Heckingbottom, Glenn Whelan, J. P. McGovern and Steve MacLean all arrived. A 3-0 home defeat to Colchester United – watched by over 24,000 optimistic soles – was not the ideal start and Wednesday's form was mixed in the early weeks of the campaign as the new side gelled together. Unfortunately for Turner, chairman Allen was under significant pressure from a takeover battle with Ken Bates – a significant number of the Owls fans supporting the deal – and he duly acted by dispensing with Turner's services and installing Paul Sturrock. The likeable Scotsman took over a team full of promise and his new charges slowly climbed the table before the inspirational signing of an unknown Southampton player, Kenwyne Jones, significantly accelerated that climb – Jones scored seven times in seven games, including on his debut when MacLean became the first Owls player since 1972 to score an away league hat-trick in a 4-0 rout of Doncaster Rovers. When the loanee returned to the south coast, Wednesday sat fourth and they would finish the league programme one place lower, clinching a place in the play-offs, for the first time, due to a dramatic last-gasp winner at Hull City in the final away game. The club's play-off campaign started on a Thursday evening at Hillsborough against Brentford, where a goal from McGovern gave his side a slender lead. The second leg was a truly memorable evening as with Wednesday fans adapting the Beatles' 'Hey Jude' tune, they cheered their favourites to a 2-1 win, Peacock and Brunt with the goals that booked a trip to Cardiff's Millennium Stadium, the temporary home of England's big domestic finals due to the rebuilding of Wembley.

SWFC team: Lucas, Bruce (Collins), Heckingbottom, Bullen, Wood, McGovern, Rocastle, Whelan, Brunt, Quinn (MacLean), Peacock (Talbot) Subs – Adams and Adamson

The club's support of 40,000 was more than double their opponents, Hartlepool United. But despite McGovern putting Wednesday ahead, it looked like the day would end in disappointment as their opponents fought back to lead 2-1, an advantage they maintained until the clock reached eighty minutes. It was then that the match changed on one incident as referee Crossley adjudged that United defender Westwood had pulled back Drew Talbot inside the area. The outcome was a red card and a penalty for Wednesday and a glorious chance for substitute MacLean. It was certainly not the best penalty the Scot has ever taken but all that mattered was that it went between the white posts and sent the game into extra-time. Within three minutes of that additional time, Whelan drove home a glorious third and in the very last minute, time almost stood still as Talbot raced onto a defensive error, rounded the 'keeper and chipped the ball into the net – cue huge celebrations among the Wednesday hordes. Captain Bullen lifted the play-off trophy and celebrations continued on the Cardiff streets well into the night after one of the most unforgettable games in the Owls' long history.

Drew Talbot said 'It's unbelievable. The gaffer told me to run channels and do my best. With the goal, I just tried to keep calm. I thought if I tried to rush I might miss it. When I saw the keeper coming I knew that if I knocked it past him I was bound to score.'

40,000 Owls fans sang 'Who needs Mourinho, We've got Paul Sturrock-O.'

Consolidation but Relegated Again as the Club's Future Hung in the Balance

Promotion meant that in the 2005/06 season, Wednesday would be the highest supported club outside of the Premier League, despite the Owls struggling all season after losing key attacker MacLean to a broken leg, suffered in preseason. Without the goals of the forward, the club could not extricate themselves from the lower end of the division and failed to find the net in twenty of their forty-six league fixtures, including a run of seven consecutive games in mid-season. Thankfully, the Owls' defence was relatively watertight and this meant that a 2-0 victory at Brighton was enough to not only relegate their hosts but also send down Millwall and Crewe Alexandra. Arguably the most memorable game of that season was a fixture against one of those relegated clubs, Millwall, in February 2006. The game saw Wednesday lose 'keeper Lucas to injury and in those days, before substitute goalkeepers, it was left to Bullen to don the gloves. He managed to keep his goal intact and then watched on as the Owls took the lead among chaotic scenes as the home side thought they had scored and celebrated appropriately. However, the referee had disallowed the goal for a push on Bullen and Wednesday poured downfield after taking a quick free-kick, with the Lions' players in hot pursuit. The ball eventually reached Frankie Simek – who for some reason found himself in the opposition area – and his miskick almost apologetically rolled over the line to cue celebration, remonstrations, disbelief and arguments in equal measure! After escaping the drop, a fit again MacLean was in the side for the start of the 2006/07 campaign but his boss Sturrock lasted only until early October, when he was dismissed after a 4-0 beating at Colchester United left Wednesday bottom. It was therefore time for yet another new manager and Brian Laws enjoyed a quite remarkable start, continuing the fine work of caretaker manager Sean McAuley, who had gained ten points from twelve. The first game of the Laws' era was a 2-0 win at Ipswich Town and by the time Wednesday took three points from Oakwell in the final game of 2006, they had broken into the top ten. Incidentally, a few days earlier Mark Crossley earned his own unique place in club history as he became the only Owls goalkeeper to score from open play – heading home in the last minute of the 3-3 draw with

Southampton. The run of results also included a game at Coventry City where, for the first time in a Wednesday league fixture, the club had two men red-carded, having to play most of the game with nine after Small and Brunt were dismissed. The dawn of a new year brought a run of five straight defeats but the Owls rallied and it was only defeat in the final away game at Birmingham City that ended a brave attempt at crashing the play-off party.

The free-scoring Owls had notched seventy league goals in 2006/07, Burton, MacLean and Tudgay all reaching double figures, but it was perhaps a sign of the ever-fragile nature of the club's finances that the popular MacLean departed, as did Brunt, and the goals suddenly dried up as, rather unexpectedly, Wednesday lost their first six games of the 2007/08 season, setting another unwanted club record. In an attempt to add some firepower, Wednesday pushed the boat out to secure the services, of former Everton striker Francis Jeffers, but he provided little solace, scoring only twice in an injury-hit campaign. Another new arrival, Akpo Sodje, briefly burned bright to help Wednesday climb out of immediate danger, but a club record run of seven consecutive draws, from mid-March to mid-April, did little to clear away the relegation clouds. A damaging defeat at Blackpool meant Wednesday had to win their final two games, and almost 32,000 were inside Leicester City's Walkers Stadium to witness a classic relegation 'six-pointer'. It was to be the Owls' day though, as goals from Bartosz Slusarski, Steve Watson and Leon Clarke secured a 3-1 win, lifting the visitors above their hosts in the relegation dogfight. A win on the final day at home to Norwich City would complete the escape. The vast majority of the biggest Championship crowd of the season (36,208) fell silent when Darren Huckerby put the Canaries ahead after just nine minutes, but a few minutes later a terrific save from Lee Grant avoided a disastrous two-goal deficit and Wednesday duly drew level from the penalty spot (Burton) before netting three times in the second half (Sahar, Burton and Clarke) to retain their status.

After that close shave, the 2008/09 season was, thankfully, far less stressful for Wednesdayites, who, since relegation in 2000, had mainly been staring at the wrong end of their respective division when it came down to the business end of the season. The campaign started with a goal after just thirty-five seconds by Tudgay while Wednesday spent the entire season firmly in mid-table, with the highlight being the momentous double over city rivals United. Sixteen wins and seventeen defeats brought a final position of twelfth but Wednesday fans were looking upwards as with new chairman Paul Strafford at the helm, and a pledge to attract much-needed investment, the club seemed to be heading in the right direction. Unfortunately, twelve months later they were literally heading in the wrong direction as Wednesday not only suffered relegation but by the end of the 2010 calendar year their entire future was in doubt as the continuing financial problems meant that administration became a distinct possibility. Against the possibility of there being no Sheffield Wednesday, relegation almost paled in significance, with a disastrous season, which saw Laws replaced by Alan Irvine, decided on the final day of the season when the Owls failed to beat Crystal Palace at Hillsborough. It was therefore back into the third tier and Wednesday looked well placed for a promotion push after a promising start to the season, the highlight being a 5-0 win at Hartlepool United and goalscoring form of loan striker Neil Mellor, who became the last man to score an away league hat-trick when he achieved the feat in a 4-1 win at MK Dons. However, those first few months were overshadowed by the stalking horse of financial disaster as in September the club's bank agreed to pay HM Revenue and Customs the £1.1 million debt, which threatened to send the club into administration. The issue would not go away though and in mid-November Wednesday were back in court to answer a second winding-up order for an unpaid tax bill of £1.4 million. Club liabilities were estimated at around £23 million and with no sign of a saviour on the horizon, several false starts and broken promises coming to nothing, the outlook was indeed bleak. It was left to interim chairman Howard Wilkinson and chief executive Nick Parker to stave off administration and a likely point's deduction. Tuesday 16 November 2010 would became a significant date in the Owls' history as it would be the support of the Co-op Bank that secured a twenty-eight-day adjournment, although the words of Judge Jacques left no one in doubt about the severity of the situation: 'You are clearly trading insolvently and you are probably doing so using HMRC's money. HMRC's money is our money. Once this perception of your behaviour takes root, you do not need a judge to say this is your last stay of execution.' Outside the court, Parker was a shaken and angry man, passionately stating that

> There are people out here who say they have money when they do not. It is now time for people to step forward and, in private, do a deal with the bank and no longer shilly-shally around and make excuses for not doing it.

His defence of the club's perilous position did, thankfully, lead the whole sorry mess to a happy conclusion, as on 27 November it was announced that former Portsmouth owner Milan Mandaric had taken over. A subsequent third winding up order was dismissed when the £300,000 liability was settled and on 14 December his takeover was rubber-stamped when shareholders voted that he could take sole ownership of Wednesday at an extraordinary general meeting. It was the dawn of a new era and a few days earlier the team seemed to respond with a 6-2 win over Bristol Rovers. It was somewhat ironic that once the club had officially changed hands, form slumped spectacularly, with a 5-1 mauling at Exeter City commencing his tenure as Wednesday supremo. Mandaric duly backed manager Irvine in the January 2011 transfer window but results continued to disappoint with Irvine departing, to be replaced by Gary Megson. The arrival of Megson did start a revival that would lead to a thrilling chase for promotion at the end of the following season, the summer signings of Jose Semedo, Chris O'Grady, Danny Batth and Rob Jones proving pivotal. The Owls ended the 2010/11 campaign down in fifteenth place but would spend the 2011/12 season in the top half of the table, after a stunning opening-day goal from another new arrival, David Prutton, helped the Owls to a 2-0 success over Rochdale. After overcoming a sticky start, which included arguably the club's worst ever defeat, 5-1 at Stevenage, Wednesday hit form, the arrival of winger Ben Marshall triggering a glut of goals from Gary Madine. By Christmas, Wednesday was firmly ensconced in the top three and it became increasingly obvious that promotion would be between Charlton Athletic, Wednesday, Huddersfield Town and Sheffield United. A spectacular 4-4 draw with the Terriers, in which Rhodes scored all the visitors' goals, did little to help either side, although by the time the Owls won 2-0 in the return fixture they had a new manager – Dave Jones controversially replacing Megson – and the race for the top two was down to just three clubs, with Charlton firmly placed to take the title. In the end, it was a repeat of those city battles for promotion of 1939 and 1950 with the Blades in the driving seat, despite having lost at Hillsborough. That win at S6 proved significant as new loan signing Michail Antonio made his debut. Two months later it was his ninety-fifth-minute winning goal against Carlisle United that suddenly closed the gap to just a point. A nerve-racking 2-1 win at Brentford followed and nerves of fans were further shredded as they watched the televised Blades versus Stevenage game. Pints went flying as United went two down, but despite drawing level they could not force a winner and suddenly promotion was in Wednesday's hands. The biggest Football League attendance of the season (38,082) saw Wednesday fans uniquely on four sides of Hillsborough and the party started when Antonio powered through to put the Owls ahead after twenty-four minutes. The celebrations really began when Nile Ranger grabbed a second and the pitch was a sea of blue at full-time as Wednesday broke their record points tally (ninety-three) and gained promotion to the Championship.

SWFC: Bywater, Buxton, Beevers, Batth, Llera, Antonio, Semedo, Lines, Treacy (J. Johnson), Madine, Ranger (Lowe) Subs – Weaver, R. Jones & Prutton

Captain Jose Semedo:

The noise was unbelievable. I remember at one point during the game we were two versus two at the back and I was calling for someone to come back and help cover, but nobody could hear me, it was fantastic. It was very emotional. This is the best thing that has happened in my career. To celebrate in my place, my stadium, with my fans, my teammates, it was unbelievable. I thought it was going to be like the derby game, a full house, but to see blue and white all over the place, I never imagined to see that. I will never forget this moment, never.

Early Struggles, Consolidation and a New Era under Chansiri and Carvalhal

The club's first season back in the Championship would be one of struggle, although they enjoyed a fine start, 6,000 bouncing fans celebrating a dramatic late comeback at Derby County and then Barcelona loan player Rodri scoring on his home debut. The likes of Anthony Gardner, Chris Maguire, Chris Kirkland, Joe Mattock and Kieran Lee all joined in the summer while the club's main target, Antonio, finally signed just before the season commenced. Wednesday equalled a club record by taking their unbeaten run to nineteen league and cup games – they had been unbeaten in the last twelve matches of the previous season – but the wheels fell off somewhat after losing at Crystal Palace and a nine-game winless run dumped Wednesday into the bottom three. They would recover though, and a dramatic last-minute win at relegation rivals Millwall in early April 2013 looked to have secured safety before another wobble meant that, for the second season in a row, Wednesday needed a win in their last home game. This time it was to secure their divisional status and the only goal in Wednesday colours from Steve Howard settled nerves and a 2-0 win secured that hard-won status. In hindsight, Jones had perhaps made too many changes to the promotion side and at the start of the 2013/14 campaign the club quickly slumped to the bottom of the table, setting an unwanted record as it was not until their thirteenth game that a league win was secured. A second victory came in early December against eventual champions Leicester City, but it was secured by new manager Stuart Gray, Jones' former assistant taking over after a loss at Blackpool. The new manager sparked a dramatic revival, a 6-0 hammering of Leeds United being a definite highlight. Safety was mathematically secured on the final day of the season, beating Middlesbrough at Hillsborough, and although Wednesday could not financially compete with several clubs in an increasingly competitive league, hopes were high that a mid-table finish could be achieved. Newcomers Tom Lees and Keiren Westwood would prove their long-term worth, although the summer was dominated by the supposed takeover of the club by Azerbaijan businessman Hafiz Mammadov. Owner Mandaric had promised to sell if a potential buyer could help the club take the next step, but sadly the whole deal eventually fell through with the prospective new owner failing to provide any of the promised money. Not unlike the early years under Jack Charlton, Gray's first priority was to shore up the Owls defence and he was rewarded with seventeen clean sheets during the 2014/15 season, which equalled the club record set in 1978/79. However, goals were at a premium – the club only netting forty-three times – with a rare three-goal haul providing the abiding memory of the season as two goals in stoppage time at Rotherham United clinched an unbelievable 3-2 win. The biggest event of the season though came off the field when in January 2015 the club was bought in a multi-million-pound deal by Thai businessman Dejphon Chansiri, his considerable fortune financing the deadline-day arrivals of Marnick Vermijl, Sergiu Bus and Filipe Melo. None of the three new arrivals made an impact but it was still a huge surprise in the summer when Gray was relieved of his duties after the club had finished comfortably in mid-table.

The new era effectively began on 30 June 2015 when Carlos Carvalhal became the club's first foreign boss. The new man at the helm was tasked by the chairman to deliver an attacking brand of football and by the end of August a multitude of new faces arrived, Wednesday's stronger financial position allowing the new manager to add players of a totally different quality to the senior squad. Included in the permanent newcomers were Fernando Forestieri, Barry Bannan, Ross Wallace, Lucas Joao and Marco Matias while several loan signings also arrived, including Jack Hunt, Daniel Pudil, Vincent Sasso and Alex Lopez. The new manager would be like a breath of fresh air for Wednesday fans as his attractive pass-and-move style of play quickly endeared him to supporters. It would be a memorable first season in charge as Wednesday went all the way to the play-off final. A terrific spell of form in October proved the catalyst for the season and as it reached its conclusion Wednesday were still in contention for a much prized play-off spot, a terrific win at rivals Birmingham City being a notable result. Four consecutive wins in late March/early April 2016 pushed the club to fifth and a top-six placing was secured after almost 32,000 watched Cardiff City beaten 3-0 at Hillsborough – a brace from Gary Hooper, who had joined permanently in January after a loan spell, clinched a play-off spot. The Owls' opponents were Brighton & Hove Albion and, on one of the most memorable Hillsborough nights in living memory, an electric atmosphere spurred Wednesday to a terrific 2-0 win thanks to goals from Wallace and Lee. Three days later the Owls somehow kept a rampant home side to a single-goal lead before another Wallace goal somewhat silenced the home support as Wednesday progressed to the new Wembley Stadium for the first time. The long-awaited visit to the rebuilt national stadium proved a memorable day for fans, despite their side slipping to narrow 1-0 defeat, with the atmosphere created by the 40,000 strong travelling 'barmy army' living long in the memory.

SWFC: Westwood, Hunt, Pudil (Joao), Lees, Loovens, Wallace (Helan), Lee, Hutchinson (Nuhiu), Bannan, Hooper, Forestieri Subs – Matias, Lopez, Sasso, Wildsmith

Dejphon Chansiri: 'The fans deserve to be in the Premier League. You are Premier League. Almost everyone who was at Wembley on Saturday came away talking more about what they saw off the pitch rather than on it. I thought those scenes were incredible – I have never seen anything like it and neither have a lot of people who have been in football for many, many years. You are all a credit to yourselves and to our club and I would like to sincerely thank every single one of you for the truly remarkable way in which you supported the team.'

Carlos Carvalhal: 'Today we didn't play as well as we have other times during the season. Hull deserved to win the game because they created chances and got a goal. At the start of the season we didn't have a lot of time as a group, but we have beaten our expectations. We have made a lot of progress in a short time and this season I think we have woken the giant. You could see after the game, when the fans were still singing, that we all know we've had a good season. After what we achieved this season we all know that we can look forward to the future. I think this club will get more respect and that is a positive thing for Sheffield Wednesday.'

After the joy and disappointment of Wembley, last summer saw several new arrivals including Steven Fletcher and Almen Abdi, while on the final day of the August 2016 transfer window Wednesday broke their transfer record when paying a reputed £5 million for Adam Reach. With Carvalhal continuing his footballing philosophy, the Owls were in and around the top six during the first half of the season, a tremendous Boxing Day win at leaders Newcastle United cementing their position, before the transfer window saw the arrival of several more new faces, notably that of Jordan Rhodes, initially on loan, with Wednesday committing to a club record fee for his services at the end of the season. After qualifying for the play-offs for the second consecutive season, hopes of a return to Wembley were dashed by Huddersfield Town in the play-offs, their Yorkshire rivals winning a penalty shoot-out in the semi-final on a dramatic night at S6. Appearances and goals (top 30):

App: A. Wilson 502, Brown 465, Finney 455, Froggatt 434, Crawshaw 418, Pressman 404, Davison 397, Blenkinsop 393, Fantham 388, Megson 386, Hooper 384, Rimmer 381, T. McAnearney 352, R. Springett 345, Brittleton 342, Worthington 338, Layton 331, Curtis 310, Young 309, Ferrier 308, D. Walker 307, Langley 295, Hirst 294, McIntosh 293, Shirtliff 292, Spiksley 292, M. Smith 282, Sterland 279, Swan 275, H. Chapman 270

Gls: Wilson 198, Fantham 146, Froggatt 139, Hooper 124, Rimmer 122, Trotter 109, Hirst 106, Spiksley 100, H. Chapman 93, Shiner 93, Ball 90, McLean 88, Sewell 87, Finney 81, Allen 76, Woodhead 72, Burgess 70, Quixall 63, L. Chapman 62, Dooley 62, Davis 59, Bannister 55, Wylde 54, Prendergast 53, D. Wilkinson 53, Ellis 52, Layne 52, Dobson 49, Quigley 49, Tudgay 49

Chapter 4

Up for T'cup: Wednesday and the English Cup

Play up Wednesday Boys! Play up Wednesday Boys! Before the season's up, you'll win the English Cup. Play Up Wednesday Boys!

There is no doubt that the introduction of the English Cup in 1871 was a major factor in the rapid growth of football in the Victorian age, the competition quickly growing to become the premier tournament in England by the early 1880s. Cup football had first started in Sheffield in 1867 – Hallam winning the Youdan Cup – and the town was first represented in the third season when Sheffield FC reached the third round. As the 1870s progressed, a handful of northern clubs started to appear – the competition was largely dominated by southern clubs in the 1870s with the obvious exception of Scots Queens Park – and Wednesday secretary William Littlehales duly sent in the club's application for the 1880/81 season. This was successful and the draw paired Wednesday with the aforementioned Scottish amateurs – Scottish teams were allowed to enter until being banned in 1887 – although the tie never went ahead with Queens Park scratching from the tournament and giving Wednesday a walkover. It was a common occurrence in the early years for teams to scratch for various reasons, usually due to the travelling distances involved or the inability to arrange a suitable date for the tie, and seven such walkovers took place in Wednesday's first season in the tournament. The second round sent Wednesday to Blackburn Rovers with the Lancashire club installed as strong favourites. It would actually be footwear that would decide Wednesday's first match in the FA Cup as conditions on the day were quite dreadful for football, a frosty playing surface combining with a 'perfect hurricane' blowing down the pitch. To combat the conditions, Rovers attached strips of felt to the soles of their boots while Wednesday decided upon a kind of leather stud and it would be the Yorkshiremen who chose correctly as the home eleven struggled to stay on their feet as a hat-trick from Bob Gregory sent Wednesday skating through, 4-0.

SWFC: W. Stacey (GK), T. Buttery, E. Buttery, Hunter, Hudson, Malpass, Winterbottom, Lang, Mosforth, Newbould, Gregory

The next round sent Wednesday back over the Pennines to a club called Turton, who were based near Bolton. This time the tie was played on a frozen pitch in dense fog but it was the away side that triumphed 2-0, taking Wednesday through to the next round, which rather confusingly contained twelve teams. The fourth-round tie was described as the 'Final of the Northern Section' and it was yet again back into Lancashire where the tie against Darwen was played in persistent snow. The game proved the end for Wednesday's first attempt at the FA Cup as, despite two goals from Gregory, they exited 5-2. It had been a great start for Wednesday in the cup but it was only the precursor to the 1881/82 season when Wednesday reached the semi-finals. Although drawn away in the first round, Wednesday did not travel out of Sheffield as they met local rivals Providence at their Quibell's Field Ground, near Hyde Park. The game, which was stopped after ten minutes when it was realised that the home side had twelve players, was won 2-0 by Wednesday but only once did the ball cross the goal line as a new rule meant that when Gregory's goal-bound shot was handled on the line by a home player, the match official awarded a goal – the rule only lasted one season when it was decided that it gave too much power to the referee. Wednesday were fortunate to receive a bye in the next round so did not play again until Staveley visited Bramall Lane in the third round, Wednesday progressing after three games, winning the second replay 5-1 at Lockwood Brothers' ground in Sheffield. Progress continued with a victory over old rivals Heeley while the home tie against Londoners Upton Park became the first major match to be played on Sheffield's traditional market day of Tuesday – the date had been avoided previously by all the local sides but the southerners did not have a Saturday or Monday free so Wednesday had no option but to play on a day when the good people of Sheffield were preoccupied with the main day of business in the town. As expected, a smaller than average crowd attended but those that did forgo the market did see a stunning 6-0 victory, with Mosforth's second-half goal lighting up the tie:

> One of the most magnificent runs ever seen, nearly the whole length of the field, was made by the little wonder, who was totally unsupported, and he did not finish his good exertions until he had put the leather between the Upton sticks.

The win took Wednesday into the semi-final and another meeting with Blackburn Rovers, at the St John's Ground in Huddersfield – more commonly known as Fartown and the home of Huddersfield RLC until the early 1990s. There was huge interest in the fixture and special trains from Sheffield ferried thousands to the match, although the one carrying the players actually arrived late, meaning the tie was delayed. The game proved a hard-fought one, ending 0-0, and after Wednesday refused the opportunity of playing extra-time, the teams reconvened in Manchester. It was before the replay that it came to light that Wednesday could already have been in the final as the match referee commented to Mosforth 'Well, Mosforth, you should not have been here today', and when the Wednesday winger queried his statement he admitted that if captain James Lang had appealed, as he usually did, then a Mosforth goal would have stood as the referee thought the ball had in fact crossed the line! It would be a case of what might have been for Wednesday as despite taking the lead in the replay the wide pitch greatly favoured Rovers' fast attackers and they hit back to win 5-1, emphatically ending a tremendous second season in the English Cup. The first tie of the 1882/83 cup run saw Gregory become the first Wednesday man to score five times in a senior game, achieving the feat in a 12-2 trouncing of Lincolnshire Cup holders Spilsby, while the next round saw the club remain in the town, facing Lockwood Brothers on Ecclesall Road. Wednesday's attackers proved far too potent for Lockwood's defence and a comfortable 6-0 win, on a frosty slippy pitch, put them into the third round for the third consecutive season. The win set up a mouth-watering fixture at Nottingham Forest where the first instance of 'protesting' took place, the home club claiming that Wednesday man Malpass had been paid 30s to play for Sheffield Wanderers earlier in the season. Wednesday had no choice but to draft in Willis Bentley and with Billy Betts making his debut, they earned a replay, the teams sharing four goals. Before that replay the Forest captain, Widdowson, travelled to Sheffield and publically offered £20 to anybody who could prove that any Wednesday players were not legitimate members. He failed to uncover any evidence and two goals from Harrison took Wednesday to a 3-2 win at Bramall Lane, although the 'Foresters' played under protest due to the playing surface, which was described as a 'ploughed field'. After losing, Forest protested again, this time about ineligible players, but they were the ones who were eventually in trouble with the authorities, being censured by the Football Association for their somewhat frivolous protestations. Wednesday though had another fourth round English Cup tie to look forward to and they again met Nottingham opposition with County travelling north. Upwards of 10,000 were expected for the tie but heavy rain significantly reduced that number, although Wednesday could have progressed without kicking a ball after they received a telegram from County, just before the game, stating that they could not raise a team. There was a change of heart though and the visitors recorded a 4-1 win, dashing hopes of further progression.

After making a considerable impact in their first three seasons, Wednesday then experienced several lean campaigns, culminating in 1886/87 when they did not enter the tournament after failing to send in their application on time. Their 1883/84 campaign commenced against local rivals Staveley and the tie was perhaps the first instance of 'giant killing' in Wednesday's history as despite being made one of the favourites for the English Cup they crashed out at the Recreation Ground in Chesterfield – the tie had been moved from Staveley after several instances of bad language and crude tackling.

A win at virtual unknowns Long Eaton Rangers got the club back into the winning habit in December 1884, but after receiving a bye in the next round, Nottingham Forest duly returned to Sheffield to gain revenge for their earlier exit, man-marking Mosforth out of the game and winning 2-1. The 1885/86 campaign proved disastrous as home side Long Eaton Rangers adapted better to their puddle-strewn pitch and after going down to ten men following an injury to Mosforth, Wednesday exited 2-0 with barely a whimper. When Wednesday restarted their English Cup campaign, they did so as a professional club and after winning a tricky tie at Belper, there must have been some apprehension when the next round sent Wednesday to Long Eaton yet again. Around 200 Wednesday fans made the short trip into deepest Nottinghamshire and they must have thought another cup upset was on the cards after Rangers took the lead. Incidentally, before the game a story is told that Wednesday could not find any pre-match food so Carl Hiller was sent on a foraging mission, returning soon after with half a stone of black pudding, which was cooked and devoured by the hungry Wednesday squad! Thankfully though, Wednesday took the game into extra-time and up popped George Waller to secure passage to the third round, which became the fourth round after the club were again lucky to receive a bye. This was common practice in the early years of the FA Cup as it was uncommon for any round in the competition, with the obvious exception of the final, to include even numbers or an amount of teams that could be easily divisible for the next stage – there were forty-one teams in the fourth round in 1887/88! For that fourth round, Wednesday made a trip into the unknown as they travelled to the Essex County Cricket Club Ground to face home side Crusaders. Despite the distances involved a noisy band of Wednesdayites followed their team, and in front of a sparse crowd their favourites dug out a 1-0 win, Carl Hiller netting the all-important goal. It was perhaps fortunate that prestige and not finances was more important in those early FA Cup forays as it cost £24 for Wednesday to fulfil the fixture but they only received a cheque, several months later, from their opponents for £8s, 4d – that cheque actually had a story of its own as it was endorsed by Wednesday and subsequently changed hands several times, even going overseas on one occasion, before, much to the merriment of the committee, it arrived back in Wednesday hands after it transpired that the club had not endorsed the cheque correctly in the first place! Wednesday did hit the financial jackpot in the fifth round when they were again sent to Nottingham where around 8,000 kept the turnstiles clicking for the meeting with Forest. The crowd included an estimated 2,000 Wednesdayites, the majority travelling on two special Midland Railway trains, which were bedecked with blue and white favours. The tie proved a titanic tussle, which looked set to go the way of the 'Reds' as Forest led 2-1 before Wednesday received a slice of luck as home player Burton was forced to retire injured. With the numerical advantage, Wednesday scored three times, Ingram completing a hat-trick without reply to book a sixth-round home tie against Preston North End. The 'war of the roses' clash was comfortably the biggest football match played so far in Sheffield and in anticipation of a record crowd, Wednesday made several improvements to their Olive Grove Ground. That work was rewarded with a record 9,000 gate, although the match only went ahead after a smallpox scare, which saw Lancashire 'experts' claim that it would be unwise for a large crowd to gather in Sheffield. However, Wednesday had the indomitable Charles Clegg in their corner and after he debunked their opinion the match went ahead, slightly delayed. One can only speculate what the crowd figure would have been if the tie had gone ahead on its original date but it was still a record attendance for a competitive football match in the town, with snow on matchday also failing to deter fans. For Wednesday, the occasion was perhaps too much for them as Preston, noticeably bigger and stronger, won 3-1. To complete a trio of ties against Nottingham teams, Wednesday were drawn away at Notts Rangers in the first round of the 1888/89 season, the home side resisting a financial incentive to switch to Olive Grove. On the same day both Forest and County were at home but the Rangers versus Wednesday tie still attracted around 5,000, Wednesdayites – an estimated 2,000 strong – again showing that it is not just in modern times that the club can rely upon a strong away following. The home side netted inside the first minute but Captain Fred Thompson levelled matters and due to a worsening snow storm, and several pitch encroachments, the referee decided against extra-time, so it was back to Sheffield. It would be fair to say that Wednesday did not expect so many fans to attend the replay, deciding against making any special arrangements, and Olive Grove was almost overwhelmed, the good-natured throng knocking one of the entrance gates down while several were perched precariously from any vantage point. The visitors resisted until after half-time but Wednesday pulled away to win 3-0 and secure yet another Nottingham tie, this time County travelling to Olive Grove with Wednesday looking for revenge for six years earlier. Another bumper crowd watched the action and the vast majority went home delighted as their favourites won again, 3-2, despite playing the last few minutes with only ten men after a bad injury to Harry Woolhouse. After the match rumours swept the town that the attacker had actually passed away but thankfully that proved to be just rumour, 'Toddles' being released from hospital the day after. The third round handed Wednesday a tough task at Dudley Road, home of Football League club Wolverhampton Wanderers, and it proved unsurmountable, exiting 3-0.

First Cup Final

The 1889/90 season was memorable for Wednesday winning the Alliance League but this was certainly overshadowed by a tremendous run to the final of the FA Cup, Wednesday becoming the first Yorkshire team to do so. The cup run began with a comfortable six-goal romp over London Swifts, Wednesday supporters sportingly applauding the away goalkeeper off the field after he had managed to keep the score down. Progress, combined with continued success in the league, ensured interest in all things Wednesday was peaking and 10,000 packed into Olive Grove to see Accrington dispatched, the abiding memory being of Wednesday 'warhorse' Betts, who retired from the match with a broken nose but returned to help his side complete the win. The issue of FA Cup protests raised its ugly head again in the third round when three games were played against Notts County with a 5-0 win for Wednesday and a 3-2 success for County both being wiped from the record books. The first win was ordered to be replayed after County lodged a complaint about the poor condition of the Olive Grove pitch while it was then Wednesday's turn to protest about the ineligibility of two opposing players, the FA ordering a third game after declaring the County men cup-tied. The tie was eventually decided on the neutral territory of the County Ground, Derby, where a travelling army of 3,500 Wednesdayites witnessed a thrilling tie, won 3-2 by the men from the 'cutlery capital'. Another County protest was duly received at FA headquarters but this was dismissed and Wednesday lined up against Bolton Wanderers at Aston Villa's old Perry Bar ground in the semi-final. Wednesday spent the week preceding the tie at Matlock and another huge travelling army were inside the ground when 'Clinks' Mumford started proceedings at exactly 3.33 p.m. The Wednesday man would be the pivotal figure as after Winterbottom had quickly levelled a Wanderers goal midway through the second half, it was Mumford who fired past Parkinson to book his side's place at Kennington Oval; Wednesday became the only club to lose a FA Cup tie but still reach the final. On the big day, many fans caught the midnight train out of Midland Station while the remainder caught the 7 a.m. service, card schools quickly forming on-board with the morning papers scanned for news of the big game. The blue and white favours of Wednesday fans could be seen all over the capital – many of the Northerners expressing astonishment at the prices in London – while the team prepared at the Haxell's Hotel on The Strand, where it was revealed that key man Winterbottom was unfit and Wednesday generally would be going into the showpiece match carrying several bumps and bruises. Ninety minutes before the kick-off around 8,000 fans were already in the ground with the serving military men conspicuous with the red uniforms on a drizzly afternoon in London – all military personnel were admitted free. The teams entered the arena, Rovers wearing an all-white kit and Wednesday in a powder-blue jersey with a white Yorkshire rose and white knickers.

SWFC: Smith, Morley, Brayshaw, Dungworth, Betts, Waller, Ingram, Woolhouse, Mumford, Bennett, Cawley

Back home in Sheffield, the town was a hive of activity as fans gathered around the club's headquarters on Charles Street and several shops regularly posted telegrams in their windows giving updates of the situation 170 miles further south. Back in London, Wednesday won the toss and decided to defend the Vauxhall Road end, but sadly the final would prove a match too far for the plucky side as uncharacteristic mistakes from 'keeper Smith meant Rovers were quickly two goals ahead. The Wednesday fans in the 20,000 crowd could be heard encouraging their favourites – shouts of 'Play up Toddles', 'Well done Clinks' and 'Play up Wednesday' reverberated around the ground – but those supporters realised that hopes of glory were well and truly dashed as Rovers scored twice more before half-time. The words 'disunion, disorganisation and chaos' were used to describe the club's attacking efforts, although spirits were lifted after fifty-three minutes when Bennett pulled a goal back. It was not the start of a revival though as the Lancastrians added two more goals to inflict a heavy and surprise defeat on Wednesday. Despite the loss, Wednesday Captain Morley was actually chaired off the field by fans, such was his outstanding display, and the club was left to reflect on a history-making cup run, which enhanced their national reputation as renowned cup fighters and arguably the best club outside of the Football League.

After making the final in 1890, more history was etched into the club annals at the start of the 1890/91 FA Cup run as Lancashire side Halliwell were beaten 12-0 at Olive Grove, which stands as Wednesday's highest ever competitive win. A financial incentive had persuaded Halliwell to switch the tie to Sheffield and on a snow covered pitch they had no response as Harry Woolhouse claimed a personal goal haul of five as the home side went goal crazy; incidentally on the same day Sheffield United lost 9-1 at Bramall Lane to Notts County, the most extreme 'Sheffield double' of all-time! A fortnight later, Wednesday made the short trip to Derby and looked like exiting the competition when they trailed 2-1 with just thirteen minutes remaining. However, a quick-fire brace from Winterbottom turned the game on its head and the thousands of Wednesday fans in the crowd started to dream of another trip to London. The subsequent home clash with Football League side West Bromwich Albion was without doubt the biggest home game staged by Wednesday in their pre-league era as interest in the tie was immense, showed by the record attendance of 16,871, which filled Olive Grove to its rafters. Fans could be seen perched in trees at the Heeley end of the enclosure as 'cup fever' gripped the town. Both teams actually occupied the bottom rung of their respective leagues but the FA Cup was the 'blue ribbon' event of the football calendar and both sides competed fiercely, Albion nudging ahead just before the half hour mark. The departure of Mumford soon after decisively turned the tie in the visitors' favour and Wednesday fans would have to wait another year. There was a false start to the club's next cup campaign as when first-round opponents Bolton Wanderers arrived at Olive Grove it was decided that the playing surface, which was frozen solid under a covering of snow, was not fit and the teams would play just a friendly game (after the pitch was covered with straw and sand) before reconvening on the following Saturday. The match was worth the wait for Wednesday fans as their team produced arguably their best display of the season to progress 4-1, in front of another bumper 16,000 crowd. The home tie against Small Heath – switched from Birmingham after Wednesday offered a £200 guarantee – was notable for the dismissal of two Wednesday men, Gemmell and Richardson, in the second half but they were already 2-0 ahead when reduced to nine men and hung on to clinch a rematch with West Bromwich Albion. What proved to be the club's last FA Cup tie as a non-league team found Wednesday 2-0 in arrears by half-time and the eventual cup winners resisted a late fightback to go through.

Wednesday's first tie as a Football League club was against Derby County and the Olive Grove faithful saw a thriller as Wednesday recovered from a two-goal deficit to force extra-time, before the incomparable Fred Spiksley fired home a last-minute winner – a 'coming of age moment' for the Gainsborough winger with fans immediately dubbing him the 'Olive Grove Flyer'. The joy of reaching the next round quickly evaporated as a subsequent protest from Derby was successful, an FA Committee ruling that Brady was ineligible. The second game took place on a Monday afternoon at the Racecourse Ground and was again decided in extra-time with the home side scoring the only goal. However, it was then Wednesday's turn to lodge an appeal, with regard to Steve Bloomer, and this was also successful with the match finally being settled at the third attempt, Woolhouse netting twice in a 4-2 win back in Sheffield; protests duly disappeared from the game after this season, the FA stating that any appeals should be made seven days before a tie. The home tie with Burnley in the next round would be remembered for the bravery of Spiksley, who was targeted by the Burnley players and forced to leave the field 'bandaged up' before the interval. At half-time, Captain Tom Brandon beseeched Fred to return to the field of play, saying 'Try and get one goal and we will keep them out at the other end.' Despite being in immense pain – it transpired that he had broken two ribs – Spiksley returned and it was he who scored the late winner. The cup draw sent Wednesday to Everton where in front of almost 25,000 the home side cruised to a 3-0 win with Man of the Match Allan keeping the scoreline respectable. The 1893/94 campaign saw Wednesday fall one game short of reaching the final, the run commencing with a 2-1 win at Woolwich Arsenal where around 200 Wednesdayites made the long trip to the Gunners' old Plumstead ground. Stoke were beaten in the next round before the Olive Grove record was smashed for the visit of league leaders Aston Villa in the quarter-finals , over 22,000 cramming in. The match became known as 'Spiksley's game' as when all seem lost he scored a stunning last-minute equaliser before, with only five minutes of extra-time remaining, setting up the winner for Woolhouse. As in 1890, Bolton Wanderers stood in their way of the final and Wednesday were installed as favourites and cheers, ringing bells and blows on penny trumpets greeted the sides when then they entered the field. The game would prove a tight and highly physical encounter, which proved controversial as Spiksley had two goals disallowed and his side exited 2-1, a late revival failing to bring an equaliser after Wanderers had taken a 2-0 lead. There was great despair at the rather unjust manner of the exit but Wednesday were back at the same stage a year later, this time facing West Bromwich Albion at the County Ground. Two comprehensive wins, 5-1 against Notts County and 6-1 versus amateurs Middlesbrough, had secured passage to the last eight where revenge was gained over Everton as another record crowd (28,000) witnessed a thrilling cup tie, Wednesday going ahead before Harry Davis was forced to leave the field injured. The ten men battled gamely on and were dealt a further blow when Bob Ferrier received a dead leg and was moved onto the wing, if only for nuisance value to the opposition. Incredibly, with virtually nine men, Wednesday scored again on the stroke of the interval and a 'backs-to-the-wall' defensive display took Wednesday through. All roads, therefore, led to the County Ground at Derby where 8,000 travelling Wednesday fans ensured the team would be fanatically backed. Not unlike a year earlier, the importance of the tie led to a somewhat scrappy and over-physical encounter that saw Wednesday man Crawshaw receive such a bad head injury that he was bandaged up for most of the game, blood constantly seeping from the wound. Unfortunately, Wednesday simply could not cope with the sheer physicality and 'professionalism' of the West Midlands outfit with a nineteenth-century example of modern 'simulation' winning Albion a penalty, from which they went ahead. They added a second goal before the break and Wednesday tumbled out.

Cup Glory for Wednesday

After one final and three semi-final losses, Wednesday finally lifted the English Cup in 1896, their run starting at Southern League Southampton St Mary's on the first Saturday in February. At the time, the Saints played their home matches at the Antelope Grounds with a record 12,000 attending the cup tie, hoping to see an upset against one of top sides in English football. The home team did take a first-half lead but within a couple of minutes they were behind as Wednesday hit back in emphatic fashion. Both sides scored again but it was the northerners who progressed to face a tough-looking home tie against league champions Sunderland. The Olive Grove crowd record was smashed yet again and the vast majority were delighted as Wednesday raised their game to beat the Wearsiders, clinching another tie against Everton. In the week preceding the game, the players were taken to Matlock for special training and it seemed to do the trick as Wednesday duly progressed to their fifth semi-final, comprehensively winning 4-0. Standing in the club's way to the final were none other than Bolton Wanderers, the club's opponents at the same stage in both 1890 and 1894. The tie was played at Goodison Park where Wednesday fans significantly outnumbered the Bolton followers, giving their favourites a huge welcome when they entered the arena. It was the Lancashire side that scored first, early in the first half, but Brash levelled up with twenty minutes remaining to secure a draw and a replay at the Town Ground in Nottingham. Yet again Wednesdayites travelled in huge numbers and they were in raptures after Crawshaw netted after only two minutes. Despite Bolton equalising there was no denying Wednesday, and they scored twice more (Davis and Spiksley) to clinch a place in the final, thousands of Wednesday fans taking to the streets and inns of Nottingham to celebrate. On 18 April 1896 fans started leaving Midland Station at 6.00 a.m. for Kings Cross and St Pancras stations, and when arriving in London hopped on the open-topped horse-drawn carriages to see the sights of the capital. The FA Cup final had been played in the north for the previous two seasons and the FA were desirous of the final returning to London, although they did not have a venue with the Kennington Oval having been outgrown by the game of football. It was at this point that they approached the owners of the Crystal Palace, who duly created a new impressive enclosure within their extensive grounds. The original all-glass Crystal Palace structure had been built in Hyde Park for the 1851 Great Exhibition and later dismantled and re-erected in a 200-acre park in Sydenham, South London. The move to Crystal Palace certainly proved beneficial as 48,836 attended the final and fans started arriving over two hours before the 4 p.m. kick-off. Unbeknown to the Wednesday fans, the team for the final had only been decided on the morning of the game as secretary Arthur Dickinson had informed the squad that if the weather was fine then Langley would play but if it was heavy, Jamieson would line-up. This led to a sleepless night for the players involved and a lack of overnight precipitation meant it was 'Mick' Langley who took his place in the club's second cup final.

> The opening of play was startling, for the Sheffielders at once bore down at top speed on their opponent's stronghold, and, at the finish of the run, Spiksley was left in possession, and with a splendid oblique shot he beat Tennant, though the latter managed to touch the ball, almost before the crowd had got settled down in their places.

The above words from the *Sheffield Independent* described a dramatic start as in around twenty seconds Wednesday were ahead, with what is believed to be the quickest goal scored in an FA Cup final. The Wednesday supporters celebrated wildly but there was consternation in their ranks just eight minutes later when Black hooked the ball towards goal and Massey could only watch it drop over his head into the goal. Another ten minutes later, though, the blue and whites were back ahead with what Spiksley considered his greatest ever strike, the darling of the Wednesday fans firing home a terrific 35-yard shot past the despairing dive of Tennant and in off the foot of a post. The shot was hit with such force that it rebounded back into play and this confused the Wolves goalkeeper to such an extent that he failed to notice that the game had been restarted! As the second half progressed Wednesday started to visibly wilt, but the 'old tin pot' was duly secured thanks to some tremendous last-ditch tackling and great saves from Massey. At exactly 5.42 p.m., referee Lieutenant Simpson blew the final whistle and celebrations of those in blue and white started in earnest. The new FA Cup (the previous one having been stolen and never recovered) was presented to Captain Earp by Lord Kinnaird, the president of the FA, and the trophy was heading to Sheffield, and Yorkshire, for the first time – the players also received gold medals. Incidentally, while the players were walking off the pitch, Wolves custodian Tennant asked Langley when the date for the replay was. 'Replay old chap, there won't be any replay, we have won the English Cup by the odd goal in three.' Tennant replied 'Get away, there were only two goals scored today.' 'Why, man alive, where on earth were you when we scored our second goal?'

SWFC: Massey, Earp, Langley, H. Brandon, Crawshaw, Petrie, Brash, Brady, Bell, Davis, Spiksley

Back home in Sheffield, Wednesday's reserve side were playing Barnsley St Peter's at Olive Grove and 4,000 fans stayed behind well after the final whistle to wait for news of the cup final. When the news came through cries of 'WE'VE WON THE CUP' broke out among the fans. Back in London, the Wednesday party returned to their rather pokey hotel and travelled back north on Monday, with crowds of well-wishers lining the train track from Derby to Sheffield, many hoping just to get a glimpse of the cup, which was now adorned with blue and white favours after Langley tied his blue and white tie – a present from Earp – around its neck! A large crowd gathered at Midland Station and down Sheaf Street and when at 5.30 p.m. the train steamed in the song 'Wednesday Boys' reverberated around the station. The cheering increased as the players alighted to board a charabanc (a horse-drawn carriage) in order to tour the streets, but this plan soon collapsed as the sheer volume of people forced the journey to be curtailed at 6 p.m. The players retired to the Royal Hotel, the thousands lining the streets of Fargate and High Street missing out on seeing the cup. After a short rest and refreshments they made a triumphal short journey to the theatre where thousands packed in to hear speeches and various presentations, every event being wildly cheered, with a nervous Earp, on behalf of the players, thanking the house very much for the very kind reception and that he was proud of his team. The curtain then, literally, came down on three days of celebration of that momentous victory.

The club's defence lasted only one game as Nottingham Forest won 1-0 at Olive Grove on a frosty, bone-hard pitch. A terrific win at Sunderland started their 1897/98 campaign, although the home fans were not happy, Langley having to be smuggled out of the ground and then the rest of the team running from the gauntlet of the unruly home fans an hour after the final whistle. It was West Bromwich Albion who again brought the cup run to a close while the club's final FA Cup tie at Olive Grove was a goalless encounter with Stoke in January 1899, Wednesday losing 2-0 in the replay. A home win over Bolton Wanderers started their FA Cup story in the twentieth century while the controversial exit to Sheffield United is documented elsewhere. In fact, the early part of the century were barrens years as Bury won at Owlerton in February 1901 with an effort that went straight through the legs of home 'keeper Massey (it should be noted that the tie was postponed from its original date after the death of Queen Victoria on 22 January 1901). Wednesday then exited to both Sunderland and Blackburn Rovers, in 1902 and 1903 respectively, before finding their cup-fighting qualities of yore to reach the last four in 1904. Wednesday went into the season as reigning champions and returned to the ground where that trophy was confirmed when they visited Home Park to face the newly formed Southern League side Plymouth Argyle. There was huge interest in the visit of the champions and the bumper crowd witnessed an end-to-end cup tie, which ended 2-2 after the home side fired home a last-minute equaliser. The fledgling club were comfortably beaten in the replay and this led to the greatest game of Vivian Simpson – who was killed in the First World War – in a Wednesday shirt as he netted a treble in the comprehensive 6-0 win over Manchester United. The left-winger was kicked from 'pillar to post' during the game but showed his undoubted talents to secure a quarter-final meeting with another Southern League club, Tottenham Hotspur. Although Spurs were a non-league side at the time, they had won the FA Cup in 1901 and the leading clubs in the Southern League were certainly on a par with many Football League teams, if not better, so the tie was certainly far from being a forgone conclusion. The game ended 1-1 in North London and just over 30,000 watched a thrilling replay as Wednesday progressed 2-0 to face Manchester City for the first time in an FA Cup tie. The tie brought the top two clubs in the First Division together, although the travelling 4,000 Wednesday fans were somewhat irritated as the tie was played at Goodison Park, with a Lancashire referee in charge – even the marching band was the same one that played before City home games! Wednesday's hopes of a third final were dashed though as City dominated from the start and were worthy 3-0 winners on their way to lifting the trophy. In a duplicate of the previous decade, Wednesday also reached the last four in 1905 but again fell short of having another crack at lifting the trophy. Their run started with a 2-1 victory at Blackburn Rovers, before a new record crowd of 36,413, including around 1,200 from visitors Portsmouth, saw Wednesday gain passage thanks to a dramatic late goal from crowd-favourite Davis. The win set up an all top-flight tie at Preston but a decision to significantly hike the admission prices rebounded as less than 12,000 were in attendance to see the teams play out a draw,

Wednesday cruising through in the Thursday afternoon replay. This meant another semi-final, the club's seventh, and as was usually the case, the week preceding was spent preparing in the Matlock area. Their opponents were Newcastle United, with the tie to be played at Manchester City's Hyde Road ground, although the streets of the city were dominated by Wednesday fans, making an almighty racket with their rattles and horns. Unfortunately greater numbers in the stands does not guarantee success and this proved the case as in a game played at breakneck speed, the tie going the way of the Geordies by a solitary goal. Wins against two more Southern League opponents, Bristol Rovers and Millwall, took Wednesday into the last sixteen a year later and they were close to another ground record when long-term rivals Nottingham Forest visited. To cope with the expected large crowd, and in response to crowd disorder in a recent home league game, the local police constabulary deployed a total of fifty-two men, who patrolled inside and outside of the ground plus Wadsley Bridge railway station. Thankfully the day passed off peacefully and the vast majority in the crowd walked home with a spring in their step, following a comprehensive 4-1 victory. Incidentally, after the tie, the club received two letters from supporters with one claiming his coat had been torn on a rusty nail as he had entered through the turnstiles, and one saying he had left his coat on a nail in the ground and forgot to take it home. Both asked to be compensated but both claims were given short shrift by the committee. For the Wednesday 'cup excursionists' the win meant a trip to Liverpool for the quarter-finals and a meeting with Everton. Those loyal supporters would have been distraught at the break though as their side trailed 4-1 with Davis also having seen his spot kick saved. All seemed lost but the team did not throw in the towel and by full-time the home side were hanging onto win by the odd goal in seven.

More Cup Glory Followed by Calamities

The 1907 cup run began with a home tie against Wolverhampton Wanderers, which Wednesday were expected to negotiate with relative ease. However, the Black Country visitors had other ideas and early in the second half they took a two-goal lead to stun the Owlerton crowd. It was then time for a remarkable comeback as Oliver Tummon pulled a goal back and, with the crowd fully behind them, Wednesday laid siege to their opponent's net, levelling through Jimmy Stewart before George Simpson drove home a glorious winner. They had just escaped an exit but were even closer to being knocked out three weeks later when non-league hosts Southampton led 1-0 with just twenty seconds left to play. It was at this point that Wednesday made one last attack and from a corner Crawshaw headed the ball down for Andra Wilson to hook it over his shoulder and into the net for a last-gasp leveller; the 300 Wednesdayites went wild. The replay was won comfortably to set up a titanic struggle with Sunderland.

The game ended goalless and led to one of Wednesday's greatest ever cup performances as, in front of a record Roker Park crowd, they progressed 1-0, despite losing Davis to a broken leg with still twenty minutes remaining and surviving a quite remarkable onslaught from Sunderland in the dying embers of the tie. Another 1-0 win against Liverpool, watched by a new ground record of almost 38,000, clinched another semi-final berth with scorer Harry Chapman chaired off the field by the delighted fans. Next for Wednesday was Woolwich Arsenal at St Andrews, with the travelling fans from Sheffield encountering many Woolwich fans that seemed 'cocksure' their side would progress to their first final; the London press could see no other result than a win for Arsenal. That confidence looked well placed as they led early on but this Wednesday team was not to be denied and a brace from Wilson and goal from Stewart clinched a 3-1 win and a third FA Cup final appearance. The venue for the final was again Crystal Palace and the increasing popularity of the FA Cup was shown with the attendance of 84,000, which dwarfed the official crowd from 1896. Opponents in that final were Everton and amazingly Wednesday's opponents in the 1907 cup run were identical to the 1896 win, with the exception of Bolton Wanderers – a quite remarkable coincidence. The influx of the northern hordes (a rather discriminatory and tiresome phrase used by the London press) duly descended on the capital again, the vast majority resplendent in their best clothes, mainly as a show of resentment towards the press' description of them in years past. The restaurants on Euston Road were jam-packed in the morning while the Houses of Parliament, Tower Bridge, the National Gallery and Westminster Abbey were all on the 'to do' list of the provincial fans. Many went to extraordinary lengths to support their team with one particular fan bedecked in an all-white linen coat and trousers with blue and white silk stripes sewn on, along with a blue and white rosette pinned upon his chest. His outfit was completed with a white and blue tall hat, decorated with knives, forks, spoons and scissors from Sheffield, and the words 'Ye old Cutlers'. The 'handsome' gentleman was one of the endearing sights of the day and his merry dance at half-time and full-time showed he could also 'trip the light fantastic'. The scene was set for a tremendous struggle and when Wednesday arrived by open carriage, their captain Crawshaw commented that his team had 'got a big job on' to beat Everton, who had been made slight favourites by the media due to their numerous international players. It was Wednesday though who scored first, Stewart heading home in a goalmouth scramble after twenty minutes, but Everton fought back to draw level. Incidentally, after the game the match referee confirmed that is was in fact Harry Chapman that had opened the scoring for Wednesday, his initial shot crossing the line before Stewart headed in, but the history books always credit his fellow attacker. The second half was an even contest but the cup was won with just four minutes remaining when Wilson's cross to the far post found George Simpson, who gleefully headed home to secure the English Cup for a second time. Several men contributed to the victory but it was captain

Crawshaw – the only man to appear in two victorious finals for the club – who despite his advancing years had the game of his life, duly receiving the trophy from the Lord Chief Justice, Lord Alverstone.

SWFC: Lyall, Layton, Burton, Brittleton, Crawshaw, Bartlett, Chapman, Bradshaw, Wilson, Stewart, G. Simpson

The ecstatic Wednesday fans were conspicuous in London town after the final whistle and the streets of Sheffield were crammed with well-wishers when the players brought the trophy home. The parade was completed this time, running through the throng of fans to reach the Town Hall, with the Corporation band playing 'See the Conquering Hero Comes' and 'Play Up Wednesday Boys'. After various speeches the team stepped onto the balcony to huge acclaim from an estimated 50,000, the biggest cheer reserved for when the trophy was lifted aloft.

It is highly likely that most fans would swap a cup win for several seasons of early exits and this befell Wednesday after their victory, crashing out at non-league Norwich City in 1908. They offered the Canaries the handsome sum of £300 to switch the tie to Sheffield but the 500 fans who followed their team to Norfolk would not have expected the holders to crash out so early, the home side winning 2-0 at their Newmarket Road ground on an ice-bound pitch, which proved a great leveller on the day – it was so bad that play had to be stopped on several occasions so players could recover from tumbling over. Wednesday got through to the last sixteen in the season that followed, beating Stoke and Portsmouth, a dramatic late double from Tummon snatching a draw on the south coast. The club could not have asked for a better draw in the next round, Second Division Glossop North End being drawn at Owlerton. The Derbyshire club had reached the third round for the first ever time and would stun the Wednesday faithful by scoring the game's only goal from the penalty spot just before half-time. To make matters worse, Wednesday were awarded two penalties in the second half but neither Brittleton nor Burton could get the leather between the posts and the club were the victim of another 'giant-killing'. It was Southern League opposition who again knocked Wednesday out of the cup a year later, minnows Northampton Town administering the '*coup de gras*' with a single goal win at Owlerton, following a scrappy goalless encounter on a waterlogged pitch. The club's tale of woe continued in 1911, Southern League side Coventry City providing the knockout blow. On this occasion though there was more than a whiff of complacency as it was later revealed that Wednesday had offered their men a £2 per head bonus if they progressed. The players decided to share the booty between the sixteen men in the squad, rather than the eleven who would play, but they seemed to be already spending the monies and forgot they had a cup tie to win. The first round draw in 1912 handed Wednesday arguably the toughest tie as they were sent to a championship-chasing Middlesbrough. The tie, though, finished goalless and the 3,614 Wednesday fans that travelled to Teeside were confident of progressing in the Thursday afternoon replay. That replay was subsequently postponed and the teams drew 1-1 in the league before Boro visited Sheffield and progressed 1-0 in the cup, a sterling defensive display meaning Wednesday just could not a find a way through their rearguard. In the two seasons that followed, Wednesday refound some of their old cup-fighting spirit to reach the last sixteen in 1913 and last eight in 1914, the former run including a 6-0 replay win over Chelsea before surprisingly exiting at plucky Second Division side Bradford Park Avenue, where a huge travelling army of 8,000 Wednesdayites watched the red-hot favourites for the completion bow out. A year later, the first-round home success over Notts County proved highly controversial due to an incident just after half-time, with the teams tied at 2-2. Wednesday won a corner, from which the ball was collected, low down, by visiting goalie Iremonger but then fans saw a rather bizarre scene as one by one seemingly the whole Wednesday team dived on top of the startled 'keeper and a huge melee ensued. While all this was going on, the referee watched on and suddenly pointed to the halfway line to indicate that the ball had been 'forced' over the line. Poor old Iremonger did not know what had hit him and was carried unconscious from the field of play after being attended to by the trainers of both sides. The decision left Notts down to ten men and there was no further scoring, County also losing a subsequent appeal to the FA about the incident. A replay win over Wolves in the next round was marred by a collapse of a retaining wall at Owlerton, which left almost eighty fans injured in a new record crowd of over 43,000. The quarter-final tie with Aston Villa set another new ground record (56,991) but it was the visitors who prevailed. The final season before the First World War saw Wolves beaten again in the second round while the impact of the conflict was shown in the third round when less than 26,000 watched Newcastle United win 2-1 at Hillsborough. It was clear that people had more important things on their minds than mere sport.

More Cup Struggles Before Controversy in the Semi-final

After the carnage of the First World War, Wednesday experienced a dreadful first season, which included arguably their worst ever cup result against North Eastern League minnows Darlington. The Owls seemed to have done the hard part by earning a replay but in front of over 52,000 – the highest gate of the season by a considerable margin – Wednesday slumped to a 2-0 defeat, the snow that fell heavily in the second half adding to the air of despondency. Despite that result, the FA Cup was still king in English football, and Wednesday's ground record was again smashed in February 1921 when over 62,000 attended the second-round replay with Everton, Wednesday having earned a creditable draw to earn a second bite at the cherry. Unfortunately the vast majority of the huge gate went home unhappy as a first-half goal put the visitors into the next round. The early 1920s were characterised by some quite amazing crowds with the ground record surpassed again in 1923 when Barnsley was drawn at Hillsborough. It was not until the 1928/29 season that the top two divisions entered the competition, as they do today, in the new revamped third round. Interest in the tie was enormous with the gates at one end of the ground closed before kick-off and several adventurous souls securing viewing points on the top of the South and North stands. When the gates closed there was thousands of disappointed fans still outside as the ground capacity was stretched to its very limit. At that point in Sheffield football history, it was the biggest gate to view a sporting event in the city (66,103). Those lucky enough to see the match witnessed a typical cup tie full of vigour, earnestness and speed, although the finer subtleties of the game were missing as the rivals locked horns. The home side looked set for another home exit when the Tykes netted just before the break but by the hour mark Wednesday was ahead and they hung on to secure a trip to fellow Second Division side Derby County, where they lost to a late goal. Wednesday was also knocked out by the club from their own division in 1924, although the loss particularly hit hard as Bristol City were bottom of the league. A brilliant display from Harold Hill took the Owls to a deserved 2-0 win over Manchester United in January 1925, with his second goal a remarkable strike as he headed the ball with such force that the opposing 'keeper hardly saw his effort as it sped past him into the net. The tie was also memorable for the appearance of the visiting mascot – a one-legged man who proceeded to hop around the pitch pre-match. The knockout was administered by city rivals United (*see* Derby chapter) while, despite Bob Brown's side winning the Second Division title, his charges were again 'giant-killed' as Division Three (North) club New Brighton won 2-1 at their Rakes Lanes ground. Wednesday took the lead through Jimmy Trotter and seemed to have retained their advantage when goalie Jack Brown brilliantly tipped a home penalty kick over the crossbar. However, the referee ordered the penalty to be retaken and Brown was beaten the second time. Despite dominating the game, on a narrow pitch in a cramped ground, it was the home side who hit the winner and Wednesday yet again failed to progress in a 'winnable' tie.

With Wednesday now back in the First Division, hopes were high that an overdue cup run was on the horizon and they did at least overcome Brighton & Hove Albion, who were now a league club, before being drawn at home to Second Division South Shields. Hero for the visitors was goalkeeper Taylor and they earned a deserved replay, with the carrot of a home tie against Swansea Town waiting in the last sixteen, although home fans were scathing of a substandard display from their favourites. The replay was certainly a case of what might have been as Wednesday hit the woodwork four times but still lost 1-0 at Horsley Hill, incredibly taking their run without an away victory in the competition to twenty years. Thankfully that particular statistic was 'put to bed' a year later when second-half goals from Jimmy Seed and Ted Harper sealed a win at Division Three (South) side Swindon Town. Sheffield United again knocked them out in the fifth round after a replay, and the club's woes in the tournament continued in 1929, in a season that Wednesday were crowned champions. The Owls did squeeze past Wigan Borough in the third round but crashed out at Second Division Reading in another story of missed opportunities. Finally, in what is regarded as Wednesday's best ever season, the club got past the quarter-finals for the first time since winning the cup, beating Burnley, Oldham Athletic (managed by Owls legend Andrew Wilson), Bradford Park Avenue and Nottingham Forest to set up a semi-final meeting with Huddersfield Town at Old Trafford. With Wednesday top of the league, a double seemed a distinct possibility, but the headlines from the game would belong to Birmingham match referee Mr Lines, whose decisions were arguably the most controversial in any single game played by Wednesday in their history, one which denied the Owls a chance of a replay. Wednesday started well and deservedly took the lead after twenty-one minutes thanks to a brilliant cross-shot from Hooper, but then the controversy began as just before the break a Huddersfield player seemingly knocked the ball to his teammate with his hand. The recipient was left-winger Lewis, who hesitated, waiting for the whistle, but then fired home to level the scores. Even at this point, the players and fans expected the whistle to order a free-kick but everybody was amazed when the referee pointed to the centre circle. If the thousands of Wednesdayites in the ground were aghast at that decision then they were furious in the final minute when, with Huddersfield leading 2-1, Wednesday made one last foray into enemy territory and Seed's pass found Allen, who scored to clinch a fully deserved replay. However, that was without the intervention of Mr Lines, as it transpired that he had blown the final whistle as the ball was literally about to cross the goal line; it was another crucial decision that went against Wednesday on an afternoon when Lady Luck deserted them.

More Cup Woe Before the Trophy Returns to Hillsborough

After that controversial exit, Wednesday were knocked out by Barnsley in 1931 while the January 1932 fourth-round meeting with Bournemouth at Hillsborough was notable as two Wednesday men, Burgess and Millership, grabbed hat-tricks in a 7-0 romp. That victory set up a last sixteen home tie with Chelsea where despite George Stephenson putting the Owls ahead, the Londoners hit back to force a replay and progress in West London, watched by just over 60,000. Second Division neighbours Chesterfield were first on the cup agenda in the 1932/33 season and the atmosphere at Hillsborough was described as 'akin to a Mansion where the Duke laid dead upstairs' as the tie finished 2-2 after late drama saw Ball's eighty-first-minute penalty strike a post and his successful follow-up shot disallowed as no one else touched the ball. Wednesday were still favourites in the replay but, on a pitch half cleared of snow, they ran the Owls ragged and the away supporters that had made the short journey were stunned that their side were four goals behind after just twenty-three minutes, the home side's tactics of utilising the snowless wings contrasting greatly with Wednesday's persistence of playing the 'short game' in the still snow-bound central areas. It was a tactical gaff that could not be corrected in the second half and although Wednesday did pull two goals back – also hitting the woodwork twice – it was far too late and they crashed out again to lower league opponents. The following campaign attracted some quite remarkable crowds, despite the somewhat depressed nature of the economy, with Rotherham United registering record receipts in the 3-0 home loss to Wednesday in the third round. Almost 46,000 were at Oldham Athletic in the next round and Wednesday looked to be heading out before Hooper grabbed an equaliser. The replay was comprehensively won 6-1 to set up a home tie with fellow First Division side Manchester City, which caused such interest that Hillsborough hosted its biggest ever crowd, 72,841, described as a 'veritable sea of humanity on all four sides of the ground'. The masses were treated to a thrilling cup tie, the teams sharing four goals, while the result meant Wednesday were seventeen league and cup games unbeaten, surpassing the sixteen-game unbeaten start to the 1899/1900 season. The home tie saw the gates closed fifteen minutes before kick-off and the aggregate for the two ties totalled over 140,000. The second game did not live up to the excitement of the first and both sides were somewhat nervous, with future Manchester United manager Matt Busby the outstanding individual on the pitch as City won 2-0.

Finally, twenty-eight years after their last appearance, the 1934/35 season saw Wednesday reach the final again, which also meant a maiden visit to the Empire Wembley Stadium, opened in 1923. The road to North London commenced with a 3-1 home win over Oldham while hopes of a run in the competition soared after a superb 2-1 win at Wolverhampton Wanderers, where Ellis Rimmer's near-post header took his side through. Billy Walker's men were promptly handed a tricky-looking tie at Norwich City, a team that had already taken their 'scalp' back in 1908. The venue for the tie was different as City now played at The Nest, a tight compact little ground, and in fact the game would prove to be its last FA Cup tie before the Canaries moved to Carrow Road. In preparation for the fixture, manager Walker was the figure behind one of the strangest games ever seen at Hillsborough, as before the trip to Norfolk he arranged a public practice game where the unemployed were invited to attend and line up at the side of the reduced pitch, three to four deep, in an attempt to replicate the cramped surrounding of The Nest. During the game, Walker bellowed instructions through a microphone from his seat in the scorebox, and this rather unorthodox approach certainly paid dividends as a late goal from Rimmer put his side through to a meeting with old rivals Arsenal. Incidentally, the game at Norwich set both attendance and receipts records with just over 25,000 somehow being squeezed into the tiny ground, with hundreds locked out when the gates were closed fifteen minutes before the start. There was again huge interest in the sixth-round tie with the Gunners and the popularity of the competition was again shown as, either side of the tie, Wednesday attracted just under 20,000 fans but over 66,000 were inside Hillsborough (20,000 applying for the 7,000 reserved seats) to see if Wednesday could progress to the semi-finals. It was again a tie of contrasts with Wednesday's grit, determination and terrific never-say-die attitude matched against Arsenal's more 'scientific' football. Home 'keeper Brown was also outstanding on the day and his display ensured that when Rimmer scored his side's second goal, with twelve minutes remaining, it proved decisive. Wednesday received the draw their fans had wished for: a tie against Second Division Burnley at Villa Park. First Division Wednesday were hot favourites to reach Wembley but supporters had heard that all before and there were pre-match nerves about the outcome. The fans need not have worried though as their side were ahead after just five minutes, Rimmer continuing his run of scoring in every round, and although plucky opponents, Burnley proved no match with Owls captain Starling truly outstanding as his side recorded a comfortable 3-0 victory, Rimmer (again) and Palethorpe netting after fifty-eight and seventy-five minutes respectively to send Wednesday to Wembley.

For many years the competing clubs in the FA Cup final have received 50,000 tickets but back in 1935 the scramble for the precious tickets was far more acute as the Football Association deemed that the two clubs could share just 20,000 tickets – 13,000 went to theatre and travel agencies with the remaining to local associations. Of course, this meant the tickets were hugely oversubscribed and Wednesday took the rather odd decision, to modern eyes anyway, of inviting two local blind men to pick out the applications from three huge drums in the boardroom. When the lucky fans were informed, the build-up to the final began, with Wednesday spending ten days prior to the game at Cleveleys – a seaside town between Blackpool and Fleetwood oft frequented by football clubs – although the season was ongoing with the club playing matches immediately prior and after the final. Wednesday had special cup final strips manufactured, although it was left to trainer George Irwin to take all the socks home and shrink them when it was found out that they were too big. The team travelled to the capital on the preceding Thursday and was driven from their Bushey Hall base on the Saturday by a driver who was immediately adopted as a lucky mascot, having driven winning sides to the national stadium on four occasions. The party had enjoyed a lunch of boiled fish before departing at 1 p.m. while Starling had a word for the Wednesday fans:

> We are full of beans, genuinely confident, and are prepared to play the games of our lives in our attempts to bring the cup back to Sheffield.

The crowd was full of fans from all corners of the UK, with hundreds of special trains arriving at stations all over London, eight coaches from Sheffield arriving at Marylebone, shouts of 'Come of Wednesday' filling the air. An estimated 20,000 travelled from Birmingham while there was even a special train from Falkirk, 430 miles away. It was noted that there seemed to be as many female supporters as male. One Wednesday fan was lucky to be there as a few days before the final he was travelling to Leeds when a fellow passenger commented that he had not been able to have a shave before his important meeting. The Wednesdayite duly opened his travel case, taking out a razor and soap, so his new-found acquaintance could look more presentable. The man proceeded to take his name and just before the final a precious ticket arrived in the post! After the usual pre-match formalities were concluded, including a passionate rendition of 'God Save the King', Wednesday won the toss and there was a sensational start after just two minutes when Hooper found an unmarked Palethorpe inside the area and he fired home. It was perhaps ironic that the only Sheffield-born man on the pitch, Albion's Walter Boyes, was the man to score next, lobbing the ball over Brown after twenty minutes. The teams were tied at the break and it was Wednesday – sporting white shirts after flatly refusing Albion's suggestion of wearing red – who went back ahead after sixty-nine minutes when Hooper's 18-yard effort, from Starling's pass, went in off the post to huge acclaim. The lead was short-lived though as just six minutes later a long-range effort from Sanford hit Nibloe and looped up and over a stranded Brown. It was at this point that the tide turned in Wednesday's favour, if superstition is to be believed, as Rimmer had left his lucky mascot – a horseshoe decorated with a lucky cat – back in Sheffield. When realising this he had doubts he would be able to continue his run of netting in every round. However, trainer Irwin had arranged for the lucky charm to be ferried from Sheffield and it arrived in the second half, and who else but Rimmer snatched the lead for his side with only three minutes remaining, heading past Albion 'keeper Pearson from a cross from Hooper; his goal meant he became the first player to score in every round of the competition in the same season. The cup was almost won and it was Wednesday's with a minute left when Hooper's shot was knocked away by the goalie only for Rimmer to fire in the rebound, rounding off a sensational 4-2 win, watched by 93,204.

SWFC: Brown, Nibloe, Catlin, Sharp, Millership, Burrows, Rimmer, Surtess, Palethorpe, Starling, Hooper

The Prince of Wales, deputising for the King, presented the cup to Starling and the Wednesday players bolted 'like lads let out of school' for the dressing rooms, the captain holding the cup aloft and the press in hot pursuit. After lifting the cup, Wednesday enjoyed a celebratory meal back at their hotel and then travelled to Brighton, where they bumped into the Albion team on the seafront, several challenging their vanquished foes to games of table football, although the results are not known. The side travelled back to Sheffield on the Monday and were met by around 100,000 fans, who cheered wildly as they made their way from the station to the Town Hall.

The blowing of steelworks whistles and buzzers had heralded the arrival of the train with one woman having dressed her baby in blue and white and when she held it up to the players they gave the cherub three cheers. The cheers reached a crescendo when Starling lifted the cup on the balcony while the victorious squad enjoyed a civic reception, complete with waitresses dressed in blue and white and even blue and white electric lights, while a blue and white flag fluttered in the breeze from the flagpole. After luncheon, the procession travelled to Hillsborough, where a reserve game was taking place, and the cup was paraded before the ecstatic fans. The celebrations were completed on the following day when at the Regent Cinema the players were presented with their cup final shirts – bearing the Sheffield coast of arms – as souvenirs of their success.

Post-Cup Hangover and Replays Galore Before War Intervenes

Defending the cup had, historically, not been an easy task for Wednesday but they were handed an ideal opportunity to get past the first hurdle when they were drawn at Division Three (North) club Crewe Alexandra. The hosts decided to double their admission prices for the eagerly awaited fixture but their move led to the smallest crowd of the day – less than 10,000, with the game ending 1-1. Freezing conditions resulted in a poor crowd for the replay – the pitch was covered with straw – and the game went into extra-time before Wednesday progressed. The fourth-round tie versus Newcastle was duly postponed and ended in a draw when played forty-eight hours later – a two-minute silence preceded the kick-off because of the death of George V. The second tie in the north-east was somewhat fractious, but on yet another bad pitch – containing more mud than grass – the club's grip on the trophy was ended on a miserable rainy day. The descent from cup winners to also-rans was quick for Wednesday as two years after the victory they were relegated, with a third-round 3-0 replay exit at Everton not a great surprise to their supporters – Wednesday conceding a last minute equaliser in the first tie. The 1937/38 season saw Wednesday exit to Burnley before, in the final season before the Second World War, enjoying eight cup ties, even though they only reached the last sixteen, due to five replays. A home draw against renowned cup fighters Yeovil and Petters United looked to be a banana skin, although Wednesday had to dump 15 tons of sand on the pitch to enable the match to be played due to the ice-bound surface. The pitch proved a great leveller and the Southern League club forced a deserved replay. A record crowd packed into the Huish, around 300 being locked out – over forty fans found a viewing point in an old Oak tree adjacent to the ground. They all came hoping to see an upset but Wednesday went through, winning 2-1, thanks to a Charlie Napier goal. Their reward was Division Three (North) side Chester at Hillsborough but the minnows again proved to be no pushovers, also earning a replay after almost 30,000 watched the

1-1 stalemate. For the second round running, the replay attracted a record crowd to the home side, just short of 19,000 cramming into Sealand Road, and the home eleven took the game into extra-time before going to a third game. The neutral venue chosen was Maine Road, Manchester, and this time there was no mistake, Wednesday winning 2-0 to set up a tough away tie at top-flight Chelsea. Unfancied Wednesday dug deep to earn a replay but on the following Monday the teams could not be separated again, two hours of football failing to see either goalie pick the ball out of the net. The cup draw tantalisingly offered the chance of a Steel City derby in the sixth round but United were defeated at Grimsby before Wednesday had their opportunity to book a place in the quarter-finals at home to the Mariners. They would have to reach the stage the hard way though as the FA, in their wisdom, decided the neutral venue for the third match would be at Highbury, North London. In fairness, the vocal support for both sides was equal on the night – the vast majority of the 51,879 crowd being neutrals – but it was a poor game, won 3-1 by Chelsea to bring the curtain down on Wednesday's exploits in pre-war cup football.

The advent of the Second World War meant the FA Cup was mothballed for six years, returning in the 1945/46 season with, uniquely, all the ties played over two legs from the first round up to and including the quarter-finals – the reason being that two legs would give all clubs extra revenue as the Football League would not restart until the following season. Wednesday – playing in blue and white hoops – was paired with Mansfield Town and, after a goalless encounter in Nottinghamshire, cruised though after all five forwards scored in a 6-1 win. Goals also flowed in the fourth round, Wednesday putting York City to the sword, netting five at Hillsborough and then six away from home. Waiting for them was Stoke City and the Potteries club won 2-0 in the first leg, leaving a lot to do in the home leg. Despite the second leg being played at 2.30 p.m. on the following Monday afternoon, an astonishing crowd of 62,728 attended, with thousands also locked out. The match, though, proved a disappointing spectacle and absence of the 'Hillsborough roar' told its own story as the teams played out a largely uneventful 0-0 tie. Just under a year later, the club would themselves be in the unaccustomed role of 'giant-killer' as they shook off their poor league form to beat top-flight Blackpool 4-1 on a near-waterlogged Hillsborough pitch. Over 62,000 were again inside the ground for the visit of First Division Everton in the fourth round and they repeated their exploits of the previous round, knocking out the Merseyside club after netting twice in the first ten minutes, goals from Froggatt and Tomlinson triggering pandemonium inside the old ground. Wednesday had played clever, fast-moving and skilful football in their cup run so far, no doubt leaving fans wondering how the side were facing a fight to stay in the Second Division! The fifth round proved a bridge too far though as a delayed tie against Preston North End – Britain was suffering one of its worse winters on record – saw the visitors comfortably win 2-0 to end hopes of more cup glory. For the next six seasons, Wednesday only progressed past the third round on two occasions, in 1948 and 1949, exiting to the likes of Portsmouth, Arsenal and Bradford Park Avenue before finding their old cup form to reach the last four in 1954. The run started with two games against Sheffield United in the third round, which brought Wednesday another local tie at home to Chesterfield. Their Division Three (North) opponents reprised their exploits of 1933 to earn a fully deserved replay, although unlike in that pre-war tie it was Wednesday who progressed 4-2 in the Saltergate replay, scoring three times in the final twenty minutes. A full house of 65,000 watched Everton beaten 3-1 in the next round and Wednesday was then drawn at home for the fourth consecutive round, Bolton Wanderers travelling to S6. Another capacity crowd was somewhat perplexed just before the break when a terrific 30-yard free-kick from Dennis Woodhead flew into the top corner, only for the referee to disallow his spectacular effort for offside. Wednesday did go ahead with only fifteen minutes remaining, Woodhead's effort being allowed this time, but Bolton levelled with only three minutes remaining to force a replay. The Owls recorded a third 'away' scalp after a perfect 'smash and grab' performance to win 2-0. This set up a last-four clash with fellow top-flight side Preston North End at Maine Road, and thousands travelled from Sheffield to support their side as hopes were high of a fifth FA Cup final appearance. Just over 75,000 were inside the ground but, unfortunately for Wednesday, the Man of the Match accolade belonged to Owls' custodian Dave McIntosh, who made a series of fine saves as the more experienced Preston side dominated from the start. Despite failing to really perform, Wednesday managed to stay in the game until the closing minutes, after having to play eleven minutes without Jackie Sewell, who had left the field with a suspected broken leg, only to return after treatment. A Jimmy Baxter goal after eighty-six minutes finally killed off the gallant Owls side and the club was left to rue a missed opportunity.

A Mixed Bag Before Another Semi-final Appearance

Wednesday were paired with non-league opposition again in 1955 when Southern League Hastings United were handed a trip to Sheffield. The days of the Southern League being on a par with the Football League had long-since disappeared but you would not have thought so as the Sussex visitors proved a very tricky opponent for an Owls team that sat bottom of the division with confidence at a low ebb. It was not until three minutes from time that youngster Greensmith netted the decisive goal. Progress to the fifth round seemed likely when the Owls led Second Division Notts County 1-0 with just a minute remaining; however, in front of over 53,000, Wednesday defender Conwell then netted but unfortunately it was at the wrong end and the teams duly reconvened in Nottingham where County scored the only goal in extra-time to progress. Wednesday failed to get past the third round in the next two years, losing to Newcastle United and then to Preston, in a second replay held at Goodison Park. It was then time for non-league opponents again, although on this occasion the Owls eased through, winning 3-0 at Hereford United – a game for which footage has survived and is widely available on social media. A delayed home tie with Division Three (North) side Hull City proved a bit trickier as Wednesday opened up a 4-1 lead only to be hanging on at the end to win by the odd goal in seven. Ordinarily the fifth-round tie at Manchester United would have received the standard coverage by the local and national media but the game in question became of huge importance due to the tragedy, thirteen days earlier, when a plane carrying the Manchester United team back from a European Cup tie, in modern-day Serbia, crashed at Munich Airport. A total of twenty-three players, staff and journalists died and it was Wednesday who were United's first opponents after the tragedy. The tie therefore received enormous coverage, home and abroad, and Wednesday were in the unfortunate situation where the whole nation was behind the home side as they started to rebuild their club. On an emotional night, a full house roared their makeshift team forward – the Manchester United programme poignantly left the home team blank – and Wednesday had no answer, losing 3-0. West Bromwich Albion ended interest in the competition in 1959 before Wednesday reached the semi-finals again in 1960, the cup run starting with a 2-1 home success over Middlesbrough where Brian Clough netted a late consolation goal. Victory over strong Midland League club Peterborough United saw them into the fifth round and progress continued after a Tom McAnearney penalty was enough to seal a win at Manchester United. Opponents in the sixth round were city rivals United and victory at Bramall Lane set up a last-four clash with Blackburn Rovers at Maine Road – both sides had lost post-war semi-finals at the ground. Although ticket allocations were identical, it was Wednesday who received the far bigger welcome when they followed Rovers out of the players' tunnel. However, it was Blackburn who dominated the first half and deservedly led thanks to Dougan's thirteenth-minute strike, although the scorer did look decidedly offside when he received the ball before firing past Springett. With the wind behind them, Wednesday started the second period on the front foot and dominated the remainder of the match. Against the run of play it was Blackburn who scored again and despite a John Fantham header, after seventy-seven minutes, it was Wednesday who again experienced the gut-wrenching feeling of losing a semi-final.

Remarkable Night at Old Trafford Before Brown's Young Side Reach Wembley

The run to the quarter-finals in 1961 would not be remembered for the replay exit to Burnley but for a remarkable evening in Manchester when Wednesday recorded one of the most incredible results in their entire history. The road to Old Trafford had commenced with a satisfying home success over Leeds United. It looked like the tie had swayed towards Manchester

United when 58,000 watched the teams draw at Hillsborough. What followed though shocked the football world as United were torn apart by a rampant Wednesday XI, teenage goalkeeper Ronnie Briggs picking the ball out of his net seven times as the visitors stunned the United faithful to win 7-2. It was the Owls biggest cup score for almost thirty years and one of Manchester United's worst home results; their fans were streaming from the ground with twenty minutes remaining. Revenge would be quick though as just over twelve months later it was the Lancashire side who were held at home, in the fifth round, before winning 2-0 at Hillsborough, Bobby Charlton sealing the victory. Over 130,000 watched the two games, showing that enthusiasm for the competition was still at pre-war levels. A much-delayed tie with Shrewsbury Town, which was postponed on several occasions in one of Britain's worst ever winter freezes, was navigated after a replay before old foes Arsenal dealt the knockout blow in round four. The less said about the 1963/64 third-round tie at Fourth Division Newport County the better as Wednesday looked comfortable before the home side levelled after forty-seven minutes – hundreds of Welsh teenagers invaded the pitch and the referee had to stop play for several minutes while the interlopers were shepherded away. The stoppage seemed to affect the home side more than Wednesday and soon after the large contingent of Wednesdayites in the crowd were celebrating as Alan Finney put the favourites ahead for the second time. However, 'keeper McLaren was having a game to forget – he was to blame for Newport's first goal – and after sixty-nine minutes his clearance went straight to Bonson, who gleefully fired in his second of the afternoon. The proverbial roof then fell in as two minutes later it was 3-2 to County and, the hymn 'Bread of Heaven' being sung in the ground, County hung on for a famous win – it was certainly one of the Owls' darkest cup days. There was no 'banana-skin' ties in the 1964/65 campaign as top-flight Everton denied Wednesday progress when grabbing an injury-time equaliser at Goodison Park in the third round. The tie was notable as it was the Owls' first appearance on the BBC's new *Match of the Day* show. The Merseyside club are Wednesday's most frequent opponents in the FA Cup and progressed easily in the replay, coasting to 3-0 success in front of another 50,000-plus gate. The Toffeemen would also play a pivotal role in the Owls' 1966 FA Cup run, which started in the third round at lower league Reading and finished in May 1966 at Wembley against the blue half of Merseyside. The aforementioned victory at Third Division Reading was sealed by a last-minute winner from Fantham, and victory at Newcastle United set up a local derby with Huddersfield Town. The Owls went behind in the first minute but hit back to snatch a late winner and set up another meeting with an old cup foe, Blackburn Rovers. To say the pitch at Ewood Park was a great leveller would be a huge understatement as on a rainy afternoon the playing surface was effectively just compacted mud, the players often struggling to keep themselves upright. That mattered little though to the 15,000-strong Wednesday following, which was almost half of the attendance, that celebrated wildly when a brace from Ford sealed a 2-1 win and a third post-war semi-final. Standing in their way of a fifth FA Cup final were a much-fancied Chelsea side, although another mudbath of a pitch at Villa Park did somewhat even out the cup tie, arguably to Wednesday's advantage. The first half was a somewhat fractious affair, characterised by several fouls and scrappy play, and this was proven by the four minutes added on at the end of the half by Bolton referee Mr Dagnall – something almost unheard of in 1960s football. Ten minutes into the second half came a moment that eighteen-year-old cup debutant Graham Pugh will never forget as he fired home from close range before wheeling away in celebration. A few minutes later the offside flag denied him a second and after Wednesday's defence, with Gerry Young outstanding, had repelled heavy pressure, several more chances were created, prompting their travelling fans to chant 'easy, easy, easy'. Those same fans were in dreamland in the final minute when another teenager, Jim McCalliog, headed home to clinch victory and a trip to Wembley on 14 May 1966. Despite the media stating that the final would be a dour affair, it was in fact one of the greatest cup finals of the post-war era, although for Wednesday it was a heartbreaking final as the trophy slipped from their grasp in a mad fourteen-minute second-half spell. Prior that point, Wednesday had impressed all present with their high-quality football and led 2-0 thanks to McCalliog's deflected shot, after just four minutes, and then a fifty-seventh-minute strike from Ford. Perhaps it was the second goal that actually cost the Owls the trophy as they seemed to slightly ease off and were punished quickly as Mike Trebilcock netted twice in five minutes to level matters – an Everton fan famously ran onto the pitch, with five policemen in hot pursuit, when the equaliser went in. Despite that double blow, Wednesday were still the best side before hearts were broken when the usually reliable Gerry Young let a long punt slip under his foot and Temple raced away to score after seventy-three minutes. There was still time, though, to save the game and Wednesday laid siege to the Everton goal, McCalliog, Fantham and Smith all going close before the final whistle brought the end to a bittersweet afternoon for Brown's young side – the sight of a hunched-up Gerry Young kneeling on the turf at full-time was an abiding memory.

SWFC: R. Springett, Smith, Megson, Eustace, Ellis, Young, Pugh, Fantham, McCalliog, Ford, Quinn

Don Megson: 'I would rather we had played football of not so high standard and won, but there is consolation in the fact that we put up an entertaining show. At two goals up, I thought we really had them. Then things did not go our way. That's the way it goes in football. I'm sorry for the supporters. We are all bitterly disappointed.'

Despite the defeat, Captain Megson took his players on a lap of honour around the Wembley pitch – a tradition that started on that afternoon –

and it was then back to the Russell Hotel for a gala banquet, a star-studded guest list including lords and their ladies, football luminaries such as FA President Sir Stanley Rous, and dozens of former players and backroom staff; eight players from the 1935 cup-winning team were guests of the club at Wembley, including captain Ronnie Starling, with five men, Nibloe, Catlin, Starling, Hooper and Walker, having attended the semi-final victory. The players did not expect much of a reception from fans on their return to the city but supporters turned out in force, an estimated 100,000 packing the streets as their specially painted blue and white coach snaked its way through the thronging masses from the station to the town hall. It was said that some of the players were close to tears, such was the welcome home, while a small band of Sheffield United fans quickly disappeared after they joined in the procession singing anti-Wednesday songs. Once the players were ensconced on the town hall balcony, manager Brown addressed the 30,000 or so stood below him: 'This was the best welcome I have seen in football. We're all surprised by it. The lads were disappointed with the result but this has been a salve to their feelings.'

A gala reception followed to honour the players who came so close to bringing the trophy back to Sheffield for a fourth time. It was wondered by the local press what the reception would have been if Wednesday had actually lifted the cup!

Close to Wembley Again Before Scunthorpe United, Villa Park and Arsenal

After the excitement of Wembley, the cup campaign of 1967 began at Hillsborough in late January, the tie against Queens Park Rangers being notable for the launch of a Wednesday mascot called Ozzie Owl, one of the first of its kind as clubs slowly started to realise the potential of marketing and commercial activities. The tie also saw the Springett brothers on opposite sides, and Wednesday cruised through courtesy of a hat-trick from Ritchie. Progression to the last sixteen followed quickly, a 4-0 home win versus Mansfield Town including an appearance for sixteen-year-old 'keeper Gary Scothorn, who at the time was Wednesday's youngest player. Memories of 1935 then came flooding back as the draw took the Owls back to Norwich City, completing a hat-trick of cup ties at the Norfolk club on three different grounds. The Canaries had dumped Manchester United out in the previous round but Wednesday were never in any trouble, winning 3-1 to set up a rematch with Chelsea. Wednesday looked set to earn a deserved replay, backed by an outstanding travelling support of 18,000, but it would be a cruel end as in the third minute of five added on at the end, mainly due to an injury to home player Tambling, Baldwin literally shinned the ball past Springett to end hopes of Wembley. The following season, Wednesday put aside poor league form to reach the last sixteen before it was Chelsea yet again who ended their interest, winning 2-0 at Stamford Bridge following an entertaining 2-2 draw. The draw for the third round in 1969 sent a buzz of excitement through the county as championship-chasing Leeds United were sent to Hillsborough. Just 2,889 short of the 55,000 capacity watched a thrilling draw, although the game was marred by fighting on the Kop, which eventually meant the police intervened to create their own version of 'no mans' land' between the scrapping youths. After the draw, Leeds was hotly tipped to progress into the next round but they didn't anticipate youngster Woodall would have the game of his life, scoring twice as Wednesday pulled off a memorable 3-1 win. Unfortunately, having got past the considerable barrier of Leeds United, they were held at home by Birmingham City before ingloriously going out in the mud at St Andrews. Of course, Wednesday tumbled from the top flight in 1970 and the FA Cup provided little solace. After beating West Bromwich Albion they were fully expected to brush aside the challenge of Fourth Division Scunthorpe United. However, the opposite happened and with a young Kevin Keegan in their ranks, the Irons pulled off a sensational 2-1 win at Hillsborough, inflicting arguably Wednesday's worst ever cup defeat. What made the result even worse for Owls fans was that the visitors deserved the win and it was a sad end for club legend Don Megson, who played his final game on one of the club's most inauspicious days.

The first two seasons of the 1970s saw away exits to higher division sides, before a run to the last sixteen in 1973 will always be remembered for a tremendous evening at Villa Park, when top-flight Crystal Palace provided the opposition in the second replay of a fourth-round tie, following two draws. Thousands and thousands of Wednesday fans travelled to Birmingham, turning the ground into a mini Hillsborough, and they were celebrating ten minutes from the end of extra-time when Joicey ran onto Sissons' through ball to complete his hat-trick, prompting manager Derek Dooley to comment:

> This is undoubtedly the greatest night of my life since my playing career ended twenty years ago last week. Right from the draw I thought we could win this one and even tonight, when we were down twice, I thought we could still do it. We thoroughly deserved the win. I do not think anyone could argue with that.

Who else but Chelsea ended Wednesday's run, the West London club again providing the killer blow in 1975 when a plucky Owls side performed heroically to lead 2-0 at Stamford Bridge before the hosts hit back to win 3-2. A year earlier, Wednesday had lost in a midweek third-round replay 3-1 at Coventry City while in 1976 they found themselves in unchartered territory, playing in the modern-day first round, negotiating tricky home ties against non-league Macclesfield Town and Wigan Athletic before exiting at second tier Charlton Athletic. Wednesday exited to another Fourth Division club, Darlington, in the 1976/77 campaign but it hardly created any column inches due to Wednesday being a Third Division club themselves. A horrible rainy afternoon in December 1977 provided another low point in Wednesday's FA Cup story as they were knocked out by non-league Wigan Athletic, at their Springfield Park ground, which left the long-suffering fans to concentrate on the club's precarious league position. The contrast a year later was quite remarkable as Wednesday, slowly being rejuvenated under Jack Charlton, earned a crack at the mighty Arsenal in the third round. The tie was at Hillsborough and was eventually given the go-ahead after volunteers helped clear the pitch of snow after a big freeze had hit Britain. There was still snow on the terracing though and during the game Gunners 'keeper Pat Jennings was mercilessly pelted with snowballs by the fans on the Kop, who were delighted as their side earned a deserved replay after a rumbustious cup tie. The Gunners were, understandably, hot favourites in the replay but Wednesday came within a whisker of recording one of their greatest results, leading 1-0 at Highbury (Wylde) only for Brady to snatch an injury-time leveller. The sides could not be separated in extra-time, so the teams reconvened at Leicester City's Filbert Street – the ground was available as the Foxes had installed a large protective balloon over the pitch to protect the playing surface as games all over the country were postponed. The third game finished 2-2 and five days later the teams shared six goals as Jack Charlton's plucky troops more than matched their top-flight opponents; the team was also backed by terrific vocal support from Sheffield as Arsenal fans were vastly outnumbered. The match eventually went the way of the Londoners after nine hours of football, although Wednesday were emphatically back on the football map, the tie proving a catalyst to the promotion campaign that followed. That marathon against the eventual cup winners was followed by early exits to Carlisle United, Newcastle United and Coventry City prior to a run to the semi-finals for the first time since 1966. It would be fair to say that Second Division Wednesday had a dose of luck in the 1982/83 campaign as the cup draw did not pair them with a top-flight club until the semi-finals, and then with a side that was heading for relegation. Wednesday almost went out in the third round, needing a second replay to see off Southend United, before wins against Torquay United and Cambridge United handed Wednesday a quarter-final tie at Burnley. A penalty save from Bolder helped earn his side a replay and on one of Hillsborough's most memorable nights, almost 42,000 roared Wednesday to a 5-0 win, Burnley simply having no answer to the Owls' devastating display. Wednesday's build-up to the semi-final at Highbury was affected by injuries with a broken leg for Ian Bailey ruling him out and skipper Mick Lyons only making the team after an eleventh-hour fitness test. It was a scorching hot day in North London and with Owls fans amassed on the North Bank there was a terrific atmosphere, the noise becoming quite deafening as Wednesday made a confident start. It was Brighton who netted first though, a spectacular 30-yard effort from Case, but Wednesday fought back to draw level twelve minutes into the second half, record signing Mirocevic gleefully firing home from close range. A place at Wembley was now up for grabs but after seventy-eight minutes it was Albion who grabbed the winner, Robinson firing home to take his side to the cup final for the first and only time. It was tough on the Owls, who had matched their opponents without really reaching the heights, but a year later a new-look side almost matched their efforts, reaching the quarter-finals. This time Wednesday did record a top-flight scalp, beating Coventry City 3-2 at Hillsborough in a delayed fourth-round tie, but were held 0-0 at home by Southampton, in what was the first game televised live from Hillsborough. Wednesday succumbed 5-1 in the replay and were controversially knocked out in the fifth round in 1985 after Ipswich Town grabbed an eighty-eighth-minute winner, the Owls defence stopping to appeal to the linesman when a cross from the wing headed towards two home players who were clearly offside; however, the referee did not blow and D'Avray fired the ball into the net to trigger protestations to the match official, which failed to get the goal chalked off as Town progressed 3-2 on an eventful night.

Another Semi-final Before Wembley Again and Again

The story of Wednesday's progression to the semi-final in 1986 centred on a young forward who had been plucked from non-league football and scored four times in as many cup ties. His name was Carl Shutt and after wins over West Bromwich Albion and Orient, Wednesday beat Derby County in a replay, Shutt scoring both goals in a 2-0 win. Incidentally, the first game at Derby proved highly controversial with the frozen surface leading to goalie Hodge receiving a head injury and allegations from County about the legitimacy of the injury. Third Division County held Wednesday to a draw but after they were dispatched at Hillsborough, Wednesday welcomed West Ham United, the match being delayed to a Wednesday evening. A terrific display from Wednesday, full of poise and power, sent them into the semi-final again with a rare goal from Worthington and another Shutt strike clinching the 2-1 victory. Two important players were absent from both the Wednesday and Everton sides for the Villa Park semi-final, Lineker and Marwood failing late fitness tests, but Martin Hodge was declared fit, recording his 150th consecutive game. The tie was evenly balanced throughout and went into extra-time after Shutt had equalised Harper's opening goal – the former Spalding United attacker headed home in front his supporters and almost climbed over the fences to acknowledge the acclaim. The game continued to ebb and flow but Wednesday hearts were broken when eight minutes into the additional time Graeme Sharp lashed home what proved to be the winner. The mid-1980s were certainly a golden period for Wednesday in the tournament as they again reached the last eight in 1987, although the run was marred in the fourth round when a terrible tackle from Chester's Bennett left England U21 defender Ian Knight with leg injuries more akin to a car crash than a football field – the multiple fractures effectively ended his career. The previous round had also been controversial with referee George Courtney, who was never a popular figure at S6, sending off Chapman but seemingly failing to take action against visiting players – the injustice felt by the Owls ensured the ten men progressed 1-0 to that ill-fated meeting with Chester. Wednesday subsequently knocked out West Ham United (again) in the next round before welcoming the surprise team of the competition, Coventry City. The Sky Blues brought an estimated 15,000 supporters with them and the tie was evenly balanced early in the second half, Gary Megson equalised Regis' early goal for the visitors. With the majority in the 48,005 crowd behind Wednesday, the Owls tore into their opponents, but every cup-winning team needs luck and they received their share after seventy-seven minutes when a shot from Houchen deflected off Mark Smith's outstretched leg and looped over a stranded Hodge. The same player accepted a late deflection off Nigel Worthington's head to clinch a 3-1 victory for the eventual surprise cup winners. For Wednesday, it was a disappointing end to their cup exploits and they were handed the rather unwelcome draw of Everton in the third round in 1988. Just eight days before the cup tie, Wednesday actually recorded their first win over Everton in twenty-three league and cup games and the confidence accrued from that result ensured they gave their old advisories a tough game, taking the lead late in the second half only for Everton to force a replay. That was not the end of the story though as the reigning league champions were surprised in the replay as Wednesday performed gallantly to force another game, back at Goodison Park. The tie was turning into one of those cup marathons so loved by fans and after Wednesday lost the toss, the teams reconvened on Merseyside for the third instalment. The tie again went into extra-time and again the sides could not be separated, a third 1-1 result seemingly handing the advantage to Wednesday. The biggest crowd so far (38,953) was inside Hillsborough to see who would play Middlesbrough in the next round and all expected another keenly fought tie. However, the absence of the ever dependable Madden at the heart of the Owls' defence proved crucial as Everton ran riot in the first half, a treble from Sharp helping his side to a 5-0 lead at the interval. Wednesday fans were left in a state of shock – it was said that the pubs around the ground quickly became packed as supporters left at half-time to drown their sorrows – and suffice to say the second period was somewhat academic with neither side adding to the score.

The 1988/89 cup campaign commenced with a 5-1 home win over Torquay United before Second Division Blackburn Rovers provided the mortal blow. Wednesday exited to Everton again in 1990, after Wednesday had experienced the strange surrounds of a dilapidated Molineux Ground where the capacity crowd was squeezed into only two stands, one of which was 40 yards from the pitch, making for a strangely subdued atmosphere. The 2-1 win in the Black Country immediately caused comparison with the FA Cup run in 1935, but those quickly ended after Everton won a high noon Sunday meeting at Hillsborough. Wednesday's run to the last sixteen in 1991 was somewhat overshadowed by progression in the League Cup but it did include one of the most exciting cup ties played by Wednesday as they led three times but had to settle for a replay after hosts Millwall grabbed a ninetieth-minute equaliser as the sides shared eight goals. Strikes from Anderson and Hirst ensured progression, but it was a weary Wednesday side, experiencing somewhat of a fixture pile-up, who were overpowered by John Beck's direct and powerful Cambridge United side in the fifth round, the 4-0 reverse to the eventual Third Division champions a sobering experience for the travelling Wednesdayites. The January 1992 tie at Preston North End saw the club play on an artificial surface for the first time in the competition but progress was brief as the delayed home tie with Middlesbrough, postponed because of snow, saw a 2-1 defeat. The 1992/93 campaign commenced with a return visit to the scene of the club's exit two years before – Cambridge United's Abbey Stadium. Bad weather again caused the original match to be postponed and Wednesday looked to be heading out again before a quick-fire brace from Harkes and Bright guaranteed safe passage to the fourth round. Sunderland were the visitors to Hillsborough but it needed a huge slice of luck for the Owls to progress, the evenly fought match being decided in the last minute when visiting 'keeper Norman inexplicably dropped a cross at the feet of Bright, who gladly accepted the late Christmas gift to put his side through. The emergence of Paul Warhurst in an attacking position had been a catalyst for success in both domestic cup competitions and it was the former defender who was on the scoresheet twice as First Division Southend United were comfortably beaten 2-0. The Owls' run in the cup was identical to their 1982/83 campaign, in so much as that Wednesday did not face a top-flight side until the semi-finals. This was because it was second tier Derby County who stood in their way in the sixth round, the teams thrilling a live TV audience as they shared six goals, a late leveller from Warhurst ensuring a replay. In the interim, the two Sheffield sides were drawn together in the semi-final and twenty-four hours after United booked their place, the Owls joined them as whom else but Warhurst scored the only goal. The biggest derby game in history is covered in detail elsewhere but the subsequent win clinched a sixth FA Cup final appearance, perennial foes Arsenal standing in their way of a fourth success. The staging of the semi-finals at Wembley did somewhat dilute the experience, especially as Wednesday had already lost to the Gunners in the League Cup final, but fans still travelled in good heart, confident that one of the best teams in the Owls' 150 years would surely end the season with some silverware. Tickets for the showpiece occasion ranged from £15 to £50 (each club being allocated 21,500) while 'The Hillsborough Crew' (actor Ian Reddington and Heaven 17's Martyn Ware) released 'If it's Wednesday it must be Wembley', which was available on 7-inch vinyl, cassette and picture disk. The London Underground and train stations echoed with 'Tricky Trev's Barmy Army' and 'We Love You Wednesday' as fans descended on the capital, just like their fellow Sheffielders had done for the first time back in 1890.

SWFC: Woods, Nilsson, Worthington, Anderson (Hyde), Warhurst, Harkes, Sheridan, Palmer, Waddle (Bart-Williams), Hirst, Bright

It was the Gunners who started better in the final, leading at half-time thanks to a Wright strike, but Wednesday hit back, with Hirst scoring his sixteenth goal of the season, firing in a left-foot shot from a Harkes cut back. As is usually the case in major finals, the thirty minutes of extra-time produced little of note and Wednesday duly enjoyed their Saturday night banquet at their team hotel, the destination of the cup still to be decided – Jeff Lynne of ELO was a member of the band that played for the players, officials, guests and dignitaries. The sides reconvened on the following Thursday evening but it proved a day of disaster for Wednesday fans, which started with terrible problems on the roads that left many stranded on the M1 and not even able to make the kick-off, which was delayed half an hour by the Football Association. They then watched their side fall behind to Wright (again) but spirits were raised when Waddle levelled after sixty-nine minutes, converting a through ball from Harkes. A pivotal moment then changed the game as Bright's miscued effort struck the post and went away to safety. At the end of ninety minutes the teams were again locked at 1-1 and the match seemed to be drifting towards the inevitable penalty shoot-out when, in added time in extra-time, the Gunners won a fortuitous corner and Owls fans were devastated as it was swung over and Andy Linighan headed past Woods; it was the cruellest way imaginable to lose a cup final and meant after sixty-three games there was nothing tangible to show for their laudable efforts.

SWFC: Woods, Nilsson (Bart-Williams), Worthington, Palmer, Warhurst, Harkes, Sheridan, Wilson (Hyde), Waddle, Hirst, Bright

'What a cruel game. I thought they did everything that could be asked and I reckon we won a lot of friends out there. They've been marvellous all season. The winning goal came from an unfortunate corner but it was a well-taken one. Linighan had a free header but I thought Chris Woods had it. He could have done no more. The pace of the ball took the ball over the line. I don't blame anyone' said Trevor Francis.

Memories of those amazing scenes in 1966 came flooding back when the team returned to Sheffield on the Friday, commencing an open-topped bus journey from Hillsborough, which snaked all the way to the town hall. Thousands of fans lined the streets, stood on top of bus shelters and even perched precariously on top of bay windows. There was a sea of blue to welcome the team back with banners, scarfs, balloons and flags before the official party enjoyed their second civic reception in as many years, although on this occasion they were not accompanied by a gleaming trophy. The following season included a replay win over Nottingham Forest before Chelsea, yet again, knocked the Owls out, winning 3-1 in extra-time at Hillsborough after a Hyde goal had earned a replay. The abiding memory of the 1994/95 cup campaign was a crazy night at Wolverhampton Wanderers after Bart-Williams had seen his eighty-seventh-minute penalty saved in the first game. The previous round had seen a heroic goalkeeping display as the Owls won 2-1 at Third Division Gillingham where Pressman was red-carded just before half-time after conceding a penalty. It was rookie goalie Key who took his place and, in what was his only senior game for Wednesday, pulled off a string of saves to ensure progression. The Wolves replay saw the teams level at the end of extra-time and Wednesday was therefore taken to their first penalty shoot-out in the FA Cup – second replays had been scrapped in the early 1990s. A place in the fifth round seemed assured when Pressman hammered home to put his side 3-0 ahead but the proverbial sky then fell in as the next three were either missed or saved and home forward Goodman converted the twelfth penalty of the night to send his side through and leave the travelling Owls fans open-mouthed. A year later, Wednesday exited with a whimper at First Division Charlton Athletic but dreams of Wembley were back on the agenda in 1997 when Grimsby Town (7-1) and Carlisle United (2-0) were beaten before a Bradford City side, containing Chris Waddle, lost 1-0 at Valley Parade. This set up a quarter-final home clash with perennial party-poopers Wimbledon, but with Wednesday ensconced in the top six of the Premier League, there were high hopes of at least getting through to the semi-finals. Wednesday had netted nine times in their previous three fixtures but it proved to be 'one of those days' as chances were missed, players were injured (both Newsome and Hyde received injuries that finished their season) and the Wombles took their chances, securing a 2-0 win. Sadly, the Owls have not reached this stage again, twenty years later.

Two Decades of Disappointment

It would be affair to say that after that loss Wednesday and the FA Cup have only been casual acquaintances who meet briefly every January before saying a tearful goodbye, usually around two weeks later. In fact, since 1997 Wednesday have reached the fifth round on only four occasions, with, ironically, two of the runs occurring in seasons where league form was dreadful – 1999/2000 and 2010/11. The 1990s FA Cup story ended with defeats to Blackburn Rovers in 1998, after another penalty kick howitzer from Pressman sealed a shoot-out win over

Watford, a Hillsborough loss to bogey cup team Chelsea in the 1999 fifth round, and an embarrassing fifth-round exit at lower league Gillingham in 2000 – the experiment of playing the third round in mid-December backfired badly when a raft of poor crowds hit the competition, less than 12,000 attending the home win over Bristol City. The run in 2000 also saw Wednesday earn penalty revenge at Wolves, winning the fourth-round replay tie on spot kicks, although hundreds of the 'barmy army' did not arrive until half-time, or later, after an M1 accident caused gridlock. The aforementioned defeat in Kent seemed unlikely at the break, when Wednesday led, but three goals in the final ten minutes left the Owls concentrating on their perilous position at the foot of the Premier League.

Exits to Southampton and Crewe Alexandra preceded a return visit to Gillingham in 2003, although the match was postponed with many fans having already reached the ground. When the teams tried again a few days later, the tie was played in almost artic conditions – temperatures were recorded of minus 10C – and on a frozen pitch a rag-tag Wednesday side meekly exited 4-1, much to the despair of the long-suffering fans who had travelled the 200 miles to deepest Kent. The last man to score an FA Cup hat-trick for Wednesday, Adam Proudlock, achieved the feat in a November 2003 first-round home tie against non-league Salisbury City, although his side subsequently crashed out to Scunthorpe United at the next stage. What followed was simply Sheffield Wednesday's worst run of form in the FA Cup as they exited in the third round for six consecutive seasons, arguably the only real highlight being in 2007 when cup-fighting days of yore were reprised as 28,000 watched the Owls hold Manchester City 1-1 at Hillsborough before losing 2-1 over the Pennines – a Lee Bullen equaliser briefly raised hopes of an upset. Considering the Owls' cup form going into the 2010/11 season, it was perhaps a surprise that Wednesday, starting back in the first round for the first time since 2004, went all the way to the fifth round, beating Southport and then Northampton Town to earn a third-round trip to Bristol City. The ensuing 3-0 win at Ashton Gate did not cause much of a ripple in the media but it was a notable result as incredibly it was the first time Wednesday had won a cup tie away from home against a team from a higher division. Wednesday was also lucky with the draw, being handed a home tie against minnows Hereford United, and two penalties from Clinton Morrison helped his side to a 4-1 win and a trip to Birmingham City. Less than 15,000 watched the Blues progress 3-0, Wednesday never really getting a foothold in the tie after conceding twice in the first seventeen minutes. Wednesday were still a League One club when they paid a first visit to Morecambe, winning 2-1 on the west Lancashire coast in November 2011, and subsequently knocked out Premier League West Ham United at Hillsborough in the third round – O'Grady netting a late winner in a game that was remarkable for eleven minutes of added time, caused by a bad injury to Julian Bennett. A home replay defeat to Blackpool ended hopes of Wembley. The two games against MK Dons in the following season's third round did not linger in any fan's memory as a turgid 0-0 at Hillsborough was followed by an equally lacklustre match, which ended 2-0 at Stadium MK.

Perhaps the biggest cup disappointment in recent years came in February 2014 when Wednesday welcomed fellow Championship club Charlton Athletic to Hillsborough with a place in the quarter-finals at stake, wins over non-league Macclesfield Town (in a replay) and Rochdale earning that crack at the last eight. Neighbours United were already in the next round and the prospect of a trip to Bramall Lane was eagerly anticipated by both sides of the city divide. It was therefore a huge disappointment when the Londoners (who gave a debut to Morgan Fox) took the lead midway through the first half. An equaliser from Leon Best got Hillsborough roaring their appreciation but you could have heard a pin drop when the visitors retook the lead and held on to inflict the *coup de gras* on the Sheffield cup derby. The last three seasons have seen early exits, although the 5,485 Wednesdayites that travelled for the January 2015 tie at Premier League Manchester City could be justified in claiming a moral victory, Wednesday leading through Nuhiu only for Milner to grab the winner in added time. The 2015/16 campaign ended in the fourth round at Shrewsbury Town, but the game was not without controversy as Wednesday led twice through McGugan only to concede a ninety-seventh-minute winner, seconds after Nuhiu had been hauled down in the Shrews area and the match official inexplicably waving away protestations. A home tie with Manchester United would have been the reward while Accrington would have travelled to Hillsborough in the 2017 fourth round if not for the small fact what the Owls lost 3-0 at Middlesbrough, in what was Wednesday's 400th game in the tournament. Both managers picked relatively strong sides but Boro opened the scoring and despite being down to ten men, scored twice more to bring the curtain down on the Owls' 137th year in the oldest professional football competition in the world. Top appearances and goals:

Appearances: Tommy Crawshaw 47, Andrew Wilson 44, Jack Brown 42, Don Megson 41, Alan Finney 39, Mark Hooper 39, Mark Smith 39, Tom Cawley 37, Ellis Rimmer 36, Mel Sterland 35, John Fantham 34, Billy Betts 33, Jack Lyall 32, Ernie Blenkinsop 31, Tom Brittleton 30, Willie Layton 30, Harry Chapman 30, Fred Spiksley 29, Tommy Walker 29, Nigel Worthington 29

Goals: Tom Cawley 22, Ellis Rimmer 18, Andrew Wilson 17, Fred Spiksley 15, Bob Gregory 14, Davie McLean 12, John Fantham 11, Mark Hooper 11, Harry Woolhouse 11, Lee Chapman 10, John Ritchie 10, Harry Winterbottom 10, Jack Allen 9, Redfern Froggatt 9, Harry Millership 9, George Simpson 9, Harry Davis (Twentieth Century) 8, Billy Ingram 8, E. Rhodes 8, Jimmy Stewart 8

Chapter 5

All-time XI

'I shouldn't object if they played football all the year round. Every time Saturday comes around in the close season I get fidgety. I am alright until 12 o'clock. After that I'm at a loose end as it were; wishing there was a football match, in which I could play or could watch. I don't think you realise how fond I am of football. To me it is the absolute king of games.'

Mark Hooper, 1933

Over 1,000 players have represented Sheffield Wednesday in competitive football and it would be perhaps foolish to just pick eleven men, especially when one considers the vast contrast in how the 'beautiful game' was played back in the nineteenth century and today's product. It has moved from a highly physical sport, which captured the hearts of the masses, to a far more technical and certainly less physical pastime, which is, however, equally as popular. Debate will always rage as to whether players of fifty or 100 years ago would even be effective in the modern game, and visa-versa, but no one will ever know the answer. Various polls over the years always end with a relatively recent player top of the pile, which is perhaps understandable, but this does tend to eliminate a large percentage of any club's all-time greats. Although this chapter title suggests the choice of just eleven players, I think it would be prudent to call up fifty players with a first-choice eleven, followed by eleven substitutes and the remainder sat in the proverbial stand, wrapped up in their winter coats, hoping to get into the matchday squad soon. I believe the following individuals should start and think they would be fairly unbeatable:

Starting XI

No. 1 Ron Springett
Wednesday has been blessed with some truly outstanding goalkeepers and the competition for a place would be a fight between Teddy Davison,

Jack Brown, Ron Springett and Kevin Pressman. There is no doubt that Jack Lyall, Martin Hodge and Keiran Westwood would also have been in the manager's plans but the aforementioned foursome could all make a claim for inclusion. Despite the attributes of his rivals, I believe it is a relatively simple task to hand the No. 1 jersey to the great Ronald Derrick 'Ron' Springett (22 July 1935), if only for the fact that he is the most capped England international in the club's 150-year history, winning thirty-three between 1959 and 1966. By the late 1950s, Wednesday found themselves in somewhat of a goalkeeping crisis, four different men having worn the gloves as they stumbled towards relegation from the First Division. It was at this point that secretary-manager Taylor – in one of his final acts before handing over to Catterick – completed arguably his greatest signing, capturing Springett for a bargain £10,000 from Queens Park Rangers. The Owls' hierarchy held Springett in such high esteem that they uniquely allowed him to live and train in London and travel up to Sheffield on matchdays. Wednesday fans quickly realised that their new 'keeper was an outstanding talent, boasting razor-sharp reflexes, bravery and almost faultless judgement. He was unchallenged as No. 1 for the whole of his Owls career, helping Wednesday challenge for major honours. His form for Wednesday quickly resulted in a call-up for the full England squad with the Londoner making his international bow against Northern Ireland in 1959. By 1962 he had surpassed Blenkinsop as the most capped Englishman while in Owls colours and was virtually unchallenged for his country until the emergence of Gordon Banks. Unfortunately for Springett his rival became first choice just before the 1966 World Cup finals – almost forty-three years later he was one of several 'non-playing' members of the victorious team to be handed medals in a ceremony at Downing Street. He appeared in 384 games before being involved in a very unique transfer, which saw his brother, Peter, move to Hillsborough from Queens Park Rangers and Ron return to Loftus Road. His popularity at Hillsborough was shown when over 23,000 attended his testimonial game in 1967. His professional career came to a close in 1969. He later ran his own decorating business while his daughter, Terry, represented England and became football secretary at Loftus Road. He passed away on 13 September 2015 after a short illness, with Wednesday dedicating their home game against Fulham in his memory.

No. 2 Roland Nilsson

The right-back position would be hotly contested between five men with 1896 FA Cup-winning captain Jack Earp, Tommy Walker, Norman Curtis and Mel Sterland all making claims to earn the starting shirt. However, I think it would be reasonable to hand the No. 2 shirt to one of the club's greatest post-war players and arguably the finest truly defensive players to ever represent Sheffield Wednesday – Roland Nils Lennart Nilsson. He was relatively unknown when signed by Ron Atkinson for just £375,000 in December 1989, but he was already a fully fledged Swedish International, having won the first of a record-breaking 116 caps in May 1986. He would add thirty-one to that tally while in South Yorkshire and finished third with his country at Euro 1992 and the 1994 World Cup. His playing career had started at hometown club Helsingborg IF (where he was born 27 November 1963) and won numerous honours while on the books of IFK Gothenburg, including a domestic 'double' and success in the 1987 UEFA Cup. It was not long before Wednesday fans learnt of his qualities as in 186 games he was virtually faultless, showing incredible timing, athleticism and superb consistency, in addition to being seemingly unflappable. Described by Atkinson as the 'best professional I have ever worked with', Nilsson was instrumental in Wednesday's victory in the 1991 League Cup final and his commitment to the cause was no more typified than in May 1993 when between the FA Cup final and replay he jetted back home to play for Sweden. He was without doubt one of the most popular players of the modern era and it was a sad day when he returned home in May 1994, the club allowing him to re-sign for his first club. It would not be the last that Wednesday fans saw of 'Rolo' though as he made a surprise return to England in 1997, signing for 'Big Ron's' Coventry City. When the teams subsequently met two seasons running, he was given a standing ovation by Wednesdayites in both the home and away fixtures. Injury eventually brought his career in England to a close, although he continued to play as a player-coach back at Helsingborg. After winning the Swedish title he returned to Coventry in a coaching capacity and was eventually appointed their manager, being rather unfortunate to be fired in April 2002 after the Sky Blues just failed to qualify for the First Division play-offs. He returned to Sweden, gaining employment with the Swedish FA, and later managed at Gothenburg club GAIS, Malmo FF (winning the title in 2011) and Danish club FC Copenhagen. Incredibly, despite his new club leading the division, in January 2012 he was replaced by the club's sporting director and has remained outside of club management since, working for the FA with specific responsibility for the U17 national side.

No. 3 Ernie Blenkinsop

To complete the full-back positions, several candidates spring to mind, the likes of Harry Burton, outstanding Scottish International Jimmy Blair, and Hugh Swift all making claims for inclusion. However, the fight for the No. 3 spot became a straight choice between Ambrose Langley, Ernest Blenkinsop, Norman Curtis, Don Megson and Nigel Worthington. All of those individuals could have been handed the old-style No. 3 shirt but it seems fitting that a man who earned the nickname of 'the prince of full-backs' should win the race. The man in question was Cudworth-born (20 April 1902) Ernest 'Ernie' Blenkinsop, who signed for Wednesday back in January 1923 for £1,150 from Hull City. The youngster's chances of enjoying a career as a professional footballer had seemed unlikely when he left school, aged thirteen, and spent the next five years down the

Grimethorpe and Brierley coal mines, almost losing his life on one occasion when a roof caved in; years later 'Blenki' revealed he was sure he'd have died if he'd not took evasive action. While still down the pit he laced up his boots again to appear for Cudworth United Methodist Club and a move to Cudworth United followed – Blenkinsop forming a left-wing partnership with his brother – before he was taken into the Football League in 1921 by Hull City. He moved for a £100 fee plus, supposedly, eighty pints of beer, but it transpired that the Tigers could not recognise they had a 'diamond in the rough' and Blenkinsop only played the occasional senior game. Thankfully for both concerned Wednesday manager Brown used his legendary eye for talent and, after seeing Blenkinsop play for City's reserve side, brought him to Wednesday. He was virtually an instant success, although his debut – in front of an astonishing 66,000 crowd for a FA Cup tie versus Barnsley – was at right-back. He quickly switched wings though and by the mid-1920s was an automatic choice, helping Wednesday to win the Second Division in 1926. He exuded style and panache, boasting great distribution, positional sense and superb timing in the tackle. It was these qualities that won him the first of twenty-six caps for England in 1928 – he is the most capped Englishman on the club's books after Springett – and was idolised by Wednesday fans. It was therefore a huge shock, in January 1934, when the current international and Owls captain transferred to Liverpool for a club record fee of £6,500, after 424 games. Supporters were not impressed, many accusing manager Walker of selling the outstanding full-back to ensure he would not replace him – at the time 'Blenki' was training to become a coach – and it was thought that the Wednesday boss saw him as somewhat of a 'stalking horse'. This, of course, was never proven and when he returned in Liverpool colours he was not only given a standing ovation but the players lined up to clap him onto the pitch, the Owls' matchday band playing 'See the Conquering Hero Comes' – all to emphasise the respect he was held in and what a big loss he'd been to the club's playing staff. He remained at Liverpool until November 1937 before retiring from league soccer in 1939 after two years at Cardiff City, the second year under a player-coach remit. During the wars years he guested for a handful of clubs, after moving back to Sheffield to work in the steel industry, and was appointed a part-time coach by the Owls in 1942, 'Blenky' also taking over as landlord of the Mason's Arms in Crookes. In 1950 he became the publican of the Sportsman's Inn in Crosspool, and coached occasionally for Sheffield United in the 1950s. Later in life he became an outstanding golfer, playing off-scratch at one point, and it was perhaps fitting that he won the championship of his local golf club just one week before his passing, aged sixty-seven, on 24 April 1969 in Sheffield.

No. 4 Tom Brittleton

While it is relatively easy to pick a goalkeeper and two full-backs, it is somewhat complicated, assuming one is using a modern 4-4-2 formation, to pick two men for the middle of the park. This complication is mainly caused by the fact that English football stuck rigidly to the old 2-3-5 (pyramid) formation from the late nineteenth century until the early 1930s, utilising three half-backs in the middle of the pitch, with two full-backs behind. In the 1930s, the WM formation, introduced by Arsenal manager Herbert Chapman, became the common formation and over the years that followed the No. 4 position eventually metamorphosed from a central defensive position to a deep-lying or box-to-box midfielder. Therefore, for the purpose of this chapter, I have classed the old-style left and right half-backs as midfield players and the old pivotal centre-back stopper as a modern-day central defender. Therefore, the first midfield slot, of which he has numerous rivals, goes to one of the club's longest-serving and highly rated right half-backs, James Thomas 'Tom' Brittleton. Born on 23 April 1882 in Winsford, Brittleton was once described as 'the perfect footballer' and during fifteen years at Wednesday was an automatic choice, showing many qualities that also earnt Brittleton five full caps for England. In modern terms, he would probably be classed as a defensive midfielder but that description would do Brittleton a disservice as during 372 games he netted thirty-three times and was renowned for his terrific shooting ability. He gave countless classy displays, characterised by superb tackling, unselfish play and tireless running. When he signed from Stockport County in January 1905, the £300 fee was a club record but he gave tremendous value; Wednesday initially had a £200 bid rebuffed by cash-strapped County before they eventually accepted a more lucrative bid, much to the dismay of their fans. He had actually built a reputation as a smart and clever inside-right and all of his early games for Wednesday came in that more advanced position, pairing up with right-winger Davis. However, at the back end of the 1905/06 season he replaced Ruddlesdin and never looked back, helping his new club to FA Cup glory and, as previously mentioned, won several representative honours; one honour he did, however, politely decline was in 1911 when he was invited by the FA to tour South Africa, Brittleton stating he'd rather spend his summer fishing – it was not without cause that Tom was once described as 'the biggest home bird you could ever meet'. He showed his remarkable fitness by playing for the Owls past his thirty-eighth birthday. He was thirty-eight years and eight days old when he made his Wednesday finale, and at the time was the club's oldest player. He subsequently moved to Stoke FC and later commented, 'However, there it is, I have had a good innings and must recognise the very unpalatable fact that I am not as young as I used to be, though understand the "too old at forty" doesn't apply to me.' Incredibly, he played another five seasons and even turned down the offer of becoming manager in 1922 so he could continue playing. Finally, at the grand age of forty-five he retired from league football and returned to his first love, Winsford United, in July 1925. His return completed a career circle that had started when he left school, aged fourteen, and became at regular at Winsford Celtic. He appeared in every position, including goalkeeper, before signing for the town's senior club, Winsford United. It was while playing for United that the bizarre intervention of a Stockport County fan led to his move to the Edgeley Park Club. The supporter in question had a sweetheart from Winsford and it was while in her company that he was impressed by the skills of Brittleton. He duly recommended the youngster to the County hierarchy and aged nineteen he signed amateur forms, while continuing to work in the Winsford Salt Works. While still on amateur forms, he showed his preferences by turning out for Winsford in a County Cup tie, rather than play for Stockport, but after signing professional forms he appeared in forty-five league games before County lost their Football League place in 1904. They bounced back into the league twelve months later but by then Tom had moved to Owlerton. When he did return to the Cheshire town it was as player-manager at Winsford United, while working at ICI, and when he retired from playing became landlord of the Navigation Inn. His son, John Thomas Jr, followed in his father's footsteps, appearing for Aston Villa in the late 1920s, while Brittleton Snr stayed in his hometown for the rest of his life, passing away on 22 February 1955.

No. 5 Tommy Crawshaw

Competition for the two central defensive positions would include many of the club's inspirational captains, from Billy Betts in the early 1890s to more recent leaders such as Nigel Pearson and Lee Bullen. One man who stands alone, though, in this position is Sheffield-born colossus Thomas Henry Crawshaw, who remains the only Wednesday player to win two FA Cup and two League Championship medals. Born in the town on 27 December 1872, Tommy started his career in local Sheffield football, but it was from Manchester club Haywood Central that he would arrive at Olive Grove, signing on 24 April 1894 – he later joked that his transfer fee was a glass of ginger ale he was given while signing the paperwork. Wednesday officials hoped that the strong-willed Sheffielder, who was a brilliant header of the ball, could be a long-term replacement for Betts and he quickly repaid their faith as within a year he was not only established in Wednesday's first team but had already won the first of ten England caps. He was simply an outstanding defender – once described as a 'glorious spoiler of the opposition' – and his wholehearted 100 per cent commitment to the cause made him hugely popular among supporters and teammates. The Ferrier-Crawshaw-Ruddlesdin back line of the period powered the club to several honours and Tommy, who for the time was a towering figure at 5 feet 11 inches, was a captain who truly led by example, showing remarkable courage and determination. During the club's second FA Cup-winning campaign, Crawshaw passed his thirty-fourth birthday, but even though final opponents Everton were favourites for the trophy, Tommy played the game of his life and rallied his team to lift the cup again. That 1906/07 campaign would be his last as a regular and his 465th, and final, appearance came rather fittingly in a derby win over Sheffield United. His loyalty was rewarded with a free transfer and it's thought by many that the announcement of his signing at a subsequent Chesterfield AGM was the only reason the Derbyshire club gained re-election into the Football League. He stayed a season at the Spireites and then appeared for Castleford, prior to being secretary of Glossop until the outbreak of war in 1914. After the hostilities, Tommy was the landlord at three Sheffield public houses but sadly, after retiring, he came upon hard times and it was reported, in 1952, that he was depending on public charity to survive. Thankfully, on hearing of his plight, his old club came to the rescue and deposited the princely sum of £50 in his bank account, which he was allowed to draw down at £1 per week. He soon recovered from his dire straits and lived another eight years, before passing away in the city on 25 November 1960, aged eighty-seven.

No. 6 Des Walker

His partner at the back would be without doubt the quickest defender to have ever played for Wednesday – Desmond Sinclair Walker. His remarkable pace, coolness under pressure, ability to read a game and sheer consistency ensures he secures the shirt. He arrived at Hillsborough in July 1993 for a club record-equalling £2.75 million fee, after having experienced a decidedly mixed time in Italian football where Walker was often forced to play at full-back. His outstanding displays for his country at Italia '90 ensured that several of Europe's elite clubs courted his signature, but Hackney-born Walker (26 November 1965) stayed loyal to his first club, Nottingham Forest, for a further two seasons before starting his ill-fated Italian adventure. He was simply a living legend for Forest, amassing 346 games in his first spell and scoring the only goal in his long career, against Luton Town on New Year's Day 1992. He was rejected by Tottenham Hotspur as a youngster but he would thrive under the tutelage of Brian Clough at Forest, quickly breaking into the first team and earning England U21 caps. He earned two League Cups and two Full Members Cup winners medals, and was an automatic choice for England for several seasons. When Francis bought him back to England it was hoped his confidence would return and he'd quickly be back on the international scene. He did return to England duty but to the amazement of Owls' fans he won only one further cap. Despite failing to add to that tally his club form was almost faultless from the day he arrived to the day he was released in June 2001, after 362 appearances. He was without doubt one of the best 'man markers' in the game and he was very much a player who was an out-and-out defender, Des very rarely adventuring over the halfway line! He was a rock at the heart of the club's defence and as Wednesday's fortunes started to wane they became even more dependent on his remarkable consistency and his uncanny ability to rescue any seemingly hopeless situation. At times he seemed to be Wednesday's defence all on his own and it was only the club's worsening financial situation that meant his career came to a close after eight seasons.

After leaving he joined Burton Albion, who at the time were a Northern Premier League club, alongside former teammate Nigel Clough, although he only played a solitary game. He would then enjoy a renaissance back at the City Ground, rejoining Forest in July 2002 and captaining them to the First Division play-off semi-finals. After adding another thirty-three games to his total he retired in May 2004, joining the club's coaching staff. But after a succession of managers he departed in January 2005, when Gary Megson took over. He then dropped out of football altogether and remarkably became a long-distance lorry driver for several years, prior to returning to the game in February 2016 when appointed academy defensive coach at Derby County. Both his sons, Tyler and Lewis, rather fittingly play for Forest and the Rams, although it is doubtful they will achieve the heights in the game of their much-respected father.

No. 7 Mark Hooper

The fight for the right-wing position is far more straightforward with a handful of long-serving wingers all featuring in the choice. The club's first great winger was early twentieth-century wide-man Harry Davis, with post-war men Finney, Waddle and even maverick winger Di Canio all challenging for a first-team spot. Despite these worthy men, the choice for the No. 7 shirt is arguably the easiest of all eleven positions as it could be none other than legend of the interwar years, Mark Hooper. His inclusion is certainly two-fold as if he had been a centre forward, his tally of 135 goals in 423 games would have brought him close to inclusion, but the fact he was an old-fashioned touchline-hugging winger makes his figures even more remarkable, guaranteeing him a place. The slightly built Hooper – he was 5 feet 5 inches and wore size 4 boots – arrived at Hillsborough on 21 January 1927 and it had required a change of heart from his new manager Brown, who, three years earlier, had scouted the Darlington-born Hooper (14 July 1901) but decided he was too small.

Hooper came from a footballing family – his uncle Charlie Roberts was a notable Football League centre half-back – while all of the five siblings, including two sisters, played football with one brother, Chris, playing reserve team football at Wednesday. He had first started to play organised football at his school and his first step into senior football came with Northern League club Cockfield Colliery in the early 1920s, in his more accustomed role of right-winger. He earned a crust as a furnace worker in Darlington Rolling Mills but a remarkable 1922/23 season alerted many clubs to his qualities as Hooper helped his side to third place in the powerful Northern League and was also instrumental in a remarkable run in the old prestigious FA Amateur Cup, the team being dubbed 'Cockfield Wonder Village' as they progressed to the semi-finals. In the season that followed he appeared regularly for Darlington's reserve side and it was inevitable that he'd turn professional at the end of the season. He would average around a goal every three games for Darlington and netted eighteen times in the 1924/25 season as his side won the Division Three (North) title. The promotion brought Hooper into direct opposition with Wednesday and a dazzling display against them in a 5-1 win at Feethams in March 1926 probably ensured Brown did have that change of heart, Hooper moving to the 'Cutlery Capital' part way through the next season. It would be the start of a glittering career at Wednesday as he matured into arguably one of the finest players of the interwar years and certainly one of the best uncapped attackers. He was a real 'bag of tricks', possessing a deceptive turn of pace, superb close ball control and outstanding crossing ability. He was also fearless, going toe to toe against opponents who were heavier and taller, and boasted a rocket-like shot that left many a 'keeper rooted to the spot as the ball flew into the net! All those qualities, of course, exclude his remarkable goals record, which saw him net double figures in seven separate seasons, including eighteen in the 'great escape' campaign of 1927/28, and one at Wembley in the 1935 FA Cup final. He also had the welcome knack of seemingly never missing a game, setting a club record of 189 consecutive appearances, which was only bettered by Martin Hodge in the 1980s. He'd replaced Welsh winger Rees Williams and Hooper would be unchallenged for over a decade, briefly switching to inside-left when young starlet Drury took his place during the 1936/37 campaign. His senior career effectively came to an end when his cartilage was removed in May 1937. Hooper then acted as player-coach for the club's Yorkshire League side, until leaving for Rotherham United in the summer of 1939. The advent of war meant that Hooper appeared in only a handful of games for the Millers before retiring in 1940 and spending the next eighteen years acting as trainer to the second team and then the senior side, before retiring in 1958 following a major operation. Since the early 1930s he also ran his own sweet and tobacconist shop on Middlewood Road and no doubt told stories to fans who called in when Wednesday were at home. He stayed in Sheffield for the rest of his life before passing away on 9 March 1974.

No. 8 John Sheridan

With Tom Brittleton taking the first midfield berth, the second place could go to at least a dozen other worthy players, such as Chapman, Stewart, Bradshaw, Marsden, Burgess, Robinson, Froggatt – the list is endless. However, for sheer passing ability there cannot be many players that could match the silky skills of John Sheridan. He arrived at Hillsborough after a disappointing spell at Nottingham Forest, where after signing from

Leeds United he was only used once by the eccentric Clough before he was rescued by Atkinson, less than three months after moving to Forest. His quality was instantly acclaimed by Wednesday fans and he quickly became a favourite as 'Big Ron's' side played some of the best football seen for years. Sadly, relegation followed but with his partnership with Carlton Palmer flourishing, Wednesday bounced straight back, Sheridan famously scoring the first-half winner against Manchester United that won the League Cup. With Wednesday back in the top flight, Sheridan (born 1 October 1964 in Manchester) was at his peak, showing his outstanding vision and a full range of passing skills, allied with an eye for a spectacular goal, including a stunning goal in a ZDS cup tie versus Sheffield United and an incredible free-kick at Luton Town. Although born in Manchester, Sheridan qualified for Eire due to his Dublin-born parents and amassed twenty-nine caps while at Hillsborough, appearing in both the 1990 and 1994 World Cup finals. He remained first choice before falling out of favour under Pleat, much to the chagrin of Owls fans. It proved the beginning of the end for 'Shezza' as he went on loan to Birmingham City. The inevitable permanent move away duly occurred, after thirty-three goals in 244 games, when Bolton Wanderers paid £225,000 to sign him in November 1996. Spells at Doncaster Rovers and Oldham Athletic ended a playing career that had started as a trainee at Manchester City before being snapped up by Leeds United, who offered Sheridan his first professional contract. He would net fifty-two goals in 267 games for the Whites, earning a reputation as one of the best players outside of the top flight, eventually earning that ill-fated move to Nottingham Forest. Since retiring in 2004, he held various coaching and assistant managerial roles before being handed his first management role at Oldham Athletic in June 2006. Three years later he moved to Chesterfield and completed the double of the League Two title and victory in the Football League Trophy before departing early in the 2012/13 season. Spells at Plymouth Argyle, Newport County, Oldham Athletic (twice) and Notts County preceded a third spell at Oldham, taking over during the 2016/17 season.

No. 9 Andrew Wilson

Any all-time XI simply could not exclude the name of Andrew Wilson, who still holds the club record for appearances and goals almost a century after he played his final game. Born on 10 December 1880 in the small village of Lendalfoot, Ayrshire, the young Wilson actually played very little organised football in his early years, just the odd game while attending Irvine Royal Academy – his family had moved to the area where his father owned a farm. After leaving school he did not play football for three years, working on his father's farm, and interest was only rekindled when he made some new friends, many of whom played for a boys' team called the Irvine Meadow Eleven. Talk among the friends was almost exclusively about football, so it was effectively peer pressure that launched the career of Andrew Wilson! By the time he signed for the club they had progressed to junior status – the Scottish equivalent of non-league football – although his career actually started at left-back, Wilson believing he was too slow to play further upfield. He spent two seasons at full-back before being transferred into the Scottish League with Clyde, earning £2 per week, such good terms that his father did not object to 'Andra' – as he became affectionately known – becoming full-time. When he was scouted by Clyde, he was being temporarily used at inside forward and it would be in a more forward role that Wilson would play for the remainder of his career. A year later, in May 1900, he made the move into English football, Wednesday paying a club record fee of £200. His debut came on the opening day of the season and Wilson was so shocked by the pace of the English game that he later commented, 'I thought it was no game for me. The speed in which it was played simply staggered me and long before the match was finished I felt perfectly certain that if that was anything like the usual pace, the sooner I got back to Scotland the better.' Thankfully his physical strength helped Wilson adapt and he would remain in Sheffield for fully two decades, accruing a 546 senior games and netting 215 goals to sit comfortably at the top of Wednesday's all-time scoring chart. He also won six caps for Scotland, playing alongside his brother David against England in March 1913, while brothers James and Alex were also professional footballers.

He was a slow starter at Wednesday but would prove to be the best value for money signing the club has ever made, blossoming into one of the best British players of the years preceding the First World War. His sheer physicality – he stood at 5 feet 10 inches and weighed over 13 stone – thunderous shot and total professionalism were some of his best qualities. He replaced Harry Millar at Owlerton, finishing his first season as top scorer with thirteen goals. Incredibly he would achieve double figures in the goals column for every season he spent at Wednesday up to 1915, when war called a halt to league soccer. For the first ten years he occupied the centre forward role, helping the club to numerous honours before being switched to inside left when Murray arrived in March 1910, although the newcomer stayed less than a year. It was the arrival of lethal fellow Scot McLean that ensured Wilson remained in his new role as the duo forged a terrific partnership that came within a whisker of leading Wednesday to the title in 1913.

Due to his long service, Wilson received a total of three benefit games (standard league fixtures where the net receipts went to the player), although bad weather always seemed to keep the attendance down. His third attempt, against Bradford City in November 1913, saw Wilson made captain for the day, receiving a huge cheer when he led the teams out, but after buying cigars and 'bubbly water', heavy rain hit the attendance. During the war, Wilson remained on Wednesday's books, working in munitions production in Sheffield, and signed a new contract in 1919 that gave him a coaching role and a scouting position. He would make one more senior appearance and in 1920 was a founder member of Hillsborough Golf Club, helping to design the new course. A few months later he retired from playing and moved to take over as manager at Bristol Rovers. He spent five years at the Pirates, earning a reputation as a quiet, deep-thinking manager, but departed after Rovers just escaped having to apply for re-election in Division Three (South). Five years in charge at Oldham Athletic followed – his charges agonisingly missing out on promotion to the top flight in 1930 when losing their final game – before a season at Stockport County brought an end to his thirty-two years in English football. He retired back to Scotland and passed away on his family homestead, Patterton Farm, Irvine, on 13 March 1945.

No. 10 David Hirst

Who to partner with Andrew Wilson was no easy task, with pre-First World War legend McLean, prolific centre forwards Allen and Trotter, 1960s sharp-shooter Layne and the club's most recent prolific forward, David Hirst, all strongly considered. In the end it was Hirst who won the race, mainly because he actually outscored his fellow nominees and is considered by many to be the club's best attacker in the modern era. It was back on 11 August 1986 that Wednesday paid Barnsley a £200,000 fee, which later rose by £100,000, for eighteen-year-old Hirst, who'd come through the Reds youth ranks to appear in twenty-nine senior games and win England Youth honours – a feat repeated by his son, George, over thirty years later. It was very much a case of 'second time lucky' for Wednesday, as a schoolboy Hirst had attended an intended two-day trial at Wednesday. After a morning's training he was asked his name by a club official and was told 'we didn't think you had turned up'. After this comment, his father said 'if they don't know you are here we may as well go home' and there ended Hirst's first association with the club. Thankfully, this experience did not affect his decision when the Owls returned and the gangly teenager, born 7 December 1967 in Cudworth, Barnsley, joined Wednesday, making his debut from the substitute's bench on the opening day of the season. His home debut could not have been more dramatic as, in front of the newly covered Kop, Hirst scored with his first touch, again entering the fray from the bench. During his first three seasons at Hillsborough Hirst was in and out of the side but fans kept seeing flashes of his obvious talents, a spectacular last-minute winner against Manchester United being an early highlight. It was the arrival of Atkinson in 1989 that proved the springboard to his Owls career as he was paired with new arrival Dalian Atkinson and duly scored sixteen times, winning the club's 'player of the year' award. After relegation, Hirst enjoyed his best season, not only scoring thirty-two times but also helping the club to League Cup glory and winning the first of three full caps for England, scoring on his second appearance. After Wednesday's promotion, his prolific scoring continued as the Owls just missed out after a surprise challenge for the title. He reached a century of goals for Wednesday in March 1992, but various injury problems then dogged his career, starting with a crude tackle from Arsenal defender Steve Bould, which broke his ankle. He was then troubled by Achilles tendon problems and scored only twenty-eight goals more before departing for Southampton, in October 1997, after 358 games, with the Saints breaking their transfer record to pay £2 million. In the interim, Hirst scored in the 1993 FA Cup final and remained a hugely popular player; even a half-fit Hirst was better than what most clubs could muster.

He seemed back to his best during the early months on the South Coast – scoring a typically spectacular goal against Wednesday – but Lady Luck then deserted him, a knee ligament ruling him out for the whole season. After failing to add to his tally of nine goals in thirty-two games, Hirst admitted defeat in his battle for fitness and officially retired in January 2000, returning back to Sheffield. Although retired, he did play a handful of games, alongside former teammate Waddle, for Brunsmeer Athletic, typically netting the winner on his debut. After hanging up his boots altogether he worked for a local independent radio station and until recently was a regular sight around the ground, helping in corporate areas and keeping a whole new generation of fans entertained.

No. 11 Fred Spiksley

The final place was simply a fight between two legends on the left, both of whom enjoyed quite remarkable careers at Wednesday. The men in question are the 'Olive Grove Flyer' Fred Spiksley and prolific goalscoring left-winger Ellis Rimmer. In the end the final spot went to Spiksley as he was not only just a remarkable footballer but was a trailblazer for a player of his time, coaching all over the world at a time when that simply did not occur, and was a larger-than-life character who lived a quite remarkable life. His amazing story was put into print in October 2016 and it is impossible to even summarise his career without doing Fred an injustice. Suffice to say that Spiksley did not receive his nickname for no reason, although his story may not have involved Wednesday at all if not for the timely intervention of player Fred Thompson. Spiksley was travelling home from Accrington, after deciding he was going to join the town's league club, when he missed the last train back to Gainsborough and was therefore stranded in Sheffield. It was at this moment that fate took a hand as he duly bumped into Wednesday player Thompson, who made Fred promise that he would not sign for Accrington before talking to Wednesday. Spiksley duly signed for Wednesday in February 1891 – for £3 per week plus a compositors job at the *Sheffield Telegraph* – and would go on to amass 321 appearances in senior matches and score 115 times, becoming the first true hero of those early Football League days. His career had started in youth football, Spiksley gaining employment as an apprentice at the *Gainsborough News*, although he showed his love of gambling and horse racing as his father had to pay a second £50 bond to secure his employment after the impudent Fred ignored his employer's instructions not to attend Lincoln races. His performances in junior football meant it was not long before the town's powerful senior club, Trinity, snapped him up and Fred achieved the unique feat of scoring in every home game in 1887/88 season. His career suffered a setback in January 1889 when, ironically in a game against Wednesday FC, he suffered a broken leg, putting him out of action for the remainder of the campaign. The lithe and pacey winger was soon back to his best form and league clubs started to chase his signature. It was somewhat of a coup when Arthur Dickinson sealed his transfer as Wednesday was still a non-league outfit.

Almost instantly he became a big favourite with fans, who revelled in his tremendous ball control – he was genuinely two-footed – superb shooting ability and lightening-quick pace; he was said to be so quick that legitimate goals were chalked off for offside as no one could believe he could get to the ball so quickly! He was quickly named the 'Olive Grove Flyer' by his adoring public and is without doubt Wednesday's greatest player of the pre-First World War era. One of England's greatest managers, Herbert Chapman, commented, 'Fred Spiksley, in my judgement, was unsurpassed both in poise and balance, and his ability to work the ball with both the inside and outside of both feet.' He was so valued by Wednesday that he was offered, and signed, a three-year deal in 1892 – this was an era where player power was non-existent and every man was either retained or released at the end of his one-year deal. Perhaps Wednesday were worried – maybe with good reason – that other envious clubs would try to pinch Fred, using whatever means possible – legal or illegal! Anyway, Fred remained at Wednesday until October 1904, helping the Owls win the FA Cup (Fred scoring twice in the final), the Second Division title and the League Championship for the first time. He had appeared in the club's first ever league fixture and formed a potent left-wing partnership with Alec Brady. Spiksley was also said to be similar in manner to a certain Chris Waddle as he was known to run from the halfway line only to stop dead once or twice before finally crossing the ball into the danger area. Like Waddle, he also was capped for England, on seven occasions, and is believed to a have scored a hat-trick against Scotland in April 1893. A leg injury eventually ended his playing days at Wednesday and he later appeared for Glossop, Leeds City and Watford while also briefly being employed as secretary at non-league outfit Southern United. The end of his playing career was by no means the end of Spiksley's story though, as over the years that followed he was declared bankrupt, charged with illegal betting, coached in Sweden and was in charge at German club FC Nuremburg in 1914 at the start of the First World War. Fred and his son were imprisoned as 'illegal aliens' but engineered an escape from captivity, with Fred next being found working in munitions in America. He returned to Europe in 1918, taking over as coach at Barcelona, while remarkably in the early 1920s he combined his coaching role at Mexican club Real Club

España with working at the Bank of Montreal in Mexico City – Fred was multilingual. Further coaching roles in England, Germany and Switzerland preceded his retirement from the game in 1929, although he was not one to sit around the house, competing in various athletic pursuits, including skating, rowing, running and swimming. He did, however, spend most of his time competing in professional handicap sprinting, taking part past his seventieth birthday, with Fred more interested in taking the money from the bookies than the actual prize money for winning the race. He lived the last few years of his life in London, after undergoing a major internal operation, and passed away on Ladies Day at Goodwood Races on 28 July 1948 – Fred supposedly backed the winner of the 3:10 race but did not survive to collect his winnings. It was perhaps fitting that his final hours were spent in pursuit of his favourite pastime, gambling, with Spiksley having lived an extraordinary life for the son of publican from a town in Lincolnshire.

On the Bench

No. 12 Davie McLean

In the race for the forward roles, centre forward David McLean was perhaps unlucky to find himself on the substitute's bench. His seasonal record was incomparable to any player of the era before the First World War with Forfar-born McLean scoring twenty-five goals in his first full season before becoming the first Owls player to net thirty league goals in a season, achieving the feat in 1912/13 – he topped the First Division scoring charts in both 1912 and 1913. Wednesday signed him from Preston North End in February 1911 for £1,000 – he was the club's first four-figure transfer – and proved a real penalty-box predator that forged a tremendous partnership with Andrew Wilson, after taking his No. 9 shirt after signing. Born on 13 December 1890, McLean played for a variety of clubs, including Forfar West End, Glasgow Rangers and Ayr, before moving to England in November 1909. He was, however, the centre of controversy in 1913 when he was perhaps an early example of 'player power' after refusing to re-sign for Wednesday unless they offered him an almost unheard of three-year contract with a guaranteed £450 benefit. Wednesday refused and an impasse ensued, McLean returning home to play for Forfar Athletic. As the season progressed the Owls struggled to replace their star centre forward and with pressure mounting from fans, the club caved in, bizarrely having to pay Forfar a £250 fee to get their man back. As soon as he returned, the goals started to flow again and he grabbed another twenty-two in the league in the final season before football was suspended due to the war. It was back to Scotland during the hostilities – he was employed in Glasgow in work of 'national importance' – where he guested for several teams, including Rangers. When peace was restored he returned to Sheffield but played

Above: The earliest known Wednesday Cricket Club photograph, dated around 1850.

Below left: The football club's first trophy, the Cromwell Cup, won in 1868.

Below right: A members' card from the 1874/75 season.

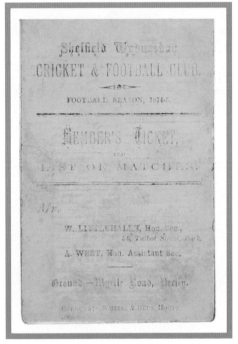

Above: The 1890 FA Cup final team wearing powder-blue shirts with a white Yorkshire rose.

Below left: Wednesday legend, Fred Spiksley: 115 goals in 321 games.

Below right: Sheffield-born Wednesday captain Tommy Crawshaw, twice an FA Cup winner with the club.

The men that brought the English Cup to Sheffield for the first time, in 1896.

The Wednesday XI before the first game at Owlerton in 1899.

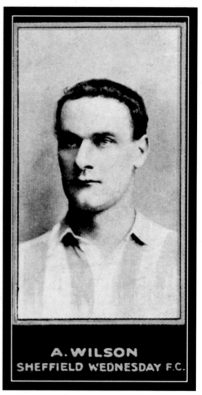

Above left: Wednesday's first 'official' matchday programme.

Above right: Andrew Wilson, holder of the club's appearance and goals record – 546 and 215 respectively.

Below: Early match action at Owlerton, September 1903.

The Wednesday attack is relieved by Williamson.

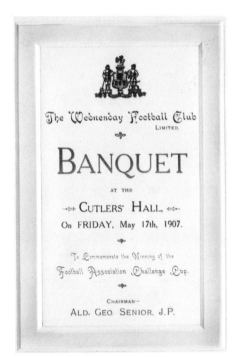

D. McLEAN, SHEFFIELD·WED

Above left: Menu from the 1907 dinner held to celebrate FA Cup success.

Above right: Prolific pre-First World War centre forward Davie McLean.

Below left: Custodian Jack Brown made 507 appearances between 1923 and 1937.

Below right: A colouratte interwar years cigaratte card image.

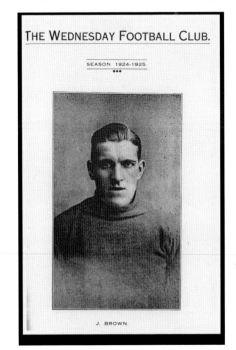

SHEFFIELD WEDNESDAY F.C. LEAGUE CHAMPIONS. 1928-29.

The 1928/29 league championship-winning side.

Thousands of caps – the Hillsborough Kop.

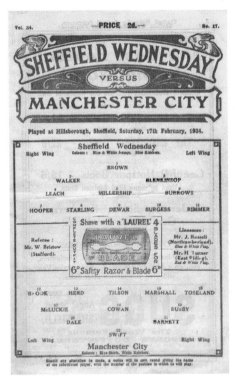

Above left: Programme from the record Hillsborough crowd: 72,841 in February 1934.

Above right: Wing wizard Mark Hooper: 135 goals in 423 appearances.

Below: Sheffield's Midland Station as the FA Cup is brought back in 1935.

SHEFFIELD WEDNESDAY

Versus

TOTTENHAM HOTSPUR

FOOTBALL LEAGUE—DIVISION II

PLAYED ON THE WEDNESDAY GROUND
SATURDAY, 1st MARCH, 1947.   KICK-OFF 3 p.m.

OFFICIAL PROGRAMME   PRICE ONE PENNY

SHEFFIELD
WEDNESDAY
F.C. Ltd.

—

NEW STAND
RESERVED

1949 - 50

Above left: National football returned in the 1946/47 season.

Above right: An old-style season ticket pass.

Below: Training at Hillsborough in January 1949.

Above left: Derek Dooley in hospital after the tragic end of his playing career in 1953.

Above right: Members' card from 1953/54.

Below left: Itinerary from the club's groundbreaking tour to the USSR.

Below right: 1966 FA Cup final.

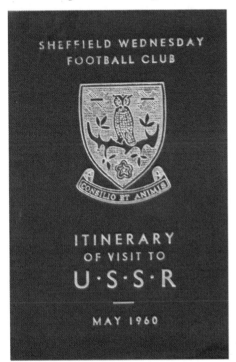

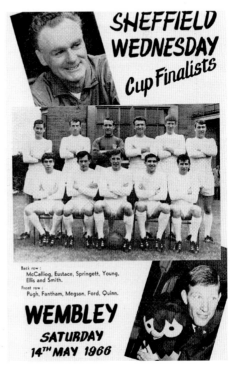

Above left: Wednesday and England international Ron Springett.

Above right: The place to be in the late 1960s/early 1970s – the Ozzie Owl nightclub.

Below left: Wednesday manager Jack Charlton being interviewed by John Motson in 1981.

Below right: A striking supporters' club handbook.

Above left: Popular forward Andy McCulloch.

Above right: January 1984: Wednesday 2 Liverpool 2.

Below: The 1991 League Cup-winning side.

The Owls at Wembley in 1993.

Fans at the 2005 play-off final in Cardiff.

Marcus Tudgay wheels away after scoring the winner at Sheffield United in 2009.

Unforgettable scenes on the final day of the 2011/12 season.

Reda Johnson and Lewis Buxton celebrate a last-minute equaliser at Derby, August 2012.

The scenes as Kieran Lee scores the decider at Rotherham United in 2014/15.

The Hillsborough 'light show' against Brighton in May 2016.

Jack Hunt, Tom Lees and Sam Hutchinson celebrate reaching Wembley in 2016.

Club owner Dejphon Chansiri and manager Carlos Carvalhal in a relaxed mood.

The Kop, 2016.

only three times – taking his tally to 100 goals in 147 games – before Wednesday accepted a record bid of £2,000 from Bradford Park Avenue in October 1919, the transfer being agreed in a Sheffield Cinema House. He played alongside his brother, George, during ninety-two games (fifty-five goals) at Avenue before returning to Scotland to end his career, while also working as a publican. He finally retired from playing in his mid-forties and was later assistant manager at Partick Thistle and scout for Huddersfield Town. He remained a celebrity in his home town and was a regular at Forfar home games until his passing on 21 December 1967.

No. 13 Kevin Pressman

The day after the club's 120th birthday, nineteen-year-old goalkeeper Kevin Paul Pressman made his competitive bow as Wednesday won 2-1 at Southampton. It would be the start of an association that, from signing professional forms in 1985, would last fully nineteen years and see the Hampshire-born stopper (6 November 1967) accrue 478 games and sit comfortably in the all-time top-ten appearance chart. It was when Pressman's family settled in Dronfield that he started to play organised football and after being spotted by Wednesday scouts he signed apprentice forms, stepping up to professional status on 6 November 1985. In his early years at Wednesday, competition was fierce, the likes of Turner, Hodge and Beresford all vying for a first-team spot. He did eventually become first choice under Atkinson but a serious injury halted that progress and ensured he missed out on an appearance in the 1991 League Cup final. The arrival of Woods meant Pressman became understudy once again but eventually his hard work and patience was rewarded as for almost a decade he remained first choice, apart from the occasional challenge for his shirt from the likes of Srnicek and Tidman. Known as a brilliant shot stopper – he particularly seemed to excel against Sheffield United – his form meant a call-up to the England squad in 1998. His thirteen-second red card against Wolverhampton Wanderers in 2000 remains the quickest dismissal in senior British football. A new three-year contract in 2001 included the position of goalkeeping coach but he relinquished the role in January 2003 to aid the Owls' fight against relegation. Unfortunately, Wednesday did fall back into the third tier and, solely from a team performance point of view, his final season proved a big disappointment as Wednesday finished in the bottom half of League One. He also faced competition from newcomer Lucas and was briefly loaned out to West Bromwich Albion before returning after his rival was injured. He was one of the thirteen players released in the summer of 2004 and appeared for Leicester City, Leeds United and Mansfield Town before retiring in July 2006. Pressman, whose brother, Howie, is a well-known voice on BBC Radio Sheffield, did subsequently come out of retirement to spend several months at Irish club Portadown, but he did hang his gloves up permanently after joining Scunthorpe United as goalkeeping coach in 2007. He was later assistant manager at Scunthorpe but, after leaving, also spent a year as Bradford City goalkeeping coach before joining Millwall, in the same capacity, in 2012.

No. 14 Alan Finney

Winger Alan Finney is second on the club's all-time appearances list behind Andrew Wilson, and his post-war tally of 504 (eighty-eight goals) will surely never be beaten. Born on Halloween 1933 in Langwith, the teenage Finney often walked the 4 miles from his Armthorpe home to watch Doncaster Rovers, hoping one day to appear for his boyhood club. His wish did eventually come true but he would serve Wednesday for almost two decades first, becoming attached to Wednesday after leaving school. He joined Wednesday's ground staff in 1948 and signed a professional contract in October 1950, while serving his two years' national service, alongside fellow 'starlet' Albert Quixall. After being demobbed in 1951 the pair made their senior debuts in the same game – at home to Chelsea in February 1951 – and would become friends and first-team regulars. The pencil-thin Finney made his debut on the right wing and would play the vast majority of his games for Wednesday in that role, although he did spend almost three seasons, in the late 1950s, on the opposite wing when Derek Wilkinson was preferred on the right. He was that rare breed of winger who was actually consistent and his tricky and pacey play ensured he remained a fixture in the first team until the mid-1960s, only losing his place early the 1965/66 campaign. He helped the Owls to second place, behind Spurs, in 1961 – he was ever-present during the club's best post-war season – although he probably did not win as many representative honours as Wednesday fans believed he should have, although he did have the distinction of appearing in the first U23 international played by England. He also won an England 'B' cap but was unfortunate when his promised testimonial game, against Sheffield United, never took place due to the Owls' run to Wembley in the FA Cup and the club's preparations for the World Cup finals. In the end, Wednesday sent a team to Belle Vue in May 1966, four months after he had been sold to Doncaster Rovers for £3,500. He had helped Rovers win the Division Four title in his debut season and played professionally for another season before 'hanging up his boots' in 1967. He continued to play for Alfreton Town and then on a Sunday with Doncaster Dentists after gaining employment at Armthorpe Colliery. He held a variety of positions at the pit, including driving the paddy, which took the men to the coalface. Later in life he became a bookmaker and continues to live out his retirement in the Doncaster area, surely satisfied that his name will forever be one of the most famous in Wednesday's 150 years.

No. 15 Chris Waddle

It would be perhaps reasonable to state that when Chris Waddle moved to Hillsborough in the summer of 1992, his arrival was not greeted with a fanfare, as many wondered if the thirty-one-year-old former England international could readjust to life in England after three successful seasons in French football. Any doubters though were emphatically proven wrong as his sheer quality shone like a beacon as he enjoyed a remarkable debut season at S6, becoming the only Wednesday player to win the prestigious Football Writers' Player of the Year award. His tremendous form made fans wonder how he was still not an England regular – he was never recalled despite repeated calls from supporters and media – but was certainly one of the best signings in Wednesday's history. His wonder goal in the 1993 FA Cup semi-final against Sheffield United will never be forgotten and at times he seemed to be able to beat the opposition on his own; a fine example is a famous game against West Ham United in 1993 when he teased and tormented visiting full-back David Burrows to distraction. He netted for the Owls in the 1993 FA Cup final replay and by the time he left for Scottish football in September 1996, Waddle had become one of the club's most popular players of modern times. Waddle was born in the north-east town of Felling on 14 December 1960, and famously worked in a factory that made seasoning for pies and sausages while playing for Tow Law Town. Despite being a Sunderland fan as a youngster, it would be with their great rivals Newcastle United that Waddle rose to prominence, after the St James' Park club paid Tow Law £500 in July 1980. His familiar gait and languid style had been apparent at an early age and his incredible trickery and mazy wingplay was refined during his early years as a professional, culminating in promotion from the Second Division in 1984. The experience of playing alongside the likes of Keegan and McDermott proved invaluable and his form was such that a big-money move to Tottenham Hotspur followed in July 1985 – Spurs paid £650,000 after fifty-two goals in 192 games for Newcastle. In North London his star rose even further and he became an established England international, although domestic honours eluded him. He became the most expensive British footballer when Olympic Marseille paid £4.25 million in 1989 and became an all-time legend in southern France, earning the nickname of 'Le Dribbleur Fou' as he helped OM to three league titles and the European Cup final. Marseille fans were heartbroken when he returned to England and Wednesdayites were similarly disappointed when he was allowed to join Falkirk by Pleat. His Football League career continued at Bradford City and Sunderland before a player-manager role at Burnley, which lasted a year, preceded a spell at his final league side, Torquay United. He returned to Hillsborough in December 1998 after being appointed to the coaching staff, but after being promoted to reserve team boss he left in the summer of 2000, having failed to land the role of first team manager. Despite ending his professional career in 1998 he continued to play in non-league football, appearing for a plethora of teams including Worksop Town and Stocksbridge Park Steels. Since leaving the professional game, Waddle has carved out a successful media career and is a regular voice on BBC Five Live's coverage of the domestic game.

No. 16 Don Megson

It was a change of position that really sparked the Wednesday career of Donald 'Don' Harry Megson, being moved from half-back to full-back by Owls boss Catterick when Megson finished his national service in 1959. Born in Sale on 12 June 1936, Megson started his playing career at Mossley prior to signing amateur and then professional forms at Hillsborough – the Owls paid his club £50 in June 1953. During a long apprenticeship, Megson played in a variety of different positions but it was sixteen reserve team games at full-back, at the behest of Catterick, which catapulted him into the club's senior side, making his debut in November 1959. Over the decade that followed he was unchallenged in the role, showing several fine qualities, including tremendous passing ability, robustness in the tackle and great all-round physicality. The flame-haired Lancastrian also played the game with a smile on his face and 'Meg' became a firm favourite with Wednesday fans and a great leader on the pitch. He was definitely unfortunate not to earn any significant representative honours and was unlucky that his 442nd, and final, appearance coincided with one of Wednesday's worst ever results – a FA Cup home loss to Scunthorpe United in January 1970. After enjoying a testimonial season he was given a free transfer in March 1970 and became player-coach at Bristol Rovers. After adding thirty-one games to his career tally he became manager in 1972, winning promotion and the Watney Cup, before moving across the Atlantic in 1977 to take over at North American Soccer League (NASL) club Portland Timbers. He returned home in 1980 and a spell in charge at Bournemouth preceded various scouting roles, including for his son Gary, prior to retirement. He continues to live in Sheffield and published his autobiography, *A Life in Football*, in 2014.

No. 17 Jack Allen

The goalscoring record of Jack Allen at Wednesday was nothing short of remarkable as, after arriving from Brentford in March 1927, he proceeded to amass eighty-five goals in only 114 appearances. He was actually better known as an inside forward before signing for Wednesday, in a career that started in his native north-east (born in Newburn, 31 January 1903) at Prudhoe Castle. Spells at Leeds United and then at Griffin Park preceded a move into the 'big time' at Hillsborough, Brown paying £750 to sign Allen. Incidentally his career in West London was marred by some fierce criticism he received from some Bees fans, which reached such a level that Brentford manager Curtis would not play him in home games and even wrote to the local newspaper, asking the fans to 'get off his back'. That was all in the distant past for Allen as when

Brown moved him to centre forward in September 1928, his career took a dramatic upturn as he simply could not stop scoring, netting thirty-five times in just thirty-seven games as Wednesday lifted the title. The deadly attacker added thirty-nine goals to his tally as Wednesday retained the league, but then came the rather bizarre situation, to modern eyes, where Wednesday brought in Ball from Manchester United and Allen started only six more league games, before being sold to Newcastle United for a considerable profit in February 1931. Financially it was a great deal but Wednesday could not secure a Championship treble and it was a case of 'what might have been' for Wednesday supporters. The rigid 2-3-5 formation prevalent in the English game was the reason why Allen and Ball only played together once and it can only be conjecture to believe that Wednesday perhaps regretted their sale of Allen as the aggressive attacker with a deadly left foot led United to the 1932 FA Cup, scoring a controversial goal at Wembley in what became known as the 'over the line incident'. He completed his playing career at Bristol Rovers, Gateshead and then Ashington, and was a publican in County Durham before passing away on 19 November 1957.

No. 18 John Fantham
The extremely strong bench continues with Wednesday's record post-war scorer, inside forward John Fantham. The Sheffield-born attacker (6 February 1939) ended his Owls career with 166 goals to his name from 434 appearances. Brought up in the Sheffield district of Pitsmoor, Fantham actually played cricket for his county but it was football where he made his name, although he was a terrific all-round sportsman, nearly becoming a professional golfer before deciding to chase a career in the 'beautiful game'. He joined Wednesday as a fifteen-year-old and a year later was elevated to the professional ranks, having already shown his many qualities, which included great strength, a high degree of skill and a real penalty-box predator's instinct. It was as an inside right that he made his senior bow but the departure of Quixall seven months later saw Fantham seize the opportunity, becoming a first-team regular and replacing another club legend, Froggatt, at inside left. As the 1960s progressed the old positional references became somewhat obsolete, Fantham becoming what we would describe today as a forward. He continued to score regularly throughout his Owls career, although honours did elude him as Wednesday finished runners-up in the league and FA Cup. Surprisingly he won only one full cap for England, although the fact that a certain Jimmy Greaves played in the same era was probably the main reason why he did not receive further representative honours. His father, Jack, had played league football for several clubs but Fantham Jr eclipsed his father's achievements to finish his Owls career as the second highest all-time scorer for Wednesday. Short spells at Rotherham United and Macclesfield Town brought his career to a close,

with Fantham then concentrating on his barbershop, which he'd opened while still playing. He later started his own machine tools business, which still trades today, while in the 1980s he coached and was then assistant manager at Hallam. He became a keen golfer in retirement, holding the course record at Beauchief Golf Club for several years, but sadly passed away on 25 June 2014 after a long illness.

No. 19 Alf Strange

Between the club's golden years of 1928–35 Alfred 'Alf' Henry Strange (born on 2 April 1900 near Ripley) was part of the famous Marsden-Leach-Strange half-back line that powered the club to two league titles. He arrived from Port Vale in February 1927, although it was as an exciting inside forward that he was signed. It was only when he moved to half-back, during the great escape season of 1927/28, that Strange almost accidently found his true position and over the next five seasons missed only six games, showing superb passing skills, a rocket-like shot and great tackling ability. His form was recognised by England, winning the first of twenty caps for his county in April 1930, and while on international duty in Italy in 1933, he famously asked, and was given, an autograph by Mussolini! He showed his all-round sporting excellence by playing cricket in the summer months, often appearing for Derbyshire County Cricket Clubs' second XI. It would not have been lost on the club's hierarchy that Wednesday could have snapped up the eighteen-year-old Strange back in 1918 when, while working down the pit and playing football for Ripley Town, he was rushed in a taxi to Hillsborough for a reserve game when the club was suddenly short of players. For an unknown reason, the official trial was never instigated and it would be many years later before he returned to Wednesday on a more permanent footing. His career began in earnest at Portsmouth where an impressive sixteen goals in twenty-four league fixtures – including five goals against Gillingham in January 1923 – earned a move to higher division club Port Vale in 1925. After arriving at Wednesday he struggled to hold down a regular place, competing with the likes of Hill and Seed for an inside forward place, but he was one of the first names on Brown's team sheet after converting to right half-back. He was also a popular fellow among his teammates as he kept chickens for most of his life and his colleagues could always be guaranteed a regular supply of fresh eggs! It was not until the 1933/34 campaign that Strange found himself out of the first team as he experienced an injury-hit season, firstly fracturing a bone in his foot before suffering a broken leg. It proved the beginning of the end for the unlucky Strange as after a twelve-week absence he returned, only to break his other leg to end a desperately unlucky season. With Walker now in charge, Strange made only a solitary appearance in the 1934/35 season – the form of Sharp keeping him in the reserves – and after twenty-two goals in 273 games he departed for Bradford Park Avenue in May 1935. It would be fair to say he never regained full fitness after the two leg fractures. After just a few months in West Yorkshire he quit the game, eventually gaining employment at Nottingham-based Rayleigh Cycle Co., coaching and playing for the works' football team and appearing for the cricket side. Incredibly, just after the Second World War, he could be found playing for Wiltshire side Corsham United aged forty-six, where his remit was captain and 'advisor-in-chief'. He later returned to his first job, coal mining, and passed away in Ripley, close to his birthplace, in October 1978.

No. 20 Billy Marsden

Left half-back Billy Marsden was arguably the greatest player in his position in the 1920s, having impressed at Sunderland before developing into an international player during six years at S6. Born in County Durham on 10 November 1901, Marsden started his working life down his local coal mine while playing amateur football at Ryhope and then Silksworth Colliery. At the time he was an inside forward and was understudy to Charles Buchan, during four years at Sunderland, before Wednesday won the race for his signature in May 1924, paying £450. He was quickly switched to left half-back, despite Marsden being predominantly right-footed, but Brown's legendary eye for talent proved reliable again as the wholehearted and enthusiastic Marsden took to his new role like 'a duck to water'. He started the 1925/26 season in the No. 6 shirt and was ever-present as Wednesday won the championship, clinching a return to the top division. After being moved into his unfamiliar role he showed great diligence and professionalism by constantly practising with his left foot. By the end of the 1920s he was simply peerless in the Strange-Leach-Marsden defensive line as his strength and pace helped Wednesday to two league titles and personal accolades for Marsden, winning three England caps. He was undoubtedly at the peak of his game when he travelled to Germany with the England side in May 1930, but his world came crashing down as during the game he accidently collided with teammate Ray Goodall and suffered quite appalling injuries, including a broken neck and a spinal injury that left the Wednesday man fighting for his life. Thankfully for the stricken player, the excellence of a German surgeon saved his life and he spent six weeks hospitalised before returning to Sheffield to recuperate. His comeback came in a November 1930 reserve fixture and he would appear in five such games before having to take the decision to retire from the game altogether, therefore prematurely ending the career of an outstanding player after 221 games. Ironically, the Owls received more in compensation (£2,000) from the Football Association than Marsden did (£750), although he did receive a reasonable sum from a subsequent benefit game in October 1931. Within three months he left for foreign shores, taking over as coach at Dutch side HBS Hague, returning home in July 1934 to take over as trainer at Gateshead. However, he soon returned to the Netherlands, coaching Be Quick FC and DWS Amsterdam before

the onset of the Second World War. It should also be noted that he did
suffer long-term damage from his career-ending injury as he occasionally
played in friendly fixtures but once collapsed when he headed a ball – he
never headed a ball again after needing twenty-four hours to recover.
He was actually assistant manager to the Dutch national side when
England declared war on the Third Reich, and when the Germans invaded
he dodged snipers' bullets to gain refuge in a barbers shop, famously
commenting that 'nobody wanted a shave though'. Along with his wife he
managed to reach the British consul and was duly repatriated back home,
leaving all of their worldly goods behind. During the remainder of the war
years he served as part-time coach at Wednesday and part-time boss at
Doncaster Rovers and then Worksop Town, prior to becoming landlord
of the Crosspool Tavern. When he died, aged eighty-one, on 20 September
1983, he was the last surviving member of that glorious 1929/30 team.

No. 21 David Layne
Not unlike Marsden, the flourishing career of David Layne was also
cut short at the peak of his powers, although the circumstances were
considerably different to the fate that befall Marsden. In the case of
Layne, his career ended due to a simple error of judgement relating to
a Wednesday game at Ipswich Town in December 1962. Three Owls
players had been approached by Mansfield Town player Jimmy Gauld to
bet on the club losing a fixture and all subsequently profited from the
subsequent defeat. In hindsight the financial benefit accrued by Layne
and his co-conspirators seemed trivial but all the players involved were
severely dealt with by the FA and the law courts, Layne spending four
months in jail and receiving a life ban from football. The scandal put an
abrupt stop to Layne's career immediately after two exceptional seasons
at Hillsborough, which had seen the bustling, hard-running goal poacher
grab fifty-eight goals in only eighty-one appearances, all his league goals
coming in the top division, such scoring not seen by Wednesday fans since
the days of Trotter and Allen in the 1920s. The Sheffield-born attacker
(29 July 1939) played in the same city boys' team as Fantham and Gordon
Banks but after a short time working in the steel industry signed part-time
forms for Rotherham United. After just a handful of games he moved to
Swindon Town and it was in Wiltshire that he received his nickname of
'Bronco'; after crashing home a particularly fierce free-kick he was said
to have 'the hardest shot in the west' and was duly named after a popular
TV cowboy. His incredible scoring record quickly earned Layne another
move – to Bradford City – and in his second campaign he netted thirty-four
league goals, a seasonal record that has still not been beaten. It was clear
that the rising star was destined for the top flight and it was Wednesday
who won the race for his signature, paying City £22,500 in May 1962.
One can only speculate what Layne and Wednesday could have achieved
if he had not been banned but the reality for Layne was unemployment
and a criminal record, although he actually played football for his prison

team. His personal life was further rocked to the core when he lost his wife in a motor accident. He remarried and worked as a publican before the FA lifted his ban in 1972, Wednesday immediately inviting him back into the fold with a one-year contract. Despite having kept his fitness levels high during those 'wilderness years', it was difficult for a thirty-three-year-old to relaunch his career and he failed to make a first-team return, a short loan spell at Hereford United marking the end of his league career. He did briefly appear for Matlock Town but worked as a publican for the remainder of his working life. He remarried his second wife, after they split up in the mid-1990s, in 2014 and now lives out his retirement in Darnall, no doubt still regretting the events of 1962.

No. 22 Ellis Rimmer
An admittedly attack-minded substitutes' bench is completed by another club legend, Ellis James Rimmer. A teenage Rimmer (born on 2 January 1907) failed to progress any further than the third team at his first league club, Everton, before moving to Tranmere Rovers after a spell in non-league soccer at Whitchurch. Further success led to several clubs expressing an interest but it was Brown who again used his terrific eye for a player by negotiating the £1,850 deal. When he joined in February 1928, the newcomer must have thought he'd soon be playing Second Division football as Wednesday were certainties for relegation. However, the 'great escape' followed and left-winger Rimmer inspired back-to-back titles as he spent just over a decade in the club's first team, scoring an astonishing 140 goals (fifth in the all-time list) in 417 games. In addition to being a prolific scorer he also created countless goals for his teammates, and in 1935 achieved the rare distinction of scoring in every round of the FA Cup, Rimmer scoring eight times, including a brace in the final. With Hooper on the opposite wing and Rimmer on the left, they formed a deadly partnership, comfortably the best wing pairing in Wednesday's history – the duo scored 275 goals, figures that would make most forwards green with envy. During his time at Hillsborough he was also capped four times by England, although his debut must have felt like he had not left the Wednesday dressing room as three of his teammates – Marsden, Strange and Blenkinsop – all played against Scotland in April 1930. He remained at S6 until joining Football League newcomers Ipswich Town in August 1938, and played four times before retiring and returning north. During the war he took a public house in Sheffield but eventually returned to Merseyside, being 'Mein host' at a pub in Formby before sadly passing away, at the relatively young age of fifty-eight, in March 1965.

In the Stands

Goalkeepers
John Edward 'Teddy' Davison (born on 2 September 1887, Gateshead) was the club's first true goalkeeping legend, playing 424 games, after

signing at the age of twenty in April 1908, from Gateshead Town. Such was his promise, Wednesday paid a hefty £300 fee for his services but within a few months he had replaced Lyall and remained there until the mid-1920s. Despite being somewhat diminutive (he was only 5 foot 7 and is the smallest goalkeeper to be capped by England) Edward, known as Teddy throughout his career, possessed all of the attributes needed for a custodian: courage, bravery, razor-sharp reflexes and great anticipation. He was held in such high esteem by his peers that Davison was known as 'Honest Ted' and it was said that 'he was a sportsman and a gentleman of the first order'. He was perhaps unlucky to appear between the posts for Wednesday just after and just before two golden periods and failed to win a medal despite having amassed so many appearances. He also served his country in the First World War, spending the majority of the conflict in France. When he was eventually replaced he moved on to non-league Mansfield Town and launched a highly successful managerial career, which first came to notice in 1931 when he led Chesterfield to the Division Three (North) title. In June 1932 he returned to his adopted home of Sheffield after accepting a lucrative offer to take over at Bramall Lane. He steered the Blades to the 1936 FA Cup final and promotion from the Second Division and is perhaps best known as the manager that signed Jimmy Hagan. He became known as the George Washington of Sheffield football (after the first president of the United States) but left in August 1952 after failing to take United back into the top flight. His managerial career ended with six seasons back at Chesterfield and he retired back to Sheffield, passing away in February 1971, having made a huge impact on both sides of the city's football divide.

His successor would be another outstanding goalkeeper as after coming to the fore with Worksop Town, John Henry 'Jack' Brown would become unopposed between the sticks at Wednesday for virtually the remainder of the interwar period. His display in a FA Cup tie versus Tottenham Hotspur alerted many clubs to his qualities and it was Wednesday who secured his signature, Brown signing on 23 February 1923 for £360. Worksop-born (19 March 1899) Brown amassed an astonishing 507 appearances, becoming one of only three individuals to exceed 500 games. His start at Wednesday was actually rather problematic – his form was criticised after some unconvincing displays – but he soon settled and from that point onwards never looked back, with Brown, known as a brilliant shot stopper, fearless and commanding, winning several honours. It was not until the spring of 1937 that he was displaced as an automatic choice and his final appearance for Wednesday came just a day after his thirty-eighth birthday. He was capped six times by England in the late 1920s and after leaving Hillsborough played only one more senior game, for Hartlepool, before retiring. He returned to Sheffield and ran a public house and newsagents before ending his working life at Dorma Tools, Handsworth. Sadly, he did not have the opportunity to enjoy his retirement as he passed away, aged only sixty-three, on 9 April 1962.

Full-backs

Over the years, Wednesday has been blessed with several outstanding right-backs with Martin John 'Jack' Earp (born on 6 September 1872) just missing out on a place on the bench. Nottingham-born Earp was an amateur player when he signed league forms for Wednesday in September 1893, having previously appeared for home town club Forest, Everton and Corinthian Causals. However, just six days after signing he penned his maiden professional contract and would develop into one of England's finest backs, becoming an automatic choice for his club and a hugely popular player with supporters and fellow players. His form ensured his predecessor, Tom Brandon, was not missed and he forged a brilliant full-back partnership with Langley. His never-say-die attitude and inspirational qualities also marked him as leadership material and in April 1896 he entered Owls folklore as the first captain to lift the FA Cup. Although totally right-footed, his pace and tenacity ensured he was a stern opponent for any opposition winger and he remained a mainstay until the club was relegated from the top flight in 1899. He did play in the first game at the club's new Owlerton ground but played only a handful more before moving to Stockport County in the summer of 1900 as player-coach after eight goals in 174 matches for Wednesday. Earp – a very private individual whom it was said got changed in a local hotel and caught a taxi to the ground – appeared in County's first ever Football League fixture but stayed for only a few months before emigrating to South Africa in January 1901. He joined the police force and is believed to have remained in the southern hemisphere for the rest of his life.

The man who replaced Earp, William 'Willie' Layton (born in Gornall, 1874), holds the distinction of playing more games for the club than any of his rivals for the right-back slot, accruing 361 games between 1896 and 1910. He only ever played league football for Wednesday and it was a twist of fate that ensured this was the case as during a long 'apprenticeship' in the reserves he worked as a miner at Blackwell Colliery – playing for Wednesday in the hope of securing a professional contract. In November 1895 he decided not to work his night shift so he would be fresh for the following day's game against Attercliffe and it proved to be literally a lifesaving decision as, during the night, an underground explosion killed seven of his workmates, Layton vowing then to commit his whole football career to Wednesday. It was during the club's maiden Owlerton season that he displaced Earp – he had previously been a temporary replacement in both full-back positions – and the well-built and quick back remained a first choice for almost a decade, part of the famous three 'Ls' of Layton, Langley and Lyall. Born in Staffordshire but brought up in Derbyshire, Layton played for Blackwell Colliery and Chesterfield before being engaged at Olive Grove. He was known as a hard but fair player, with a fierce kick, and he helped Wednesday to clinch two league titles and a FA Cup in the first decade of the twentieth century. He was best known for a unique scissor kick, which he employed to clear the ball out of defence, and remained at Wednesday until retiring in 1910, taking over as landlord of the Butchers Arms at Whitwell. Despite Midland League Worksop Town chasing his signature he instead agreed to play for local village side St Lawrence, becoming a popular figure with the locals after becoming the first player to commit to the new season, being made captain in the process. Layton, whose brother Arthur played for several league teams and was the grandfather of former Carlisle United owner Michael Knighton, then made a decision that shocked both his family and friends as in 1912 he set sail for a new life in Australia. During the perilous crossing he met and married again – despite not being divorced – and lived the rest of his life 'down under' working as a miner in Sydney before ill health curtailed that occupation, Willie passing away in April 1944 in New South Wales.

The club's next outstanding right-back was Thomas 'Tommy' Walker (born on 4 March 1902), who was first choice for the majority of the interwar years, scoring three times in 287 games. Born in the village of Cross Crols, Stirlingshire, Walker started his footballing career in local football and arrived in England in 1924 at Bradford City. His debut for Bradford was somewhat bizarre as he was sent from the field after having supposedly punched a Fulham winger, who had accidentally collided with the goalkeeper – even the Cottagers winger told the referee that he'd simply collided but the stubborn official refused to change his mind! Walker would certainly have been pleased to secure a career as a professional footballer as, earlier in his life, while working as a miner, he was stuck underground when a roof caved in, only escaping after crawling on his stomach to safety. He was subsequently a big hit at the Bantams and Wednesday duly recruited him, paying £1,900 for his signature in February 1926. He quickly formed a superb full-back partnership with the incomparable Blenkinsop, which included the ability to read the game, a brilliant knack of intercepting the ball, great athleticism and genuine pace. One of twelve children sired by his ex-Hearts footballing father, Bobby, Walker became well known at Wednesday for his 'Scotch Kick' – a kind of overhead kick that he used to clear his defensive lines. He provided a multitude of goalscoring centres for the likes of Trotter and Allen, and in 1929 became the first ever Scottish player to represent the Sheffield Association in their regular meeting against his home association. He also formed a great double act with winger Hooper and it was a surprise that he never won full international honours. He would remain as a player at Hillsborough until July 1937, when he was appointed assistant trainer to Sam Powell, but his first-team career had long-since come to a close after a spectacular 'falling out' with manager Walker, prior to a FA Cup tie at Wolverhampton Wanderers in January 1935. All the players had already gone out onto the pitch when the duo locked horns and Walker was instantly dropped; he played only twice more. It was an unfortunate end to his senior career but Walker would remain at Wednesday until 1967, working in the Sheffield steelworks in the Second World War, although poor health meant he was demoted from his assistant role in 1958. When manager Brown rearranged his backroom staff in March 1967, Walker was a casualty, the club kindly letting him use a club-owned property for the remaining six years of his life, Walker passing away on 7 March 1973.

Ambrose Langley was a member of the famous 'Three L's' backline of the early twentieth century and arrived at Wednesday in the summer of 1893. He was born in Horncastle on 10 March 1870 and progressed through various junior clubs before signing for Grimsby Town in 1889. Incidentally, one of his early teams was a side called Blue Star, which was financed solely through donations and subscriptions with all the young players having to give a guarantee that their sister would make them all, rather fittingly, a blue- and white-striped shirt to play in! By the early 1890s he was building a reputation as a fearless, uncompromising full-back and after gaining more experience in the tough Northern League with Middlesbrough Ironopolis, he signed league forms for Everton. Bizarrely though, and fortunately for Wednesday, they decided to release him a few weeks later, stating they had decided he was too slow. A move to Aston Villa broke down after he refused to undertake a medical on a suspect knee, and it was third time lucky when he was captured by Wednesday. Over the next eleven seasons he emphatically dismissed any worries about his fitness by being almost ever-present, winning several honours in the process. He was certainly a no-nonsense individual and early in the twentieth century found himself summoned to Preston Police Court after he'd become irritated by the constant barracking of a Preston fan behind his goal. To get near to the supporter he decided to take a goal-kick and when close enough swung his arm back, catching the fan fully in the face and giving him two black eyes! On the day of his case he paid £7 to settle the matter, although there is no record of Langley being suspended for any matches. He eventually succeeded Earp as team captain and remained a regular until injury allowed newcomer Burton to take his place, Wednesday insisting that he got his fitness back but did not play reserve-team football. This meant he was not 'match fit' when he did return to the starting XI and after undertaking some scouting and admin work he left for Hull City in April 1905, after fourteen goals in 318 appearances. He was player-manager at City, although the prefix ended in December 1905, and he almost led them to the top division in 1910 – it was once said that he rowed across the Humber to beat a rival to a player's signature! He returned to Wednesday in April 1913 as assistant-secretary, and acted as temporary first-team trainer during the years of the First World War. After the war he led Huddersfield Town to promotion from the Second Division and the final of the FA Cup and spent his later life as a publican, running the Cricketers Arms on Bramall Lane and then the Pheasant Hotel on London Road, passing away, aged sixty-six, on 29 January 1937.

The Owls' first outstanding post-war left-back was Norman William Curtis (born on 10 September 1924 in Dinnington). He had started his working life as a 'butcher's boy' and duly joined the Royal Navy in 1942, serving during the remainder of the hostilities as a wireless operator/gunner on vessels that escorted aircraft carriers in the Far East. After surviving the war unscathed he underwent a successful trial at Midland League Gainsborough Trinity, moving to the town where he gained employment as an engineer. He joined Wednesday on 23 January 1950 for £1,250, and within a year had broken into the club's senior side. He replaced stylish right-back Swift and became known as somewhat of a footballing schizophrenic as the quiet well-spoken man off the field became a larger-than-life bundle of energy on the pitch, which meant a catalogue of left-wingers wished they had not tangled with Curtis. He had a great ability to recover well when his opponent had seemingly broken away while his strength in the tackle ensured he remained an automatic first choice before losing his place to Megson. He did occasionally also turn out at right-back – most notably in the 1954 FA Cup semi-final – while he was also the club's emergency goalkeeper, long before the concept of a substitute custodian became reality in the 1990s. In fact Curtis was synonymous with the kick from 12 yards as he was well known for an outlandish penalty-taking technique, which often involved running, sometimes from inside his own half, and fairly hammering the ball past the goalie, who was probably best advised to get out the way. He did not earn the nickname 'Cannonball Curtis' for no reason!

Mainly due to his versatility, Sheffield product Melvyn 'Mel' Sterland would claim a place in the squad. Sterland, who signed his maiden professional contract for the Owls in October 1979, made his debut while he was still an apprentice but it would not be as a centre forward – his preferred position as a teenager – that Sterland would become known, as in 1981 he was switched to a attacking right-back role by coach John Harris, and his career flourished from that point forward. He really came to the fore during Wednesday's promotion-winning campaign of 1983/84 when his rampaging runs from right-back and flowing locks earned him the affectionate nickname of 'Zico' from fans – after the famous Brazilian attacker. The club's management also handed him the rather uncomplimentary nickname of 'The Flying Pig', mainly due to his rather ample frame! He also won the first of seven England U21 caps and scored the penalty, against Crystal Palace in April 1984, which clinched promotion. Sheffield born on 1 October 1961, Sterland was the archetypical story of 'local boy made good', having been brought up as a Wednesdayite on the Manor Estate, while starting his playing career in local Sheffield football – in one season he netted 144 goals for his two sides. After making the breakthrough into the senior side he became an automatic choice at full-back and one of the most popular Wednesday players in their entire history, amassing 347 games and scoring forty-nine goals. He always carried a significant goal threat from right-back and netted outstanding goals, a length of the field effort against Arsenal in 1988 being his most memorable. Six of those goals came when he started the 1988/89 season as a centre forward, showing why he had been scouted in that position as a teenager, while in November 1988 he won his only cap for England. He became the first Owls player to be capped by England since Springett and probably would have spent his entire career at Hillsborough if not for a 'falling out' with new manager Eustace over the issue of team captaincy. He was placed on the transfer list and despite Atkinson taking over he left for Glasgow giants Rangers, Wednesday receiving a club record £800,000. He stayed in Scotland for only a few months – playing enough games to win a Championship medal – before linking up again with Wilkinson, this time at Leeds United. He earned promotion and won a League Championship medal in 1992 before a succession of injuries forced his retirement from the professional game in 1994. He did, however, continue to play in semi-professional football and enjoyed two successful campaigns as player-manager of Boston United before an administrational error cost the Pilgrims a place in the National Conference. He continued to play with the likes of Denaby United, Hollinsend Amateurs and, finally, Hallam, before hanging up his boots. He later played a part in football film *When Saturday Comes*. In 2003 he was lucky to survive after a blood clot travelled from his leg to his lung, Sterland being saved by emergency surgery. Since ending his playing days, Sterland has held a variety of jobs and still supports the club, contributing a column to the matchday programme for every home fixture.

The most recent candidate for the left-back spot is former Northern Ireland international Nigel Worthington, who between 1984 and 1994 amassed 417 appearances, as well as winning fifty caps for his country – the highest tally of any player in Owls' history. Born in Ballymena on 4 November 1961, Worthington started his playing career at Ballymena United – while working for tyre company Michelin – and he lifted the Irish Cup with his side in 1981. It was while guesting for Linfield that he was spotted by Notts County manager Jimmy Sirrel and in the same year as being voted Northern Ireland Young Footballer of the Year he moved to Nottingham for £100,000. It was not long though before Sirrel was replaced at Meadow Lane by a certain Howard Wilkinson and on 7 February 1984 the Owls' paid County a 'get your money back' fee to sign the highly rated Worthington. He'd already received plaudits for his sheer consistency at full-back and also possessed that unflappable quality. Less than three months after moving to Sheffield, Wednesday were back in the top flight and he would play the vast majority of his games in the higher grade, apart from that memorable 1990/91 campaign when 'Irish', as he was affectionately known, helped his club to promotion and the League Cup. By the early 1990s, Worthington had actually switched to a more midfield role and created a partnership with Phil King down the left-hand side, the duo being a crucial facet of Wednesday's successes of the early 1990s. In 1992 he was named the inaugural Northern Ireland player of the year and represented his county in the 1986 World Cup finals, eventually finishing his career with sixty-six caps. After just over a decade at Hillsborough, in June 1994 he became yet another player to renew links with Wilkinson at Elland Road, joining Leeds United. The move was not really the success that Worthington had hoped as he was effectively only a squad player, used only occasionally, and would spend his final playing years at Stoke City and then Blackpool, where he was appointed player-manager in July 1997. After just over two years at Bloomfield Road he enjoyed the best years of his managerial career at Norwich City – his first game in charge was back at Hillsborough in January 2001 – as in 2004 he led the Norfolk club into the Premier League. They immediately dropped back down and when it became apparent that the anticipated immediate return was not likely, he was dismissed. A brief spell at Leicester City was followed by just over four years as boss of the Northern Ireland side, winning just nine of 41 games in charge before resigning in October 2011. A cousin of fellow manager Brendan Rodgers, Worthington's last managerial role was at York City where a mixed stay included an appearance in the 2014 League Two play-off semi-finals before a dip in form resulted in his resignation in October of the same year.

Centre Halves/Central Pivot (No. 5)

Despite winning several England caps, George Wilson failed to even make the substitute's bench, mainly due to the fact that he hardly played any top-flight football for Wednesday. It seems bizarre, to modern eyes especially, that Wilson won his first cap for England while playing for a mid-table Second Division club (Wednesday) and accrued a further eleven before dropping into regional football in 1925 – one could certainly not accuse the England selectors of the time of picking players from the top flight on reputation alone. His arrival at Wednesday was a surprise to many as the Preston-born half-back was on the books of First Division Blackpool and had been mentioned for possible international selection. However, Wilson and Blackpool had a falling out in the spring of 1920 and he was quickly snapped up, Wednesday paying a club-record fee of £2,500 for the intelligent, inspirational and hard-working defender. A son of a Blackpool Police detective-sergeant, Wilson was utilised as a centre forward at his first few clubs, which included Fleetwood and Morecambe, and also in his early years at Bloomfield Road. However, after being converted to centre half in the 1914/15 campaign, he became an automatic choice. A decorated war hero – he was awarded the Belgium Medal of Honour for his bravery – he was handed the captaincy at Blackpool and seemed set for a successful career in the First Division. He arrived at Hillsborough with Wednesday desperately trying to stave off relegation but, after this proved impossible, he played almost all of his 196 games in the second tier. His England honours came after he impressed in an international trial match and his leadership qualities were such that he was handed the Owls' captaincy. He emerged as the club's best pivot half-back since Crawshaw and after five years was awarded his benefit, his popularity shown with a club record £650 raised. It was at that point that relations between Wednesday and Wilson deteriorated, the former offering £8 per week for the following season and the latter rejecting the offer. With Wednesday unwilling to budge, it seemed that Wilson was on his way out but his destination shocked the football fraternity as Third Division (North) minnows Nelson captured his signature, paying a £2,350 fee, which was not only a record fee for Nelson but also for the third tier of English football. Again, from a modern perspective, this moved seemed crazy for him to drop even further down the leagues but in the days of the maximum wage, the offer of a public house in Nelson was the sole factor that clinched the move. He stayed for two seasons before retiring in 1927, aged thirty-five, and returning to Blackpool. He became a licensee at the Mere Park Hotel but passed away just a few months after his retirement, in November 1961.

Thankfully for Wednesday, they had two ready-made replacements for the departed Wilson, Frank Froggatt captaining the club to the Second Division title in 1926 before right half-back Fred William Kean was moved to the No. 5 position and became another Wednesday great. Ironically, he won six of his seven England caps while still being used in his old position, becoming the first Sheffield-born player to play for his country since Crawshaw. Before breaking into league soccer he served in the First World War, initially being sent home after it was found that the patriotic Kean had lied about his age. He was eventually conscripted and served in the Navy before returning home unscathed. He duly played in non-league football at the oldest ground in the world and for the oldest club in the world, Hallam FC and Sheffield FC respectively, before moving into the Southern League at Portsmouth. He played only a solitary friendly there and within a few days was back in Sheffield after Brown moved to Wednesday and quickly brought Kean with him. He had been an inside forward but Brown had different plans for his new signing and after switching to half-back he built a fine reputation. In March 1923 the Owls provided England with two half-backs in their 6-1 win over Belgium, Kean making his debut. His upright running style made him instantly recognisable on the field and his no-nonsense attitude endeared him to fans. He took over the club captaincy in 1927 but when Tony Leach took his place near the end of the 1927/28 season, he was on borrowed time, eventually moving to Bolton Wanderers for a record £5,600. Many Wednesday supporters were greatly disappointed to see the popular Kean depart but it proved a great piece of business as Wednesday lifted the First Division title a few months later. In 1929 he won the FA

Cup before four years at Luton Town preceded a player-manager spell at Sutton Town. He returned to Sheffield and worked as a publican for the rest of his life, passing away in the city on 28 October 1973.

As was the case with Wilson and Kean, Owls boss Brown always had a contingency plan in relation to half-backs and the departure of Kean was not felt due to the outstanding form of newcomer Sheffielder Tony Leach. The old-fashioned-style stopper – not many opposition players got past his broad and bulky frame – had actually been plucked from local club Wath Athletic, winger Wilkinson joining Wednesday on the same day from the same club. The hard-working Leach would serve an apprenticeship of almost eighteen months in the reserves but after breaking into the first team he never looked back, showing many qualities that included ferocity in the tackle, great pace and intelligence. By the early 1930s he had developed into one of England's greatest backs, winning two England caps. His debut for his country, in October 1930 against Ireland at Bramall Lane, must have been slightly surreal as he did not have to travel outside of Sheffield and the England XI also contained teammates Strange, Blenkinsop and Burgess! His time at Wednesday came to close in the summer of 1934 following a contract dispute, and he dropped into the Second Division at Newcastle United. He also appeared for Stockport County, Carlisle United and Lincoln City and after his playing career ended, he worked as a builder in Hull and died near Doncaster, aged sixty-four, in January 1968.

Like his contemporary Layne, the career of Peter Swan was ended by the 'bribes' scandal. The impact was even greater on the central pivot as he had already won nineteen caps for England, before a bout of tonsillitis ended his run in 1962. He already had 286 Owls appearances under his belt before the story broke and like Layne was banned for life, in addition to serving the same four-month custodial sentence. It was a sad end to his top-flight career, which had seen the tall and imposing defender progress from Doncaster junior football to sign amateur forms at Wednesday while working at Armthorpe Colliery. Six months later he stepped up into the full-time professional ranks and duly made his senior bow. His early career was interrupted by national service but after being demobbed, he replaced Gibson in the side during the Second Division title-winning season of 1958/59. He made such an immediate impact that England U23 honours were quickly followed by full caps, as he became part of the famous back line of McAnearney-Swan-Kay. Purely in football terms, the loss of Swan and Layne was a grievous blow to Wednesday and for Swan, who gained employment at a local bakery before going into the licensing trade. When his ban was lifted in 1972 he also returned to Hillsborough but unlike Layne did return to the club's first XI, adding fifteen more games to his tally before joining Bury in July 1973. His playing days did not end, however, when he left Gigg Lane as he was a Wembley winner in the FA Trophy in 1975 while player-manager of Matlock Town. He later held managerial roles at Worksop Town, Buxton and Matlock (again) and continued to play in charity games into his late fifties. He worked in the licensing trade for many years and in 2006 co-wrote his biography *Setting the Record Straight*. He is now retired and sadly, since the mid-2000s, has been suffering with Alzheimer's disease.

Both Mark Smith and Peter Shirtliff came through the club's successful youth teams of the late 1970s, the former becoming an apprentice at his boyhood team in 1976. The cool and composed defender was elevated to the professional ranks in March 1978 and just over a month later made his debut. He had moved from midfield to defence when Ashurst was in charge and subsequent manager Charlton enjoyed the benefit of that positional switch, the classy and consistent Smith becoming an automatic choice. He entered the record books in the 1979/80 promotion season when he successfully converted eleven penalty kicks, beating the record set by Ball in the 1930s. He helped Wednesday to promotion in both 1980 (he was named in the PFA divisional team) and 1984 and also won five England U21 caps. He was an irregular starter in the latter years of his Owls career, as competition came from the likes of Madden, Hart and, of course, Shirtliff, but enjoyed a testimonial game before, after twenty goals in 350 appearances, leaving for Plymouth in the summer of 1987 for a £170,000 fee. He returned to South Yorkshire two years later, signing for Barnsley, and made appearances for five other league sides before taking over at Meadow Lane as reserve team manager in 1994. He was later caretaker and then assistant-manager to Sam Alladyce at County and then forged a fine reputation in youth football, first at Barnsley and then back at Wednesday, where he was appointed academy coach in July 2003. In September 2004 he was the Owls' caretaker manager for one game, Smith commenting that it was an honour to manage the club he had supported and played for. He left in 2006 and since has remained a much-respected coach in youth football, working at Sheffield United, running his own junior coaching sessions in Chapeltown, Sheffield, and now works for Chesterfield, where he was also briefly caretaker-manager in November 2013.

His contemporary Shirtliff also made his Wednesday debut in 1978, although he was still a trainee, turning professional two months later. He would actually enjoy two separate spells, leaving for Charlton Athletic in August 1986 before being bought back by Atkinson in July 1989. During his first spell, Shirtliff became a popular and consistent performer, playing in the same side as Smith as Wednesday regained their top-flight place. Competition from Knight and Lyons meant that when Wednesday returned to the First Division, Shirtliff was mainly utilised at full-back, and when relations with the club broke down in 1986 after discussions over a possible testimonial game, he moved to Charlton. He was made captain and famously scored the goal that kept the Londoners in the top flight in 1987, in the days when the play-offs involved clubs from two different divisions. After returning to S6 he enjoyed arguably his best spell, winning the League Cup and promotion, before a broken arm meant he was forced to miss the 1993 FA Cup final. Soon after, he severed ties with Wednesday, after thirteen goals in 359 appearances, to join Wolverhampton Wanderers and, like Smith, later signed for Barnsley, appearing thirteen times as the Tykes earned promotion to the Premier League. He was subsequently appointed coach and then assistant manager at Oakwell, leaving in 2001. Since then Shirtliff has held a variety of backroom roles at clubs such as Birmingham City (under Francis), Leicester City and Mansfield Town (under Palmer). He was also manager at Mansfield Town with his last role being at Bury, where he was coach and caretaker-boss before leaving in 2013.

The final defensive player in the all-time squad, Nigel Graham Pearson, proved an inspirational member of the 1991 side. He joined Wednesday after impressing for Shrewsbury Town in a September 1987 League Cup tie against the Owls and duly signed for Wilkinson's side, quickly replacing May and forming a solid centre-back pairing with Madden. He eventually took over the captaincy and became a key member of the side during that glorious 1990/91 season, netting twelve times and being voted Man of the Match in the League Cup final. He remained 'the heart and soul' of the team under Francis and his steadying influence was missed during Wembley defeats in both domestic cup finals in 1993, a broken leg suffered in the League Cup semi-final denying him the opportunity of a return visit to Wembley. Despite his time on the treatment table it was a real shock to Wednesdayites when the Nottingham-born player (21 August 1963) was sold to Middlesbrough in July 1994. He immediately captained Boro to the First Division (Championship) title in 1995 before having the unfortunate experience of not only losing in both domestic cup finals but also being relegated from the Premier League. He was again on the losing side for the Teeside club in the 1998 League Cup final and was tipped to return to Wednesday as assistant to Atkinson, with a view to taking over the reins when 'Big Ron' retired. However, the departure of Atkinson in May 1998 ended those plans, Pearson subsequently forging his own management career, beginning at Carlisle United in December 1998. He stayed in Cumbria for only six months though and was then recruited by Gary Megson as first team coach at Stoke City (1999–2001) and spent two years as assistant-manager at West Bromwich Albion (2004–06). He also had the distinction of coaching the England U21 side in the first ever game played at the new Wembley Stadium. After spells as caretaker-manager at both West Bromwich Albion and Newcastle United (twice), it was clear he was destined for a significant No. 1 position, which duly occurred when he took over at Southampton. His tenure was brief, however, and he was soon in charge at Leicester City, leading them to immediate promotion from League One and the Championship play-off semi-finals in 2010. However, he subsequently left for a brief spell at Hull City, before returning to the King Power in

November 2011. The Championship title was duly won in 2014 and the Foxes then recorded one of the most remarkable escapes from relegation in 2015 to retain their Premier League place. He had forged a remarkable team spirit and was unfortunate to be fired following an off the field incident involving his son, James, during a preseason tour of Thailand. He is credited by many as being a major factor in Leicester's fairy-tale capture of the Premier League in 2016. Pearson was quickly back in the game, appointed at Derby County. However, a dispute with the Derby hierarchy meant his stay was brief, Pearson leaving in October 2016 with County struggling at the wrong end of the table.

Midfielders/Inside Forwards/Left- and Half-backs

A plethora of midfield men failed to make the matchday cut with two of the club's early greats, Harry Chapman and Harry Davis, being prime examples. In fact, of all the men to miss out, Chapman was perhaps the best inside forward, being unsurpassed in Wednesday colours before the First World War. In fact, such was his quality that he was dubbed 'the finest inside-forward of his day, not to be capped' and it was surprising he never received international recognition after scoring 100 goals in 299 appearances. His early years were spent in local non-league football, at Kiveton Park, Worksop Town and Attercliffe, before moving to Wednesday in the summer preceding the club's first season at Owlerton. He showed his enthusiasm in a preseason public trial game when a rather overzealous tackle on Ambrose Langley left the youngster with a severe 'dressing down' from his experienced teammate. Chapman was a real rarity of his generation as he was highly adaptable, able to play in any of the attacking positions and in defence, and his qualities were numerous, including an incredible work rate, real pace and a peerless tactical brain. The partnership he developed with right-winger Davis saw the two dubbed 'the marionettes', such was their synchronisation. He was the vital cog in the Wednesday side that won back-to-back First Division titles and lifted the FA Cup. Born in Kiveton Park in 1879, he could boast a very famous brother, Herbert, who is revered as one of the greatest managers of all-time, taking both Huddersfield Town and Arsenal to top-flight titles. For Harry, he remained an automatic choice into his early thirties and after taking over as player-manager at Hull City in 1911, played for another two campaigns before finally retiring after failing to recover from a broken kneecap. He was appointed secretary at Hull late in that season and within a month also took the managerial reins when Langley – who had scalded him in that practice game many years earlier – handed in his resignation. He was in charge just over a year but his story had a sadly abrupt end as he contracted tuberculosis and, after two years fighting the disease, died 29 September 1916, tragically followed by his wife, leaving their two sons orphaned. The other half of that famous wing partnership, Harry Davis, also progressed through local junior football before signing for Barnsley in 1897. The Oakwell club's committee were somewhat hesitant to pay a fee for a youngster untried in league soccer but he proved a great signing, Barnsley receiving forty times that fee when he moved to Wednesday. The diminutive Davis – he stood 5 feet 4 inches tall – arrived at Wednesday a year after his namesake had retired from football (the other Harry Davis serving between 1892 and 1899) and became a huge favourite with those early Owlerton crowds, who dubbed Harry 'Joe Pluck', such was his wholehearted attitude and courage on the field of play. He possessed a deadly shot and was a real individual, fans often in stitches of laughter when, after being tackled, he performed his 'party piece' of sliding, on his back, 10 or more yards with hands and legs up in the air! His form earned three caps for England but his highly committed play did mean he picked up more than his fair share of injuries; he missed the 1907 FA Cup final after suffering a leg fracture. Unfortunately he failed to recover from that broken bone, leaving a year later to take over a public house at Wadsley Bridge, remaining in the trade until the start of the First World War. He survived the conflict, serving in the Army for the duration, and ran a newsagents shop until passing away in October 1945, aged sixty-five.

Another outstanding attacker of the same period was Gateshead-born James 'Jimmy' Stewart. The inside left was spotted playing for Gateshead North East Railways FC and duly invited for a trial. It only needed a solitary reserve-team appearance for the Wednesday officials to realise they had a great talent on their hands and Stewart – nicknamed 'Tadger' as a youngster – was quickly tied to a professional contract. He broke into the Wednesday side during the 1903/04 title-winning season but it would not be until part way through the following season that he became a permanent fixture. Despite not being a regular, he enjoyed a memorable 1906/07 season when in addition to winning two caps for England he also scored four times, including the opening goal in the FA Cup final. He netted thirteen league goals in the season that followed but Wednesday fans were shocked when he refused to sign a new deal, after sixty goals in 141 games, despite the club offering him the maximum wage. It was clear he wanted to return to his native north-east and Newcastle United was his destination, Wednesday receiving a club record £1,000 fee – a small profit on the £32 they paid six year earlier! He won the league and was a losing FA Cup finalists for United before his career ended as player-manager at North Shields after a season at Glasgow Rangers. After retiring he became a commercial traveller and then a publican. Later in life he worked as an accountant while also occasionally scouting for Derby County. He died in Durham on 23 May 1957.

While Stewart's Wednesday career lasted only six years, Jackie Robinson spent twelve years at Hillsborough but appeared in a dozen games less. The reason, of course, was the advent of war, to which Robinson lost his greatest years. Wednesday fans who can still remember the days of

Robinson class him as the greatest player they have seen in an Owls shirt and one can only speculate the heights he could have achieved if not for the conflict. It must be said though that those may not have been achieved for Wednesday as the club sold several promising youngsters in the late 1930s – George Drury being a prime example – although it's believed some of those sales were made so they could fend off approaches for the mercurial Robinson. He arrived at Hillsborough in October 1934, after spotting him by accident when scouting another player, and after signing it quickly became clear that Robinson was a real talent, possessing great ball control, an unerring eye for goal, tremendous pace and a mesmerising body swerve. He made such an impression that he was handed his debut aged just seventeen years and eight months at West Bromwich Albion, borrowing the boots of team captain Ron Starling and scoring to signal his arrival. He was still a teenager when capped by England, scoring on his debut, and was a shining light as Wednesday tumbled out of the top flight. He was also in the England side that was controversially forced to give the Nazi salute before a game in Germany, although he scored twice in a 6-3 win. He netted nineteen times as Wednesday just missed out on promotion and returned to the north-east when war was declared, guesting for Newcastle United and Darlington, while enrolling in the Home Guard. His career at Hillsborough had not ended though and he returned in 1942, enjoying a quite remarkable season, netting six hat-tricks in a tally of thirty-five goals in just thirty-two appearances. His incredible form took Wednesday to the War North Cup final and just reminded fans of what league football had been denied due to Mr Hitler. In the war years he totalled ninety goals in 110 games and it was a surprise when he moved to Sunderland for £6,800 in October 1946. He spent three years in the top flight at Roker Park and ended his career in regional football at Lincoln City; a broken leg suffered on Christmas Eve 1949 meant he never played again. He returned to his home county to work in the building trade and was later a publican, before ill health meant early retirement and his subsequent passing in July 1972 in Shiremoor, aged only fifty-five.

During Robinson's exploits in wartime football, Wednesday signed a nineteen-year-old player from Sheffield YMCA. His name was Redfern Froggatt and he would become the club's next outstanding talent, scoring 148 goals to set a post-war scoring record, which was only surpassed by Fantham. He played 458 games for Wednesday but sadly his father, former Owls player Frank, only saw Redfern play in wartime football, but he was alive when his son was spotted playing in a five-a-side competition in Millhouses Park and recruited to the Hillsborough ground staff. He continued to train as a draughtsman but was subsequently signed as a part-time professional and became a regular for Wednesday – his job was a reserved occupation so he was not called up. After the war he joined Wednesday full-time and over the next fourteen seasons was an established first-team player, proving to be a genuine all-round talent, capable of scoring and creating goals and a constant threat to opposition defences. England caps followed – four in total – with Froggatt playing alongside his cousin, Jack, on every occasion. Although usually utilised at inside left, 'Red' played all along the front line with around a third of his goals coming when he was out on the right wing; when challenged for his first-team spot by Sewell and then Quixall he moved positions to retain his place. His final two seasons saw Froggatt mainly restricted to Central League soccer, passing on his vast experience to the club's youngsters, and wound up his career at Stalybridge Celtic, prior to a benefit game against Ajax Amsterdam. After his playing days ended he was employed at an oil company and subsequently lived out his retirement in Sheffield, passing away on Boxing Day 2003.

Relatively new players such as Barry Bannan, Fernando Forestieri and Kieran Lee (Carlos Carvalhal suggesting in October 2016 that he 'might be from another planet') were all considered for one of the final spots but their lack of top-flight football for Wednesday, which does pervade throughout the players picked, means they don't – they hopefully can make the squad in future years. Another spot therefore belongs to the 'golden boy' – due to his blond locks and boyish looks – of Sheffield football in the 1950s, Albert Quixall. His career drew parallels with Jackie Robinson as he was also seventeen years old when he made his debut and was also capped by England at a tender age. He came through the Wednesday ranks, making a scoring debut in February 1951. By the 1953/54 campaign he was established at inside right and perfect ball control and intelligent play brought five England caps. He helped Wednesday to two promotions but it was increasingly difficult to hang onto Quixall as Wednesday bounced between the top two divisions. A third relegation of the decade, in 1958, proved decisive and in September 1958 he left for a Manchester United side that had been decimated by the Munich Air Crash. The Owls did not undersell Quixall though and United had to break the British transfer record to get their man, paying £45,000 for his signature. He netted fifty-one times in 165 games for United and won the FA Cup in 1963. After spells at Oldham Athletic and Stockport County he ended his playing days in non-league football at Altrincham, and duly settled in the Greater Manchester area, starting his own scrap metal business, which he ran until retirement.

Another man unable to force his way into the matchday twenty-two was Thomas 'Tom' McAnearney, who between 1951 and 1965 amassed 382 appearances for Wednesday, scoring twenty-two times. During a five-month period the club actually signed two McAnearney brothers from Dundee junior soccer, Jim following his older brother Tom. It would be the older sibling (born on 6 January 1933 in Lochee, Dundee) who would prove to be the exceptional player of the pair, the £490 fee Wednesday paid to Dundee North End a real bargain. He was part of the

Swan-Kay-McAnearney back line, which helped Wednesday to the runners-up spot behind the great Spurs team of 1961. During his first few seasons, McAnearney challenged Gannon for the No. 4 shirt and it wasn't until his rival returned to Irish football that he became established, partnering the likes of McEvoy and O'Donnell. The emergence of Swan and Kay in the late 1950s helped to cement McAnearney's place in the first team and over the next six seasons he showed his outstanding qualities, which included a superb range of passing skills and genuine pace. He was made team captain in the early 1960s. He eventually lost his place to the emerging Eustace and made only a handful of appearances during the reign of Brown, eventually being sold to Peterborough United in November 1965. He stayed less than six months at United, ending his playing days at Aldershot, where he was appointed player-manager in March 1966. It was not long though before he was back at Hillsborough, being appointed assistant manager to Marshall in October 1968. He was briefly caretaker-manager and was retained by new boss Williams, before moving to take over at Bury in 1970. After heavy investment in the squad in the hope of avoiding relegation did not have the desired effect, he returned to Aldershot, enjoying relative success. After leaving in January 1981 he briefly scouted for Chelsea before returning to Aldershot to work as a postman. Later in life he returned to Sheffield, enjoying his retirement on the golf course, passing away on Valentine's Day 2012.

The final place in this category was down to interwar star Harry Burgess and popular midfielder Carlton Palmer. Both men exerted a significant influence on the side they were members of, although Burgess was a highly talented inside forward while Palmer was a hard-working box-to-box midfielder, more associated with the modern game. If only for historical balance, Palmer gets the nod, the West Midlands-born player having started his career in non-league football before moving to West Bromwich Albion. He arrived at Hillsborough for a club-record fee and was an automatic choice for the next five seasons as Wednesday challenged for honours. His work in the side was not often acclaimed by football 'experts' but he was a vital member of that team, winning the ball, breaking up the opponents' play and generally being a nuisance to them. He would experience three spells at Wednesday, leaving for Leeds United in 1994 before returning on loan, from Coventry City, in February 2001, then rejoining again on a permanent basis. During those years he amassed a total of 286 games, netting eighteen goals, and was perhaps the most unlikely player in Wednesday's history to score a hat-trick, achieving the feat in a 1991 game against Queens Park Rangers, which left Wednesdayites disbelieving. He was unfortunate that suspension cost him a place in 1991 League Cup final and he was also on the losing side in both domestic finals in 1993. While at Wednesday he was capped eighteen times by his country and remains one of the most popular players in the club's recent history. After spells at the likes of Southampton, Nottingham Forest and the aforementioned Coventry City he moved into management, taking over as player-manager at Stockport County. A similar spell at Mansfield Town ended his management days in 2005 and he would later set up a football academy in Dubai and coach in China, in addition to media work. In December 2016 he hit the headlines after a five-hour heart operation saved his life with the fifty-one-year-old expected to make a full recovery.

Forwards

It is perhaps a reflection of the number of outstanding players Wednesday have had on their books that Jimmy Trotter – one of only two Owls players to top the First Division scoring charts – could not even squeeze into the matchday twenty-two. He achieved the feat in 1926/27, scoring thirty-seven times, while it was his goals that pulled Wednesday out of the Second Division in 1926, Jimmy also contributing thirty-seven of the club's eighty-eight. He had arrived in February 1922 after his previous club Bury were forced to part with him due to financial problems, but patiently spent two seasons in the reserves as first-choice centre forward. Binks blocked his path to the senior side, starting only eleven games in almost three years. When his rival departed in September 1924, the path to the first eleven was open and Trotter took the chance in emphatic fashion, grabbing seventeen goals in the remainder of the season, as well as becoming the first Wednesday player to score five in a single game, achieving the feat against Portsmouth in December 1924. Born in Easington in 1899, Trotter was spotted playing for Parsons Turbine Works, moving to Bury in 1919, and followed in the footsteps of pre-First World War scoring hero McLean, the only other Wednesday man to top the First Division standings. Trotter was lethal in the penalty area and he became a hero among Wednesdayites, supporters even inventing their own terrace chant to sing his praises. It was during the 1927/28 season that he started to lose his automatic place as first Harper and then Allen were brought to Hillsborough. He managed to see off the challenges of Harper but this was not the case with Allen as he spent two seasons in the reserves, before moving onto Torquay United in 1930. His playing days ended at Watford and after working as a masseur he returned to the game when former teammate Seed appointed Trotter 'A' team trainer at Charlton Athletic. Inside a year he was promoted to first-team trainer and remained in the role until taking over as manager in 1956. He was in charge when Athletic lost their top-flight place in 1958 and in October 1961 paid the price after three failed attempts at regaining their place. He retired altogether after departing the valley and passed away at the age of eighty-four, in St Albans, on 17 April 1984.

Another forward in the stands held a unique place in the Owls' long history as when Jackie Sewell arrived from Notts County, for £35,000 in March 1951, Wednesday broke the British transfer record to capture his signature – the only time Wednesday have been involved in raising the transfer bar in British football as a purchasing club. What is perhaps surprising is that when he was signed Wednesday were actually fighting relegation, his capture seen as one last desperate effort to avoid the drop. The big financial gamble failed to pay off despite the outstanding inside forward scoring six times in the final ten games, but the skilful and direct attacker netted twenty-three in the following season as Wednesday bounced back. He had first come to national attention in the late 1940s when his partnership with Lawton, at Notts County, powered the Meadow Lane club to the championship of Division Three (South). When you consider that Sewell had not played any top-flight football until joining Wednesday, it does make the fee paid even more remarkable, Eric Taylor obviously confident in his quarry's potential. Sewell left County after 104 goals in 193 games and Taylor's faith was quickly justified as Sewell was capped six times by England, although his last two appearances came in the seismic defeats to the magical Hungarian team of the era. Back in club football he proved to be an ever-willing worker on the field, which, combined with a deadly shot and great ball control, marked him as one of the club's key players in early 1950s. In total he scored ninety-two goals in 175 games – a scoring ratio that compares favourably with all of the club's great forwards – but relegation from the top division in 1955 made it difficult to retain his services and he returned to the First Division, moving to Aston Villa. He won the FA Cup in 1957 and his playing days in English football came to a close at Hull City in the early 1960s. His playing career continued though as he flew to Lusaka, in Northern Rhodesia (modern-day Zimbabwe), to help form a new team after being asked by a former teammate. He actually stayed in Southern Africa for over a decade, also being appointed player-coach of the national team, and also worked various other jobs, which included car salesman. He eventually returned to the UK in 1973 and lived in Nottingham for the remainder of his life. In 2010 his biography was published and he passed away in September 2016 at the grand age of eighty-nine.

It would not be fair to exclude the incomparable Derek Dooley from any summary of the club's best players as his incredible rise and tragic fall could not have been more dramatic. Of course, he also later managed Wednesday, which is covered elsewhere, but he will mostly be remembered for his scoring feats in the early 1950s, specifically the 1951/52 season when Dooley set a seasonal goals record that will never be beaten. His playing career had started after he left school, turning out for Sheffield YMCA and Firth Park YM while training to be a mechanic for hearing aids. He did eventually sign as an amateur for Lincoln City and actually trained twice a week at Bramall Lane; United's manager at the time, ex-Owls legend Davison, tried unsuccessfully to sign him while the teenager actually appeared in a friendly game for the Blades. Like on so many other occasions, fate played a role in Dooley's route to Hillsborough as the terrible winter of 1946 resulted in the season being extended by two weeks. However, the extension only applied to professional players, so Dooley was a free agent, being snapped up by Wednesday after a former player recommended the youngster. The 6-foot 3-inch-tall red-haired centre forward literally towered above his teammates and over the next two seasons Dooley, who possessed pace, a great eye for an opening and a powerful shot in both feet, scored dozens of goals in 'A' team and reserve football before being handed a senior debut against Preston North End. He failed to impress though and it was back into the shadows for the Sheffield-born attacker, Derek scoring forty-nine goals in the 1950/51 season, which included all eight in a Yorkshire League fixture. He also made a single appearance in that season but it was third time lucky when he was reintroduced into the side in October 1951, after Wednesday had suffered a stuttering start. He scored a brace against Barnsley and it was the beginning of an unbelievable run that saw him finish the season with forty-six league goals from thirty games, and also score in nine consecutive league fixtures – another club record. His feats saw crowds at Hillsborough soar (he was so popular that in September 1952 thousands of fans decided to attend a steel city reserve derby at Bramall Lane rather than watch the first team at Hillsborough) and he not only became a true phenomenon in the English game but also one of the most talked about players. After Wednesday regained their top-flight place he initially struggled in the higher grade but quickly showed his quality by scoring sixteen times in twenty-eight league games prior to a match at Preston North End in February 1953. Of course, it is well known what happened on the fateful day in Lancashire as Dooley broke his right leg, contracted gas gangrene, and three days after the match, his surgeon took the decision to amputate his leg in order to save his life. The football world was stunned and Wednesday fans disbelieving that their hero would never play again. For Dooley it was a terrible blow but the club and supporters rallied around the stricken player and at least he had no immediate financial worries after 55,000 attended his benefit game in March 1955. There is no doubt that Dooley was a real 'one-off' with his like not seen before or since, rightly earning the tag of a 'Wednesday great' after scoring sixty-three goals in precisely sixty-three games.

To say the final player to make this rather inflated squad could perhaps be described as a 'wildcard' entry does indeed rather describe the Owls career of the outrageously talented Italian Paolo Di Canio. Until August 2016 he remained the club's highest ever transfer outlay – £4.5m to Glasgow Celtic in August 1997 – and for the considerable fee Wednesday received arguably the most exciting, and certainly skilful, player to wear the blue and white shirt in the last two decades. The Roman (born on 9 July 1968) counted Juventus, Napoli and AC Milan among his clubs when he first arrived on British shores in Glasgow in 1996. Like at all of his previous clubs, the fiery, passionate and temperamental Di Canio became a huge favourite with the Parkhead fans and was named Scottish player of the year in what proved his only full season. The departure of manager Burns unsettled Di Canio though and after a fallout with the Celtic board he did not return for preseason training. A few weeks later he was on his way to Hillsborough. He joined up with compatriot Carbone and not only finished his debut campaign as top scorer but was also voted player of the year after truly entertaining the Owls fans – an outrageous goal at Southampton being a lasting memory. However, there was a reason why Di Canio played for so many clubs in his career and was never capped for Italy, which was simply that he did not take too kindly to figures of authority, such as managers, directors and referees! During his career he had various fallouts with a succession of individuals but is perhaps best remembered for the incident in September 1998 when his Owls career ended in a few seconds of madness. It was in a home game against Arsenal that Di Canio, after being red-carded, proceeded to push over the match referee and the result was a £10,000 fine and a mammoth eleven-game ban. He would not add to his seventeen goals in forty-eight games for Wednesday as the club and player reached an impasse, after he failed to return to England when his ban expired with, Wednesday taking a hard line and suspending him without pay. For a player that did not particularly like authority, this seemed ill-advised and within a few weeks it was West Ham United's gain and the Owls' loss as he joined the Londoners in a cut-price £2-million deal. He actually remained in East London for four years, being loved by the fans and tolerated by management, and became a huge cult hero with Hammers fans. Harry Redknapp stated that he 'does things with the ball that make you gasp. Other footballers would pay to watch him train. Di Canio is an entertainer. When he is focused and in form, few can rival his invention, skill and technique'. Ironically, considering his various brushes with authority, he was handed a FIFA Fair Play award in 1999 after failing to score into an empty net when an opposition goalkeeper was lying injured in the penalty area. After fifty-one goals in 141 games he returned to Italy via a brief spell at Charlton Athletic, and announced his retirement in March 2008. He was surprisingly appointed boss at Swindon Town in 2011 and led them to promotion from League Two before departing in February 2013, with Town in the top half of League One, after falling out with the club's board over the sale of players. He almost immediately took over at struggling Premier League club Sunderland and despite saving them from the drop was fired early into the following season. He has remained out of football since that day but despite playing so few games I think he deserves the final place in the fabulous fifty, despite the comments of his one-time manager Ron Atkinson, who said about Di Canio: 'Managing Paolo is like trying to keep the lid on a volcano – bloody hard.'

Chapter 6

League Cup Stories

'I knew I had struck the shot well but I thought the 'keeper had saved it. I'm pleased to score the winning goal but full credit to the lads. We won this for the fans. The atmosphere was unbelievable.'

John Sheridan, 21 April 1991

Although the Football League Cup was the idea of FA secretary Sir Stanley Rous, it was Football League secretary Alan Hardaker who proposed the competition, mainly as an extra revenue stream when the league was reorganised, which never actually took place. At the time, attendances at English football matches had started to fall and with most clubs now having floodlights, it was seen as an ideal way to revitalise the domestic game. The trophy was paid for personally by the Football League President Joe Richards but it experienced a difficult birth as the tournament was widely criticised and several of the major English clubs, including Wednesday, declined their invite to enter. As the decade progressed the Football League Cup had still not curried favour with the game's bigger clubs and it was at this point that the Football League, who now had more negotiating power with the FA and UEFA due to the introduction of the competition, effectively threated the European association with withdrawing their clubs from the Fairs Cup unless the League Cup winners were guaranteed a place. It was a bullish, or foolish, stand taken by Hardaker but both parties got around the proverbial table and the outcome was that from 1967 the winners had direct entry into European football, the only caveat being that they had to be a top-flight club. It was perhaps ironic that three of the next four winners, after the European prize was introduced, did not enter as two were outside of the First Division – Queens Park Rangers and Swindon Town – and a third, Leeds United, had qualified for Europe through their league position. It was 1968 winners Tottenham Hotspur who were the first to qualify with every league member, except for Manchester United, now entering, the final moving to Wembley in 1967 significantly increasing the kudos and participation. By 1971 it was compulsory for all ninety-two clubs to enter with the prize now on offer being the old Fairs Cup, rebranded as the UEFA Cup.

Due to the lack of 'senior' clubs entering in the early days, several smaller sides enjoyed their 'moment in the sun', the likes of Rotherham United, Rochdale and Norwich City (who had still to play at the top level) all reaching the final, which was played over two legs. It was on the back of England's World Cup win that many clubs had a change of heart, Wednesday having previously stated that they thought the competition 'lacked a little something' and that 'it had not caught the imagination of the public'. The Owls also thought it created fixture congestion that the average fan could do without. Despite their reservations they did throw their 'hat into the ring' for the 1966/67 tournament – the top-flight clubs did not enter until the second round – and were rewarded with a home derby clash with Rotherham United, managed by former Wednesday trainer-coach Jack Mansell. Despite poor weather, a healthy 20,204 crowd attended that first ever fixture with the Owls fielding the following eleven: R. Springett, Smith, Megson, Eustace, S. Ellis, Young, Usher, Pugh, McCalliog, Davies, Quinn.

Wednesday went into that inaugural game missing key players Fantham and Ford and were somewhat disgruntled when Davies' seventy-fifth-minute goal was controversially chalked off after another player was deemed to be interfering with play. They were made to pay with just forty seconds of the game remaining when the Millers counter-attacked and from a resultant free-kick, Casper drove home the winner. The 1967/68 season draw handed Wednesday a trip to Third Division Stockport County and it was Wednesday who progressed 5-3, although they were given a mighty scare by the battling home side. A comfortable home win over Barrow secured a place in the last sixteen but that was as far as the Owls managed, being held 0-0 at Hillsborough before exiting 2-0 at Stoke City. The rest of the decade saw Wednesday face two lower league clubs but were also knocked out by both, the biggest embarrassment being in September 1968 when they made the long trip to Devon, just a few days after beating Manchester United 5-4 in a league game. It seemed to be a case of 'after the Lord Mayor's show' for Wednesday as they crashed 3-1 to the minnows – the victory was described as triggering the biggest celebration in Devon since the introduction of cream teas and pasties! The meeting with Third Division Bournemouth at Hillsborough in September 1969 proved another evening to forget as the visitors, missing five regulars, forced a draw after Owls defender Ellis inexplicably headed into his own goal, which meant another long trip south for the replay. Unfortunately the Owls simply did not compete in the second game, in front of an enthusiastic 15,894 crowd, and for the third time in only four seasons they were dumped out by a minnow – the club probably now regretting that decision to enter the tournament three years earlier!

1970s

While the sixties had not been too kind to Wednesday in the League Cup, the following decade was also a 'mixed bag' with more humiliating exits mixed together with two runs to the last sixteen, both when the Owls were a Third Division club themselves. There was no disgrace exiting, in a replay, to top-flight Chelsea in September 1970 while a semblance of revenge was dished out a year later when the Owls won 2-0 at Rotherham United. However, the League Cup was still not providing games of quality and the first forty-five minutes at Millmoor were described as a 'disgrace to football' due to the poor quality fare on offer and a whistle happy referee. The second half did improve and goals from Sissons and Sinclair secured the Owls' first win in the competition for four years. In hindsight the Wednesday players would probably have preferred exiting in South Yorkshire as they were subsequently humiliated in Cumbria as Carlisle United inflicted a 5-0 defeat. Wednesday went into the game sitting bottom of the Second Division and it showed as they were overpowered by a more committed home side who taught the 'poor little rich kids' a footballing lesson, leading 4-0 after thirty minutes. The only consolation was that the hosts were in the same division and they would be beaten in a Second Division fixture just over six weeks later. The 2-0 home win over Third Division Bolton Wanderers in September 1972 was remembered for a virtuoso display of wing play from Henderson, while an exit at top-flight Wolves was not helped when Wednesday conceded a penalty and an own goal inside a two-minute period! Wednesday were again struggling in the bottom half of the Second Division table when the League Cup draw paired them with Bournemouth for a second time. The sides would meet on three occasions, which included two replays, but the aggregate attendance of less than 26,000 suggested there was very little enthusiasm for the games. The first tie ended 0-0 on the south coast before the lowest Hillsborough crowd since the Second World War (5,883) saw a late equaliser from Bournemouth force extra-time after a 2-2 scoreline. Thankfully the Owls were winners on the night as manager Derek Dooley correctly guessed the coin toss for the venue, the next game duly taking place at Hillsborough two weeks later. There was no doubt that the sides were well matched, despite the lower league status of the Cherries, and the third game again went to extra-time before Prendergast forced home the 104th-minute winner to earn a trip to First Division Queens Park Rangers. Sadly, like the win over the Millers two years earlier, the next round only offered abject humiliation, although the score at Loftus Road was tied at 2-2 just before half-time after Wednesday had scored through Knighton and Prendergast to wipe out the host's advantage. It was 3-2 to Rangers at the break but Wednesday were then swept away by a four goals in eight minutes burst and ended up on the wrong end of an 8-2 thrashing. The 1-0 loss at basement division club Scunthorpe United in August 1974 seemed almost regulation in comparison to that disastrous evening in West London, although it did perhaps reflect the club's terrible struggles of the mid-1970s and their chronic paucity in front of goal. The 1975/76 season saw two-leg ties introduced and Wednesday scored twice in the second period to win 2-0 at Fourth Division Darlington. By that season the Owls were only a division higher than their opponents but it was still a huge disappointment to the loyal Wednesday fans, who turned out to record a reasonable 7,452 Hillsborough crowd when the Quakers won the return leg 2-0 to force a third match. If any game summed up the club's struggles of the 1970s, it was this tie as the visitors showed a surprising lack of ambition and seemed content to exit with a whimper. They did not count on such a woeful display from the home side though with manager Burtenshaw the only winner on the night, the coin toss again resulting in a third game at Hillsborough. If the long-suffering Wednesdayites expected better in the third match, they were sadly disappointed as a display from their team, described as 'bereft of imagination or skill', contributed to a desperate 120 minutes, including extra-time, before the crowd did get some excitement with a penalty shoot-out. The fans did not realise at the time but the shoot-out was not only the first in a League Cup tie but the first time ever in a senior English game that this system was used to settle a tie; it had previously only been used in the Watney Cup back in the early 1970s. In keeping with the evening, Prendergast missed the first shot but the visitors scored all of their five penalties, Wednesday exiting 5-3 after another calamitous evening.

Wednesday were certainly overdue a decent run in the competition and that finally occurred, ten years after they had first entered, in the 1976/77 season. A comfortable 3-0 aggregate win over Grimsby Town negotiated the first round and handed Wednesday a second League Cup visit to Molineux to face First Division Wolverhampton Wanderers. Finally, the giant-killing boots were worn by the Owls as they shocked their hosts by taking an early lead through Potts. Wolves seemed somewhat complacent and a resolute defensive display from Wednesday ensured they held that lead until Parkin levelled with seventeen minutes remaining. This Len Ashurst team, though, would not be denied and after eighty-two minutes popular attacker Wylde scored from close range to complete a memorable victory. Wednesday were therefore through and a home tie with Elton John's Fourth Division Watford side, who were about to commence their inexorable march through the divisions. A 3-1 win ensued with Owls fans rather optimistically singing 'we're going to Wembley' as their side reached the last sixteen for the first time for a decade. The draw was certainly unkind to Wednesday as it sent them to Second Division Millwall; the Owls fans, aboard twelve coaches that travelled from Sheffield, were certainly not relishing a trip to the Old Den as it was not exactly the friendliest of grounds in the mid-1970s! The brave few that made the journey did get beck to Sheffield relatively unharmed but sadly their side crashed out, slipping to a 3-0 defeat after conceding twice in the opening fifteen minutes. During the run in the 1976/77 season the Owls were also enjoying a good season in the league but it was the total opposite in the season that followed as progress in the competition was in sharp contrast to the Owls' awful league form. The unexpected progress started with a first-round tie against Doncaster Rovers, Wylde becoming the first Wednesday player to score a League Cup hat-trick in a 5-2 Hillsborough win. The visitors' nineteen-year-old rookie 'keeper was at fault for four of the Owls' goals and he let in another three in the second leg as Wednesday cruised through. Incidentally both legs of the first round were played before the season commenced – a regular occurrence until the early 1980s. The draw handed Wednesday a trip to Second Division Blackpool and another 'giant-killing' looked on the cards as Wednesday led 2-1 with just a minute to go. However, the game then exploded into controversy as despite looking to have tripped defender Dave Cusack, Tangerines forward Bob Hatton ran through to score. Wednesday were incensed, Cusack commenting that 'I had Hatton beaten and it was obvious what happened – I have got the mark on my leg to prove it.' The consolation was that Wednesday did have a replay and they debunked their poor league form by winning the second tie 3-1, delighting their fans with a display of real gusto to reach the fourth round for a third time. Wednesday fans, after years of struggle, craved a glamour game and they were duly rewarded with a home tie against Everton. It was like the good old days were back at Hillsborough as a season's best crowd of 36,079 had the turnstiles ticking, bringing much needed revenue to a club that was still struggling financially. The Owls were understandably rated as 200-1 outsiders but a display full of grit and endeavour ensured the Toffeemen couldn't settle, the proverbial roof lifting off the old ground when Tynan equalised Lyons' goal after thirty-five minutes. The visitors pulled away in the second half to win 3-1 but manager Charlton was a pleased man, commenting 'We frightened them occasionally, and it was all good experience for the lads. They are a bit sick at the result but they enjoyed the atmosphere and the crowd. Now we've got to play with that sort of spirit in all our league games'. The club's run in the FA Cup dominated cup football in 1978/79 but Wednesday did play four games in the League Cup, although three were required to see off the initial challenge of Doncaster Rovers. The scrappy first game was rather fittingly settled at Belle Vue by an own goal from home defender Robinson with Hornsby also seeing his penalty saved. That goal looked to be sending Wednesday into the next round as the second leg was tied 0-0 with literally seconds left; however, Rovers netted the winner with virtually the last kick and a third game was required, frustratingly meaning the Owls' opening league fixture had to be postponed. On this occasion it was Rovers who won the choice of venue so it was back to

Doncaster for the third episode, fittingly won with a Hornsby goal, the midfielder atoning in the best way for his earlier profligacy from the penalty spot. The second round meant a first League Cup visit to an Aston Villa side containing Gary Shelton, and it was the future Owl who scored the only goal of the night, in a game watched by over 31,000, as Wednesday fought superbly but exited. The decade ended with four more games in the competition, two-legged tussles with Hull City and top-flight Manchester City. The Hull first leg saw new signings McCulloch, King and Mellor all make their debuts but a Curran goal was not enough to secure an advantage for the second game, City levelling in the second half. The return at Boothferry Park swung the Owls' way in the second half as another Curran goal secured a 3-2 aggregate win and the aforementioned tie against the blue side of Manchester. Wednesday secured a 1-1 result in the first leg at Hillsborough but were desperately unlucky not to knockout City in the second leg as, with only two minutes left, they led through Smith's eighty-minute penalty. The proverbial ceiling then caved in as, incredibly, Henry scored twice in those last 120 seconds and Wednesday were left stunned.

1980s

The '80s would be much kinder to Wednesday with only one rather embarrassing exit and the quarter-finals reached for the first time, on four separate occasions. Before Wednesday reached the dizzy heights of the last eight, there was the small matter of a Sheffield derby at the start of the 1980/81 campaign. Just under 50,000 fans attended the two-legged tie, Wednesday completing a 3-1 aggregate victory, but the club was on the wrong end of an upset in the next round when Fourth Division Wimbledon won 2-1 at Plough Lane in the first leg. Thankfully, Wednesday recovered sufficiently in the second leg to squeeze through 4-3, although it did need a last-minute winner from Curran. This set up another visit to Hillsborough for Watford and they gained revenge for their 1976 exit, although it was they who needed a last-minute goal to go through. The 1981/82 League Cup started much later in the season and with Wednesday exempt from the first round, they did not start until 7 October, the latest the Owls have started in the competition. Unfortunately it was not worth the wait as fellow Second Division outfit Blackburn Rovers knocked the Owls out 3-2 on aggregate; the teams drew 1-1 at Ewood Park (Brotherston missing a late penalty for Rovers) and then a goal from ex-Owl Lowey helped them clinch a place in the next round. The following campaign proved important in the club's League Cup history as they reached the fifth round for the first time, despite needing extra-time to overcome Fourth Division Bristol City in the second round. Despite winning the first leg in Bristol 2-1, Charlton was not a happy man, questioning the attitudes of several players who seemingly did not pay attention as City forced the tie into extra-time in the Hillsborough return. It was a dismal showing from Wednesday against a team ninetieth in the league and without an away win all season, and despite a goal from Taylor sending Wednesday through they were met with jeers from the Kop at the full-time whistle – Wednesdayites had not been impressed! The draw sent Wednesday to Crystal Palace in the renamed Milk Cup, and poor finishing from the home side contributed greatly to the Owls progressing 2-1, thanks to first-half goals from the two Garys, Megson and Bannister. The fourth-round draw paired the two south Yorkshire clubs left in the tournament, Wednesday and Barnsley, together at Hillsborough. The 33,354 crowd was higher than any league game played by Wednesday in that season and they were treated to a fiercely fought encounter, which included six bookings, and was won by an early strike from McCulloch. Thousands travelled from Sheffield for the quarter-final clash at Highbury but the tie proved a bridge too far, Wednesday failing to create any clear-cut chances and, despite a gutsy display, went down 1-0.

That taste of the latter stages of the competition wetted the club's appetite and they repeated the feat a year later, overcoming Darlington, Preston North End and Stoke City to set up a mouth-watering Hillsborough game against League Champions Liverpool. A 3-0 stroll in the first leg against Darlington effectively wrapped up the tie – Wednesday eventually winning 7-2 on aggregate – and Howard Wilkinson's troops eased past Third Division Preston to set up a visit to First Division Stoke City. The Owls were backed by a vociferous following at the Victoria Ground but the game was a real non-event until Bannister fired past ex-Owl Fox to put Wednesday in front, six minutes after half-time. It roused the home side but despite chances falling to both sides it was the Wednesdayites who celebrated in the away end. Wilkinson commented about the away following: 'The players were thrilled ... they were fantastic. After that win I think the kettle is back on the boil'. The fifth-round home tie against Liverpool proved to be one of the most memorable games played at the ground in the last fifty years. A huge 49,357 crowd attended and they were treated to a thrilling topsy-turvy game with future Owl Nicol putting the holders in front only for Megson and Bannister to put the home side ahead. Wednesday was then agonisingly close to extending their lead – Shelton missing when it looked easier to score – before the Reds stormed back to equalise and take the tie back to Anfield. The replay was best remembered for the 12,000 Wednesday fans who braved the snow-bound Woodhead and cheered their side from the first to last minute. The 3-0 defeat was almost incidental as the Sheffield hordes repeatedly sang 'we'll be back' and they were proved correct. A year later the Owls supporters were again dreaming of Wembley after reaching the last eight for the third season running, Wednesday easing past local rivals Huddersfield Town and squeezing past Second Division Fulham to set up a home tie with Luton Town. The subsequent 4-2 victory put the Owls in the last eight again. The tie will always be remembered for the feat of Andy Blair as he became the first, and only, Owls player to score a hat-trick from the penalty spot. The midfielder had missed his previous penalty, having taken over spot-kick duties from Sterland, but fired home on fifteen, fifty-one and seventy minutes to put his side 4-0 ahead and a guaranteed place in the fifth round. The draw pitched two First Division sides together with Wednesday being drawn at Chelsea. Bad weather meant the tie was postponed but when it was played Owls 'keeper Hodge was the hero as his penalty save, from Dixon, earned Wednesday a replay. The teams reconvened at Hillsborough and fans were again treated to a thriller, although for Wednesday supporters the overriding feeling was one of frustration as a 3-0 half-time advantage was lost and it needed a last-minute penalty from Sterland to force extra-time after a breathless 4-4. The extra thirty minutes failed to separate the two heavyweights and so it was back down to West London where Wednesday hearts were broken as old foe Mickey Thomas scored a last-minute winner.

After the drama of those quarter-finals, Wednesday came back down to earth with a bump in the 1985/86 campaign as, after beating Brentford over two legs, they travelled to deepest Wiltshire, to face basement division Swindon Town, sat third in the top flight. The cup showed little respect for league placings though as Wednesday crashed out, a former non-league forward called Peter Coyne scoring the only goal. The following season saw the Owls pay a return visit to Stockport County, almost twenty years after the previous League Cup tie, although it was not to Edgeley Park but Manchester City's Maine Road. The reason was because Stockport, in their wisdom, had decided to switch the second leg to their neighbour's much larger ground so they could maximise the crowd and subsequent revenues. Unfortunately they had probably hoped the first leg would have been a bit closer than the 3-0 win secured by Wednesday, the tie becoming almost dead and buried with a poor crowd of only 2,089 attending the second leg. The fans rattled around in the stadium but it was a night to remember for Colin Walker as after entering the fray as a half-time substitute he proceeded to bag a hat-trick to become the only player to achieve the feat from the substitute's bench for Sheffield Wednesday. The actual game ended 7-0 – the Owls' biggest away win since a 7-2 FA Cup success at Manchester United in 1961 – but the run ended emphatically in the third round as they were beaten 4-0 at Everton, having Lawrie Madden sent off for two yellow cards with the score at 2-0. The 1987/88 League cup campaign will perhaps be best remembered for two individuals – Pearson and Hodge. The former came to the fore in the second-round tie against Shrewsbury Town, although it was not his feats for the Owls that caught the eye but his sterling performances for Wednesday's opponents in both legs; he made such an impression with Wilkinson that Pearson was signed within three weeks of Wednesday completing a 3-2 aggregate win. The third round again paired Wednesday and Barnsley together, this time at Oakwell, but Tykes old boy Hirst returned to haunt his former club, scoring a diving header winner against a home side that contained Stuart Gray. Often controversial referee George Courtney – who had left Wednesday fuming after red-carding Lee Chapman earlier in the year – was again the centre of proceedings in the fourth-round tie at Aston Villa after he sent off Megson, just thirty-six minutes into the game. The game against their Second Division opponents was tied at 1-1 when he was ordered off but Wilkinson's side rarely buckled, digging in to keep Villa at bay. A West goal duly put the Owls ahead and they hung on for probably the best result of the whole season, earning a home game with Arsenal in the last eight. Sadly the clash with the Gunners was a poor affair and will only be remembered for the sixty-seventh-minute speculative shot from Winterburn, which went straight through the body of the usually dependable Hodge to win the match. The Owls exited at the second round stage in the 1988/89 season after losing 2-0 at Blackpool (the curse of the ex striking again with a goal from Cunningham) and, with caretaker-manager Eustace in charge, went out on away goals after winning 3-1 in the second leg. The decade ended in spectacular style as after being held 0-0 at Hillsborough by Fourth Division Aldershot, Wednesday filled their boots in the second leg to record the biggest away win in their history, 8-0, with goals for Whitton (four), Atkinson (three) and Shakespeare. In the next round the Owls were again hit by the late, late show – as per Manchester City a decade earlier – as after Hirst had put Wednesday ahead with only four minutes left, Derby still won as Saunders netted twice in the remaining time to dump Wednesday out.

1990s

The new decade saw the club not only (finally) get past the quarter-final stage of the tournament but go all the way to win the trophy. The run to the final had started with a tie, in the renamed Rumbelows Cup, at home to Brentford, won with second-half goals from Hirst and Pearson. It was a slender lead to take to their Third Division opponents but it was 'job done' when Francis and Pearson scored in the first eighteen minutes, Wednesday eventually winning 4-2 on aggregate. The third-round tie at home to fellow Second Division club Swindon Town included a debut for new US player John Harkes but the game fizzled out into a 0-0 stalemate and the Owls were faced with an unwanted midweek trek to Wiltshire. On this occasion, though, the single-goal win was Wednesday's, with Captain Pearson scoring his third goal in the tournament, after just ten minutes, to earn a place in the last sixteen. A juicy tie awaited the Owls with top-flight Derby County handed a trip to Hillsborough. A healthy crowd watched the action but the home fans were not impressed as

Wednesday failed to perform and the tie petered out into a draw, despite Hirst having put his side in front after just fourteen minutes. The Owls were a changed team in the replay on a night that was memorable for two individuals, one on and one off the pitch. Off the field of play TV cameras focused on a rather portly supporter who had decided to watch the game, in freezing conditions, with his shirt off – so began the long association with the Owls for Wolverhampton's Tango. More importantly his team had a match to win and they went ahead after thirty-two minutes with an unbelievable 35-yard thunderbolt from John Harkes, which left Peter Shilton grasping for thin air as the ball flew past him into the top corner. The home side levelled but Williams fired home the winner, earning the Owls their first win at the Baseball Ground for forty-two years. Manager 'Big Ron' said after the game that 'You will go a long way before you see a better goal scored anywhere than that.' The Owls boss had seen Coventry City manager Terry Butcher before the game and told him that 'he wouldn't fancy playing Wednesday in the next round' and they certainly did not relish their visit on a night of passion and drama at Highfield Road. The Owls' tremendous away record – they had won twelve matches on the road before the quarter-final – looked set to be extended as Wednesday dominated the vast majority of the game and deservedly led from the eighth minute after Pearson's goal. It was a long time to hang onto a slender lead and the nerves of the travelling fans were somewhat shredded at the full-time whistle as City threw everything at Wednesday, Man of the Match Pearson clearing off the line in the dying embers of the game. Despite the late scare the win put the club into the semi-finals for the first time and a two-legged clash with top-flight Chelsea. As both legs were to be televised, it meant a very early start for the thousands of travelling Wednesday fans after the game was set for a Sunday noon kick-off. The early alarm call was worth it though as Wednesday produced another outstanding away-day display with Pearson and Shirtliff a rock at the back and the whole team taking the match to a somewhat surprised home team. Goals for Shirtliff and Hirst put Wednesday on the brink of Wembley and the job was completed, just three days later, in front of an ecstatic 34,669 at Hillsborough. It was truly a night to remember as Wednesday responded to the emotionally charged fans by ripping into their visitors and scoring twice near half-time to effectively put the tie to bed. Pearson opened the scoring and was yet again Man of Match as his inspirational captaincy spurred the team forwards. It ended 3-1 to the Owls, Wilson and Williams with the other goals, and all eyes were on Wembley on Sunday 21 April for Wednesday's first major final since 1966, against Manchester United.

With Wednesday still chasing promotion to the top division, the date at Wembley was almost just another crucial game but twenty-five years without a trip to the national stadium meant it was certainly NOT just another game. It is well documented how Atkinson's pre-match preparations worked wonders, including having a comedian on board the team bus to Wembley, and the players were left in no doubt how Wednesday fans felt as Wembley Way was a sea of blue and white with no red and white to be seen. It was Wednesday's big day out and although the actual game was not particularly sparkling, it was Wednesday who won the tactical battle, the now fit again Nilsson working together with Harkes (who had replaced the dreadfully unlucky Palmer, who was suspended after being sent off at Portsmouth) to snuff out the threat of danger man Sharpe. When Sheridan fired home in the thirty-eighth minute, the Owls fans went wild and nails were chewed to the bone as they hung on to that precious lead, Turner superbly turning over McClair's header as the game entered the last ten minutes. There was just time for a cameo appearance from 'winger' Lawrie Madden before match official Ray Lewis blew the whistle. Wednesday had won the cup; cue massive celebrations from 30,000 Wednesdayites in the ground!

'Any of my players could have been man of the match. They all did their job brilliantly. I told my lads to savour the occasion and we had a smashing time in the two days before the final. It didn't bother me that it was United who we beat. They had pressure but never controlled the game. We were brave enough to keep our nerve and there wasn't one bad performance from my team out there,' said Ron Atkinson.

Pearson won yet another Man of the Match and while Wednesdayites travelled home, no doubt hoping to arrive back before closing time, the players attended a post-match reception at Wembley conference centre before the celebrations continued at a London hotel, where around 400 people gathered – it had been a grand day out.

Cup Winning Season Teams:

Brentford: Pressman, Nilsson, King, Palmer, Shirtliff, Pearson, Wilson (McCall), Francis, Hirst, Williams, Worthington

Brentford: Pressman, Madden, King, Palmer, Shirtliff, Pearson, Wilson, Sheridan, Francis, Williams, Worthington

Swindon: Pressman, Harkes, King, Palmer, Shirtliff, Madden, Wilson, Sheridan, Hirst, Williams (Francis), Worthington (McCall)

Swindon: Pressman, Harkes, McCall (Madden), Palmer, Shirtliff, Pearson, Wilson, Sheridan, Hirst, Williams, Worthington

Derby: Pressman, Harkes, King (Williams), Palmer, Shirtliff, Pearson, Wilson, Sheridan, Hirst, Francis, Worthington

Derby: Pressman, Harkes, King, Palmer, Shirtliff, Pearson, Wilson, Sheridan, Hirst, Williams, Worthington

Coventry: Turner, King, Worthington, Palmer, Shirtliff, Pearson, Wilson, Sheridan, Hirst, Williams, McCall

Chelsea: Turner, Harkes, King, Palmer, Shirtliff, Pearson, Wilson, Sheridan, Hirst, Francis (Williams), Worthington

Chelsea: Turner, Harkes, King, Palmer, Shirtliff, Pearson, Wilson (McCall), Sheridan, Hirst, Francis (Williams), Worthington

Manchester United: Turner, Nilsson, King, Harkes (Madden), Shirtliff, Pearson, Wilson, Sheridan, Hirst, Williams, Worthington

After the high of actually winning the trophy, Wednesday had the small problem of defending their prize, which started with a 4-1 aggregate win over Leyton Orient, all the goals being scored in the second leg. The next round paired the Owls with fellow top-flight side Southampton and Wednesday looked set to progress, thanks to a Hirst goal, but a late equaliser from Shearer earned the Saints a replay. The trip to the south coast proved disappointing as a goal from Horne was the only one of the game and the holders bowed out. There is always another season though and 1992/93 campaign saw another appearance in the final. The run commenced against Division Two·(League One) side Hartlepool United with new signing Bright among the scorers in a comfortable 3-0 home success. Despite it being only early October, Wednesday fans who travelled to the north-east wished they had taken their thermal underwear as the freezing cold wind whipped off the North Sea as the Owls went 2-0 ahead – Bright scoring after just twenty-two seconds – only for the game to end all square. It was Leicester City next at Hillsborough and Wednesday were at their very best, crushing their visitors 7-1 with five different players on the scoresheet in a clinical display of finishing that marked them down as one of the favourites. Queens Park Rangers were easily brushed aside in the next round to set up a quarter-final at Ipswich Town. A diving header from Sheridan early in the second half put the Owls in the driving seat but it was another game, in an increasingly cluttered fixture list, when another ex-Owl, Steve Whitton, netted a late penalty. Over 26,000 were inside Hillsborough and Paul Warhurst, recently converted from a defensive role, continued his scoring hot streak by netting the winner and clinching a second semi-final appearance. It would be fair to say that the first-half display by Wednesday in the first leg of the last four games at Blackburn Rovers was the best forty-five minutes of football seen by an Owls side in living memory as they recovered from an early goal to comprehensively outplay their hosts and race into an unassailable 4-1 lead. There were a few nervous moments in the second leg, no more so than when Rovers took a surprise lead and then Nilsson's miscued back pass beat Woods and hit the foot of a post. Second-half goals from Hirst and Bright, though, safely saw the Owls through to another Wembley day, on Sunday 18 April 1993. Opponents were George Graham's Arsenal and in front of 74,007 it looked like another fairy-tale win was on the cards after John Harkes netted after just nine minutes, becoming the first US national to score in a major cup final at the venue. It was not to be though, Merson levelling and Morrow grabbing the sixty-eighth-minute goal that proved the winner for the Gunners. A bullish John Harkes commented, 'We'll come back and win the FA Cup. We can play better and I think we will beat them next time. For my goal you pray for that sort of situation with the ball coming out like that. I just thought of whacking it and keeping it low and it went straight in.'

   SWFC: Woods, Nilsson, King (Hyde), Palmer, Anderson, Harkes, Wilson (Hirst), Waddle, Warhurst, Bright, Sheridan

Two appearances in League Cup finals in just three years was a remarkable feat for a club that had not got past the last eight before reaching the 1991 final. Wednesday certainly had a taste for the competition and another great run came in the following season. It started with a final visit to Bolton's old Burden Park ground, the Owls having to borrow the home side's gold away kit after the match referee decreed that Wednesday could not wear their black and yellow away shirt. The First Division (Championship) hosts gave Wednesday a scare, taking the lead through a spot kick, but a late diving header from Bart-Williams ensured parity. A Bright goal sent the Owls through but another two games were required to see off Middlesbrough, Wednesday needing a late equaliser from Palmer to earn a replay in the first tie at Ayresome Park. The replay against Boro was equally troublesome, the visitors taking the game into an additional thirty minutes before Palmer was again the unlikely hero as he volleyed home the winner with five minutes remaining. For the fourth-round tie at Queens Park Rangers the Owls again sported a gold away kit but this time it was from their own kit bag as they wore a natty strip, which was never seen again. It proved lucky as with just three minutes remaining, and the game tied at 1-1, rapidly emerging midfielder Ryan Jones ran fully 35 yards to get on the end of a great Worthington cross and powerfully head home a glorious winner. It was his fifth goal of a breakthrough season with home manager Gerry Francis tipping the Owls to win the trophy. The cup draw gave Wednesday fans the one tie they did not want – Wimbledon at Selhurst Park – but they still travelled in good numbers despite the gate being less than 9,000. Manager Francis picked probably the tallest Wednesday side in their history in an attempt to combat the home side's direct style, and Wednesdayites that did make the awkward journey to Croydon witnessed a real rarity – a goal from Bright from outside the area, his spectacular late strike sending Wednesday through to another semi-final. The draw for the last four gave Manchester United an opportunity to gain some revenge for the 1991 final, although the tie seemed finely balanced after the first leg at Old Trafford finished 1-0 to the hosts, an early Giggs goal being the difference. The second leg was delayed due to heavy snow but the inaugural Premier League champions showed their undoubted class to score twice early on and register a convincing 5-1 aggregate success.

   Wednesday came back from that disappointing semi-final to reach the last sixteen for the next two seasons, although their nemesis Arsenal provided the knockout blows in both seasons. The Owls squeezed past

Bradford City in the early stages of the 1994/95 campaign and then beat Southampton at Hillsborough before losing 2-0 at Highbury. A year later a treble from Bright was the highlight of a 7-4 aggregate win over Crewe Alexandra before the Owls made their first visit to Millwall's new ground. Wednesday had a quite terrible record at the Old Den but left with a 100 per cent win record at the new one, Pembridge and Whittingham netting in a 2-0 win. The Owls actually scored at Highbury in the fourth round (Degryse) but it ended in the usual way, the Gunners winning 2-1. It was probably in the late 1990s that the League Cup started to lose some of its kudos, with both clubs and supporters, poor crowds watching Wednesday crash out early in three consecutive seasons, commencing with a 2-1 exit to Oxford United in September 1996 with less than 7,500 inside Hillsborough for the first leg. Wednesday had Manchester City loan player Nigel Clough in their side for the first leg tie at Grimsby Town in the following September but it was a terrible night as the Mariners recorded a convincing 2-0 win, leaving Wednesday with a mountain to climb in the second leg. Wednesday were so woeful on the night that the loyal band of travelling fans started singing 'it's just like watching Blackpool' – they were not eluding to the club's bright orange away kit! That deficit proved unsurmountable despite a 3-2 win on the night, and the trio of embarrassing exits was completed in 1998 when Cambridge United won at Hillsborough and secured a draw at home to progress on aggregate. The home tie became famous for the post-match 'fancy-dans' comments of Danny Wilson, which many believed, including Di Canio himself, was aimed at the fiery Italian who had a bad night and was criticised for not passing to his teammates. It certainly showed a rift between the pair and it was only ten days later before Di Canio's frustrations boiled over in the infamous match against Arsenal. It was perhaps ironic that the Owls' relegation season included another run to the last sixteen of the competition after paying a first visit to Stoke City's new Britannia Stadium in the second round. The First Division home side held the Owls to a goalless encounter before Alexandersson netted twice in the return game to secure a 3-1 aggregate success. The season as a whole was an unmitigated disaster but remarkably, in a twelve-day period in early October, Wednesday fans saw their favourites score nine times in two games, four coming in the third-round tie against another First Division side, Nottingham Forest, as Wednesday bucked their dismal league form. The win handed the Owls a trip, rather unsurprisingly, to a First Division club with Bolton Wanderers lying in wait for the Premier League's bottom club. For the Owls it was an evening when Lady Luck was definitely not on their side as controversial refereeing decisions saw penalty claims turned down and a goal from Sibon mysteriously chalked off. To rub salt into the wounds, Wednesday, rather fortuitously it must be said, did get a penalty with only ten minutes left, but Owls fans could only watch in disbelief as De Bilde's effort was saved. In a game littered with errors and little penalty box action, the cup tie was settled by a single goal with Wanderers progressing.

2000s

The 2000/01 season would be the final one to include two-legged ties, other than in the semi-finals, with too many 'dead rubber' second legs and increasing fixture congestion being the main reasons behind the changes. Despite having just been relegated, Wednesday were still seeded and faced Oldham Athletic in the second round, winning 8-2 on aggregate, although the irony was not lost on Wednesday fans as the two victories came during a club record run of eight consecutive league defeats. The wins did provide some light relief from those league troubles and the cup draw was welcomed by both sides of the Sheffield divide as Wednesday drew United at Hillsborough. A crowd of 32,383 attended the tie and it proved a 'rip-roaring' encounter that, as you would expect, contained its fair share of robust tackles, although the referee only handed out three yellow cards. The hero of the hour would be a man who'd only just arrived in the city, as new signing Ekoku scored twice, netting the 112th-minute winner. The fourth-round draw rather mischievously handed the Owls a trip to Upton Park and a reacquaintance with erstwhile winger Di Canio. It was expected that the lower league strugglers would buckle under the attacking might of the Hammers but Wednesday again saved their best for the League Cup as they secured a shock 2-0 lead just after half-time. With Di Canio behind every West Ham forward thrust – Owls fans serenading him with 'Paolo, Paolo what's the score' – they did pull a goal back and it needed a terrific rearguard display to deservedly earn a rather unglamorous trip to Birmingham City in the quarter-finals. The second city club was managed by ex-Owl Francis and proved their tag as favourites to be correct as they outplayed an Owls side who were a pale shadow of the cup-fighting team that had got the club so far. The last time Wednesday reached the last four of the competition came in the following season, in another campaign where the cup run was in sharp contrast to poor league form. With two-legged ties confined to history, the Owls played in the first round for the first time in twenty years, and were handed a trip to Bury. The build-up to the game was dominated by the sad news that young professional Tom Staniforth had died suddenly – the players all wearing black armbands – and the 1,000-strong travelling Wednesday fans paid tribute to him in, chanting his name constantly during the second half and at full-time. The tie proved a comfortable evening, the Owls winning 3-1, with the reward a home game against Premier League Sunderland. The tie was also overshadowed with tragedy as it was played the day after the infamous 9/11 terrorist attacks on the World Trade Centre. After observing a minute's silence, the sides duly served up a thrilling tie, which Wednesday would win 4-2 after extra-time, and will always be remembered for an outrageous 20-yard overhead-kick goal from young Italian forward Di Piedi, just two minutes into the additional thirty. The memory of Staniforth was featured as when Morrison scored from the spot he lifted his shirt to simply reveal the word 'Stan' on a t-shirt underneath; the thrilling victory was a fitting tribute to the popular defender. Fellow Division One club Crystal Palace were drawn at Hillsborough in the third round of the renamed Worthington Cup and the tie provided excellent entertainment with the sides sharing four goals, again after extra-time, and was duly settled in a penalty shoot-out, Wednesday progressing 3-1 with 'keeper Pressman yet again the hero, saving three penalties to earn a trip to Aston Villa. By the time the game was played, manager Shreeves had departed and it was Yorath at the helm for the trip to Villa Park. The Owls' remarkable run continued though as a first-half goal from Ekoku proved enough to knock out a second Premier League club and secure a quarter-final berth. The draw was kind to Wednesday as they were pitted against a fellow First Division outfit, this time Watford, at Hillsborough. The game would prove memorable for Hamshaw as he scored one of the best goals seen at the ground in modern times, collecting the ball just outside his own penalty area and running fully 70 yards before firing in off a post from the edge of the opposition penalty area. He would not have been in the side if Wednesday had not been hit by injuries and suspensions, but his goal broke the resolve of the visitors and Wednesday netted twice in the last two minutes to complete an eye-catching 4-0 success. Just short of 31,000 fans were inside Hillsborough for the first leg of the semi-final against Blackburn Rovers, but Rovers showed their Premier League class by securing a 2-0 half-time lead. However, roared on by a noisy home crowd, the Owls rallied in the second half and were applauded off at full-time, despite only having an Ekoku goal to show for their efforts. For the second leg, Wednesday was hit by an injury crisis in the goalkeeping department and Heald was drafted in at the last minute to make his debut in a cup semi-final. The Owls fought gallantly in the second leg but never really looked likely to close the aggregate gap, eventually exiting 6-3 over the two legs. The latter stages of the game also proved controversial as a black cordon of riot police marched into the ground and promptly stood in front of the 5,000 away fans, blocking the view of the pitch for hundreds and leading to flurry of complaint letters to Wednesday, Blackburn and the Lancashire Police in the days following the tie.

The rest of the naughties were a barren period for Wednesday as they progressed past the second round on only one occasion, comprehensively exiting 3-0 to Everton in September 2007. Before then, the Owls were beaten at home by Leicester City in the 2002/03 season before a 2-2 home draw with Hartlepool United ended in a 5-4 loss on penalties, current Brentford manager Smith missing the decisive penalty for Wednesday in the rebranded Carling Cup. The 2004/05 run commenced with a win over Walsall before academy coach Smith was in temporary charge, after the sacking of Sturrock, for the trip to Coventry City. The temporary boss gave a first-team debut to full-back Greenwood and after a minute's silence for Brian Clough, who had passed away that week, Wednesday fought well but could not prevent the almost standard loss at Highfield Road, the hosts scoring the only goal. The Owls were drawn at basement club Stockport County in the first round of the 2005/06 campaign and were given a real fright, the hosts twice levelling the tie before a Proudlock brace in extra-time squeezed his side through. In the second round visitors West Ham United were ahead inside seventy-five seconds and the tie looked dead and buried when they went 3-0 ahead after sixty-three minutes. However, Wednesday staged a quite remarkable fight back and a crazy four-minute period saw them reduce the arrears to a single goal before Graham's close-range shot crashed against the crossbar! A frenzied end saw Lee Peacock denied by Hammers 'keeper Hislop before the visitors broke away to kill the game with a fourth goal. The home tie with Wrexham, which the visitors won 4-1, will go down as one of the club's worst ever results in the competition, but two players will forever remember that August evening as both David McClements and Matt Bowman came off the substitute's bench to register their only senior appearances for the club. The aforementioned run to the third round in 2007/08 commenced with a 3-1 local derby win at Millmoor before revenge was secured over Hartlepool United with substitute Folly netting a dramatic winning goal in the last minute of extra-time. Wednesday were drawn with Rotherham United for the fourth time in the League Cup in the following season, and Wednesday fans were celebrating a place in the next round when their side led 2-1 going into the final minute of extra-time. However, our neighbours have a tremendous record in recent years at S6 and they conjured up a last-gasp leveller before Esajas missed the decisive penalty as the Millers progressed 5-3 on penalties. The August 2009 3-0 home success against Rochdale was remembered for an incredible goal from Esajas, which saw the Dutchman volley in, from fully 30 yards, a long punt upfield from Wednesday 'keeper Grant. The second-round tie at Port Vale was equally forgettable as the Owls were reduced to ten men in the first half – Francis Jeffers seeing the red mist descend and being red-carded for headbutting a Vale player – and his depleted side slid out 2-0.

2010s

The 2010s did not bring much joy until the club's terrific run to the last eight in 2015/16, with a home game against Bury starting the story. Wednesday won 1-0 but were embarrassed in the next round, losing 4-2 at Scunthorpe United. The integrity of the competition was certainly badly hit in the following season when it was decided to televise the club's home game against Championship Blackpool, moving the fixture to a Thursday night in the process. Just over 5,000 attended the tie with both managers effectively fielding reserve teams, Wednesday handing debuts to kids Nyoni and Tumility plus new signing Uchechi. What followed was a turgid 0-0 with the only excitement coming after 120 minutes when the Owls progressed 4-2 on penalties, which did little for the credibility of the tournament. The draw sent Wednesday back to Ewood Park and any latecomers would have missed most of the goals as Premier League Rovers were three ahead after seven minutes, a real old-fashioned thrashing looking likely. Luckily for the Owls, the hosts took the foot off the proverbial pedal and Morrison pulled a goal back to leave the final score somewhat respectable. The 2012/13 season saw the League Cup revert back to the days of the late 1970s/early 1980s with the first-round games being played before the league season commenced, Wednesday travelling to Oldham Athletic. Wednesday handed debuts to four players, including Kirkland and Maguire, but was rocking against the League One hosts, losing 2-0 after twenty-six minutes. The Owls were handed a lifeline on the brink of half-time but another debut boy, Slovenian Pecnik, proceeded to fire the penalty high over the bar. Whatever was said at half-time, though, had the desired effect as Wednesday stormed back, scoring four without reply. A home tie with Premier League Fulham was next on the agenda and an early Madine penalty was enough to beat the Londoners, although there was an audible groan from the travelling Wednesdayites when the draw sent their team to Southampton in the third round. A hardcore of 698 fans made the long midweek trip to the south coast but they had little to cheer, Wednesday slipping out without a whimper to a Rodriguez brace. The 2013/14 season saw Wednesday and Rotherham United drawn together yet again, for the fifth time, with the away draw meaning Wednesday visited the Millers' new New York Stadium for the first time. It proved a sobering experience for the travelling Owls fans as a poor display, in which Portuguese left-back Floro made his debut, ended in a 2-1 defeat.

The 2014/15 season will probably be remembered for two visits to the home of champions Manchester City, in both domestic cups, the third-round tie in the League Cup seeing a bizarre 7-0 beating, despite going into the half-time break goalless. The route to that Etihad thrashing started with a 3-0 home win over Notts County before two much-changed Burnley and Wednesday sides clashed at Turf Moor in the second round. In front of less than 5,000 (over a thousand travelling from Sheffield) a late penalty from Nuhiu won the tie and gave the club a Premier League scalp and a lucrative, if somewhat sobering, trip to the blue side of Manchester. In the following season the Owls made big headlines in the tournament as they knocked out two Premier League sides in that memorable run to the quarter-finals. The run started with a comfortable 4-1 success over Mansfield Town before a trip to

Newcastle United was secured with a win over Oxford United. Both teams made several changes for the St James' Park clash but it was the near 5,000-strong travelling support who were celebrating at the final whistle, a late McGugan goal enough to win the tie. Owls boss Carvalhal commented, 'We know we beat a very good team with a very good coach in their stadium, so of course we are very happy about that. We picked these players to show a different face in relation to the last three matches. We tried to play more compact, block all the ways for Newcastle and with four very quick attackers. I am very happy with the players. They were perfect in the strategy that we brought to this match.' The draw finally gave Wednesday fans a tie they craved – one of England's biggest clubs, Arsenal, at Hillsborough. Over 35,000 packed into the ground to welcome the Gunners and the evening proved one of Wednesday's best in fifty years of competing in the tournament, a terrific display seeing a much-changed Arsenal side beaten 3-0. The opening goal was a great team effort involving Bannan, Pudil and scorer Wallace and goals from Joao and Hutchinson wrapped up the win and really announced that Wednesday were on their way back. It was left to Carlos to again sum up the night: 'I am very happy about the players and for the club, it is an important victory for the club. It was a full stadium, with a new generation of fans. We deserved what we got.' The fifth-round draw sent the Owls to Stoke City but it proved a bridge too far as Wednesday, disrupted by an injury to Lees, exited 2-0. The story of the club's fifty-years in the League Cup ended on an August 2016 evening at League Two club Cambridge United – Wednesday somehow managing to face United as, bizarrely, both clubs were in the northern half of the draw. The Owls made fully ten changes from the opening weekend league win over Aston Villa but the shadow side greatly impressed and a Joao goal looked to have taken the club through before the hosts scored a last-minute leveller. Wednesday, including debutants O'Grady, Buckley, Murphy and Hirst, then looked to be heading for a penalty shoot-out, but United scored again in the last minute of extra-time to make the journey home seem that much further.

Chapter 7

European Days

'Before the kick off, the noise was even better than Wembley. It was unbelievable. The fans have been fantastic. They have also turned out in force for the three home games we have had in a week and we must thank them for that. It's just a shame we weren't able to get the right result for them this time. Being in Europe has been a good experience for us. It's given us a taste for more and made us want to be in there again next season.'

Nigel Pearson, post-Kaiserslautern, November 1992

After being introduced in 1955, the European Cup was a huge success with the outstanding Real Madrid team of the era winning the first five tournaments. Also founded in the same year was the International Industries Fairs Inter Cities Cup (better known as the Inter-City Fairs Cup or just the Fairs Cup), which evolved from friendly games played between cities who had staged trade fairs. In the early years it was competed for by city teams, such as Birmingham, Lausanne and Vienna. As the games were scheduled to coincide with trade fairs, it took three years for the competition to reach a conclusion with the city of Barcelona (effectively FC Barcelona) eventually beating a London XI 8-2 on aggregate. The brainchild of Swiss Pools promoter Ernst Thommen, Italian Ottorino Barassi and FA General Secretary Stanley Rous, the second tournament was completed in just two years with Barcelona beating club side Birmingham City. The competition became a seasonal tournament in the 1960/61 campaign and in the summer of 1961 the rules were altered to allow three teams to enter from each country, although still on an invitation-only basis. The tournament was not run by UEFA and only came under their banner in 1971 when the competition was rebranded as the UEFA Cup. It was at this point that Sheffield Wednesday received an invitation to compete, the club experiencing their first taste of competitive European football, joining teams from fourteen other countries. That first step into European football in the early 1960s was very much a stride into the unknown as there was none of today's wall-to-wall TV coverage, and very little was known of Wednesday's first opponents, French side Olympique Lyonnais. The competition was split into four groups with the winner progressing to the semi-finals, but the games were not played on a 'round robin' basis but instead in a knockout format, which meant defeat in the first two-legged encounter ended participation in the competition. The Owls were placed in a seven-team section with holders AS Roma handed a bye.

The club's first competitive game in Europe duly took place at the Municipal Stadium, Lyon, in September 1961 and the first forty-five minutes proved a shock as the hosts showed a high skill level to race into a 3-0 interval lead, civil servant Eugene Njo-Lea – a 40 million francs signing from St Etienne – grabbing two and Angel Rambert opening the scoring. The action was watched by a crowd of around 5,000 and the Owls were glad of the interval after being somewhat off the pace of the game. What was said by Buckingham certainly had the desired effect and Wednesday were quickly back in the tie, Young seeing his header hit the crossbar and rebound for the attacker to fire home. A minute later, Young saw an effort hit the woodwork again and the Owls made it 3-2 after sixty-three minutes when Ellis headed home. The intensity of the game had certainly increased and several late tackles and 'continental' body checks by the hosts went unpunished by the Swiss referee, although the Owls were not 'shrinking violets' as they retaliated in kind. After conceding two goals the hosts switched to a tight 4-4-2 formation and chances somewhat dried up for Wednesday, although they were still the dominant side – at times Springett was the only player in the Owls half. However, there was still a 'sting in the tail' for Wednesday as in the final minute Lyon counter-attacked and Nestor Combin scored from an acute angle to suddenly put a different complexion on the night's proceedings, Buckingham commenting at full-time that 'It was drummed into us that it never pays to take the opposition cheaply. We must always go all out for 90 minutes, not play just half the time.' That late goal meant the Owls needed a positive start in the return leg but they instead had a calamitous beginning as right-winger Robert Salen nipped in to extend the visitors' lead. The goal silenced the excellent crowd of 30,303, watching the first ever French side to visit Hillsborough, but within three minutes Wednesday received a slice of luck as a Fantham flick header, from Megson's free-kick, caught Lyon 'keeper Hughes out of position and dropped over his head into the goal. From that point onwards, Wednesday were a different side and produced a typical display of cup tie football, showing power, skill, guts and a physical presence. By the twenty-minute mark it was 3-1 (Griffin and a McAnearney penalty) and despite being on top throughout, the tie overall was still level as the game entered its final fifteen minutes, with tension starting to show on both sides. There would be a few more twists yet though as Wednesday nudged ahead after seventy-eight minutes when Man of the Match Dobson scored. Within a minute the tie was back to all square, the ball cannoning off several Owls defenders before Jean Djorkaeff netted, only for Fantham to head home again with five minutes remaining. The Owls' fifth goal was hotly disputed by the visitors and the ball was sat in the back of their net for several minutes as they remonstrated with the Scottish referee. When a new ball was procured the game was played to its conclusion and left the Wednesday fans with a taste for more European action after a thrilling victory. Wednesday's reward was a mouth-watering tie with holders AS Roma.

Roma provided a completely different test to Lyon with the powerful Italians using the defensive Catenaccio system, allied to several top-quality players and a well-known propensity to be highly physical in the tackle. The Owls' fans appetitive for European football was certainly shown in the opening leg as a bumper 42,589 crowd watched the proceedings. The first period would be a story of Owls domination, winger Finney a persistent thorn in the visitors' crown, and missed a hatful of chances in the opening exchanges in addition to a fine goal from Fantham after six minutes. Wednesday scored twice more in that first period with centre forward Young netting after thirty-two and thirty-five minutes, the latter goal a brilliant exhibition of one-touch play, which had the dazed Italians chasing shadows. Unfortunately the second half quickly degenerated into somewhat of a 'kicking match' as the Italians proved all the stereotypes to be correct as they committed foul after foul with Wednesday receiving little protection from the Belgium referee, Mr Blavier. In an era when bookings were a rarity, it perhaps showed the ferocity of Roma's onslaught that Argentinian-born forward Lojacono was sent from the field after sixty-five minutes after a particularly unsavoury challenge on Kay. The Italians were lucky not to have more men sent off and they also conceded a fourth goal – Young completing his hat-trick after seventy-nine minutes – to virtually seal their own exit and Wednesday's progression to the quarter-finals. There was, however, still the small matter of the second leg to play, with Wednesday officials expecting a 'hot reception' both on and off the pitch. The build-up to the return game was dominated by Roma's interest in Owls winger Craig but the issue was put to one side on the night with Wednesday's vowed intention to grab an early goal – to completely kill the tie off – almost working after five minutes. In the end the game became somewhat of a 'dead rubber' with Roma not playing with the intensity of the first leg and the Owls quite happy to soak up pressure and break on the Romans. The game did have a late goal – Swan scoring in his own net after eighty minutes – but the severe and noisy barracking the home fans gave their side at full-time, as they trooped off the pitch, perfectly summed up how comfortably the Owls progressed, setting up a glamour tie with Spanish giants Barcelona. Incidentally, after the tie in Rome the home team's manager, Mr Gianni, cooled his club's interest in Craig, commenting that they found him 'rather slow'.

It would be over two months – on 28 February 1962 – before the Catalans rolled into town and anticipation was almost at fever pitch as the Spanish side was packed with a multitude of internationals from the likes of Spain, Uruguay and Brazil, many arriving for huge fees. The local press dubbed them the 'red millionaires' as it emerged their debts could be as high as £1 million (a colossal amount in those days), although that situation was tempered somewhat by the valuation of their famous Nou Camp Stadium and their star-studded side, worth around double their alleged liabilities. A Spanish club had never played at Hillsborough with the added mix of being a competitive fixture leading to Owls officials hoping for a 60,000 full house. Unfortunately the good old British weather then intervened and Sheffield was covered with 2 inches of snow, putting the tie in jeopardy and forcing the visitors to train indoors at a Sheffield University gym. There was no further snowfall but the icy conditions decimated the anticipated attendance, which totalled just 28,956. However, those that did attend were treated to one of the greatest games seen at Hillsborough as the outstanding passing skills and movement of Barcelona were pitted against the British qualities of determination, work rate and sheer enthusiasm. It was the visitors who struck first, Villaverde firing past Springett after fifteen minutes, but Wednesday, who were showing Barça far too much respect in the early stages, levelled after twenty-eight minutes thanks to Fantham's classic diving header from a pinpoint Young cross. From that point onwards the tie was end to end, the Catalans retaking the lead after thirty-five minutes of play with Brazilian Evariste de Macedo brilliantly chipping Springett from 20 yards. Wednesday rallied again though and the game was all square at the interval as Finney drilled home a left-footed equaliser. There was no chance of the second period living up to the action-packed opening half and the contest became more physical with the evocatively named visiting player Julius Cesar Benitez lucky not to be sent off early in the second half after a dreadful tackle on Finney, the German referee only booking the offender. After fifty minutes the Owls went ahead after a great run from Hardy set up Fantham, who made no mistake, and the remainder of the game saw the home eleven on the front foot but unable to grab a fourth goal, instead taking a slender lead to Spain. There is no doubt that Wednesday faced a huge task in the second leg with a crowd of 75,000 packed into their hugely impressive home ground. Realistically the Owls needed to score an early goal but they were immediately under pressure and the superior passing of the home side led to an early goal, Evaristo de Macedo scoring after eleven minutes. It was 2-0 after thirty-four minutes (Hungarian Sandor Kocsis) and the remainder of the tie saw Wednesday throw everything at their hosts without creating any significant chances, although some strange decisions from the Swiss referee did them no favours. There was no further scoring and in the end Barcelona, backed by a fanatical home crowd, deserved to progress, but it proved a glorious end for the Owls in their first ever foray into European football.

The Owls' run to the last eight of the Fairs Cup ensured they received an invitation from the organising committee for the following season and Wednesday looked forward to another European campaign. However, unwelcome interference by the English Football Association immediately put Wednesday's participation in doubt as they effectively banned the Owls from competing, nominating Everton, Burnley and Sheffield United even though the cup committee had invited Wednesday, Birmingham City and Everton. At the time the FA and their continental counterparts did not see 'eye to eye' but the FA's stance was widely criticised in the UK as they dug their heels in and refused to compromise. The fact that more English teams had been invited than any other country did not seem to resonate with the governing body and while all parties were at loggerheads, the provisional draw paired Wednesday with German club Victoria Cologne. All of the clubs involved were furious at the FA's stance but at a Football League committee meeting held in August 1962, the ban was confirmed with only Everton allowed to participate. Wednesday immediately called an emergency board meeting and subsequently appealed, without success, to both the Football League and the FA. Sadly, Wednesday could only watch from the sidelines as the tournament kicked off with both club and supporters denied the chance to experience more top-class European football, in addition to the not inconsiderable revenue stream.

After the controversy in the summer of 1962, it was perhaps no surprise when the FA allowed Wednesday to compete in the 1963/64 season after the Fairs Cup committee handed out another invitation. The first-round draw paired Wednesday with Dutch side DOS Utrecht with the first leg in the Netherlands. Wednesday had met Dutch sides on numerous occasions in friendly fixtures but it was another trip into the unknown as far as competitive football was concerned. DOS translated to 'strength through fitness', but the visitors showed they had learnt greatly from their experience of two seasons previously and coasted to a comfortable 4-1 win, effectively clinching a place in the next round. Wednesday visited just five weeks after city neighbours United had played in a preseason game and a healthy crowd of 15,000 attended the fixture to see if their side could upset the favourites from the Steel City. In fairness, the Dutch fans were treated to a highly professional display full of endeavour and aggressive football, with goals from Holliday (five mins), Layne (twenty mins), Quinn (fifty mins) and a sixty-seventh-minute own goal from home defender Mijnais ensuring a comfortable evening for Wednesday. A consolation goal from Jackie Westphaal did little to dampen spirits among the Owls ranks as it was very much a case of 'job done'. Twenty days later came the return in Sheffield with Wednesday fresh from an excellent 3-0 win over West Ham United on the previous Saturday. After the game the visitors' coach, Austrian Willy Kment, revealed that on the plane to England he'd discussed that DOS needed a quick goal but it was Wednesday who scored first, inside ten minutes, when Layne fired home after an impudent back-heel from Dobson. It would be a night to remember for Layne for good and bad reasons, as he completed a hat-trick in the second half, netting after thirty-three and fifty-seven minutes, the third coming from the penalty spot. His night ended in agony though with twenty minutes remaining after a firm challenge from Rooders resulted in a bad fall and a dislocated shoulder, the centre forward being stretchered from the field. A crowd of 20,643 watched the action with Dobson also netting as the Owls repeated the score in Utrecht, completing an 8-2 aggregate win and safe passage.

Unfortunately, Layne had not recovered from his injury for the second-round tie against German part-timers Cologne and the Owls were also short of Fantham, who was recovering from a cartilage operation. Pearson and Derek Wilkinson filled in for the duo for the first leg in Western Germany and it looked like they'd been sorely missed as a tremendous display from the hosts resulted in a 3-0 half-time lead, thanks to goals from Christian Muller, Heinz Hornig and a Hans Sturm spot kick. The many Wednesday fans in the crowd – several with blue and white banners – could only watch on as the hosts totally dominated the game from kick-off until eighty minutes was on the clock. It was then that a remarkable transformation took place as, after being overwhelmed, the Owls suddenly rallied and after eighty-three minutes, Pearson wriggled his way through the German defence to reduce the arrears. Suddenly, the hosts were rocked and two minutes later it was 3-2 as Pearson scored again, his corner going straight in. Incredibly it then needed a remarkable save from Schumacher, from McAnearney, to stop Wednesday levelling but it had still been a remarkable recovery and gave real hope for the return match. The task for the Owls was still, however, a difficult one as Cologne arrived as leaders of the newly formed German Super League (later rebranded as the Bundesliga) and boasted a staggering eight German internationals in their side, plus the current German footballer of the year – Captain Hans Schafer. Just over 36,000 attended the second leg and the overwhelming majority were celebrating after seventeen minutes when Layne, back from injury, brilliantly back-headed Young's cross to level the tie on aggregate. However, no matter how hard Wednesday pressed they could not force a second goal and as the match progressed it was the visitors who grew in confidence, levelling through Karl-Heinz Thielen fourteen minutes into the second half, the right-winger sprinting onto a long ball and outpacing Swan to fire home. Wednesday visibly wilted after that leveller and the Germans dominated the rest of the game, scoring again through Wolfgang Overath – one of only four players to have finished first, second and third in World Cup finals – after sixty-five minutes. The game was up for the Owls and there was no further scoring as Cologne advanced, reaching the semi-finals before being knocked out by Valencia.

It would be almost thirty years before Wednesday were back in Europe, a third-place finish in 1992 being sufficient to see the Owls return, this time in the UEFA Cup. Wednesday were effectively handed a bye in the first round after they were paired with Luxembourg club Spora, ranked sixty-third of the sixty-four competing teams, in the competition draw in Geneva, Wednesday being given a home tie first. The Owls' opponents were the archetypal side of part-timers, including a banker, cook, plumber, waiter, publicity manager and decorator, while they had to catch an afternoon flight to Sheffield as they waited for their most experienced player – goalkeeper Patrick Felten – to finish his job as a teacher, on the first day of the Luxembourg school year. Surprisingly, considering that Spora was the second most successful club in their country with fourteen league titles, their side did not contain any full internationals. It was a mammoth task for the minnows and watched by a crowd of 19,792 (the ground capacity being slashed by UEFA to around 28,000) they quickly fell behind to Waddle's first goal for Wednesday. However, you could hear a pin drop two minutes later when an error from Shirtliff allowed Joao Augusto da Cruz to equalise and send the visitors into wild celebrations. It would, however, be the only positive they would take from the evening as in a totally one-sided contest the Owls rattled in another seven goals to complete an 8-1 win, one of the biggest margins of victory in the club's long history. Goals came from Anderson (two), Bart-Williams (two), Warhurst (two) and Worthington, although the game did not provide a happy memory for Warhurst as he was lucky to even survive the game after a dramatic incident after netting his second goal after seventy-four minutes. After bravely heading in a Bart-Williams cross he was accidentally punched by visiting 'keeper Felten and collapsed to the turf. It quickly became apparent that the situation was dire as the asthmatic and unconscious Warhurst turned blue and went into spasm after 'swallowing his tongue'. It was only the skills of club physio Alan Smith that saved his life, as he managed to free Warhurst's airways and was quickly rushed off the pitch and direct to hospital. Thankfully a brain scan confirmed there was no lasting damage, Warhurst later commenting that he remembered challenging for the ball but nothing else until he woke up in a hospital bed. Incredibly the stricken player actually returned to the Wednesday side for the return game and watched by around 2,000 travelling Owls fans, actually headed in his side's second goal after thirty-four minutes. The journey to the principality was not an easy one for Wednesday fans as mainland Europe was still fearful of English fans' reputation for crowd disorder and many, many hours were spent on coaches as the authorities moved them from place to place. The official coaches set off from the Middlewood Training Ground at 1.30 a.m. on game day and reached Luxembourg via the ferry from Dover and drives through northern France and Belgium. Sadly, not many fans got the chance to soak up the pre-match atmosphere as the twenty-six coaches (the twenty-seventh having broken down at the Belgium border!) were held back by the Belgium constabulary, 30 miles from the Stade Municipale, only arriving at the ground just before kick-off. The level of support that Wednesday took no doubt surprised the hosts and the somewhat frosty reception did start to thaw after the locals realised that their fear was unfounded.

Manager Francis sent a mixed side to Luxembourg and it was the livewire attacker Watson who put the Owls ahead after the home 'keeper fumbled a corner. As they did at Hillsborough, the home team did equalise quickly, the scorer at Hillsborough, Cruz, finding the net again. The entire game was played almost exclusively in Spora's half – Francis commenting that he was disappointed that Spora 'played with seven at the back' – and Wednesday could not have wished for a gentler reintroduction to European football than the eventual 10-2 aggregate victory.

The second-round draw handed Wednesday a far tougher task as Bundesliga club Kaiserslautern stood in the way of progression. The first leg in Germany proved a memorable and highly controversial evening as French referee Joel Quiniou took centre stage and made a number of dumbfounding decisions that left the Owls camp furious. The tone for the game was set in just the second minute when Nigel Pearson accidentally stumbled into an opponent and received a yellow card! The night did not go sour immediately for Wednesday though as after just five minutes a great cross from Waddle saw Hirst head home to briefly silence the amazingly noisy home Kop. Within a minute the referee made his first error as a great tackle on home attacker Witcczek by Anderson, just outside the area, was incredibly interpreted as a penalty by the referee, who was behind play and seemingly awarded a free-kick on the edge of the penalty box. However, despite a divot in the turf revealing where the tackle was made, he changed his mind and Funkel fired home. The next howler from the official came just before half-time and effectively handed the tie to the home side as Hirst and home defender Haber tangled in the area and the home player went to the floor like the proverbial 'ton of bricks'. The referee was totally unsighted but he seemed to give in to the intimidating atmosphere and rushed over to brandish a red card. Owls' players had to be restrained, such was their anger, and two early goals in the second half, from Marin and Witeczek, left Wednesday staring at a heavy defeat. Thankfully no further damage was done and the return game looked set to be a feisty affair, judging by the absences of handshakes at the final whistle. The second leg took place fifteen days later and Wednesday – missing the suspended Hirst and injured Bright – knew they needed an early goal to have any chance of reaching the third round. A sellout 27,597 crowd packed into Hillsborough and, allied with a rousing rendition of the 'Dambusters Theme', they went some way to replicating the incredible atmosphere in the Fritz Walter Stadium. Thankfully the referee from the first leg had been replaced by Hungarian Sandor Puhl and with the crowd fully behind them, Wednesday went at the Germans and after several chances went ahead after twenty-seven minutes through Wilson. Chances came and went to extend that lead but Hillsborough fell silent when the visitors broke away and Witecez drove home an equaliser after sixty-two minutes. All was not lost though as within three minutes a sublime free-kick from John Sheridan re-established Wednesday's advantage. The Owls continued to push but it was to no avail and when Zeyer levelled again, after seventy-six minutes, fans knew that the Owls' European campaign was coming to an end. The tie ended 2-2 with Wilson commenting that 'It was always going to be difficult. A lot of things went on in Europe with the diving and antics of the Germans but now they have proved what a good side they are. We did well to get the goals we wanted but they were very quick and very difficult to break down.'

After three campaigns in European football, the club's fourth experience could not have been more opposite to those great nights against the likes of Barcelona, Roma and Kaiserslautern. The club's campaign in the 1995/96 Intertoto Cup went all the way back to 1961 and three men: Malmo FF chairman Eric Persson, Ernst Thommen (co-founder of the Fairs Cup) and Austrian coach Karl Rappan, who founded the International Football Cup – dubbed the 'cup for the cupless'. The competition took place in the summer months and was heavily promoted by Swiss newspaper *Sport*, gaining its name from the German word for football pool, *Toto*. Initially, UEFA did not give their support to the competition, finding its direct links to betting somewhat tasteless, but they did eventually give permission for the tournament to go ahead, although they had no direct influence. The first winners were Ajax and the competition was played for mainly by Central European and Scandinavian teams, until UEFA had a change of heart in 1995 and officially took the tournament under their administrational wing. The format was changed so that the two finalists won a place in that season's UEFA Cup, with all continental associations required to enter three teams. In England, there was much scepticism about the relaunched cup and initially all Premier League sides rejected the offer of competing. However, subsequent pressure from UEFA, which included a possible ban on English clubs in European competition, forced the FA's hand and three clubs, Wednesday, Tottenham Hotspur and Wimbledon, agreed to enter. Confirmation of competing in the tournament immediately created several headaches for the Owls as firstly the opening game was scheduled before the players reported back for preseason training and secondly the Hillsborough pitch had been dug up and would not be ready until August 1995. To complicate matters even further, the Owls did not officially have a team manager, being embroiled in a legal battle with Luton Town over David Pleat. Other than having no players, manager or ground, Wednesday were ideally placed to make a major impact on the competition!

The tournament format saw five teams in twelve groups, with each side playing each other once, two home and two away. The 1995/96 competition included the return of Yugoslavian teams to European football after the UN embargo ended, while Welsh, Scottish and Irish club also entered. Wednesday were placed in Group 1 with the opening game scheduled for Saturday 24 June 1995 against Swiss club Basel. With most of the club's senior players on holiday, Wednesday had no choice but to quickly sign several players on a non-contract basis (with a £250 match fee), including the likes of ex-Bradford City goalkeeper Bowling, ex-Miller Brien and former Halifax Town defender German. A sprinkling of contracted men, such as Hyde and Stewart, and several youngsters completed the 'rag-tag' bunch that travelled to Switzerland under the guidance of youth coach Clive Baker. The short notice and sheer distances involved meant that Wednesday fans were conspicuous by their absence, only around a hundred making it to the St Jacob Stadium for their side's rather low-key re-entrance into European football. They faced a full-strength home side, containing three full internationals, but a spirited and tenacious display from the Owls meant they only lost by a solitary goal, scored by Rey after sixty-eight minutes. Coach Baker commented after the game that 'in terms of effort and attitude, our lads were a credit to themselves and the club. I couldn't have asked anymore from the lads. If we could have held out for another five minutes or so we would have probably got a draw. I have no complaints about the result though. It was a patchwork side but they performed magnificently'. It would be two weeks before Wednesday played the second match in the group and by this time Pleat was in charge of first-team affairs and Wednesday's first-team squad had all reported back, albeit just twenty-four hours earlier. Hillsborough was not available though, so Wednesday moved into Millmoor to host Polish visitors Gornik Zabrze. The atmosphere in the 5,592 crowd was more akin to a preseason friendly than a competitive game, with fans sporting their newly bought home shirts, which had been released on the morning of the fixture, and basking in the gloriously sunny weather. The fans were treated to an entertaining afternoon, Wednesday keeping possession for long spells of the game and taking the lead after twelve minutes when Gornik defender Krzetowski sliced the ball over his own 'keeper. A tremendous half-volley from Szemonski levelled matters but it was Wednesday who led at the break when Bright converted a Nolan cross. A goal from Waddle and a comical own goal from Owls goalie Woods completed the scoring, leaving Wednesday back in with a chance of getting through the group – only the group winners were guaranteed to qualify plus the four best runners-up. In reality the Owls needed to win at German side Karlsruhe a week later to have any chance of winning Group 1 and Wednesday had a third different management team in place for the trip, head coach Danny Bergara and chief scout Mick Mills looking after team matters. In sweltering heat, Wednesday more than matched their hosts at the Wildpark Stadium, situated in the middle of woodland. Cheered on by around 150 fans in one corner of the stadium, the Owls started brightly only to be hit by a stunning goal after just five minutes when future West Ham United manager Bilic fired into Woods' top left-hand corner from 30 yards. Around 13,000 watched the tie and it would be fair to say that the home side probably deserved the win, but they were denied with nine minutes left when a great cross from Waddle was expertly guided into the 'keeper's bottom-right corner from 6 yards out by Bright. Wednesday duly hung on for a vital point but knew nothing less than a win in the last game would keep feint hopes of progression alive. On another sunny afternoon in Rotherham, Wednesday were wearing their new 'Ajax-style' home kit and gave a debut to new signing Pembridge for the visit of Danish side AGF Aarhus (short for Aarhus Gymnastikforening). A crowd of 6,990 witnessed the action and saw a much more powerful display from the home side than in the previous home fixture as goals from Mark Bright (two) and a wonderful strike from Dan Petrescu sealed a 3-1 win. It was a thoroughly professional display from Wednesday, delighting new boss Pleat, who observed that 'we took a bit of a kicking in the second half'. The only real black mark on the day was the late red card for Bright for retaliation after being stamped on by ex-Norwich City player Mortensen. Thankfully the red card only counted in European competition and Pleat joked that 'He'll be under a suspended fine. Next time he is sent off in a European competition he'll pay double.' Unfortunately for the Owls, Bright did not get the chance to play further in the competition as, despite the win, Wednesday finished runners-up in their group and were only ranked eleventh of the twelve second-placed teams, therefore bowing out after a totally different European tour than previously experienced.

Appearances:
Finney 10, Megson 10, R. Springett 10, Swan 10, Young 8, Dobson 7, Hyde 7, Johnson 7, T. McAnearney 7, Fantham 6, Kay 6, Woods 6, Waddle 5+1, Holliday 5, Craig 4, Harkes 4, Warhurst 4, D. Wilkinson 4, Palmer 3+1, Wilson 3+1, Anderson 3, Atherton 3, Bright 3, Hardy 3, Hill 3, Hirst 3,Layne 3, Nolan 3, N. Pearson 3, Walker 3, Watts 3, Worthington 3, Sinton 2+1, Watson 2+1, Briscoe 2+1, M. Williams 2+1, Ellis 2, M. Pearson 2, Quinn 2, Sheridan 2, Bart-Williams 1+2, Whittingham 1+2, Barker 1+1, Jemson 1+1, Nilsson 1+1, Bowling 1, Brien 1, Francis 1, German 1, Griffin 1, Holmes 1, Pearce 1, J. Pearson 1, Pembridge 1, Petrescu 1, Poric 1, Pressman 1, Shirtliff 1, Stewart 1, A. Williams 1, Bailey 0+1, Faulkner 0+1, (198)

Goals:
Fantham 5, Layne 5, Bright 4, Young 4, Warhurst 3, Anderson 2, Bart-Williams 2, Dobson 2, M. Pearson 2, Waddle 2, Ellis 1, Finney 1, Griffin 1, Hirst 1, T. McAnearney 1,Petrescu 1, Quinn 1, Sheridan 1, Watson 1, Wilson 1, Worthington 1, Own goals 3 (45)

Chapter 8

The Boss

'If Wednesday were doing well then supporters would want to speak to me about *our* team but if they were doing badly then they wanted to discuss *my* team.'

Bob Brown

Although not a team manager or head coach in the modern sense of the terms, Arthur Joshua Dickinson was without doubt the main figure behind team selection and the overall management of Wednesday FC from the late nineteenth century until 1920. While many years later Eric Taylor was handed the moniker of 'Mr Sheffield Wednesday', it would perhaps be fair to say that Dickinson could have been called 'Mr Wednesday' as he made a similarly huge impact on the club, who he served unpaid for virtually all of his life. Born in Sheffield late in 1851, Arthur was one of six children, although he was the only son born to cattle trader father John and mother Sarah. It's believed that Dickinson first joined the club around 1876 and was increasingly influential before being officially appointed as financial secretary in 1887, playing a significant role in the move to Olive Grove. The leasing of Wednesday's first permanent ground also coincided with Dickinson's appointment as honorary financial secretary, while in 1891 he was handed all secretarial duties. In the late nineteenth century the secretary had a wide remit of responsibilities, which in Dickinson's case included scouting trips across the Scottish border to source playing talent; in one such instance, in September 1891, he was forced to run from a mob of baying Dumbarton fans and forced to take refuge in a Glasgow hotel for two days to let the effects of two black eyes and a bloody nose and face recede.

He subsequently oversaw the club's election into the Football League (he was the only honorary secretary in the competition), two FA Cup wins and back-to-back league titles. It was said that during the Olive Grove years he would take home the match receipts and stuff them under his bed in readiness for the bank opening on a Monday morning. It would perhaps be surprising to learn that Dickinson fulfilled all of his various roles at the club on a purely part-time basis as he worked full-time running his Sheffield cutlery business. When Wednesday changed from an incorporated to a limited liability company in June 1899, the first share was bought by Dickinson and he was charged with the task of arranging for the purchase of land at Owlerton. Known as a man not prone to small talk, who took praise and criticism with equanimity, Dickinson also loved the country life and cycling, although his main passion in life was Wednesday as he remained a bachelor. Not only did Dickinson devote his free time to Wednesday but also served on several different other football-related bodies, including the FA Council, Football League Management Committee and International Selection Committee. Known to have an encyclopaedic knowledge of the rules of the game, Dickinson worked tirelessly through the First World War to ensure Wednesday remained in business. But after forty-four years of service he stepped down on 18 May 1920. Despite his resignation, Dickinson remained a familiar face around Hillsborough, representing the club on official business. He also continued to act as courier on home matchdays, taking the gate receipts to the bank. It was while on club duty – attending a Football Management Committee meeting in London – that the master administrator met his untimely death, collapsing and dying instantly after signing the register in the Euston Hotel on 4 November 1930. Aged seventy-nine, he left a remarkable legacy with his sterling service of over fifty years incomparable to any other figure in the club's history.

His departure led to the arrival of Wednesday's first 'official' secretary-manager, Robert (Bob) Brown, whose appointment was announced on 24 June 1920. Born in Hebburn in 1872, Brown was one of seven children sired by coal-mining father Thomas and his wife, Catherine. After successfully training as a cabinetmaker he married wife Mary and settled in his home town, with sons Thomas and Robert adding to the family ranks. It was in August 1905 that Brown first became connected to Wednesday after accepting the position of scout for his local region. It is believed he was working in a north-east shipyard at the time but after successfully recommending a string of fine players he moved his family to Sheffield after being appointed assistant secretary in 1908. He stayed in Sheffield for three years, gaining valuable experience under the watchful eye of Dickinson before moving to take over the role of secretary-manager at newly relegated Southern League Second Division side Portsmouth in 1911. He joined Pompey at a time of trouble – the club was threatened with liquidation until they decided to carry on at a specially convened meeting – but a series of highly successful signings by Brown resulted in the club being immediately promoted back. His time at Portsmouth was without doubt a resounding success as in the first season after the First World War he led them to the Championship of the

Southern League, becoming one of the founder members of the Football League Third Division. However, Brown would not lead Portsmouth in the Football League as a disagreement with the board of directors on future policy resulted in his resignation and a move to take over at fellow league new boys Gillingham.

Within weeks though Brown would return to Hillsborough and forge a reputation as a tough disciplinarian but a man who had the total respect of his players. He found a club on its knees after a terrible 1919/20 season and it would take several seasons before he could rebuild the team sufficiently to mount a promotion push. The transformation was not without its problems but Wednesday won the Second Division in 1926 and consolidated in the higher grade. Unfortunately it looked like the Owls were coming straight back down in 1927/28 but after performing the 'great escape', Wednesday won the title. A year later the title was retained, amassing record points, and only some bizarre refereeing decisions denied them a place in the 1930 FA Cup final and a chance to become the first team to complete the double in the twentieth century – Brown later commented that this was his greatest regret. For the next three seasons, Wednesday remained a major force and many of his signings would go on to help the club lift the FA Cup in 1935. However, Brown did not live to see the triumph as in the summer of 1933 his wife, who had still not recovered from a major operation years earlier, suffered a seizure while on holiday and passed away. It left Brown a broken man and he never recovered from the loss, being taken ill at a reserve-team game in September 1933 and subsequently diagnosed with high blood pressure. With his overall health deteriorating, he duly tendered his resignation on 21 September 1933 to end the reign of one of Wednesday's greatest ever managers, responsible for assembling arguably the club's greatest ever side. After leaving, he remained in Sheffield, living on Wadsley Lane, and did recover some of his health, acting as a scout for several clubs. It was while fulfilling this role for Chelsea that Brown collapsed on the platform at Leeds station on 7 March 1935, with what transpired as a cerebral haemorrhage, and was rushed to Leeds Royal Infirmary. Sadly, he only survived a few more hours and passed away in the early hours of the following day, leaving a legacy at Wednesday that should never be forgotten.

It was a hard act to follow for the club's next permanent boss, and new man William (Billy) Henry Walker certainly enjoyed a long honeymoon period, after taking over the reins from caretaker-manager Joe McClelland, before the tide turned against him. Born in Wednesbury on 29 October 1897, Walker first started playing football for his school side, and was capped at schoolboy level by his country despite almost dying from consumption while still a teenager. After leaving school Walker, whose father, George, played for Wolves, started work at an engineering company and played for various local junior sides. He was eventually spotted by scouts of Aston Villa and signed as a part-time professional in March 1915. The First World War meant he could not turn fully professional for over four years but duly stepped up to full-time status in May 1919. It would be the start of a truly glorious career, which saw the inside forward score twice on his debut and go on to amass 244 goals in 531 games – the goals tally still stands today as a record for the club. He ended his first season with an FA Cup winners' medal and would also appear in the 1924 FA Cup final before becoming the first England player to score in an international at the newly opened Empire Stadium (Wembley). He would win a total of eighteen senior caps, scoring nine times. He achieved the rare feat of scoring a hat-trick of penalties in a league game – against Bradford City in November 1921 – and is considered by many to be the greatest ever Aston Villa player.

He was still a Villa player when he was appointed at Wednesday on 8 December 1933, immediately hanging up his boots. There was much surprise among supporters at his appointment, particularly as he had no managerial experience, but he 'hit the ground running' as a Wednesday side, which had slipped to nineteenth position during the managerial hiatus, won three games in succession while a twelve-game unbeaten run lifted them into mid-table. His first full season in charge proved memorable as his charges finished third and Wednesday lifted the FA Cup. Unfortunately for Walker, and Wednesday, the cup success proved a real high point as from that point forward the team struggled to compete, only just avoiding relegation in 1936. Fans pointed to the fact that Walker had sold several stalwarts – such as Blenkinsop and Ball – but had not replaced them with men of sufficient quality and this certainly seemed a reasonable hypothesis as a year later Wednesday were relegated. Sadly, this did not lead to happier times and after a heavy loss at Barnsley, which sent Wednesday to the foot of the table, he faced angry shareholders and subsequently resigned on 7 November 1937. After a few weeks out of the game he was appointed secretary-manager of ambitious club Chelmsford City on 24 January 1938, who wanted his experience to help them move from amateur to semi-professional status and gain admission into the Southern League. This was achieved but Walker stayed for only a few months before tendering his resignation in October 1938. In March 1939 he was back in the 'hot seat' and would remain manager of Nottingham Forest until June 1960. During the war years, he actually pulled on his boots again – scoring in a December 1939 game against Stockport County at the age of forty-two and also playing as a goalkeeper – and took Forest to the 1951 Southern section title. Promotion to the top division followed in 1957 and Forest would also win the FA Cup in 1959. He was known for his quietly effective and unassuming managerial style – in addition to his ever-present pipe – and after vacating the manager's chair, remained on Forest's committee until suffering a stroke in October 1963. He never fully recovered and passed away in Nottingham on 28 November 1964. His legacy to the game was perhaps best summed up by the then FA chairman, Dennis Follows, who commented that 'he represented all that was best in the game'. From an Owls point of view his time in charge was somewhat of a rollercoaster but he remains, over eighty years later, the last manager to win the FA Cup.

The link with Aston Villa continued with the club's next managerial appointment when former boss James (Jimmy) McMullan filled the Hillsborough vacancy on 3 January 1938. Born in the Scottish village of Dunipace on 26 March 1895, McMullan was one of the greatest players to be produced by Scotland, captaining the famous 'Wembley Wizards' side that beat England 5-1 in 1928 – before the game captain McMullan famously said to his players 'All I've got to say is go to your bed, put your head on your pillow and pray for rain.' Those prayers were answered and on a heavy pitch the diminutive Scots side took on the conditions like 'a duck to water' and totally overwhelmed England. Like the vast majority of his contemporaries, centre-half McMullan started his working life down his local coal mine, while also playing junior football with local side Denny Hibernian. A spell at Third Lanark followed before in November 1913 he signed for Partick Thistle, launching a professional career that would lead to sixteen caps. He went straight into the first eleven at Partick and was unlucky to miss the 1921 Scottish Cup final after being injured on international duty. A subsequent dispute with Partick led to a sensational move into English non-league football in the same year, after Maidstone United's chairman travelled north to secure McMullan as player-manager – he moved despite not even knowing where Maidstone was on the map of England! In his first season he led United to five different trophies, although in February 1922 it was reported that his family were summoned from Scotland as McMullan was dangerously ill. Thankfully he pulled through and made more headlines when he persuaded former Scotland international James White to join the Kent club – he later signed three more Scottish League players to continue the drain of playing talent. His side retained the Kent Senior Cup but it was obvious that McMullan's career was suffering in non-league football and he resigned for Partick Thistle. The second spell at the Glasgow club enhanced his reputation further and he was transferred to Manchester City in February 1926. It was at the Maine Road club that he flourished in a new inside forward role, although his first few weeks saw his new side relegated from the top flight and suffer defeat in the FA Cup final. By the end of the year though McMullan asked to be placed on the transfer list, with the hope of securing a move back north, but the fee demanded by City ensured that there was little interest. Thankfully, he settled into Lancashire life, although in September 1931 it was reported again that McMullan was gravely ill, suffering from pneumonia, and his condition was described as 'critical'. However, the Scot was clearly a fighter and he was soon back in the Manchester City side, where he remained until successfully applying for the player-manager job at Oldham Athletic in 1933. One of his final games for City came in the FA Cup Final where his second chance of securing a winner's medal was thwarted by Everton. He only stayed for a season and actually faced Wednesday in a FA Cup tie, earning a replay before exiting. The next destination for McMullan, who was known to be a quiet man of considerable charm and modesty, was Villa Park where in May 1934 he was appointed as the club's first secretary-manager. The hierarchy were keen for success and handed McMullan considerable funds to help achieve that aim but those hopes failed to materialise and in fact the total opposite occurred as Villa ended his first campaign in mid-table before being relegated in 1936 for the first time in their history. In October 1936 he tendered his resignation but McMullan – who stood only 5 feet 5 inches – was quickly linked to several managerial vacancies before taking over at Division Three (South) Notts County in November 1936. He only remained at Meadow Lane for just over a year before, in late December 1937, Wednesday offered him the vacant position at Hillsborough, the Scot joining a few days later.

He arrived at Wednesday with the team struggling in the Second Division and fortunes did not improve significantly as Wednesday finished in the same position they were when he took the reins – seventeenth. During the summer of 1938 he started to mould his own side, signing the likes of Hunt and Napier, and his new-look team performed admirably and was involved in the race for promotion until virtually the last kick of the campaign. Hopes were therefore high that Wednesday could regain their top-flight place but football matters paled into insignificance as war engulfed Europe. All contracts were declared null and void and while the conflict raged McMullan worked in a local factory, while fulfilling his Wednesday duties on a part-time basis. In difficult circumstances he managed to field a competitive side during the first three seasons of the war but in April 1942 the club announced that they would not be renewing his contract in the summer, 'owing to the continuance of the war and being desirous of reserving the club's resources to the best advantage'. The club also stated that the 1941/42 campaign had been disappointing with gate receipts much reduced. His tenure as Wednesday boss therefore came to a somewhat abrupt end and, surprisingly, he did not return to football in any capacity, remaining in Sheffield and working in industry until retirement. He passed away, in a Wadsley Bridge residential home, on 28 November 1964 – the same day as his predecessor, Billy Walker.

It would be perhaps fair to suggest that the departure of McMullan was more financial related than any other factor and it was therefore no surprise when team matters were handed over, temporarily, to a member of what was now a skeleton staff at the club – former assistant secretary Eric Woodhouse Taylor. Fittingly, Taylor was born in Sheffield on a Wednesday – 22 May 1912 – and would serve the Owls for almost the whole of his working life, earning the fully deserved moniker of 'Mr Sheffield Wednesday'. Like his predecessor, Dickinson, Taylor made a huge impact on club history, both on and off the field, and is one of a handful of individuals to have truly shaped the modern-day club. Brought up close to Hillsborough, Taylor was a passionate Wednesday fan from a young age and would often slip into the ground and watch the final few minutes. After leaving school he joined a law firm but in 1929 spotted an advert in the local press, which was asking for an office boy at a football club. He duly applied and was delighted to learn it was 'his' club where the position was and in September of that year he joined Wednesday, working under Brown – it is believed that the role was created by Wednesday as a small reward for lifting the championship. His wage was 7s 6d but Taylor learnt so much from Brown that in October 1934, when assistant secretary Joe McClelland left, he was promoted to the vacant position, aged only twenty-two years old, to work under new secretary-manager Walker; he was later briefly in charge of first-team duties after Walker left. In 1938 he married Emmie with club trainer Sam Powell one of his three best men. The wedding reception was held at the ground, a rare privilege in those days before corporate entertaining.

He was held in such high esteem that in the summer of 1942 he was appointed part-time secretary-manager after chairman Turner shuffled his administration to compensate for the departure of McMullan. By this time Taylor was employed at Sheffield company Howell's Tube Works and would hold down both positions until the end of the hostilities. His first season in charge proved to be the club's most memorable in wartime soccer as Wednesday reached the 1943 North War Cup final and scored freely with legendary attacker Jackie Robinson ensuring bumper crowds inside Hillsborough. He made such a positive impression that on 14 June 1945 new chairman Fearnehough handed Taylor the role on a full-time basis. There is no doubt that Taylor could not be classed as a 'hands-on' manager as he left the day-to-day training of the players, and matchday tactics, to several experienced coaches, men such as Knox, Brown and Marshall – the latter two prior to their managerial spells at Hillsborough. He was more involved in the scouting of players and negotiating of transfers while the first task in post-war football for Taylor was to rebuild a side that had ended the pre-war years so close to promotion. Unfortunately, Wednesday struggled in that first peacetime campaign and only just avoided the ignominy of relegation to Division Three (North). A recruitment campaign then started in earnest and for the remainder of the 1940s he assembled a side that would earn promotion in 1950. He was not afraid to spend the club's money either as the transfer record was broken several times including a British transfer outlay on Sewell. Despite signing several outstanding players in the 1950s, the decade was characterised by a series of promotions and relegations as Wednesday bounced between the top two divisions. It would be fair to say that

Taylor became even more influential – showing a remarkable flair for organisation and administration – when in 1958 the Owls board decided to reduce his ever-increasing workload and appoint Harry Catterick to deal solely with team matters.

This meant a new secretary/general manager position for Taylor and he would thrive in his new role, quickly formulating plans to totally transform the ground into one of the best in Europe. The awarding of the 1966 World Cup finals was another factor in the redevelopment of Wednesday's home and the meticulous Taylor travelled to grounds all over the world to gain valuable knowledge; he even flew to the 1962 World Cup finals in Chile to see how the games were staged to ensure that Hillsborough would be first on the list when the FA picked grounds. His first major building project had been the construction of a new North Stand before Leppings Lane was redeveloped. His organisation at the finals saw Wednesday handed the award of the best of all the provincial grounds. It was an immensely proud moment for Taylor who had done so much to totally transform Hillsborough in five years. Two years earlier, in April 1964, Taylor had experienced sharply contrasting emotions after a news story broke, implicating players Layne and Swan in a bribery scandal. The duo would eventually be jailed and banned for life by the FA while the impassioned and highly emotional speech Taylor made, before the home game with Tottenham Hotspur, would forever be remembered by fans. With his reputation enhanced even further after the World Cup, he was approached with an offer of a lucrative salary to become the executive secretary of the new North American National Professional Soccer League (NASL), which was set to start in 1967. After considering the offer, the pull of Wednesday proved too strong and he turned down the opportunity. However, less than a year later his tenure at Wednesday was almost ended permanently when in July 1967 he was involved in a serious car accident, from which he was lucky to survive. He was driving along Rivelin Valley Road when a car came careering down the notoriously steep Hagg Hill – a road that links Crosspool to Rivelin – and hit his car, causing the vehicle to overturn after crashing against a tree. He was recovered from the wreckage and needed several months of treatment, which included the reconstruction of his right hand, although he did lose a finger. Unfortunately for Taylor his work off the field was not replicated on the pitch and 1970 brought relegation, fans somewhat unfairly criticising Taylor for the club's demise. Before the end of the 1973/74 season, Taylor had announced his intention to retire and duly ended forty-five years of service. He was appointed vice-president on his departure and intended to work for the club on a consultancy basis – his experience being invaluable. Sadly, only a few weeks after leaving, he started to experience health issues and passed away on 23 September 1974, at the relatively young age of sixty-two. His death was mourned by all in the football world and his reputation in the game was poignantly shown when Revie brought what was virtually the full England team for a benefit game for Taylor's family – his wife only passed away last year, having reached her hundredth birthday back in 2012. His legacy to the club is immeasurable while his sons, Bob and Andy, keep his allegiance alive, both having been Wednesday season ticket holders for many years.

The Owls' sixth manager, Henry (Harry) Catterick, and the first without the added responsibility of general club administrative duties, would prove to be one of the club's greatest, although his stay at S6 would be relatively brief – in the hire and fire culture of modern-day football, his reign of just under three years would qualify for the proverbial gold watch! Born in Darlington on 26 November 1919, Catterick started his footballing career at Stockport County (where his father, Henry, was a coach) and after also appearing for Cheadle Heath Nomads he signed professional forms at Everton just before the outbreak of the Second World War. Described as a 'bustling centre forward', his association with the Toffeemen would remain for the rest of his life, Catterick serving as player, team manager and general manager until the mid-1980s. Prior to turning professional, he worked as an apprentice marine engineer. He boasted an excellent record in wartime football for Everton, scoring fifty-five goals in just seventy-one games. It was not until August 1946 that he made his Football League debut but competition was fierce and in fourteen years he accrued only seventy-one appearances, netting twenty-four goals. Two broken arms also did little to help secure a regular first-team place and he left in December 1951 after accepting the role of player-manager at Crewe Alexandra. His playing career ended at the conclusion of his first season in charge at Gresty Road, although he subsequently moved to Rochdale in June 1953 after the club directors agreed to cancel his contract. He remained in charge for five years but, rather surprisingly, when his later managerial record is taken into account, he was never close to mounting a promotion charge from Division Three (North), although his side was never threatened with re-election either.

When he applied for the vacant Wednesday job it was perhaps more in hope than expectation, but he made a huge impression on chairman Andrew Stephen and therefore became Wednesday's first team manager. It was to Stephen's great credit that his faith was emphatically repaid as Catterick led Wednesday to immediate promotion with a record for points (sixty-two) and goals (106) established; although he officially started work at Hillsborough on 1 September 1958, he was in charge as the new campaign kicked off. The new man at the helm quickly made a big impression with club officials, players and fans alike, proving a single-minded, tough, uncompromising, astute and inspirational manager. He was, however, a complex character who was somewhat of an authoritarian figure and shied away from the public glare, especially the media, which often meant he did not receive the accolades of his peers.

During his spell in charge at Wednesday and Everton he recorded more points in the top flight than anyone else, including Shankly and Busby, but has never really been mentioned in the same breath as those well-known individuals, his introverted personality and distrust of the media no doubt being contributory factors. Despite his strong and weak points, there is no doubt that Catterick was an outstanding manager and at Wednesday he took the club to fifth place and an FA Cup semi-final. He gelled together an Owls side that then provided the famous Tottenham 'double side' of 1960/61 with their only creditable challengers, although Wednesday did eventually have to settle for the runners-up spot – a finish that has not been bettered since. Sadly, Catterick was not in charge to receive the plaudits as a worsening relationship with the club's board – he later commented that if they had sanctioned the purchase of centre forward Joe Baker he believed Wednesday would have won the league – led to his dramatic resignation with just four games remaining. He cited differences with the board, although within days he'd moved to Merseyside to take over at Everton, quickly returning as his new side won at Hillsborough. He was booed by some fans as he took his seat in the director's box, while comparisons with Atkinson's acrimonious departure, and subsequent quick return, are hard to ignore, although it would be fair to say his 'welcome' was far more hostile some thirty years later.

His coach, Tommy Eggleston, moved with Catterick and a few months later club captain Kay also travelled across the Pennines. It did not take Catterick long to build a title-winning side at Goodison Park – they ran away with the league in 1963 – and he came back to haunt Wednesday in the 1966 FA Cup final. Dubbed 'the silent man of football', Catterick would sign several club legends – men such as Ball, Harvey and Kendall – and saw his side lose in the 1968 FA Cup final before lifting the League Championship for a second time in 1970. He once commented that he was a 'miserable-looking fellow' and there is no doubt that he never really developed a warm relationship, despite his successes, with the Everton supporters. He did, though, uphold Everton's tradition of cultured attacking football throughout his rein. In January 1972 he suffered a heart attack, many believing that the stress of Everton's poor season was a contributory factor, and Catterick believed it was over a year before he fully recovered. However, in April 1973, he accepted a non-executive director role and was effectively general manager until leaving to take over at Preston North End in August 1975. In two years at Deepdale he steered the Lilywhites to back-to-back top-ten finishes before retiring in May 1977. In a strange way it was perhaps fitting that Catterick died at his beloved Goodison Park, collapsing on 9 March 1985 after watching Everton play Ipswich Town. He will forever remain a legend at Everton while his spell at Hillsborough, even though no honours were accrued, must be seen as one of the most successful in the club's history. He was buried in the graveyard of St Anne's Parish Church, Lancashire, with his gravestone bearing the Everton club motto of '*Nil satis nisi optimum*' – 'nothing but the best is good enough'.

The personalities of Catterick and his replacement, Victor (Vic) Frederick Buckingham, could not have been further apart as Wednesday's new manager exuded charm and flamboyance. He arrived at Hillsborough from Dutch club Ajax, although weeks earlier had promised to become Plymouth Argyle's new manager before a friend informed him that the Wednesday job was vacant. He duly managed to persuade Argyle to release him from their verbal agreement and took over at Wednesday on 8 May 1961. He started work on 1 June and in three years showed himself to be a man somewhat ahead of his time, being influenced by former England boss Winterbottom and his experiences of managing on mainland Europe. He was known as a manager that almost gave free rein to his players on the pitch, and promoted a passing style, while also relying on his players to react and adjust to game situations. His management style was rightly perceived as a precursor to the total football philosophy, which was later refined by the outstanding Ajax team of the early 1970s. With Wednesday having finished runners-up prior to his appointment, expectations were high among fans, but that debut season could be classed as a success as despite not challenging for the top spot, Wednesday finished in a comfortable sixth place and reached the last eight of the Fairs Cup. However, his laid-back persona did hide a fierce determination and this was shown in March 1962 when he somewhat sensationally slated his own players on the front page of the *Sheffield Star*, commenting 'it's just not good enough, as a team they have got no skill and in the long run hard work will never make up for that deficit'. It's not known if this outburst proved divisive or not but he did remain at Wednesday for two more seasons, posting another sixth-place finish in 1963. What proved his final season was overshadowed by the 'bribes scandal', but before that story broke his days seemed numbered as he had fallen out with star goalkeeper Springett – the Owls later rejected his transfer request after he cited grievances with Buckingham. After the meeting, Buckingham was asked if he was going to resign or the club was going to let him go, to which he replied 'both are possible'. It was also reported he had a frosty relationship with chief scout Mansell and his fate seemed sealed when his assistant, Gordon Clark, left to take over at Peterborough United. This proved the case on 9 April 1964 as he was informed by Wednesday that his contract would not be renewed, Buckingham leaving almost immediately in a season where Wednesday, with Eric Taylor in caretaker charge again, finished in sixth spot for the third season running.

Born in the London borough of Greenwich on 23 October 1915, Buckingham had appeared at centre-half and half-back for Tottenham Hotspur after joining them in 1934. He amassed 128 appearances in the years preceding the Second World War. During the conflict he guested for a variety of clubs while serving in the Royal Air Force. He also played twice for England during the hostilities but did not receive a cap as they were not awarded by the FA in wartime. The summer of 1946 was spent coaching in Norway and he subsequently coached Tottenham's youth side (Stanmore), the Middlesex FA, and Oxford University prior to 'hanging up his boots' in 1949 to concentrate on coaching. His first coaching job was for famous amateur club Pegasus (a combined team from Oxford and Cambridge universities) and under his guidance the students went all the way to Wembley in 1951 to win the FA Amateur Cup. This success raised Buckingham's profile considerably and within a few weeks he was appointed manager at Division Three (North) club Bradford Park Avenue. He guided Avenue to eighth place in his first season before in February 1953 announcing his resignation to take over at top-flight West Bromwich Albion. His stock continued to rise at the Hawthorns as in Buckingham's first full season he came agonisingly close to completing the elusive league and cup double for the first time since 1897. Albion topped the table with only three games to go but inexplicably secured only one more point and had to settle for runners-up spot. A few days later the FA Cup was secured at Wembley and the debonair manager continued to play the fast and exhilarating football that became a hallmark of his teams throughout his career. He was greatly influenced by the outstanding Hungarian side that humiliated England, greatly admiring their intelligence on the ball, ball retention and speed at which they passed. He later commented, 'Don't worry about who was supposed to have marked whom. Just remember that if you are the nearest player then you go for the opponent with the ball. Whether you are playing well or badly, all of you must want the ball and look for it'.

He remained in the West Midlands until his surprise resignation in June 1959 with his destination also somewhat unexpected – Ajax Amsterdam. It would be fair to say that his style of management was perhaps more suited to foreign shores and he achieved immediate success, leading his new club to the league title. His successful career continued with the Dutch Cup secured twelve months later, while his first spell in the Netherlands was perhaps better remembered for his 'discovery' of Johann Cryuff. When his two-year deal expired he returned to British shores and after leaving Wednesday in 1964, returned to Amsterdam after being reappointed at Ajax on a lucrative three-year deal. However, within a few months he was back in England, taking over at Fulham in January 1965. His spell at Craven Cottage would test his managerial qualities as the Cottagers struggled at the wrong end of the First Division table; he left in January 1968. For a man widely regarded as one of the finest coaches of his generation, Buckingham would spend the rest of his career on foreign fields, spending just under two years in charge at Greek club Ethnikos. He was much loved by supporters in Greece, his outgoing nature and generous spirit allowing him to integrate fully in the local culture, and he impressed sufficiently with the football club to be appointed by Spanish giants Barcelona in December 1969. He halted some poor form from the Catalans and in 1971 took them to success in the Spanish Cup and runners-up spot in the league. One of his greatest feats at Barcelona only came to fruition after his departure, as while in charge he negotiated first refusal on Ajax star Johann Cryuff – at the time there was a ban on foreign imports in Spain – with the transfer eventually taking place in 1973 for a world-record fee. He had handed the Dutch master his senior debut in 1964. After leaving Barcelona in 1972 he spent two more years at Seville and then ended his career back in Greece, taking charge of Olympiacos and Rodos before retiring back home to England in 1980. In retirement he always followed the fortunes of former club West Bromwich Albion – he held shares in the club – and passed away on 26 January 1995 in the Sussex town of Chichester. His influence on the histories of both Ajax and Barcelona cannot be understated and he was a man who showed the world that football could be played with expression and enjoyment.

His successor was a face not unfamiliar to Wednesday fans as Alan Winstone Brown had served as coach under Taylor in the early 1950s. The son of a painter and decorator, Brown was born in the town of Consett on 26 August 1914, and spent his childhood days in nearby Corbridge. It was the time of the Great Depression so his hope of becoming a teacher failed to materialise as his parents could not afford to pay for higher education. As his school only played rugby, his Saturdays were spent playing the oval ball game in the morning before playing football in the afternoon for youth club Spen Black and Whites. The younger cousin of England and Huddersfield Town centre-half Austen Campbell, it was a recommendation from Campbell that led to Brown signing his first professional contract, at Huddersfield in March 1933. He was never a regular though and after fifty-seven games left to join the police force, serving for two years before returning to play a handful of games for the Terriers before the Second World War. He immediately joined the Royal Air Force but the conflict seemed to advance his football career, unlike the vast majority of his peers, as he played as a guest for a variety of clubs, appeared in inter-services games and FA representative matches, and was even twelfth man for England. The naturally athletic Brown became a wanted man and in February 1946, six weeks after being demobbed from the RAF, he became a record signing for Burnley. He would enjoy a great first season as his new side won promotion from the Second Division – he was a mainstay in a defence that conceded only twenty-nine goals – and also reached the FA Cup final. A few months later he captained a Football League side against their Irish counterparts. In October 1948 he moved to Notts County for £12,500. However, he failed to settle at Meadow Lane, commenting 'Personally, I have never played so bad in my life,' and just ten weeks after joining asked to be placed on the transfer list. He eventually secured his release after just thirteen appearances and returned to Burnley to open a catering business and rejoin the police force. Despite his playing career coming to a close it was not the end for Brown as on 23 January 1951 he accepted an offer from Wednesday to take over as coach from the deceased Knox, launching a career that would eclipse his playing days and see him lauded as an innovative tactician allied with an 'iron man' reputation, greatly respected by his fellow professionals with a huge passion for the game. He once described the game of soccer as 'one of the biggest things to happen in Creation'.

During the war, Brown had spent some time in Sheffield as a PE instructor and also coached for the Sheffield & Hallamshire FA, so his familiarity with the city no doubt helped his decision to move back into football full-time; the chairman of the FA, Sir Stanley Rous, also recommended he took up the position. He would spend just over four years at Wednesday, gaining valuable experience, and coached the club to promotion in 1952 before leaving in August 1954 to return to Burnley as manager. While at Turf Moor he forged a reputation as an astute manager who was also a hard taskmaster – it was said that Brown's name was a byword for truth, frankness and discipline. When taking over at Turf Moor it was suggested that several of the first-team players were not overly ecstatic at his arrival but any egos were soon bruised after Brown started to help dig the foundations for Burnley's new training pitch and 'volunteered' the players to do the same. Brown believed that integrity and industry should be compulsory and ensured that every club he served embraced the same philosophies. While at Burnley he also became known as a man who showed faith in youth, although his hand was often forced as he was working with one of the smallest playing budgets in the top flight. Despite the constraints he still secured three consecutive top-ten finishes and it was considered a coup when his boyhood club Sunderland persuaded him to take charge in July 1957. His new club was still reeling from an investigation over illegal payments and had only just avoided relegation. Unfortunately for Brown his debut season saw Sunderland relegated and it would be six years before they returned, sealing promotion back in 1964. Surprisingly he decided to resign and move back to Sheffield to fill the vacant position created by the departure of Buckingham, starting on 1 August 1964. He was handed a generous five-year deal with the remit of pushing Wednesday back into the top six and cultivating the club's youth policy. There is no doubt that Brown – who despite his steely exterior possessed genuine warmth – will be remembered for the number of youngsters that he introduced into the team, culminating in a run to the 1966 FA Cup final. Despite the loss to Everton, Brown commented,

> I am proud of my team. They showed what they can do, and I'll tell you this: They will be back again. Nothing will stop that. They're young

lads mostly, five under 21 and one just 21. They could be playing for Wednesday again in the next six or seven cup finals, and probably more than that. I am disappointed for them today. They tried ... how they tried. I'm the proudest man in the world because of them. After all, defeat doesn't mean everything. If you have to be beaten in the Cup, what better time than in the final. Getting to Wembley was their big achievement.

A big surge in Hillsborough crowds followed the cup run and a great start saw Wednesday soar at the summit of the division, but it didn't last, the Owls ending the season in mid-table. Fittingly, Wednesday was top of the table when they celebrated their centenary but had slipped into the bottom half before Brown tendered his resignation on 8 February 1968. He denied he was leaving to rejoin Sunderland but a few days later did indeed return. As was the case back in 1958, Wednesday accompanied Sunderland out of the First Division in 1970 and despite Brown being in the process of rebuilding the club he decided it was time to leave in November 1972, parting by mutual consent; just a few months later, nine of 'his' players were in the Sunderland FA Cup-winning team. He would spend one more season as a manager, at Norwegian Club Ham-Kam, before retiring to Bodmin, Cornwall. However, the football bug would not go away and he quickly returned to the game after being persuaded by Plymouth Argyle to become their chief coach, remaining until 1977. His second retirement proved permanent and during that period he penned a coaching manual entitled *Team Coach*, which was published after financial assistance from his former clubs and players who he managed – the likes of Dooley, Clough and Eustace. His finals years, blighted by poor health, were spent in Devon where he passed away on 9 March 1996 in Barnstaple.

  Before the end of the 1960s Wednesday would have two further men in charge, commencing with the appointment of Brown's former assistant John (Jack) Gilmour Marshall. As with Brown, Marshall was already known to Wednesday officials as he served at Hillsborough as chief scout/physiotherapist from January 1955 until moving to take over at Rochdale in October 1958, replacing Catterick, who had travelled the opposite journey. Born in Bolton on 29 May 1917, Marshall had only rejoined Wednesday for a second spell a few days earlier and suddenly found himself as caretaker-manager. However, within seventy-two hours he accepted, although somewhat reluctantly it must be said, the post on a permanent basis, officially taking charge on 11 February 1968. He inherited a relatively young side sat fairly comfortably in mid-table, and although he failed to recruit any new faces, he was able to tinker sufficiently to ensure Wednesday were not drawn into a relegation battle. He was actually in hospital having his appendix removed when Wednesday beat Manchester United 5-4 at Hillsborough in August

1968, but this game was certainly a highlight of what proved a very challenging season for Marshall as he had to contend with several players submitting transfer requests and Wednesday's form being patchy. Despite these troubles, Marshall's side was comfortably in the top half of the table before Arsenal dished out a 5-0 beating at Hillsborough. That embarrassing home defeat was heavily criticised and it seemed that Marshall could not lift the gloom that seemed to pervade around Hillsborough as the 'brash young things' of the Brown era did not seem to be maturing into the top-class players his predecessor had hoped for. When Marshall found out that Wednesday did not intend to renew his contract, he decided to cut his losses and resigned on 18 March 1969, with Tom McAnearney taking over as caretaker for the last eleven games of the season. He returned to his former club Bury as manager but found his position untenable less than three months into the job when a flurry of new directors were co-opted onto the board. Marshall was shown the door, financial constraints being the official reason for his departure. Within a few months he was back at another old club, Blackburn Rovers, where he would serve as physiotherapist from July 1970 to his retirement in 1979. In later life he returned to South Yorkshire, passing away on 1 January 1998 in Rotherham.

His career had started in the early 1930s when he was spotted playing for Bamber Bridge and signed professional forms at Burnley in November 1936. His secondary career of a poultry farmer, therefore, fell away and Marshall went on to make his league bow just before the Second World War. He subsequently joined the Royal Air Force but was almost immediately posted to Egypt, which severely curtailed any possibility of significant wartime football – he married his wife, Elsie, in January 1941 before being posted abroad. When the conflict came to a close he could not break back into the Burnley side and was eventually forced to retire in 1949 after suffering a serious leg injury. After his playing career ended he worked for Bolton Wanderers as a scout and then full time for an engineering company, while also studying massage and physiotherapy. After completing his studies Marshall joined Wednesday's coaching staff – he was also assistant manager for the national 'B' team – prior to taking over as boss at Rochdale. His debut season ended in relegation but despite this black mark on his CV, Marshall was headhunted by First Division Blackburn Rovers, joining them seven games into the 1960/61 campaign. His task was to rebuild the side that had reached the 1960 FA Cup final and he quickly forged a reputation for trying players in different positions and building a team that played an entertaining brand of football. He was nicknamed 'Jolly Jack' by some of the Rovers players and his team – dubbed the 'Marshall misfits' – surprised the football world by topping the table on Boxing Day 1963 – winning 8-2 at West Ham United to reach the summit. With resources relatively scarce, it was virtually impossible for Marshall's side to maintain a title challenge and they duly fell away to finish just behind Wednesday in seventh place. The 1965/66 season proved a turning point as after Wednesday knocked Rovers out of the FA Cup they also suffered relegation from the First Division. Marshall started the new season without a contract and the 'writing was on the wall' when former Owl Quigley was brought in as coach; Marshall left to rejoin Wednesday after various problems behind the scenes. He remained the only manager to take Blackburn close to the league title in post-war football before Jack Walker's millions financed their 1995 success.

At the time, the appointment of Daniel (Danny) Thomas Williams as the new Wednesday manager, on 17 July 1969, was seen as a real coup as he'd enjoyed a highly successful spell at Swindon Town, which culminated in promotion from the third tier and a stunning win over Arsenal in the 1969 League Cup final. His managerial stock was therefore at a real high and he seemed the perfect fit as Wednesday looked to finish the 1960s on a high and get themselves back into the upper echelons of the First Division table. Unfortunately for all parties concerned his tenure at Hillsborough would be relatively brief as relegation in 1970 was followed by his dismissal on 15 January 1971 with the team struggling in the bottom half of the Second Division table. For Williams – who projected a happy-go-lucky persona – his lack of First Division management experience certainly counted against him but he did join a club whose team was in a transitional period with several stalwarts approaching the end of their careers while several others were looking for a move away. This was combined with a youth policy that had stalled somewhat, while problems behind the scenes meant that Williams probably didn't appreciate the scale of the job when he agreed to move from Wiltshire. He did clear out several of the 'old guard' but unfortunately his dealings in the transfer market only seemed to make the situation worse as the likes of Brechin City winger Willie Lawson was clearly not up to the standard required. Wednesday were duly relegated and also humiliated in the domestic cups by Bournemouth and Scunthorpe United, the early exits no doubt hastening his departure. His exit was by no means cordial and both parties would disagree over his severance package for almost two years before he finally accepted a £10,000 compensation payment.

His unhappy spell at Wednesday was preceded by the aforementioned success at Swindon Town and a remarkable playing career that saw the outstanding wing-half/inside forward accrue a club record 621 appearances for his only club, Rotherham United. Born in Thrybergh on 20 November 1924, he left school aged fourteen to work in a local coal mine and started to play football for Silverwood Colliery and a club called Wath Wanderers, which at the time acted as a nursery team for Wolverhampton Wanderers. Surprisingly his undoubted talents were not recognised by Wolves and he started attending twice-weekly trials at Sheffield United. However, he ceased training with the Blades as his last bus back to his home village of Dalton left at 9 p.m., which meant Williams had to walk all the way home. A short time later he attended a successful trial at Rotherham United and duly signed part-time professional forms in the spring of 1943. It would be the start of a remarkable career that saw Williams spend twenty-three years at United as player, coach, trainer and manager; his loyal service marks him out as one of the club's greatest, if not the greatest, figure in their history. During his playing days he rejected advances from Arsenal and Liverpool, while in 1952 he was called into the senior Wales team before it was pointed out that despite his surname he was in fact not Welsh! The wartime regulations linked to coal mines finally ended in 1951 so Williams joined the Millers on a full-time basis and was immediately part of the side that won the Division Three (North) title. He was also a vital cog in the Millers side that came agonisingly close to promotion to the top flight in 1954/55 when in an incredible Second Division season the top five clubs finished with just two points between them, Rotherham missing out by a goal average of just 0.191. Known for his strength and stamina, he remained in the Rotherham senior side until retiring at the end of the 1959/60 season. One of his last games for United was actually at Hillsborough when his side famously beat Arsenal in a FA Cup replay, with 'local hero' Williams the star player. After ending his senior career, he was immediately appointed player-manager of the club's second team. He also opened a sports shop in the town, which became a valuable source of income for life after football. He had already gained a FA coaching badge but in 1962 informed the club that he intended to leave to concentrate solely on his business. However, a twist of fate ensured this did not occur as manager Johnson resigned and Williams was asked, and agreed, to take over on a temporary basis. The position proved far from temporary and he stayed in the 'hot seat' until January 1965 when he tendered his resignation, as a matter of principle, after several of his emerging young players were sold despite his objections.

After his departure, Williams briefly retired from football altogether, moving to Bournemouth, but after six months was appointed manager of Swindon Town in August 1965. He was handed the task of rebuilding the Swindon side that had been relegated from the Second Division, and it took Williams four years to get Town out of the Third Division, during which period his side gained a reputation as giant-killers in the cup competitions, including a famous 3-1 FA Cup win over a West Ham United side that contained several of England's World Cup-winning side. After leaving for Wednesday, he returned for a second spell at the County Ground in March 1974 after a fairly undistinguished spell at Mansfield Town. On his return he released twelve players from the squad and missed out on promotion by just two points in the 1974/75 campaign. After several mid-table finishes, he became general/commercial manager in May 1978 and was briefly back in charge at the beginning of the

1980/81 season as caretaker. He remained at the club until May 1985 when he retired back to Bournemouth after forty-two years in the game.

For the club's next managerial appointment, Wednesday promoted from within as Derek Dooley MBE moved from a commercial role to take charge of first-team affairs on 29 January 1971. His spectacular and ultimately tragic playing career is well documented while his behind the scenes role at Wednesday began in the early 1960s when, while working as an assistant sales manager at Dronfield bakery Gunstones, he spent several midweek evenings coaching the club's youngsters. He later became Wednesday's first development fund manager and his appointment was generally welcomed by fans as he was still a popular figure. Dooley, born in Sheffield on 13 December 1929, faced a difficult task with Wednesday struggling in the second tier, but within an eighteen-month period he totally revamped the side, introducing crowd-pleasing players such as Henderson and Joicey. He was known as a manager who liked his side to entertain and this was certainly the case in this second full season when Wednesday stayed in the top six for virtually the whole season until slipping in the final few weeks to finish tenth; they received countless plaudits for their swashbuckling football and regularly topped the table during the early weeks of the campaign. The brand of football was just what Wednesdayites needed after several seasons of struggle and Dooley – known as a reflective, pipe-smoking boss – looked set to lead another promotion push in the season that followed. Sadly, the 1973/74 campaign was beset with problems from the first whistle, a mystery virus, loss of form and injuries ensuring the anticipated promotion push never materialised with Wednesday instead fighting to stay in the Second Division. A winless nine-game run up to the Christmas period – influenced greatly by the virus that swept through the club and even affected Dooley himself – left the Owls just above the relegation places but fans were still upbeat that Wednesday would pull out of trouble and regain their promotion chasing form of the previous season. Dooley though would not be in charge at the Boxing Day home game against Hull City as two days earlier he had been controversially dismissed by Wednesday, the timing of the sacking being roundly condemned by all parties, including the media and the vast majority of fans. The club's new chairman, Matt Sheppard, had only been in the role for a matter of weeks when the guillotine came down and the insensitive nature of the dismissal proved a bitter pill for Dooley to swallow and, perhaps unsurprisingly, it would be almost twenty years before he set foot back inside Hillsborough.

After his departure, Dooley briefly worked as a sales rep for a footwear manufacturer before becoming one of a handful of individuals to cross the Sheffield divide after accepting the Blades' offer to become commercial manager in November 1974. His appointment would start a long association that remained for the rest of his life – Dooley joining the board of directors in 1983 after surviving a heart attack. He became managing director and chief executive in February 1986 and was at the club when the Blades earned promotion to the First Division and became founder members of the FA Premier League. He retired in 1992 but quickly returned for two separate spells as chairman before finally retiring for good in 2006, three years after being awarded a MBE for his services to football. He had already been made a freeman of the city and after his passing, on 5 March 2008, Sheffield's new ring road was named the 'Derek Dooley Way'; Wednesday renamed their club restaurant 'Dooleys' and United erected a statue behind their South Stand all in honour of a man who was, perhaps uniquely, loved by both sides of the city's football divide.

The Owls' next managerial appointment was crucial as, with matters on and off the field in a state of decline, it was vital that the correct man was handed the reins. Despite the likes of Ron Atkinson and Brian Clough being mentioned in dispatches, Wednesday took a huge gamble by appointing another individual with no managerial experience – Queens Park Rangers coach Stephen (Steve) Burtenshaw. It would be fair to say that Wednesday fans greeted the move with a mixture of surprise and disappointment as many, unrealistically or not, had hoped for a 'big-name' appointment to arrest the slow decline of the 1970s. The new man, appointed 28 January 1974, was born in the Sussex town of Portslade-by-Sea on 23 November 1935 and started his playing career in youth football, captaining both the Sussex and Brighton boys' sides before joining the ground staff at Brighton & Hove Albion, turning professional in November 1952. Described as a 'solid half-back', Burtenshaw made his first-team debut for the Seagulls in January 1954 and remained at Albion for the whole of his career, amassing 252 appearances. He won the Third Division in 1958 and started his coaching career, after being encouraged by his manager George Curtis, when he was appointed player/assistant coach in 1964. One of the players he coached was Howard Wilkinson. He retired in December 1966 and a year later moved to Arsenal after being appointed reserve team manager, working with head coach Don Howe. When Howe moved to become West Bromwich Albion manager in July 1971, Burtenshaw moved up the ladder to replace him. In September 1973 he was on the move again, this time becoming head coach at Queens Park Rangers, and it was while working at the club that he was recommended by none other than legendary Tottenham Hotspur manager Bill Nicholson.

There is no doubt that he had built up a big reputation but his somewhat radical coaching methods immediately alienated several players, and after only a few months there were questions asked about his man management skills. Only a few weeks after taking over he watched his side thrashed 8-0 at Middlesbrough and needed a goal on the last day of the season to avoid relegation. Although disaster was averted, the 1974/75 campaign proved to be arguably the worst ever season for

Sheffield Wednesday as they only won five games and were relegated with several games remaining. After such a calamitous season, it seems surprising that Burtenshaw started the following campaign still at the helm, but patience was running out at board level and the axe finally fell on 1 October 1975, after Wednesday slipped to the wrong end of the table, winning just two games from the first eight.

He subsequently returned to coaching, joining Everton in the summer of 1976, and was briefly caretaker-manager at Goodison Park. He was promoted to assistant manager to new boss Colin Lee but his managerial record suffered a decisive blow in May 1979 when after Queens Park Rangers were relegated he was sacked, fulfilling only ten months of a three-year managerial contract. He would never manage again but returned to football as chief scout/coach at Arsenal in the mid-1980s, laterally under George Graham. He found himself in 'hot water' in 1995 when was found guilty, along with Graham, by the Football Association in an illegal payments scandal involving John Jensen and infamous agent Rene Hauge in 1992. By the time the story broke, Burtenshaw was chief scout back at Queens Park Rangers and was fined £10,000 for his involvement. In January 2001 he suffered a stroke but recovered to scout for Manchester City manager Kevin Keegan and, despite having supposedly retired, for old club Arsenal.

After the disastrous reign of Burtenshaw the next Wednesday boss had the unenvious job of trying to simply stop the rot and drag the club from the wrong end of the Third Division table. After having appointed two inexperienced managers, the club decided it was time for experience, with Leonard (Len) Ashurst resigning at Gillingham to take up the managerial reins on 16 October 1975. His move from the Kent club was not, however, without problems as Wednesday were issued with a writ by Gillingham in February 1976, citing an illegal approach for Ashurst, and it was not until July 1977 that compensation was agreed, Wednesday paying £5,000. The managerial career of the Owls' new boss had literally started at the bottom as when appointed manager of Hartlepool United in 1971, his club sat last of the ninety-two league clubs. He had joined the Victoria Park club as a player-coach in the previous year and served a valuable managerial 'apprenticeship' at United, working tirelessly to drag his club off the bottom of the table, although they still had to apply for re-election. With limited resources he managed to improve United's finishing position every season he was at the helm and this relative success earned him a move to Gillingham in June 1974, who had just been promoted to the Third Division. He steered his new side to a top-half finish before finding the Wednesday job too tempting to turn down, despite the troubles Wednesday were experiencing on and off the pitch. When he arrived at S6 he found almost sixty professionals on the payroll and the immediate problem of trimming the squad with little money to play with.

After moving north, he did steady the ship and a run of home wins culminated with a victory over Southend United, which ensured Wednesday avoided dropping into the bottom division. He hit the headlines in January 1976 when he agreed to his coach, Tony Toms' suggestion of a taking the players for a night on the Yorkshire Moors for survival training – it was probably an early example of a 'team building' exercise, although Ashurst did not take part due to illness, and victory in the next game perhaps proved it was also a worthwhile exercise. He was also laid low for a fortnight later in that season due to pneumonia and was nursed back to health at home as Toms took charge of first-team affairs, going four games unbeaten before Ashurst returned to oversee four consecutive losses. He would work tirelessly to turn around the club's fortunes, clearing out several underperforming players and greatly improving Wednesday's youth scheme, a laudable policy that would bear fruit at the end of the 1970s. His first, and that proved to be his only, full season at Hillsborough finally gave the long-suffering fans something to smile about as victory in the preseason Shipp Cup competition was followed by a greatly improved league position, the Owls winning twenty games to remain in the top half of the Third Division table all season – he had brought in the likes of Tynan, Rushbury and Walden and also handed a debut to Chris Turner. There was genuine hope a promotion push would follow but unfortunately a bad start to the following campaign saw the axe fall, Ashurst being dismissed on 5 October 1977; the decision was made by the club's directors on the team coach returning from Port Vale the night before.

He was out of the game for nine months before taking a call from Fourth Division Newport County manager Colin Addison, informing him that he was leaving to become assistant to Atkinson at West Bromwich Albion and did Ashurst want his job. Of course, he answered in the affirmative and took over in June 1978. In his second season he led them to promotion from the Fourth Division and success in the Welsh Cup, discovering a young John Aldridge in the process. County's success in their domestic cup opened the door to European football in the 1980/81 season and Ashurst's side grabbed several headlines as they progressed all the way to the last eight of the European Cup Winners' Cup. He was unfortunate to be sacked by County in February 1982 – it was more a financial than football decision – and was quickly employed at their local rivals, Cardiff City. Ironically he attended his testimonial at Newport before taking over at Ninian Park the following day. He could not save them from relegation but his charges were promoted straight back into the Second Division in 1983 before Ashurst took over at struggling top-flight Sunderland in March 1984. He ensured they avoided the drop and led them to the 1985 League Cup final, losing to Norwich City, but it was a bittersweet season as relegation followed. Unsurprisingly he paid the price for the team's failure and over the ensuing years coached in the

Middle East at the Kuwait Sporting Club and then the Wakrah Sport Club (Qatar). In the late 1980s he was assistant manager to ex-Owl Mullen at Blackpool and then spent almost two years back in charge at Cardiff City, being dismissed after relegation and yet more cost cutting. Subsequent coaching roles at non-league Weymouth and in Malaysia were followed by a return to his old club in Qatar where he was hospitalised after the team bus was attacked on the road from Iraq to the Gaza Strip – the co-driver of the coach was killed but Ashurst escaped with only minor injuries. Spells at Weymouth and Weston-super-Mare brought the curtain down on his managerial career, Ashurst resigning from the latter in August 1998 to become a FA academy assessor.

Later in life he became a 'match delegate' for the FA Premier League and eventually retired to the north-east, writing his memoir *Left Back in Time*, which was published in 2009. His managerial career saw Ashurst manage 1,089 club games and in 2014 was recognised for the feat by being inducted into the LMA (League Managers Association) Hall of Fame; he became the twenty-third manager to pass the 1,000-game mark. It had been a long road for Ashurst, which began when he was born in Liverpool on 10 March 1939, and whose playing career commenced in the summer of 1954 when he joined the ground staff at Liverpool. He was also an all-round sportsman, representing Lancashire at cricket, while also working as a trainee compositor in the printing trade. He subsequently won seven England Youth caps in the winter game but his career stalled somewhat when he was not offered a professional contract by Liverpool. However, within a few weeks he had signed amateur forms for Wolverhampton Wanderers, although his stay in the West Midlands was brief, moving to Sunderland after having to play a single game for Prescot Cables to trigger his release. His new manager was Alan Brown and over the next fourteen years he amassed 458 games, placing Ashurst second in the club's all-time appearance list. The outstanding full-back was capped at U23 level by England and helped Sunderland to promotion in 1964 before accepting a player-coach role in March 1971, leaving for Hartlepool United. He was rewarded with a testimonial game against Newcastle United before commencing his managerial career.

After several 'false starts', Wednesday's revival finally started with the appointment of John (Jack) Charlton OBE as Ashurst's replacement – it was actually his predecessor that recommended him to Wednesday's board of directors. It was the following home game with Chesterfield on 8 October 1977 when supporters first became aware that 'Big Jack' was in the frame for the job and he duly decided to join after the match, actually changing his mind after being overwhelmed by the reaction of Wednesdayites to his presence. He was a hugely popular figure, his World Cup-winning exploits in 1966 ensuring football immortality, playing alongside his brother Bobby in the triumph. He was brought up in the town of Ashington (8 May 1935) and was somewhat of a rebel at school, once accidently shooting a fellow pupil after bringing his air rifle into the playground! As far as football was concerned, his career began with his home town's YMCA team. He came from a famous football family: four of his uncles – Jack, George, Stan and Jim Milburn – played professionally and his mother's cousin, Jackie Milburn, was one of England's greatest players. His home town relied totally on the local colliery and life was tough for the Charlton brothers – Bobby, Gordon and Tommy – who had to share a single bed. His father worked down the mine and had no interest in football but his mum, Cissie, regularly played with her sons and Jack became a lifelong Newcastle United fan after being taken to St James' Park. In later years Charlton remarked that, 'This part of the world produced its fair share of footballers, and nobody was particularly impressed if a lad went away to play professional football. In fact, we never used to say going away to play football, we just said "going away."' He subsequently turned down the chance of a trial at Leeds United and started his working life down nearby Lindon Pit before quickly realising that a life underground was not for him, deciding to join the police force. It was at that point that fate took a hand as he was due to be interviewed for the constabulary on a Friday but also due to attend a trial at Leeds (where his Uncle Jim was left-back) the day before. He was subsequently asked by Leeds to play in the youth team on the following Saturday and the rest is history; the uncompromising and rugged centre-half spent his entire career at Leeds, accruing 629 league games (seventy goals) between 1952 and 1973, an incredible figure for any player of any era. During that time, he earned the nickname of 'giraffe' due to his 6-foot 2-inch frame and won a plethora of honours, being capped thirty-five times by his country, making his debut against Scotland in 1965. He retired from the international stage after the 1970 World Cup finals and brought the curtain down on his club career in the summer of 1973.

Within weeks he was approached with an offer to take over at Second Division Middlesbrough and he enjoyed a remarkable first campaign as a manager, Boro romping away with the championship to finish fifteen points clear. He was named manager of the year for his achievement, the first time a boss from outside the top division received the accolade, and was also awarded an OBE. Unlike many great players, Charlton proved that he would also be a success off the field and twelve months later he'd led the Teeside club to seventh place in the top division, just five points behind champions Derby County. A run to the semi-finals of the League Cup and Anglo-Scottish Cup success followed before Charlton called time on his spell at Middlesbrough in April 1977, resigning to spend more time with his family and indulge in his love of hunting and fishing – he stated that four years was long enough to spend at any one club. However, the football bug was well and truly alive in the highly respected Geordie and after returning from a Caribbean holiday he made it known that he was looking to get straight back into work. It was on the back of this announcement that Wednesday director Roy Whitehead invited Charlton to Hillsborough and led to his appointment with the Owls bottom of the old Third Division. His first task was to make Wednesday harder to beat, using the old adage of building from the back, and this had the effect of his side steering clear of the relegation places to secure a relatively comfortable mid-table finish. It would be fair to say that Charlton's early Owls sides were not overly blessed with flair, but clean sheets ensured points, and the 1978/79 season saw Wednesday's profile rise considerably after the five-game FA Cup ties against Arsenal. Those games helped Charlton add several new faces to the squad, men such as Curran, McCulloch and Mellor, and a burgeoning youth policy contributed to a memorable promotion from the third tier in 1980. Charlton would break his own 'four-year' rule by remaining at Wednesday until May 1983, during which time the Owls came close to promotion. Wednesday also reached the last four of the FA Cup and he left with the good wishes of fans, who realised the sterling work he'd done to lift the club from the bottom of the Third Division to the brink of the top flight.

After taking a sabbatical from football he returned as caretaker-manager at former club Middlesbrough in March 1984, but left after steering Boro to safety. In the summer that followed he somewhat reluctantly accepted the managerial position at Newcastle United, after Jackie Milburn had brokered the deal, but never settled and various disagreements with fans led to his resignation after just a season. After his unhappy experience at St James' Park he vowed never to manage at club level again, but it was not the end of his career as in 1986 the opportunity arose to become part-time manager of the Republic of Ireland. At the time, association football was very much a poor relation to Gaelic football in the Emerald Isle but in almost a decade in charge, Charlton completely changed the sporting fabric of the country as he led Eire to consecutive World Cup finals and became a hugely popular figure. When Charlton took over, new FIFA eligibility rules had just been introduced that allowed a canny Charlton to draft in virtually a whole team of experienced players, many of whom had never set foot in Ireland, and introduce a direct brand of football that resulted in qualification for a major tournament for the first time: Euro '88. A win over England in those finals increased Charlton's popularity even further as his side just missed out on a place in the semi-finals. By the 1990 World Cup finals the sport had become dominant with virtually the whole population glued to their TVs to see Charlton's team reach the last eight. After reaching the 1994 World Cup finals in the United States, Charlton was made a freeman of Dublin and after retiring in 1995 was handed the highest honour the Irish state could bestow upon an individual: an honorary Irish citizenship. After retirement he received more honours, including induction into the English Football Hall of Fame and the erection of a life-size statue of Charlton at Cork

Airport, complete with his fishing tackle and caught salmon in his hand. He continues to live out his years in Northumberland, while in June 2015 he shed tears of joy after receiving a rapturous standing ovation at the Dublin friendly between Eire and England.

The fine efforts of Charlton had laid the foundations for a return to the 'big time' for Wednesday and this occurred just a few short months after Howard Wilkinson was appointed manager, on 24 June 1983. Born in Sheffield on 13 November 1943, Wilkinson was brought up in the Sheffield district of Netherthorpe and started his playing career as an amateur at Sheffield United before his form for Hallam led to a professional contract at Wednesday, signing on 25 June 1962. The winger initially played reserve-team football in his first two years but did eventually break into the first eleven early in the 1964/65 campaign. The former Abbeydale school pupil and England schools international impressed at outside right but could not secure a regular first-team spot and left for Brighton & Hove Albion in July 1966 after twenty-two appearances. It would be fair to say that Wilkinson's managerial successes far outshined his deeds on the football pitch as a relatively modest career ended at Boston United in the early 1970s (he added 129 games to his CV on the South Coast), who he joined in May 1971 after being handed a player-coach role. The decade would see Wilkinson forge a reputation as one of the best managers outside of the professional game after leading Boston to back-to-back Northern Premier League titles and a NPL League Cup win, after taking over the reins in 1972. While in charge, Wilkinson gained a degree in physical education at Sheffield University, while he spent two years at Mossley (1977–79) and also taking charge of the England semi-professional side, leading them to the Four Nations title in 1979. The almost inevitable step into the Football League came with a coaching position at Notts County in December 1979, where during a spell as assistant-manager he was promoted to the position of England U21 manager. When Sirrel left the manager's post at Meadow Lane in July 1982, it was Wilkinson who stepped into his shoes, beginning an association with former teammate Peter Eustace and physio Alan Smith, Wilkinson appointing them as coach and physiotherapist respectively. He kept County in the top flight during what proved his only season in charge as the chance of managing his boyhood club was impossible to resist. Wednesday failed in their pursuit of Watford manager Graham Taylor with Wilkinson commenting, 'for the board to try for Graham Taylor indicates to me that they are a good board. It was sensible thinking'.

The Owls had been outside of the top flight for thirteen years but Wilkinson's all-action, hard-working and super-fit side hit the ground running and quickly shot to the top of the table. Wednesday did not lose until late November and never dropped out of the top two positions for the remainder of the campaign. Wilkinson's direct style of play was not popular with some critics but Owls fans were in raptures as their side regained their place at the pinnacle of English football and became a force in the top division. He was subsequently offered a highly lucrative position at Saudi club Al-Ittihad but he remained loyal to Wednesday, although he knew that investment in the side was needed. Unfortunately for him, and Wednesday fans, the club's board was somewhat reluctant to open the coffers with chairman McGee no doubt still affected by the disastrous financial position the club was in when he took charge. Unsurprisingly, Wilkinson became frustrated by the lack of investment and another offer, this time to work in Greece, was again rebuffed but he did eventually leave on 10 October 1988, when ambitious Leeds United came calling with a financial war chest. Wilkinson commented that his new club was 'like an old Saville Road suit, frayed at the edges. Like a Rolls Royce in a breakers yard'. For long-standing Wednesday fans, it was a case of déjà vu as he repeated the feat of Catterick, in the early 1960s, by taking his new club to the Division One championship, just beating the Owls to the top spot, and into European competition.

He earned the affectionate nickname of Sergeant Bilko (after the old TV character of the same name) at Leeds due to his discipline and fitness regime, and remained at Elland Road until September 1996 when he was sacked after a poor start to the season, fan unrest never having dissipated after a lacklustre defeat to Aston Villa in the League Cup final a few months earlier. In January 1997 he renewed his links with the FA after being appointed as the governing body's first technical director. During his spell with the FA he was twice briefly caretaker-manager of the national team and for a short time was in charge of the U21 side. He left in October 2002 to replace Peter Reid at Sunderland but his spell on Wearside was not a happy one, Wilkinson resigning after just six months with the Black Cats bottom of the Premier League. A two-month spell in charge at Chinese club Shanghai Shenhua ended his managerial career, while back in the UK he was briefly first-team coach at Leicester City and non-executive director at Notts County before being appointed chairman of the League Managers Association in September 2007. His career turned full circle in January 2009 when he returned to Hillsborough as technical advisor to new chairman Lee Strafford and was temporary chairman from May 2010 until the club was saved from administration by Milan Mandaric. He played a key role in the club's rescue, helping to broker a takeover deal, and remains the only individual to hold the distinction of serving Wednesday as player, manager and chairman.

After the success of the Wilkinson years, the club promoted from within that successful managerial set up with assistant Peter Eustace, handed the reigns after a short spell as caretaker – Wednesday publicly chased several other targets without success. Several managers were linked but after being publicly rebuffed, the Owls turned to their former player. Unfortunately, his tenure as Wednesday boss would become the shortest in the club's history – lasting a mere 109 days – and a run of poor results, dressing-room unrest and fan discontentment eventually led to his departure on 15 February 1989. While in caretaker charge he took the Owls to a League Cup win over Blackpool and top-flight victory at Southampton but after being handed the post on a permanent basis he could only muster two more wins. The lack of victories meant Wednesday slid down the league table and it was almost inevitable the beleaguered Eustace was dismissed, ending an association with the club that had started back in March 1961 when he signed apprentice forms after impressing for his local club, Stockbridge Works. He was born in the Sheffield suburb on 31 July 1944 and began working as an apprentice mechanical engineer at the local steelworks, before signing professional forms in June 1962. It was former Owls player Slynn who recommended the teenage Eustace, after he started working at the steel plant and saw his obvious potential. He started his playing career as a defensive wing back before moving to a more attacking midfield role. By the middle of the decade he was an automatic choice in midfield – impressing as Wednesday reached the 1966 FA Cup final – and his stylish play made him much sought after, eventually leading to a call-up to the full England squad in 1968. Unfortunately, a freak accident – he collided with a friend while skiing on the hills around Stocksbridge – ruined his chances of a cap and despite being called up twice more he never did win that elusive honour. When new manager Danny Williams took over at Hillsborough, he stated Eustace was the club's best player but just over six months later, in January 1970, promptly sold him to First Division rivals West ham United for a club record £95,000 fee. He totalled 281 games for Wednesday, scoring twenty-six times, and was actually named player of the year by Wednesday fans despite his departure, perhaps showing what a key player he was. The move to East London though did not really work and he returned home to sign on loan for Rotherham United in March 1972. He returned to Wednesday in the summer of 1972 but failed to really recapture his previous form and after relegation to the Third Division, ended his professional playing career at Peterborough United. He actually came back to Hillsborough for a third time, on trial in May 1976, but after failing to earn a contract he retired, after a brief spell at Worksop Town.

After calling time on his playing career, Eustace spent three years working at his father-in-law's building company in Stocksbridge before coming back into the game in 1979 when being recruited by former teammate Knighton, as a coach at Sunderland. His new club was immediately promoted to the top flight and three years later he was back in S6 as assistant to another former teammate, Wilkinson. After his short tenure in charge at Hillsborough, Eustace was appointed to the coaching staff at Leyton Orient and held an identical role at Charlton Athletic before returning to Brisbane Road as assistant manager to Frank Clark.

When Clark moved 'upstairs' he was handed the reins and spent three years in charge – selling Bart-Williams to Wednesday – and remained until being dismissed in April 1994. He subsequently became West Ham United's international scout and later worked as an independent scout, before a relatively short spell scouting for Wednesday was ended in July 2003 when he was made redundant as a cash-strapped Wednesday cut costs – he later took the Owls to an employment tribunal (after chief executive Kevan Walker famously stated the only job available for Eustace was that of office cleaner). His appeal was rejected and his connection with Redknapp was duly reignited as he joined Portsmouth, leaving just after the 2008 FA Cup final. He later ran a public house in the Derbyshire village of Hope and now lives out his retirement.

After the turbulent reign of Eustace, Wednesday's next appointment was nothing short of inspired as they secured the services of larger-than-life character Ronald (Ron) Frederick Atkinson. Although born in his mother Nancy's home city of Liverpool on 18 March 1939, his family moved to Birmingham just days after his birth and four years later his engineer/toolmaker father, Fred, and mum gave him a little brother, Graham. As a youngster Atkinson inherited his father's love of sport and was brought up in an era when children spent the vast majority of their spare time outside, playing football and cricket, messing around in the local woods and generally enjoying the great outdoors. While a youngster, Atkinson was taken on alternative Saturdays to watch Birmingham City and Aston Villa before a strong allegiance to the latter was formed, which remained in adulthood. His playing career started at school and continued at Brookhill Boys Club; he also played in his father's works team when just twelve years old, being drafted in at the last minute after the side were short of players. After gaining employment at a local tool company, he played for the works XI and eventually signed for Aston Villa, after a spell at Wolverhampton Wanderers. Unfortunately, the teenage wing back failed to break into the senior side during three years and was one of fifteen players released in the summer of 1959, Atkinson later commenting that 'our pictures were all in the Sports Argus. The page looked like Interpol's most wanted list'. Also released was his brother and the siblings would duly sign for non-league Headington United and seemed destined for a career outside of the Football League. Within three years though, his new side – renamed Oxford United – was a league club, being voted in by a large majority in 1962. In the intervening years, Atkinson – nicknamed Tank – had captained the side from central defence and led United to back-to-back Southern League titles, although attempts to gain admittance into the Football League proved unsuccessful. After they did gain admittance, Atkinson took his Oxford appearances to a club record 562, while also working for many years as a sales representative, selling bathroom suites and then commercial paints. His career at Oxford ended in 1971 and a short spell as a player at Witney Town preceded his first managerial role as player-manager of Kettering Town in December 1971. Promotion to the Southern League quickly followed and further success gave 'Big Ron' his first taste of life in the Football League as manager at Cambridge United. By now he had decided to concentrate solely on a career off the field of play, while at United he famously sold a player to Barry Fry for a case of champagne! He was quickly forging a reputation as one of the best up-and-coming managers and he moved into the top flight when taking over at West Bromwich Albion in January 1978 – after rejecting an offer from Elton John to take over at Watford. He was the perfect fit at the Hawthorns as his penchant for attacking and entertaining football was matched by some of the outstanding players at his disposal, including the 'three degrees' of Regis, Cunningham and Batson. He enjoyed great success, although tangible trophies did prove elusive as Albion reached the last four of the FA Cup, the last eight of the UEFA Cup and finished third in the First Division.

In June 1981 Atkinson took over at Manchester United and over the five years that followed was unofficially crowned 'King of Bling' due to his penchant for gold jewellery, sunbeds, flashy suits and parties – he was also called Mr Bojangles due to his gold ring and bracelets. However, behind his media image was an outstanding manager and he guided United to two FA Cup wins and only departed, in November 1986, after failing to deliver the 'Holy Grail' of the league title. After almost twelve months out of the game he made a surprise return at West Bromwich Albion but the lure of the Spanish sun proved irresistible and after just six weeks in charge he left to take over at Atletico Madrid. It is not known if Atkinson was aware of the club's president's penchant for hiring and firing managers but after just ninety-six days, despite taking Atletico from third bottom to third, he joined the long list of managers fired by Jesus Gil. It was after his spell in Spain that Atkinson strolled into Hillsborough on 15 February 1989, signing a short-term deal. His brief was to simply keep Wednesday in the top flight and after several moves in the transfer market this was achieved with Carlton Palmer a notable newcomer. He signed a one-year extension in May 1989 and over the months that followed added several quality players, such as Sheridan and Nilsson, and Wednesday fans were treated to an entertaining brand of football not seen since the early 1960s. Unfortunately, the adage of 'you're never too good to go down' proved pertinent as a late slump saw them tumble from mid-table to suffer an agonising relegation. Managerial staff and players vowed to get Wednesday back up immediately and the 1990/91 season proved hugely memorable as Wednesday achieved the double of promotion and cup success, Atkinson becoming the first and only Owls boss since 1935 to win a domestic trophy.

Optimism was rife among fans but the bubble quickly burst in dramatic style as Atkinson resigned to take over at boyhood club Aston Villa, after initially vowing to stay. The manner of his departure meant he was vilified by the vast majority of Wednesday fans and years later admitted that he made a mistake. He did bring Villa some silverware, winning the League Cup in 1994, but departed six months later, sacked by Villa chairman 'Deadly' Doug Ellis. After saving struggling Coventry City from relegation he eventually moved upstairs to become director of football in November 1996. The backlash from the manner of his departure from Wednesday in 1991 had long-since dissipated when he surprisingly returned on 14 November 1997, taking over from Pleat. Even so, there was still a mixed reaction to his return but four consecutive wins on the field soon changed the minds of the doubters. He duly saved Wednesday from relegation, also showing his legendary eye for a player by signing Alexandersson for a bargain £750,000, and plans were in place for former captain Nigel Pearson to serve as his managerial apprentice. However, it was not to be as it became known that Wednesday did not intend to renew his contract and his final game in charge ended in an injury-time defeat at Crystal Palace in the final game of the season. His managerial career was coming to a close as a brief spell at Nottingham Forest ended in June 1999, Atkinson already having launched a career in football media. He became a popular TV pundit, working with ITV Sport, and uttered several famous quotes including 'Well, either side could win it, or it could be a draw' and 'I never comment on referees and I'm not going to break a habit of a lifetime for that prat.' His mainstream TV career came to an abrupt halt in April 2004 when he was forced to resign after an off the air comment about Chelsea player Marcel Desailly was broadcast to various countries in the Middle East. His media career did continue, mainly with cable broadcasters and more recently MUTV, while he was even a member of the Celebrity Big Brother household in 2013, becoming the second person evicted. His last footballing role was a brief spell as consultant at Halesowen Town while he now lives out his retirement, with wife Maggie, in the leafy Birmingham suburb of Barnt Green.

The sudden end of Atkinson's first spell in charge opened the door for Trevor John Francis to secure the position, while also continuing to prolong his distinguished playing career – he remains Wednesday's only player-manager. He had initially arrived as a player under Atkinson, signing on a non-contract basis on 23 January 1990 after a turbulent and short spell in charge at Queens Park Rangers. His time at Hillsborough brought the curtain down on an outstanding career on the field, which had seen the lightening-quick, agile attacker – born in Plymouth on 19 April 1954 – make his debut for Birmingham City at the tender age of sixteen. In February 1971 he became the youngest player to score four goals in an English league game and he became an all-time Birmingham City legend with 133 goals in 329 games. He helped City gain promotion to the top flight and in 1977 received his first call-up for the national team, winning the first of fifty-two caps. A highly successful loan spell in the North American Soccer League with Detroit Express followed in the summer of 1978, and his nineteen goals in only twenty-two NASL games made him the hottest property in the English game – Brian Clough eventually had to smash the British transfer record when paying £999,999 for his services in February 1979. Clough wanted to pay a pound under the magic million to ensure Francis was not known as the first £1-million player; taxes though did push the fee above the magic number. His impact at the City Ground could not have been more dramatic as he scored the only goal as Forest lifted the European Cup. Injury cost him an appearance in the 1980 final and he was dogged by injury in the early 1980s, prior to a £1.2 million move to Manchester City in September 1981. His stay in Manchester was brief before just over five years in Italian football, at Sampdoria and then Atalanta, preceded a return to the UK and six months in the colours of Glasgow Rangers. After initially joining Queens Park Rangers as a non-contract player, he was appointed player-manager but his spell in charge proved controversial as, although he scored regularly on the field, he experienced problems with his players and was roundly criticised when he fined a player for being at the birth of his child. He was dismissed early in 1990 and was thrown a lifeline by Atkinson, offering him the chance to prolong his playing career. During just over eighteen months as a player at Hillsborough, Francis provided several memorable cameo appearances as he was mainly used from the substitute's bench: despite his age he would often show admirable pace and proved a real handful for many Second Division defences.

The shock departure of Atkinson saw a dramatic change of role for Francis, as after an unsuccessful move for Ray Harford, he was appointed manager on 18 June 1991. He took over a side that was full of confidence and contained several players of top-flight quality and it was perhaps no surprise that he enjoyed a tremendous debut campaign, leading the club to third place and qualification for the UEFA Cup. During his time in charge, Francis signed several 'high-profile' players, such as Woods, Waddle and Walker, and the 1992/93 season will always be remembered for some of the scintillating football played by Wednesday as they just fell short of winning a major trophy. The problems for Francis started when he really failed to replace the 'old guard', the likes of Palmer, Pearson and Nilsson leaving and the replacements not being of the required quality. A season of struggle in 1994/95 left Wednesday in lower mid-table. The problems were exacerbated by a clash of personalities in the dressing room and seemed to reach a nadir when Nottingham Forest won 7-1 at Hillsborough. He survived that debacle but it proved a mere stay of execution as on FA Cup final day he was dismissed. After departing, he briefly worked as a TV pundit before going back into management at former club Birmingham City. It was a case of so near, so far for Francis at St Andrew's as he led City to three First Division (Championship) play-off semi-finals but failed to win the ultimate prize of promotion. He was also in charge when they lost the 2001 League Cup final on penalties to Liverpool, and later in the year tendered his resignation. His final job in management came with almost two years at Crystal Palace before leaving on Good Friday 2003. Since then he has worked in the media, spending twenty-one years with Sky Sports before moving to BT Sport in 2015, while in April 2012 he recovered from a heart attack – his wife sadly passed away in 2017. A year later his son, James, was acquitted of burgling the home of former Villa player Lee Hendrie, while in 2014 Francis was awarded the highest civic honour in Birmingham, a star on the city's Walk of Stars, joining the likes of ELO's Jeff Lynne and comedian Jasper Carrott.

After the departure of Francis, the preferred candidate was Luton Town boss David John Pleat, although his chairman, David Kohler, did not necessarily agree. In the previous three seasons Luton had been relegated and then just only twice avoided the drop into the third tier, so it was therefore somewhat of a surprise when he took over at Hillsborough. His move north was a drawn-out affair as Luton initially gained a court injunction to stop Pleat taking the job; the matter eventually went to a FA tribunal where a compensation package was agreed. He had earned a reputation for attacking football while in charge at Tottenham Hotspur but his first season at Wednesday proved one of struggle, Wednesday spending all of the campaign in the lower half of the table and only mathematically ensured safety on the final day. A stunning start to the following season provided a springboard to a much-improved season as only a late collapse in away form denied European qualification. Pleat had already broken the club's transfer record to bring Carbone to S6 and set another record when Di Canio arrived. However, during his tenure, the likes of Sheridan and Waddle departed while his man-management skills were called into question as the likes of Ritchie Humphreys failed to build on his early promise. The start of the 1997/98 season saw Wednesday struggle to create enough chances for the Italian duo and by early November Pleat was on his way back to White Hart Lane, as director of football, after a 6-1 beating at Old Trafford.

His Wednesday tenure proved to be Pleat's final role in club management – other than three spells as caretaker at Tottenham – which ended a playing and managerial career that had started back in 1962 when Nottingham-born Pleat (15 January 1945) joined his boyhood heroes Forest after having impressed for England schoolboys. While studying for his O levels at school, he was dubbed the 'new Tom Finney' by the media, while the winger also won England Youth caps but he failed to make the desired impression on the senior side and was sold to Luton Town in 1964. Despite being a virtual ever-present in his first season, Town were relegated to the bottom division and he would then suffer various injury problems, including a broken leg, while a back problem also surfaced, which would hamper the remainder of his career. A free transfer to Exeter City followed and he was in the Grecians side that knocked Wednesday out of the League Cup in 1968. His fitness problems meant he dropped into non-league football in 1971, following a season at Peterborough United, where he was initially player-manager at Nuneaton Boro – he was recommended to the club by Brian Clough. His stay at Nuneaton was relatively brief though and after a short spell as a journalist he returned to Luton Town in a coaching capacity. A promotion to chief coach came in 1977 and two months later he was handed the managerial reins. His all-out attacking style of football earned him many plaudits while in charge at Kenilworth Road and his team ran away with the Second Division title in 1982. A year later he was central to one of the iconic football images of the 1980s as he sprinted and bounced across the Maine Road pitch after Town had retained their newly won status. Town continued to 'punch above their weight' and Pleat took them to a FA Cup semi-final in 1984 and then a remarkable ninth-place finish. This earned him a chance at Tottenham Hotspur where his almost revolutionary formation – Clive Allen the only striker with a five-man midfield – took Spurs to third in the league, the semi-finals of the League Cup and Wembley in the FA Cup final. Unfortunately for Pleat, lurid tabloid headlines about his personal life meant he was forced to resign in October 1987, although he was back in the game at Leicester City two months later. With the Foxes facing relegation to the Third Division, Pleat was sacked in January 1991 and would then spend four fairly unremarkable seasons back at Luton Town before taking over at Wednesday. After leaving Hillsborough he remained at White Hart Lane until July 2004 and subsequently acted as advisor to Portsmouth manager Alain Perrin in April 2005 and then worked as a consultant for Nottingham Forest from 2006 until 2011. Since departing Hillsborough back in 1997 he has continued to be a regular on various media platforms, working as a co-commentator for Radio 5 Live as well as penning a regular column for *The Guardian* newspaper.

After the brief return of Atkinson had saved the club from relegation, Wednesday turned to another former player, Daniel (Danny) Joseph Wilson, after he'd impressed with Barnsley. His spell at Oakwell was his first managerial role after moving from Hillsborough in the summer of 1993, after fourteen goals in 137 games, to effectively become assistant to his former teammate Viv Anderson. A year later he was appointed manager and built one of the Tykes' best ever sides, winning promotion to the top flight in 1997. They came straight back down but his work had not gone unnoticed and he was appointed Wednesday boss on 6 July 1998, much to the chagrin of Barnsley supporters. Wednesday chairman Dave Richards was the main protagonist behind the move and it was generally welcomed by Wednesdayites, Wilson enjoying a 'honeymoon period' due to his popularity as a player. His first season in charge avoided the relegation troubles of the previous campaign and Wednesday ended the season comfortably placed just below mid-table. That final position was perhaps more praiseworthy when you consider that fiery attacker Di Canio only appeared for a handful of games after being banned by the FA in September. It was clear that Wednesday needed to bring in reinforcements but this is where Wilson's rein took a significant turn for the worse as his dealings in the transfer market were both expensive (the contract costs became a financial millstone until the club was taken over eleven years later) and provided little value, the likes of De Bilde, O'Donnell, Donnelly and Sibon all failing to contribute significantly due to injuries and lack of form. This influx proved disastrous for Wilson and Wednesday and the club quickly slipped to the bottom of the league, spending the rest of the season trying to avoid the drop. In January 2000 four Wednesday-supporting MP's called for his dismissal but it was not until March, the month after chairman Richards resigned, that the axe fell with Wednesday staring relegation in the face.

It was a sad ending for a player whose son, Laurie, came through the youth ranks at Wednesday, who had been popular during three years at Wednesday, after having been signed from Luton Town in August 1990. During his stay he showed all of his qualities, which included a great range of passing, an inspirational and wholehearted attitude and a real never-say-die ethos – he once completed a game at Manchester City despite having two broken ribs. He earned the nickname of 'Didwell', due to Alan Parry's iconic commentary in the 1991 League Cup semi-final, and continued playing at Oakwell before ending a career that had started back in the mid-1970s at non-league Wigan Athletic. He was born there on 1 January 1960 and was an associate schoolboy at Sunderland before returning home to sign for the Latics. He moved into the Football League at Bury in 1977 and only missed one game in three seasons, caused by a red card he received in the Shakers 5-1 defeat at Hillsborough in February 1980. A move to Chesterfield followed but financial problems at Saltergate meant they had no choice but to accept an offer from Nottingham Forest for his services in January 1983. He began well at Forest, starting the first nine games, but the rather unpredictable Clough then dropped Wilson and he never played another senior game for Forest. Loan spells at Scunthorpe United and Brighton & Hove Albion ended with a permanent move to the latter. His career really started to blossom on the south coast and he won the first of his twenty-four caps for Northern Ireland, qualifying as his father was a player at Derry City and met and married a local girl. A move into the top flight at Luton Town was next and Wilson was among the scorers when his side shocked Arsenal to win the 1988 League Cup. A year later he was back, Luton losing to Nottingham Forest, and subsequently experienced a mixed time in 1990 as he helped his side retain their First Division status, sending Wednesday down in the process, before joining the club he'd help condemn to relegation.

After his spell in charge at Hillsborough ended, he was quickly back in football, taking over at Bristol City in 2000, and rather uniquely stayed for the duration of his four-year contract, twice leading City into the play-offs but ultimately failing to gain promotion. Two years in charge at Hartlepool United followed, including a promotion season, before taking charge of MK Dons and then Swindon Town. He led the Wiltshire club to the 2010 League One play-off final but dreams of promotion were dashed as Millwall won 1-0. As often occurs, Swindon struggled the season after missing out on promotion and with Town in the lower reaches of the division, Wilson resigned in March 2011. Just over two months later he returned to Sheffield, joining Sheffield United in May 2011, and again took his club to Wembley in the play-offs, losing to Huddersfield Town. After leaving in April 2013 he returned to Oakwell for a second spell in charge, remaining until February 2015. During his time at Barnsley, in December 2014, he was inducted into the Football League Managers Hall of Fame after becoming the twenty-fourth individual to manage 1,000 games in English football. He joined fellow former Wednesday bosses Ashurst and Atkinson as members of the select band of managers, diplomatically commenting at the time that 'I have been fortunate to work with some very good chairmen who put their faith in me. It goes without saying how privileged I feel to join such an elite group of managers who have reached the 1,000 match milestone.' Within a few weeks Wilson departed from Oakwell and was appointed Chesterfield manager in September 2015, staying for eighteen months before leaving in January 2017.

Former coach Peter Shreeves was handed the unenviable job of trying to save the club from relegation, on a caretaker basis, but after the inevitable drop, Wednesday handed the job of restoring that treasured top-flight place to Liverpudlian Paul Steven Jewell, the new man taking charge on 21 June 2000. Born on 28 September 1964, the striker had started his playing career with home town club Liverpool but failed to secure any first-team appearances before moving to Wigan Athletic. He grabbed thirty-five goals for the Latics and would spend the remainder of his career in the colours of Bradford City. He became a big crowd favourite at Valley Parade and appeared in over 250 matches, netting over fifty times, before being co-opted onto the backroom staff and eventually taking over as manager in 1998. He was handed a relatively big transfer budget and surprised the football world by clinching promotion to the Premier League for the first time. It was perhaps a bigger surprise that he kept City in the top division but took the unusual step of stepping down a division to join the Owls after a disagreement with the City chairman, who had described the club's finishing position of seventeenth as a 'disappointment'. He was subsequently placed on 'gardening leave', while the clubs agreed a compensation package, and like his predecessor Wilson, was warmly welcomed by Wednesdayites, hoping for a quick return to the Premier League. Unfortunately that hope proved totally unrealistic as Jewell probably did not realise how threadbare and low on quality the Owls squad actually was. Jewell's reign at Wednesday could perhaps be described as 'right man at the wrong time' as the club lurched from crisis to crisis, setting a new club record of eight consecutive league defeats. With finances deteriorating quickly behind the scenes, Jewell was forced mainly to wheeler deal in the loan and free transfer market, with limited success. His inevitable departure came on 12 February 2001, with Wednesday bottom of the First Division (Championship) after a 4-1 defeat at Wimbledon, and showed his qualities over the next two years as he took his new side, Wigan Athletic, into the second tier for the first time. Two years later he guided them into the top flight for the first time and kept them there for two years, securing a win at Sheffield United in his final game in charge in May 2007 to retain that status – he'd also led them to the 2006 League Cup final. His managerial career continued to be 'boom and bust' as he was handed the job of Derby County manager in November 2007 with the Rams already rooted to the foot of the Premier League. His first win came, ironically, in the FA Cup against Wednesday and after Derby went down with a record low total of eleven points he resigned on New Year's Eve 2008. A spell at Ipswich Town followed (Jan 2011–Oct 2012) while in January 2015 he was bizarrely on West Bromwich Albion's coaching staff for just a week before departing, after being asked to take a pay cut. He has remained out of the game since that sudden exit, appearing occasionally as a TV pundit.

A familiar face was handed the reins after Jewell's departure as Peter Shreeves, who had initially joined Wednesday back in June 1996 as first-team coach and stayed until September 1998, also taking charge of a solitary game as caretaker in November 1997. He then returned as temporary manager after the sacking of Wilson and was appointed assistant to Jewell in 2000. It was therefore Shreeves who was handed the task of saving Wednesday from relegation and it was a feat he comfortably achieved, thanks in part to the inspirational signings of Palmer and Soltvedt. The Welsh-born Shreeves (30 November 1940 in Neath) was rewarded with a permanent two-year contract but lasted only a few months, resigning on 17 October 2001 with Wednesday back in trouble, commenting 'with the limited resources available to the club, the last few weeks have been very tough. In the best interests of Sheffield Wednesday and myself, I felt the honourable thing to do was to offer my resignation'. Although Welsh born, his mother was evacuated to Islington during the war and the inside forward would start his playing career at amateur club Finchley, later appearing in the Football League for Reading, in addition to spells at Wimbledon and Stevenage Athletic. A broken leg at Reading ended his playing days and he worked as a taxi driver and then a games teacher during the early 1970s before starting a coaching career at Charlton Athletic. He was employed in various backroom roles over the years that followed and after ten years at Tottenham Hotspur he was appointed manager in 1984. He led Spurs to third place in his first season but was replaced by Pleat in March 1986. He subsequently coached at Queens Park Rangers and was then assistant manager to Francis before being assistant at Watford and then under Yorath for the Welsh national team. He returned to Spurs as manager in 1991 but could not repeat the FA Cup winning feats of Terry Venables and was shown the door again after Tottenham finished in the bottom half of the table. Three years as assistant manager at Chelsea followed before he joined up with Wednesday for the first time. After taking over he found a dispirited dressing room, many players having thrown in the towel already, and despite his best efforts Wednesday dropped out of the Premier League. Described as a 'typical London boy', he returned to the capital to take charge of Barnet in February 2002 but resigned in 2003 to end his time in the day-to-day world of professional football. He later worked as a Premier League delegate (assessor) and experienced brief backroom roles at Grays Athletic and back at Barnet before retiring from the game altogether.

The next man handed the task of reviving the club's fortunes was former Welsh international Terence (Terry) Charles Yorath, who had initially followed Jewell from Bradford City. He was appointed on a caretaker basis, stepping from his former role as assistant to Shreeves, and within a month, on 21 November 2001, was handed the role on a permanent basis. He did succeed in saving Wednesday from relegation but for fans his appointment smacked of the 'cheap option' and his first full season in charge proved disastrous as Wednesday slumped to the foot of the division after winning only twice in the opening sixteen games. Wednesday sat one place off the bottom after Millwall won at Hillsborough and with five minutes of that game remaining a female Owls fan famously tapped on his shoulder and said 'Terry, you're a lovely man but please do the best thing for Wednesday and resign.' A day later he tendered his resignation and the Owls were looking for a fourth manager since being relegated. Yorath, born in Cardiff on 27 March 1950, came back into management as assistant at Bradford City in June 2003, leaving by 'mutual consent' in December 2006. He was later director of football at Margate where brother Dai and nephew Dean had both played, and subsequently spent just under a year in charge before a run of bad results ended with his resignation in September 2009.

His departure from the Kent club brought the curtain down on a career that had started back in 1967 when the flame-haired midfielder signed his first professional contract at Leeds United. As a teenager, he had been picked to represent Wales at both football and rugby and it needed the persuasive powers of his father and elder brother to sway Yorath away from the latter. He started to train with Cardiff City but it would be in Yorkshire where his career really started after signing apprentice forms at Elland Road. He experienced a frustrating start to his senior career, struggling to win a regular place and was still on the fringes when, in November 1969, he won the first of fifty-nine caps for Wales – he appeared in only fourteen league games between 1967 and 1972. He did, however, appear as a late substitute for Leeds in their shock 1973 FA Cup final loss to Sunderland and by the mid-1970s had not only become a regular but was also captain, helping United to the title in 1974 and an appearance in the 1975 European Cup final; he became the first Welshman to appear in the prestigious final. A fee of £125,000 took him to Coventry City in 1976 and the hard-tackling midfielder then spent eighteen months at Tottenham Hotspur before joining NASL club Vancouver Whitecaps. His first experience of coaching came while at the Canadian club and he returned to Yorkshire after securing the role of player-manager at Bradford City in December 1982. He took City to the Third Division championship in 1985 but the success was overshadowed by the terrible Valley Parade fire that claimed fifty-six lives and left countless others injured – Yorath was injured after jumping out of window after helping to evacuate a supporters' bar. In July 1986 he returned to Wales to take over at Swansea City and after play-off success in 1988 accepted the part-time role as manager of the national side. A shock return to Bradford caused the Swans to issue a court injunction but the whole episode ended with Yorath back in Yorkshire and his new club paying a fine set by the Football League. Unfortunately for Yorath, new owners meant he was sacked in 1990, prompting a return to Swansea! A run of nine consecutive defeats led to another departure, in December 1991, which in turn led to his appointment as full-time Wales manager. Working alongside Shreeves, he came agonisingly close to taking his charges to Euro '92 but his life was tinged with tragedy when in 1992 his fifteen-year-old son, Daniel, died in his arms while the pair were kicking a ball around his back garden – a rare heart condition proved to be the reason for his death. It would be a moment that understandably haunted Yorath – his daughter, Gabby, a well-known TV presenter, later revealed that her father had suffered over twenty years of depression due the loss of his son. His personal life seemed to have hit rock bottom in 2004 when, three times over the legal limit, he knocked down a pedestrian, narrowly escaping a custodial sentence, while divorce from his wife occurred after thirty-six years of marriage. Away from his personal heartache, Yorath remained in charge of Wales, taking them to their highest ever FIFA ranking, prior to 2016, during forty-one games. After narrowly failing to qualify for the 1994 World Cup finals his contract was controversially not renewed. He remained in Wales to become general manager at Cardiff City, later taking over team affairs, before a surprise move to become head coach of the Lebanon national side. He succeeded in lifting the country from the backwaters of world football and subsequently returned to the UK, becoming assistant manager at Huddersfield Town. A further spell at Bradford City followed, prior his move to Sheffield, while he now lives out his retirement back in Leeds.

After several false dawns the appointment of Christopher (Chris) Robert Turner, in hindsight, provided the catalyst that would get Wednesday back on track and lead to that memorable day in Cardiff, although Turner had long-since departed. When being appointed on 7 November 2002 he became the sixth former player to manage the club, having originally joined Wednesday as a trainee in March 1975. He made his first-team bow, aged seventeen, in August 1976 – he'd signed professional forms thirteen days before – and the agile goalkeeper would quickly become a firm favourite with fans. Incredibly Turner played in fifty-two senior games in his first season, earning several England Youth caps, but subsequently had to fight for the No. 1 spot with new arrival Bolder. Despite Wednesdayites clearly favouring Turner, it was his rival that Charlton eventually installed as first choice and Turner moved to Sunderland in May 1979. He went on to represent Manchester United after over 200 games for the Wearside club, where despite fierce competition he accrued seventy-nine appearances before returning to Hillsborough in September 1988. Over the next three seasons he'd compete with Pressman for the first-team jersey and the pair would trade places, with Turner earning a League Cup-winner's medal in 1991. After taking his Owls appearance tally to 205, his playing career ended at Leyton Orient – moving to the London club as part of the Bart-Williams deal – where he became assistant manager and then co-manager. A spell as youth team boss followed at Wolves while a successful spell in charge at Hartlepool United preceded his return to Wednesday, for a third time. He was immediately faced with the difficult task of saving Wednesday from relegation but eight wins proved insufficient. It seemed that his faith in many of the relegation squad was not justified as despite a bright start his charges slumped into the bottom half of League One, remaining there to finish in a highly disappointing sixteenth. It was clear to all that major surgery was needed on the squad and what followed was one of the biggest 'clear outs' in club history as thirteen players were released. This draconian measure meant Wednesday had to rebuild and Turner proved adept in the transfer market, signing the likes of MacLean, McGovern, Whelan and Bullen. Unfortunately for Turner his new-look side failed to gel immediately and he was perhaps unlucky to be fired on 18 September 2004, following a 1-0 home loss to Bournemouth. After departing he was handed the task of saving Stockport County from relegation but it proved impossible and he departed, with County five points adrift at the bottom. A spell as director of sport and then caretaker-manager back at Hartlepool followed, while just before Milan Mandaric arrived he was the public face of an ultimately unsuccessful bid to buy Wednesday. From

December 2011 he held the position of chief executive at Chesterfield, after being hired by the man who fired him at Hillsborough, Allen, but in 2017 he relinquished his CEO role to become director of football, leaving altogether a few weeks later.

The replacement for Turner, Paul Whitehead Sturrock, proved to be one of the most popular managers in recent times, aided greatly by the club's promotion from League One just a few months after his arrival. The Owls' new manager was born in the small farming community of Ellon, Aberdeenshire, on 10 October 1956 and a career in football seemed unlikely until he attended a Scottish Junior game, aged fourteen, and was asked by the manager if he could play as they were short of players. The rest is history as he scored twice and evolved into one of Scotland's best attacking players of the 1980s, later spending the whole of his professional career at Dundee United, amassing 571 games (170 goals) for the Tangerines, in addition to twenty Scotland caps, appearing in the 1986 World Cup finals. Affectionately known as 'Luggy', he was forced to retire injured in May 1989 but during the decade had helped United to the league title in 1983, the final of UEFA Cup in 1987 (losing to Nilsson's IFK Gothenburg) as well as winning two League Cups and reaching four Scottish Cup finals. It was a golden period for United and after his playing career ended he was appointed to the Tannadice coaching staff, remaining until November 1993 when he took over at St Johnstone. He totally revamped the club and in 1997 finished a mammoth twenty points clear at the top. The pull of Dundee United proved too strong, however, as he returned as manager in 1998 but the sale of his top scorer proved a mortal blow as he resigned two games into the 2000/01 campaign. A hugely successful spell at Plymouth Argyle followed – the Devon club won promotion twice in three seasons – before moving to Southampton for his first taste of Premier League football. Sadly, his time on the south coast was a decidedly unhappy one and he departed after just thirteen games in August 2004, being appointed at Wednesday on 23 September 2004. By the end of the season Wednesday had qualified for the Football League play-offs for the first time, and he certainly motivated the previously underperforming side – the likeable Sturrock enjoyed the highlight of his managerial career as his side earned promotion. However, Wednesday were still suffering financially but Sturrock overcome a plethora of injury problems to steer Wednesday to safety in their first season back in the second tier. He signed a new four-year contract in September 2006 but was surprisingly shown the door on 19 October 2006 after a damaging 4-0 defeat had left the Owls bottom. His dismissal left many Wednesday fans dismayed – flooding the local radio station to express their disappointment – and they were perhaps justified as what was virtually 'his team' ended the season in the top half of the division. He was quickly snapped up by Swindon Town and promotion in 2007 led to a return to Plymouth in 2008, the same time when he publicly admitted that he suffered from a mild form of the degenerative brain disease Parkinson's. He could not repeat the success of his first spell at Argyle and moved into a commercial role after being relieved of his duties in December 2009. A relatively successful spell at Southend United ended in March 2013 – Sturrock declining the club's offer to lead the team out at Wembley in the final of the Football League Trophy – and just three days as a consultant at Torquay United preceded his most recent managerial appointment, boss at Yeovil Town between April and December 2015.

Not unlike Sturrock himself, new manager Brian Laws inherited a side that was not short on quality but perhaps low on confidence. This was proven as after taking charge on 6 November 2006 his new side went on a tremendous run of form, which only ended on the penultimate Saturday of the season, when a late push for the play-offs stalled at Birmingham City. It should also be noted that academy director Sean McAuley was put in temporary charge after Sturrock's departure and his haul of ten points from four games could also be seen as a major factor in Laws' early successes. He would experience a mixed spell in charge at Hillsborough with a season of struggle in 2007/08 commencing with a club record six straight losses and safety secured on the very last day. The 2008/09 campaign was a rarity for the Owls in recent times – one where Wednesday finished firmly entrenched in mid-table – although the double over Sheffield United, for the first time in almost a century, was a definite highlight and made Laws popular among Wednesdayites. Incidentally he had an extra incentive to be successful at Hillsborough as his second wife, Jane, was the daughter of a Sheffield steelworker, who he'd met while at Scunthorpe after she had moved to the town with her family. Unfortunately, Wednesday was still suffering a huge financial hangover from the Premier League days and with finances tight, Laws' recruitment was limited, leading directly to a season of struggle, the Owls sliding down the Championship table as the 2009/10 campaign progressed. Despite being backed by the majority of fans, his departure became inevitable after a damaging 3-0 loss at Leicester City on 12 December, Laws leaving by mutual consent the day after, following five consecutive defeats. He was not out of work long though, with his destination a surprise as he joined Premier League Burnley, being in charge as they lost fifteen of eighteen games to tumble out of the top flight. He started the following season still in the hot seat and managed his 700th game in league football before a downturn in results led to his departure. A spell as director of football at Irish side Shamrock Rovers followed in 2012, before he joined Scunthorpe United, lasting just over a year before being dismissed in November 2013. Born in Wallsend on 14 October 1961, Laws' playing career started at Burnley and after turning professional he broke into the Clarets' side in August 1980, remaining a regular at right-back until being sold to Huddersfield Town in August 1983. After a spell at Middlesbrough he came under the unique tutelage of Brian Clough at Nottingham Forest, his new manager famously telling the new recruit that 'I've never seen you play son. I'm going on the recommendation of Ronnie Fenton. So if you're crap, Ronnie signed you. If you're good, I signed you.' Under Clough he would enjoy the best period of his career, appearing in over 150 games and winning the League Cup twice, the Full Members Cup and also being a losing finalist in the League Cup and FA Cup. Relegation from the newly formed Premier League saw Clough depart and Laws fall out of favour, eventually accepting the post of player-manager at Grimsby Town in 1994. His spell at Blundell Park was best remembered for an incident with Italian Ivano Bonetti, which triggered an urban myth that Laws threw a plate of chicken wings at the fiery attacker, breaking his cheekbone, after a dressing room bust up. Years later Laws revealed that it was a plate of sandwiches that were thrown by Bonetti before Laws retaliated! He lasted another six months at the Mariners, fired after a poor start to the 2006/07 campaign, before returning solely to playing duties, appearing for Darlington and then Scunthorpe United prior to being appointed manager at the latter in February 1997. He would enjoy a successful spell in charge, winning at Wembley in the League Two play-off final in 1999 and also gaining promotion from League One, just over a year after he was sacked and then reinstated twenty days later, as a power struggle behind the scenes was eventually resolved. After almost ten years at Glanford Park he moved to Hillsborough, Allen commenting that 'I like him, he comes from the Clough camp. I'm a great admirer of the Clough camp.' Since his second spell as Scunthorpe boss ended he has yet to return to management, being a regular co-commentator on both BBC Radio Nottingham and Sheffield.

After Laws' departure, Wednesday again turned to Sean McAuley to take temporary charge and he was at the helm for two games before former Preston manager James Alan Irvine was appointed on 8 January 2010. His two years in charge at Deepdale (November 2007–December 2009) was relatively successful, taking Preston to the Championship play-offs, but he faced an increasingly more difficult task at Wednesday, with the side at the bottom of the league and finances almost at breaking point. His coaching career before taking over at Deepdale encompassed five years as assistant manager to Moyes at Everton, where he forged a reputation as one of the finest young coaches in the British game. He'd arrived at Goodison Park after being youth team coach at Blackburn Rovers, where his playing career had ended in 1992, and then academy director and first-team coach at Newcastle United, following Dalglish from Ewood Park. He signed a three and a half-year deal at Hillsborough but his spell in charge severely tested a man with relatively little managerial experience and, despite winning four of his first five games, he could not save Wednesday from relegation. Briefly, in early February

2010, Wednesday scrambled out of the bottom three places but only two more victories followed and relegation was confirmed on the last day of the season. With little or no money to hand, Irvine brought in several experienced players during the summer of 2010, such as Morrison and Teale, and the new season started positively as Wednesday topped the early table. As winter beckoned the club's perilous financial positon became the main talking point but the future looked brighter when, just days before Mandaric took over, Wednesday beat Bristol Rovers 6-2 to jump back into the top two. However, this proved a false dawn as a run of five consecutive defeats was only masked slightly by a run to the last sixteen of the FA Cup. His forays into the transfer market in January also proved, in hindsight, somewhat disastrous, and forty-eight hours after a loss at Peterborough United he was dismissed by the club's new owner, on 3 February 2011.

It was perhaps no surprise that his destination was again Goodison Park, Irvine being appointed academy Director in July 2011, before he was appointed as manager at Premier League West Bromwich Albion in June 2014. His move to the Hawthorns certainly caused a few raised eyebrows in football circles, in addition to sheer disbelief among the Baggies fans, and his doubters were no doubt proven correct as he lasted only seven months and was fired after gaining only four wins in nineteen league fixtures. A spell as assistant manager at Blackburn Rovers followed after his 'gardening leave' at Albion had expired, before he was appointed to his current role, as first-team coach at Norwich City in July 2016, serving as caretaker-boss later in the season, and also at the end of the following season. His career off the pitch had followed a playing career that had started at Queens Park in the late 1970s. Locally born Irvine (12 July 1958) studied for the qualifications required to become an insurance broker but these fell by the wayside when the archetypical 'tricky winger' earned a move to Everton in 1981. He subsequently played for Crystal Palace, Dundee United (alongside Sturrock) and Blackburn Rovers before starting his coaching career of almost twenty-five years.

The club's seventh appointment since Premier League relegation was certainly a popular arrival as Gary John Megson took over the reins. The self-confessed Wednesday fan was appointed on 4 February 2011 and meant it was a third spell after twice being signed as a player. Born in Manchester on 2 May 1959, he spent his early years in Sheffield before his football career began in the West Country after his father took over as Bristol Rovers manager. The flame-haired, stylish midfielder appeared for several youth sides – also playing for Gloucestershire boys – before he signed as an apprentice at Plymouth Argyle in 1975. Within two years he was handed a professional deal and after impressing greatly in senior football he was snapped up by Everton in 1980 for £250,000. His career stalled somewhat at Goodison Park before joining Wednesday for

£108,500 in 1981. He shone in three years at Wednesday, missing only a handful of games and helping his boyhood club regain their top-flight place, and became a great favourite with Wednesdayites. It was therefore a surprise when he decided to join Nottingham Forest, soon after promotion, but he would then endure a nightmare four months before being snapped up his old boss, Charlton, at Newcastle United after being 'frozen out' at the City Ground – Clough famously commented that Megson 'could not trap a bag of cement'. He returned to Hillsborough in December 1985 and would take his appearance tally to 276 before leaving for Manchester City, during the turbulent rein of Eustace, the pair having a very public fallout. During a spell at Norwich City he was appointed player-coach, assistant manager and then caretaker-manager before leaving in 1995. He returned to solely playing with spells at Lincoln City and Shrewsbury Town prior to hanging up his boots and returning to Carrow Road as manager in December 1995, after a brief spell on the Bradford City coaching staff. His first experience of management proved unhappy with Megson fired in June 1996.

He subsequently spent a season in charge at Blackpool before two years at Stockport County. He was sacked after the County chairman accused him of applying for managerial vacancies while still employed and he was unlucky to leave Stoke City after the club was taken over by an Icelandic consortium, who quickly brought in their 'own man'. His departure from the Potteries preceded his best spell in club management – at West Bromwich Albion – where he twice took the Baggies into the Premier League during four years in charge. A fallout with the Albion chairman led to his departure before a spell at Nottingham Forest ended in February 1996. He was back in the game at Stoke City, being appointed coach by Pulis in June 2007, but stayed only a few weeks before being headhunted by Leicester City. Ironically, his first win in charge at Leicester was a 2-1 success back at Hillsborough but Bolton Wanderers subsequently, very publicly, chased him to take over. After Wanderers were rebuffed twice by Mandaric he did eventually leave, resigning after just forty-one days and nine league games in charge. He would be in charge of Bolton for just over two years, although his relationship with the club's supporters, despite keeping Bolton in the Premier League and to the last sixteen of the UEFA Cup, degenerated to such an extent that a poor start to the 2009/10 season led to fans catcalling the honorary Yorkshireman, who later commented about the Bolton fans that 'they did not like him and he did not like them'. His inevitable departure occurred in December 2009 and after both parties could not agree on a compensation package, he was placed on 'gardening leave' for a year. When this eventually expired he was approached for a third time by Mandaric with an offer of employment – back in 2000 he'd agreed to take over at Mandaric's Portsmouth side before deciding to turn down the post in the interests of his young family. It was no surprise that he was delighted to secure his 'dream job' at Wednesday. His first game in charge was a home fixture against MK Dons and Wednesday played so poorly in the first half that Megson abandoned his watching brief from the stands to visit the dressing room and whatever he said certainly helped as the Owls fought back to draw. The remainder of the season was simply about ensuring the club was not sucked into a relegation battle, and this was achieved. The summer of 2011 saw Megson revamp the squad, his most notable signing being Semedo, and Wednesday immediately positioned themselves in the top half of the table and launched a promotion challenge, eventually going 'toe-to-toe' with City rivals United. As the season progressed it seemed more likely that it would be the Blades that would grab the coveted place and even after a Chris O'Grady goal beat United at Hillsborough, in late February 2012, the Owls were still trailing their rivals, sat in third place. It was then that the most unexpected event occurred as Mandaric decided a change was needed to add additional momentum to the promotion chase and Megson was dismissed on 29 February 2012. It is open to conjecture if Wednesday would have caught United if Megson had still been charge – which of course they did under the next manager – but he could leave satisfied, having taken Wednesday from mid-table mediocrity to genuine promotion contenders in just over a year. He returned to football in July 2017, as assistant head coach at West Bromwich Albion.

As Wednesdayites digested the sudden departure of Megson, Mandaric was quick to fill the void, appointing David (Dave) Ronald Jones as Wednesday boss twenty-four hours later. The new man had the rare pleasure of taking over a team chasing promotion and he was at the reins as Wednesday started to close the gap over United, eventually leading to a joyous promotion. It was a dream start for Jones and he subsequently kept Wednesday in the Championship thanks to a last-day win. It would be fair to say that Jones was never particularly popular with Wednesday fans – his somewhat introverted persona being a sharp contrast to that of Megson – and despite the club being in relatively new hands, his budget remained one of the lowest in the division. This led to a plethora of loan signings and Wednesday experienced a bad start to the 2013/14 season, culminating in a 2-0 loss at Blackpool, which triggered his departure on 1 December 2013.

Born in Liverpool on 17 August 1956, Jones started his career as a defender at Everton and was actually told by Harry Catterick he was being released when aged sixteen, only for the whole management team to be sacked forty-eight hours later. The teenager decided he would just go into training the following week and not mention anything of that conversation – the plan worked superbly and he duly made his debut aged seventeen! After eighty-six games he moved to Coventry City in 1981 but a serious knee injury meant his playing career at the highest level was cut short – Jones ended his professional career at Hong Kong side Seiko before playing twice for non-league Southport, where he was appointed assistant manager during the 1986/87 campaign. He subsequently moved on to Mossley and Jones broke into league football at Stockport County in July 1990, being handed the role of youth coach. His big chance came in March 1995 when first-team boss Begara left and Jones was installed as his successor. He would enjoy great success at County as he led them to promotion to the First Division (Championship) in 1997 and also on a headline-making run to the semi-finals of the League Cup. It was one of the clubs his side vanquished on that run, Southampton, that was his next employer and he managed to keep the Saints in the Premier League before his time came to an unfortunate end in 1999 after he was arrested on charges of child abuse relating back to the late 1980s, when he briefly worked as a care worker. He pleaded his innocence from the start and when the case eventually went to trial the judge immediately threw it out of court, stating that it should never have even reached the trial stage. Despite his innocence being proven, Jones was initially suspended, pending the result of the court case, and did not return, eventually being dismissed and subsequently losing an employment tribunal case. It had been a nightmare period for Jones and his family but he was back in football in the summer of January 2001, taking over at Wolverhampton Wanderers. After heavy recruitment, Wolves looked set for automatic promotion in 2001/02 before an inexplicable loss of form resulted in close rivals West Bromwich Albion pipping them to promotion. The dip in form was compounded by defeat in the play-off semi-finals but there was a reversal of fortunes in the following campaign as a poor start was followed by a tremendous late run of form that put Wolves in the play-offs. They reached the final, beating Sheffield United to clinch a return to the top flight after an absence of eighteen years – therefore fulfilling owner Jack Hayward's wish of seeing his club back at the 'big table' of English football. Unfortunately, they went straight back down and as hopes of a quick return slowly diminished he was dismissed in November 2004.

He returned to management at Cardiff City in 2005 and remained in south Wales for six years, during which time he led them to only their second FA Cup final. Despite a large turnover of players (Glenn Loovens being one of the high-profile players to depart) City remained a competitive force in the Championship, with defeat at Hillsborough, on the final day of the 2008/09 season, seeing them miss out on the play-offs. A year later they went all the way to the play-off final, only to lose 3-2 to Blackpool, and there was more play-off heartbreak in 2011, which ended in a semi-final defeat to Reading. It seemed only when, not if, City reached the 'promised land' but Jones would not be at helm when it did finally occur, having been sacked in May 2011 after Cardiff was taken over by Vincent Tan. After his spell at Wednesday he returned to the Welsh capital as advisor to Tan in January 2014 and unsuccessfully applied to take over as manager of the Ivory Coast national team in the summer of 2015. He was briefly in charge at Hartlepool United before departing in April 2017.

In the aftermath of Jones' departure, Wednesday appointed his former assistant, Stuart Gray, as caretaker. He had been appointed No. 2 in December 2012 after having held a variety of coaching and managerial roles, which included stints in charge as a caretaker at Aston Villa, Wolverhampton Wanderers, Burnley and Portsmouth, plus on a permanent basis at Northampton Town. Born in the Yorkshire village of Withernsea on 19 April 1960, Gray started his playing career at Nottingham Forest, earning a reputation as a versatile player, mainly being utilised as a midfielder at Forest while playing at centre-half and full-back during four years at Barnsley. Four years at Aston Villa followed, during which time he won promotion and was in the side that finished runners-up to Liverpool in 1990. He took his league appearances to just shy of 300 before a serious Achilles tendon injury brought a premature end to his career in 1993, after playing a solitary game for Bognor Regis Town. He was subsequently co-opted onto the coaching staff at Southampton and in June 1994 moved to the Black Country to take over as reserve team manager at Wolverhampton Wanderers. His family could not settle in the West Midlands though and he returned to Southampton, initially as community officer, before teaming up with Jones for the first time after being appointed as reserve team boss. He was promoted to assistant manager in the following year and despite the departure of Jones he remained on the Southampton coaching staff when Hoddle took over in January 2000. When Hoddle was lured away to Tottenham Hotspur in March 2001, the popular coach was handed the reins on a caretaker capacity and was appointed permanent manager in a season where Southampton said goodbye to their old Dell Ground. He was in charge as Southampton moved into St Mary's Stadium but the Saints' chairman at the time, Rupert Lowe, dismissed him after just three months – early results were poor – after becoming somewhat panic-stricken at the possible financial ramifications of falling out of the Premier League after the huge investment in the new ground. After losing his position, he became first-team coach at old club Aston Villa before being briefly assistant caretaker manager at Crystal Palace in November 2003. When Ian Dowie took over from Symons, Gray again joined up with Jones, moving to Molineux as first-team coach and then assistant manager. A spell as caretaker-manager followed and when Glenn Hoddle took charge he reverted back to his previous role, prior to taking charge of Northampton Town in January 2007. He stayed at the Cobblers until being dismissed in September 2009 and would serve Burnley and Portsmouth in various roles, including caretaker-manager at both, until again being reacquainted with Jones at Wednesday. He was part of the management team that just kept the Owls in the Championship at the end of 2012/13 and when handed the reigns he guided Wednesday to a superb 2-1 home success against promotion-chasing Leicester City. He duly presided over a remarkable run of results, which included eleven games unbeaten, that pushed Wednesday, who were six points off safety when he took charge, to the relatively comfortable position of ninteenth. He also steered the club to the last sixteen of the FA Cup and those set of results ensured Mandaric effectively had no choice but to hand Gray the position on a permanent basis – he was officially appointed on 25 January 2014. He was still working under the same financial constraints of previous managers but with a lack of forward quality he relied on a 'rock-solid' defence, recording Wednesday's best finish since promotion in 2012. His side equalled the club record for clean sheets (seventeen), although goalscoring was a definite problem. With new Thai owners at the helm, most Wednesdayites expected Gray, who had fashioned a great team spirit and was popular among the playing staff and supporters, to be given the funds to add more creativity and firepower to the side. However, this was not the case and on 15 June 2015 it was announced he had departed Hillsborough. After leaving he joined Fulham as senior coach in December 2015, and was in the running to take over at Rotherham United before Neil Warnock was appointed in February 2016.

The club's next managerial appointment surprised both the media and Wednesday fans as Wednesday's new owner handed the role to a virtual unknown, to English fans, in Portuguese Carlos Augusto Soares da Costa Faria Carvalhal. The club's thirty-first boss therefore became the first non-British manager to be in charge and it would be fair to say that his appointment was not universally popular among supporters, especially after it was revealed that he had not managed in club football for three years, working as a technical director for United Arab Emirates club Al Ahli for the previous two years. On being appointed he commented, 'Working in England is something I have dreamed of since I was a child. I am so very happy to be with Sheffield Wednesday and like everyone, I am here to succeed. My football philosophies match those of the chairman and we want everyone behind us with all our supporters packed into the stadium for our first match of the season against Bristol City. We are now working very hard on the training field, the players are giving everything towards the first game, which is the next game, and that is always the most important one.' It would also be fair to say that he was the club's first head coach with his only responsibility being the playing side, leaving such items as contract negotiations and dealing with agents to other club employees – replicating the continental system favoured in other European countries. He may have been a surprise appointment but his affable and friendly disposition quickly charmed all parties, perhaps buying himself some time to rebuild the Owls side, although the club made a poor start to his first season at the helm, registering only one win in the first seven league fixtures. It quickly became apparent that Carvalhal had also made a big impression on the playing personal and complete with a new style, which concentrated more on a continental pass and move ethos, Wednesday surged up the table while also progressing in the League Cup – an unforgettable 3-0 win over Arsenal at a sold-out Hillsborough being the definite highlight. He was duly named Capital One manager of the tournament and his stock rose further as Wednesday clinched a place in the Championship play-offs. It was instant success for the personable Carvalhal, who it had become apparent was a deep thinker who believed in the collective, alluding to those principles after meeting Arctic Monkeys lead singer Alex Turner, stating that he would not be successful without his other band members. In fact, Carvalhal's quotes proved to be 'manna from heaven' for local journalists with comments such as 'I don't know what's happened in the house of my neighbours, but I know what's happening in mine. We are feeling positive, training very well and are fresh' (before the play semi-final versus Brighton) and 'In the Championship, if you sleep one minute your opponent will kill you. So I am here to wake everybody up.' After qualifying for the play-offs, Carvalhal steered Wednesday to Wembley but his side just could not take the final step. Despite the defeat, his debut season coaching in England had been a success and further significant investment in the squad, during the summer of 2016, saw the Owls again try to regain that precious top-flight place; he was also handed a new contract in April 2016 in recognition of that success.

The Owls' new boss was born in Braga, Portugal, on 4 December 1965 and started playing football at school, eventually signing for his home town club, aged eighteen, after finding his niche as a centre-half. Over the next fifteen years he had three separate spells at SC Braga and also appeared for a variety of other clubs, including Porto, Beira-Mar, Chaves and Tirsense. When Carvalhal retired from playing in 1998, the former Portugal U21 player had 259 league appearances to his name and went straight into his first coaching role at his last club, Espinho. He lasted just over a season in that post and duly coached at Freamunde and Aves before hitting the headlines in 2002 when his third-tier club, Leixoes, reached the final of the Portuguese cup. His side lost to Sporting Lisbon in the final but Carvalhal's reputation had been greatly enhanced and after experiencing European football with Leixoes he took over as coach at recently relegated Vitoria Setubal in 2003. He achieved instant success, coaching them to promotion, and this prompted another move, to Belenenses in 2004. Further spells at SC Braga and Beira-Mar followed before in the 2007/08 campaign, while in charge for second time at Vitoria Setubal, he enjoyed his best season as a coach, taking the Sadinos to sixth place in Portugal's top division, also qualifying for European football, and success in the inaugural final of the League Cup. After that success it was a surprise that he decided to coach abroad for the first time, moving to Greece where he took over at Asteras Tripolis. His stay was brief and after a short spell back home at Maritimo, Carvalhal was handed his biggest job in Portuguese soccer: interim boss at Sporting

Lisbon in November 2009. After failing to gain any ground on champions Benfica he was not handed a new contract and moved instead to the rather unpredictable animal that is Turkish football. In 2011 he moved to one of the country's biggest clubs, Besitkas, initially as assistant but found himself in charge after manager Tayfur Havutcu was suspended after being embroiled in a match-fixing scandal. He did eventually return to the 'hot seat' and it proved the end of Carvalhal, who spent a brief time in charge at Istanbul club Basaksehir before spending two seasons as technical director for United Arab Emirates club Al Ahli. Carvalhal, who is married to nursery teacher Maria and has a son and daughter, only sees his family occasionally, mainly during international breaks, but states this is just a 'fact of life' for a modern coach and is something that he has become accustomed to. In 2014 he wrote his coaching manual and manifesto entitled *Soccer: Developing a Know-How*, which shows his meticulous approach to the game. His second season at Hillsborough saw Carlos improve the club's finishing positon again while there was agony in the play-off semi-final before he signed a new contract in advance of a third tilt at promotion in 2017/18.

Managerial Records (League Only):

Manager	Years	P	W	D	L	F	A	Win %
Dickinson	1891–1920	840	352	172	316	1314	1247	42%
Brown	1920–33	552	248	126	178	977	823	45%
McClelland*	1933	11	2	2	7	14	25	18%
Walker	1933–37	165	53	48	64	236	269	32%
Taylor*	1937	9	5	2	2	14	7	56%
McMullan	1938–42	61	28	15	18	110	82	46%
Taylor	1942–58	504	182	120	202	874	899	36%
Catterick	1958–61	122	69	29	24	260	146	57%
Taylor*	1961	4	1	0	3	4	8	25%
Buckingham	1961–64	124	57	26	41	229	186	46%
Taylor*	1964	2	1	1	0	4	2	50%
Brown	1964–68	153	53	39	61	208	209	35%

Jack Marshall	1968–69	46	12	16	18	46	60	26%
T. McAnearney*	1969	11	0	5	6	7	16	0%
Williams	1969–71	67	16	16	35	71	114	24%
Dooley`	1971–73	122	39	31	52	150	168	32%
Young*	1973–74	5	1	4	0	6	5	20%
Burtenshaw	1974–75	66	13	16	37	66	105	20%
J. McAnearney*	1975	2	1	1	0	6	3	50%
Ashurst	1975–77	92	31	27	34	101	112	34%
Knighton*	1977	1	1	0	0	1	0	100%
Charlton	1977–83	253	101	79	73	345	288	40%
Wilkinson	1983–88	214	95	56	63	309	264	44%
Eustace	1988–89	17	2	7	8	12	27	12%
Atkinson	1989–91	99	38	30	31	131	120	38%
Francis	1991–95	168	65	54	49	242	211	39%
Pleat	1995–97	89	26	28	35	116	147	29%
Shreeves*	1997	1	1	0	0	5	0	100%
Atkinson	1997–98	24	9	5	10	29	32	38%
Wilson	1998–2000	67	18	13	36	68	98	27%
Shreeves*	2000	9	3	1	5	11	14	33%
Jewell	2000–01	31	7	5	19	33	58	23%
Shreeves	2001	28	9	8	11	30	38	32%
Yorath	2001–02	49	13	15	21	51	68	27%
Green/Burrows*	2002	1	0	0	1	1	3	0%
Turner	2002–04	84	24	27	33	101	125	29%

Sturrock	2004–06	95	31	29	35	113	113	33%
McAuley*	2006	4	3	1	0	10	7	75%
Laws	2006–09	143	49	38	56	180	192	34%
McAuley*	2009–10	2	0	1	1	2	4	0%
Irvine	2010–11	49	17	12	20	65	65	34%
Megson	2011–12	54	25	11	18	81	73	46%
Jones	2012–13	74	26	21	27	97	95	35%
Gray	2013–15	76	26	24	26	88	87	34%
Carvalhal	2015–	92	43	26	23	126	90	47%
Totals to end of 2016–17		4682	1796	1187	1699	6944	6705	

*Caretaker

Chapter 9

Grounds

'Sheffield Wednesday has lit a torch. Wednesday have started
something which, I hope, other clubs will follow.'
FA Secretary Sir Stanley Rous, opening of North Stand, August 1961

Of course, Wednesday have resided at their much-loved Hillsborough
home for the last 118 years but many supporters will not realise that
Owlerton, as it was named when Wednesday moved in, was in fact
the seventh venue used by the club, starting with a simple pitch in the
Highfields district of the town. Initially it was thought that the newly
formed Wednesday FC played all their games on a piece of land situated
where the modern-day Highfields library stands, roughly at the junction
of London Road and Abbeydale Road. However, further research has
uncovered the fact that at that time this area mainly consisted of green
spaces, broken by the occasional building, such as Highfield House and
Mount Pleasant. South of the aforementioned Mount Pleasant, which still
stands today, was an area called Cremorne Gardens – where modern-day
Mount Pleasant Road runs north to south – and it seems likely that
Wednesday played those early matches just east of these gardens, which
disappeared generations ago. This would place the pitch, and it would
have been nothing more than an unkempt pitch with no facilities, just
across the old route taken by London Road in an area with Highfields
Library to the north, Asline Road to the south and Cremorne Gardens
to the west – approximately where Highfield Place, Holland Road and
Colver Road are today. The major clue with regard to the club's early
home came with the discovery that prominent on the land in question
was a building called Parkfield House, owned by local solicitor Harry
Chambers. The significance of this gentleman was that in October 1857
he hosted the historic meeting that saw the world's oldest football club,
Sheffield FC, formed, Chambers being a player and secretary. It therefore
seems realistic to believe that such a gentleman so keen on the new sport

of association football would surely have been sympathetic to a request from the officials of the fledgling club to play on land adjacent to his residence. An educated guesstimate would therefore put the slightly sloping pitch (the area fell away to where Queens Road was eventually constructed) just below St Barnabas Church, close to where the current day medical centre is situated. Sadly, no contemporary evidence has ever come to light about that pivotal first home, other than a comment by early player, and future club chairman, Charles Clegg, who many years later revealed that he had to change into his playing attire behind a bush and pay a local youngster a few pennies to make sure his clothes did not disappear! Regardless of where the actual playing surface was situated, the Highfields district provided Wednesday FC with a vital base, the first game – on 12 October 1867 – seeing all the newly registered playing members facing each other in an inter-club fixture. The first Highfields fixture to be advertised in the local press was a January 1868 game against Broomhall, although it does seem highly likely that Wednesday did play another club earlier than that date but, sadly, no record has survived. The first match result to be reported was a return game with Mechanics (the club's first ever opponents) with the away side winning by a solitary goal to Wednesday's four rouge points. The first recorded goal by a Wednesday player came in January 1870 – 'little Frank' Butler scoring against Pitsmoor – while a few weeks later Wednesday hosted back-to-back games on the same day, both ending in draws against Broomhall and Pitsmoor respectively. The 1869/70 season would be the final one at Highfields – Ward netting the final Wednesday goal – as the increasingly popular club 'upped sticks' and moved the short distance to set up home at a pitch adjacent to Myrtle Road.

The club's new home was situated on a piece of land at the corner of the newly built Queens Road and Myrtle Road with the Midland Railway lane to the north. Thankfully, several contemporaneous reports reference the club's new abode, confirming that Wednesday played on a sloping pitch, towards an old quarry, roughly around the Myrtle Road/ Midhill Road area, not far from the Heeley City Farm. One downside to the new ground was that the access road was sometimes inches deep in mud and in 1876 local residents signed a petition to parliament in the hope of resolving the matter! The new pitch actually overlooked the site of their future Olive Grove home while it is believed that the venue was shared with the MacKenzie Club; in February 1871 it was reported that Wednesday had played Broomhall on a pitch above where MacKenzie Club had played earlier in the day, clearly stating the venue must have consisted of at least two pitches. Thankfully, a handful of club documents have survived from that era, one particular receipt revealing that for the 1875/76 season, Wednesday paid just over £8 to Mr Bailey from Bank Farm, Heeley, for the rent of the field from 1 October to 1 March. Wednesday would remain at Myrtle Road for the vast majority of the 1870s, during which period they rose to become one of the most prominent and best-supported teams in the town. That success prompted a need to move to larger premises. Wednesday moved out in the summer of 1877, although they did return briefly in January 1882, hosting two friendly games. It is also a little-known fact that in November 1870 Wednesday played a game against Derby, not at Myrtle Road, Bramall Lane or Highfields but at Hillsborough, almost thirty years before the district was even mentioned as a possible home! The Queens Hotel Grounds was situated behind the public house of the same name, at 401 Langsett Road, opposite Hillsborough barracks and near to Hillsborough corner. The ground was mainly utilised for cricket but was also used for athletics, pigeon shooting and other sporting activities before being developed for housing in the twentieth century.

After outgrowing Myrtle Road, Wednesday's next home was the larger Sheaf House Ground, although it should be noted that from 1872 the club started to use the biggest ground in the town – Bramall Lane – on a regular basis, mainly for more prestigious games as admission could be charged. It was perhaps no coincidence that Wednesday's first game at the venue was in the same year that the cricket ground's owners installed turnstiles! When construction was completed, cricket enthusiasts were delighted to find a ground, which would be unsurpassed in the north of England, boasting an exclusive side (where United's South Stand was subsequently built) that contained several viewing platforms, while the John Street side boasted a large structure, which included four publican tenants below and covered accommodation above. Low wooden sheds were also erected on that side to act as dressing rooms. When football started to grow in the mid- to late 1860s, Bramall Lane hosted the world's first ever cup final – Hallam FC lifting the Youdan Cup in 1867 – while Wednesday themselves lifted the Cromwell Cup a year later at the same venue. These games were both pre-dated, however, by a meeting between Sheffield FC and Hallam, played at Bramall Lane back in December 1862, in a unique charity game to raise funds for the Lancashire Distress Fund for cotton workers – the county had been severely hit with soaring unemployment by an acute shortage of cotton due to the American Civil War. The early years of Bramall Lane saw the ground struggle financially, with the man behind its construction, Michael Ellison, even having to pay some of the rent from his personal pocket – unbeknown to the general public. Thankfully, those financial difficulties were overcome with the formation of the county cricket club, which was based at the new ground, a significant aid. During the 1870s the ground was extended and better dressing rooms constructed while early in 1885 a new covered shelter was erected, used mainly by football fans to shelter from the inclement winter weather. By the early 1880s, Wednesday were playing virtually all of their matches there, including their first ever home FA Cup tie, and continued to do so until turning professional in 1887.

The 1880s up until 1887 had seen Wednesday use the Sheaf House Grounds, which were located in the shadow of Bramall Lane, behind the public house of the same name, which still stands today. The ground's name derived from a grand house built by Daniel Brammall in 1816 (the aforementioned pub), with the land behind subsequently developed into a sporting venue. Wednesday initially spent five years at the venue, the first match being played in October 1877 against Exchange Brewery in a Sheffield Challenge Cup tie. In 1879 and 1880 Wednesday hosted four-a-side tournaments at the ground – the winners receiving silver watches and the runners-up gold lockets – but Wednesdsday effectively deserted the venue in the early 1880s with only a solitary game played there in the 1880/81 campaign. It was clear that Bramall Lane had become the preferred venue so it was perhaps surprising that another ground move occurred for the 1882/83 campaign, Wednesday moving across town to a pitch near to the modern-day Endcliffe Park, near the Hunter's Bar roundabout.

Their new home, called various names including Hunter's Bar, Robert's Farm or Rustling's Farm, was only used by the club for three years and even then, only for relatively minor games and reserve matches. Its various names suggested the pitch was very close to the modern-day Hallamshire Tennis Club with Rustling's Farm located next to the present-day junction of Ecclesall Road and Rustlings Road, which runs around the southern side of Endcliffe Park. Contemporary reports described the ground as 'near to a bathing dam in Endcliffe Park' with fans' memories collaborating to point to Endcliffe Park, which was opened in 1884 when the weir was damned to create pools for bathers. Wednesday christened their new home with a 5-0 win over Thurlstone in November 1882. The history books group Hunter's Bar and Sheaf House together as grounds used only occasionally by Wednesday and it would be the club's next move that would truly shape the club as Wednesday moved onto the national scene and moved to a 'proper' football ground that befitted their status.

The club's adoption of professionalism in 1887 was welcomed by the vast majority of players and supporters but it created a real financial headache for the club's hierarchy as they suddenly needed to increase revenue without any obvious solution. The major problem surrounded their use of Bramall Lane as the ground authorities took a large share of the financial cake – Wednesday sometimes only seeing a sixth of the matchday takings – with receipts from FA Cup ties thought to be shared equally between the venue and two teams. It was obvious that moving permanently into Bramall Lane was not an option so Wednesday officials took the brave decision – when you consider the club had only been professional a matter of weeks and were not blessed with huge cash reserves – of revealing plans to build their own ground, where all revenues would flow direct into club coffers. Incidentally when Wednesday quit Bramall Lane, the ground saw a large drop in revenues and this was the main reason that a new club was formed – Sheffield United – to plug that financial gap. It would again be the Duke of Norfolk who aided the sporting folk of Sheffield as he agreed to lease Wednesday a piece of, admittedly swampy, land just off Queens Road, on the north side of the Midland Railway line. The club signed an initial seven-year lease and despite some fans claiming Wednesday would struggle to get more than twenty supporters to make the trip from the town centre, the club formed a ground and management committee charged with the task of creating a football ground in time for the new season. The task was not an easy one as previous tenants, Nether FC, had found that several springs bubbled just under the playing surface and a footpath ran through the pitch towards a footbridge that ran over the railway line and onto Queens Road, via several gardens. Wednesday would spend the not inconsiderable amount of £5,000 in that summer as firstly the footpath was diverted, before the various brooks were covered, the complete field drained and the whole area enclosed; turnstiles were also installed. Wednesday also erected a large covered standing enclosure on the railway side, which held around 1,000, although access to the actual ground was not ideal – fans had to enter over railway bridges from either Myrtle Road or Charlotte Road (Olive Grove Road had not been constructed yet). When completed, Wednesday's new home boasted a rather uneven pitch with a cinder track, 6 foot wide, running around its perimeter. The club would use the nearby Earl of Arundel & Surrey Hotel (now a cycle shop) as their dressing rooms, walking to the ground in full kit, while readiness for the new season was shown when Wednesday announced season tickets were available, priced at 10s 6d. The ground had already been named Olive Grove, after a prominent house that lay north east of the enclosure, and the club held its collective breath to see if supporters would follow their team to the edge of town. Thankfully they need not have worried as 2,000 attended the opening game, played on a Monday afternoon, and as the nineteenth century progressed average crowds would increase to almost five figures as Wednesday became a league club and achieved FA Cup success. Over the years that followed, various improvements were undertaken, beginning just a few months later when Preston North End rolled into town for an FA Cup tie. A brook on the elevated north side was covered, creating extra standing capacity for 1,500, while a new stand was also hastily erected so 9,000 could squeeze in for the hugely anticipated clash. In the summer of 1889 the original stand was freshly painted blue and white with the words 'Sheffield Wednesday' emblazoned on the roof, despite the club being simply Wednesday FC, while covered accommodation was erected at the Heeley end. The pitch was relaid a year later and the refreshments concession put out to local tender – it is not only in recent years that the club has moved between in-house and contracted-out catering! When Wednesday was elected into the Football League the committee decided to significantly upgrade their Olive Grove home with local contractors Mastin & Sons employed to construct a new brick stand, which when completed was said to be one of the best in the league. The new edifice provided 1,000 covered seats plus a railed enclosure at the front, which fans could access for an extra 6*d*. The players also had the luxury of getting changed at the ground as the new stand included dressing rooms, in addition to baths plus a committee and refreshment room. At both the Sheffield and Heeley ends, the standing area was increased and upgraded plus the uneven playing surface was finally flattened and extended. Total costs for the work was around £2,000 but Wednesday were confident that higher gates would more than repay the expense, an opinion that proved correct. A charge of 6*d* was levied for all league games and Wednesday moved into the Football League era with a ground the envy of many of its fellow members.

Over the intervening years, Olive Grove became a much-loved home, so fans were concerned in July 1896 when fears were first aired that the club may be forced to move grounds due the expansion of the railway. These fears were allayed though by the Sheffield Corporation (council), who stated that the Midland Railway only owned a 10-foot strip of land next to the line and Corporation owned the remainder. It was therefore a huge shock when in the summer of 1898 it was announced that the club's lease, which was due to expire on 29 September 1898, would not be renewed with the rumoured extension of the northern line going ahead after all, regardless of the Corporation's earlier assurances. The railway company and the Corporation did allow Wednesday to stay for the remainder of the season but club officials were left with the difficult task of starting again from scratch, as they had done back in 1887, and construct a ground that ensured Wednesday could preserve league status. Decades later a brass plaque was erected at the sight of the modern-day Olive Grove Council depot, which reads:

Olive Grove, home of Sheffield Wednesday 1887-1899

Sheffield Wednesday's first ground after they adopted professionalism was here at Olive Grove, on land leased from the Duke of Norfolk. In a twelve year stay they emerged as one of the countries leading clubs, joining the Football league in 1892 and bringing the FA Cup to Yorkshire for the first time in 1896. Winger Fred Spiksley – the 'Olive Grove Flyer' – scored both goals in that 1896 triumph and epitomised the spirit of an era which ended when the site was required for the expansion of the Midland Railway line.

The ground situation was the main topic of conversation between Wednesday fans and it seemed to have been solved when it was announced, in August 1898, that the club was returning to their former

Sheaf House home, having agreed a rent with prospective new landlords Mappin's Brewery. All that was required was the consent of the local magistrates at the Brewster Sessions (the annual meeting for all matters regarding the licensing trade) but supporters were dismayed when it was revealed that no application had been made by the club as the brewery company had suddenly hiked up the price and talks had therefore collapsed, Wednesday officials believing Mappin's was taking advantage of their increasingly desperate position. So it was back to square one with their final season already underway. Within a few weeks it emerged that Wednesday had identified two possible sites with one, Owlerton, highly controversial as it was a considerable distance from the town centre, badly served by public transport, and nowhere near the Heeley end of the city where the vast majority of the club's support resided. To gauge public opinion, Wednesday handed out over 10,000 ballot cards at the November 1898 home game against Aston Villa with the results relatively close, Carbrook attracting 4,767 votes to Owlerton's 4,115. Both of the possible sites were available for £5,000 but despite the poll result and opinions in the press, it would be the words of club chairman George Senior that effectively ended the debate, the successful steel magnet commenting that, 'the working men who followed Wednesday got enough mucky air down Attercliffe way during the week without being asked to go there on Saturday afternoons as well'. The issue was effectively decided when he added, 'if you take 'em down Attercliffe you won't get a penny o'mine, But if you take 'em to Owlerton, you can have as much brass as you want'.

His remarks turned a club meeting and he was backed by the Clegg brothers – Wednesday were moving out of the town centre! The club duly called a Special General Meeting at the Maunche Hotel on 6 April 1899 to announce plans to not only convert the club into a limited liability company but to also raise £5,000 through the issuing of share capital. The news that all Wednesday fans had waited for came from the lips of President Holmes, who disclosed that the funds raised would be used to buy the land for their new home, at High Bridge, Owlerton. The land was owned by Sheffield silversmiths James Dixon and was originally offered at a premium price per acre before the owners decided to accept a much more moderate sum for the 10-acre plot of meadowland, Wednesday eventually paying £4,783 for the deeds, financed mainly by a £3,300 mortgage secured by club stalwart Charles Clegg. At a director's meeting in May 1899 architect John Lancashire (who became the son-in-law of chairman George Senior in 1901) was instructed to prepare plans for the laying out of the new enclosure at Owlerton for football, cricket and athletics – thankfully the land was relatively flat and well drained, so Wednesday did not have the initial problems associated with Olive Grove – with secretary Dickinson having already arranged for the purchase of the freehold land. Not unlike the move to Olive Grove years earlier, doubts were raised that fans would not travel to the new ground but at the time the Owlerton, Hillsborough and Wadsley districts were all rapidly expanding, although transport links were still poor and amenities somewhat sparse. The former problem was quickly solved as in 1901 the tramline was extended to reach Wednesday's new abode; this followed a promise made by Sheffield's Lord Mayor, who was also chairman of the Tramways Committee, that if Wednesday moved in he would push through the extension of the line to serve the new ground. The land was bordered to the west by Leppings Lane, which at the time boasted a 'capital' carriage bridge, to the east by Penistone Road and to the south by the winding River Don, with suggestions of the new ground's name including Wardsend (a sub-district of Owlerton) and Owlerton. Of course, the latter name stuck and in the summer of 1899 the club appointed usual contractors, Mastin & Sons, who employed seventy or eighty men to ensure the ground would be completed in time for the new season. The first expense was £730 for 'laying out' of the ground before the stand at Olive Grove was moved, literally brick by brick, to be erected on the south side – it was rather unsurprisingly referred to as the 'Olive Grove Stand' by Wednesday fans, before it was pulled down in 1913. The playing surface was raised around 2 feet, railings were erected around and the majority of the ground was enclosed, including turnstiles and entrances at the east and west ends. The enclosure was duly named 'Wednesday Football Ground, Owlerton' with a subsequent 'house warming' party seeing Chesterfield beaten 5-1 in the opening fixture.

Those early works concentrated on getting the ground up to a minimum standard and once the season had commenced further major works were undertaken, with a new stand built on the north side, designed by city architects W. H. Lancashire & Sons and again built by Mastin & Sons. The new structure was substantial, being part brick and part steel (strangely the steel came from Glasgow and not Sheffield), and went virtually the whole length of the pitch, measuring 290 feet and boasting seating for 3,000. It was designed 'with a tendency to the crescent formation in order to afford a free and uninterrupted view from all vantage points'. To complete the new addition, a grassy standing enclosure was created at the front of the structure for around 2,500 spectators, which was made possible as the stand was somewhat innovative as all the entrances were at the rear, as opposed to the norm in those days of front access. The entrances were also evenly spread, allowing an equal distribution of fans, while the media would have been delighted to find a section for the newspaper men, able to hold up to fifty gentlemen of the written word. It was certainly a substantial structure as underneath could be found large dressing rooms, a cycle room, tea and coffee room, male and female toilets, referee's room, and even bathrooms that contained showers and baths, the latter boasting a 'wave attachment'. A refreshment room was also franchised for £70 to Mr and Mrs Donohue, the same family that ran a popular alcoholic concession at Bramall Lane. A large entrance door and new turnstiles were also erected on Penistone Road with the total bill adding up to £2,674, although for their money the club had one of the most modern, if not the most modern, stand in English football – the fact that it was over sixty years before it was replaced was testament to its quality. Early in 1900, Wednesday moved its main matchday operations across from the Olive Grove Stand (the old structure being downgraded to a 3d stand) while by 1903 the grassy enclosure was converted to concrete terracing and a cover had been erected over, with ten pillars installed to hold the new roof. That wasn't the end, though, of the extensive development of the ground in those early years as the Leppings Lane end saw a small covered stand erected with a corrugated roof, which provided shelter for around 3,000 fans. This was built at the top of a grassy bank, which itself was around 50 feet from pitch perimeter railings. This was eventually extended and joined up with the North Stand. In a short space of time Wednesday had built one of the finest stadiums in England and in 1912 they were awarded their first FA Cup semi-final when West Bromwich Albion beat Blackburn Rovers.

The Wednesday hierarchy, though, did not seem content to 'sit on their laurels' as in 1913 they announced ambitious plans to build a huge new South Stand. The stand was designed by famous Scottish architect and engineer Archibald Leach, who during his working career was commissioned to design and oversee the building of new stands at many of the biggest clubs, including Aston Villa, Arsenal and Glasgow Rangers. It was also a large financial outlay as the total cost was just short of £18,000 (£17,884 to be exact), which included £500 to Leach, £4,969 to the builders Henry Freckingham & Sons, £1,395 for Glasgow Steel, and £5,850 to contractors Sheffield-based Hodkin & Sons (who still trade today after being founded a year after Wednesday FC was born). The new stand ran the whole length of the south side and not only provided 5,600 covered seats but a standing enclosure at the front, which was reckoned held up to 11,000. The old stand had been sold to the club's builders for £65 while the new structure was totally incomparable to its predecessor, boasting such amenities as luxury dressing rooms, club offices and even a billiards rooms. The stand was opened, roofless, in September 1913 and was finished two months later, with the 'cherry on the cake' being a decorative ball, inscribed with the club's 1866 (wrong) date of formation, and the words 'The Wednesday Football Club Ltd'. It was also in September that Wednesday let it be known that from that date forward the title of the club's home would change from Owlerton to Hillsborough. Early in 1914, after the stand had fully 'dried out', the club reversed the move of fourteen years earlier, moving 'lock, stock and barrel' from the north to south – a structure that was being lauded as the finest in England. In the summer that followed a further £800 was spent on extending and installing concrete terracing at the Kop end, mainly as a result of the February 1914 FA Cup tie against Wolverhampton Wanderers when a retaining wall on the Penistone Road embankment gave way and resulted in seventy-five casualties. Wednesday's rapid ground developments was rewarded with another high-profile game when the 1920 England vs Scotland international was staged.

In the late 1920s it was the turn of the Leppings Lane end to be redeveloped with the small 1899 structure demolished to be replaced by not one but two new structures, a small north-west corner shelter and then a grand covered terracing, which provided standing for 12,000 fans. Wednesday again splashed the cash to bring the ground capacity up to 80,000, spending £2,373 on the smaller stand in 1927 and £7,233 on its bigger brother, in the summer of 1928. It was the vision of architects, who designed the Olive Grove Stand many years earlier and the North Stand, of city firm Chapman & Jenkinson, with the 90 tons of steel required supplied by Sheffield firm Charles Rose Ltd. To complete the Sheffield supply line, city firm Henry Freckingham & Sons were again employed to undertake the works, forty employees working daily in the hope of getting the alterations finished before the start of the 1928/29 season. This proved an impossible task, mainly as they only started work in late June 1928, as the covered terrace required thousands of bricks and 20,000 roof slates, in addition to the sundry materials required to build toilets, a refreshment room and storerooms. The last job was to erect, on the roof top, a large scoreboard, which, in conjunction with the matchday programme, updated fans on the half-time scores in other matches around the country, via a specific letter of the alphabet. When the works were finished, Hillsborough could boast covered accommodation for 20,000 fans, the highest in the UK.

It would not be until the mid-1950s that further work on the ground took place. In the summer of 1954 the club employed Sheffield firm Husband & Co., paying the contractors £15,000 to install a floodlighting system. At the same time the Kop was also upgraded with the whole area terraced to the top. The new lights were first publically used for Derek Dooley's benefit game in March 1955, when 55,000 attended to help the stricken forward and witness floodlight football for the first time. After Eric Taylor relinquished the manager suffix of his secretary-manager role in 1958, the club's development of Hillsborough went into overdrive, the 1960s seeing Hillsborough change dramatically with two sides of the ground totally rebuilt. At the forefront of the development to the north and west side of the ground was the aforementioned Husband & Co., led by Sir Henry Charles Husband, who were responsible for the design of Jodrell Bank Observatory. The city firm also had a real claim to fame as they were consulting engineers for the building of the bridge – in the Sri Lankan town of Kitulgala – for the 1957 Oscar-winning film *The Bridge on the River Kwai*. They were perhaps better known in their home city for their sterling work undertaken at Wednesday, commencing with the design of a new 10,008-seat cantilevered North Stand, which when built had no better in Europe. Wednesday announced ambitious plans to replace the old North Stand in 1960, hoping to raise most of the required capital through a new issue of debenture stock, which offered an attractive 6 per cent rate and also allowed the holder to purchase the same seat for any match at Hillsborough, whether this involved Wednesday or not. At the time the game was in a state of flux with the maximum wage about to be scrapped and the realisation that facilities at all football grounds needed to be upgraded. Wednesday also focused on the probability of staging further special and representative matches, although some supporters did criticise them on laying too much emphasis on that particular byproduct of construction.

The old stand was subsequently demolished, although for Wednesday it was rather unfortunate timing as the club had a three-sided ground for the whole of the 1960/61 campaign, the club's best post-war league season. The new stand ran the whole length of the pitch and was built by Sheffield firm George Longdens, using 508 tons of steel, 115,000 bricks, 4,000 tons of reinforced concrete, and 30 miles of Beachwood seating. The most visible part of the structure though was the huge cantilevered roof, which reached 16 feet beyond the first of forty-eight rows of seating, and was intended to offer protection to all of the seat holders from the vagaries of the British winter. The impressive new stand was ready for the start of the 1961/62 campaign and was officially opened by FA secretary Sir Stanley Rous, before the game against Bolton Wanderers on 23 August 1961. For the occasion, Wednesday flew eighteen rooftop flags, which included a Football Association and Owls flag plus one for every country the club had played in, namely the United Kingdom (England, Northern Ireland, Scotland and Wales), Eire, Isle of Man, Belgium, Denmark, Sweden, Germany, France, Holland, Soviet Russia, Switzerland and Nigeria. Just days before the stand was opened the club's chairman, Dr Andrew Stephen, commented at the Annual General Meeting that the project 'marked another milestone in the long history of the club and paved the way for other striking developments such as the provision of social amenities and pleasant entertainment, and extensions of covered accommodation.' The new addition to the ground certainly proved popular with Wednesdayites as a record £30,000 worth of season tickets were sold for the stand and the FA secretary gave the club considerable praise, commenting that 'If other clubs take this (the stand) as an example, there will be no need to lament the absence of spectators from football matches.' Secretary Taylor was a hugely proud man on the evening and ensured his legacy would never be forgotten by ensuring the gangway letters aligned in the middle of the stand to spell ET, his initials and that of his wife, Emmie.

The catalyst for the next development was the awarding to Hillsborough, in October 1963, of four matches for the 1966 World Cup finals. Plans were quickly formulated to demolish the Leppings

Lane stand and replace this with a 4,471 all-seated one, with a standing enclosure at the front. The club again paired with Husband & Co. to design the new structure, Rotherham company Tarmac Civil Engineering winning the contract to construct the latest upgrade. The total cost of the project was £109,036 with Wednesday receiving some financial help from the government, although the vast majority was from the club itself, partly financed by the 'shilling a time' development fund. The new stand, including a 75-foot cantilevered roof, was first used for the Switzerland vs West Germany game in July 1966. The awarding of the World Cup to England also meant alterations to the South Stand with the terracing converted to seating, thanks to 850 slabs of pre-cast concrete and 3,356 seats, in what would became known as the South Stand 'uncovered seating' until the mid-1990s. This area was first utilised in the November 1965 game versus Liverpool, around 2,000 supporters taking the opportunity to try out the new seats. After the successful staging of the World Cup, Wednesday continued to upgrade Hillsborough as six months after staging the tournament, the old north-west corner stand was replaced by a terracing that cost £29,000 and connected the North Stand to the West Stand. During the 1960s Wednesday also built a gymnasium behind the North Stand, opened their own restaurant – built on concrete stilts behind the South Stand – installed an electronic scoreboard at the back of the Kop, and in May 1968 the 'Ozzie Owl' social club was opened, becoming a much-loved meeting place for Wednesday fans, especially after being reincarnated as the 'Ozzie Night Owl', which offered wining, dining, dancing and cabaret until 2 a.m.

The remarkable transformation of Hillsborough in the 1960s left the club with the highest number of seats at any English ground and as Wednesday fell on hard times in the 1970s, on and off the pitch, the revenue from hosting various FA Cup semi-finals brought in vital income; the ground also hosted a League Cup final replay and was used by Northern Ireland in 1973, at the height of the 'troubles' in Northern Ireland. The ground was also set to host replays of both the European Cup final and FA Cup final during the decade, although neither went ahead after the games were decided at the first attempt. It would not be until Wednesday regained their top-flight place in 1984 that plans began to formulate to develop an area of the ground that was without doubt the most underdeveloped area – the Kop. Subsequently, in February 1986, Wednesday announced that they intended to the roof the terrace, ending the days when fans were drenched to the skin while watching their favourites. It was Eastwood & Partners who was tasked with designing the new structure, with Ackroyd & Abbott handed the contract to build the roof. The club received £500,000 from the Football Trust towards the overall cost of £850,000, and one of various fundraising events was a 'Raise the Roof Fun Run' held in April 1986. When supporters attended the opening home game of the 1986/87 season, they could not have failed to have been impressed by the site that met their eyes as the Kop had been hugely extended to create more of a square shape, and a huge roof installed, stretching almost all the way out to Penistone Road. Works had started in the summer of 1986 and involved the demolition of a part of the Kop, nearest to the North Stand, so a huge crane could be brought on site, enabling the huge steel bars to be lifted, which supported the metal sheet roof. The old uncovered Kop had a capacity of 16,850 but the new roofed Kop could boast an astonishing capacity of 22,000, easily the largest in Europe. Over 17,000 were on the Kop for the first match, the new structure being officially opened in December 1986 when Her Majesty the Queen did the honours – over 40,000 attended to witness the royal blessing. Incidentally it was the second time the Queen had visited as just two years after her coronation, in 1954, she made a state visit to the ground, commenting that 'it is a very nice name' after enquiring about the club's origins.

The terrible events of 15 April 1989 changed English grounds forever with capacities slashed across the board, especially with regard to standing areas. For obvious reasons, the Leppings Lane terrace was closed for two years before in 1991, with the help of a £480,000 government grant, Wednesday spent £850,000 to install 2,494 seats, extend the roof, and build new turnstiles and a police room. In the previous summer, Wednesday had spent over £400,000 on various ground improvements, which included new crush barriers for the Kop, new fire alarms and £10,000 on emergency lighting. The move to all-seater stadia was virtually completed by 1993 when the Kop was redesigned and 11,120 seats installed, with 'The Owls' and an Owl design included as white seats on a blue canvas – the latter disappeared in the summer of 2016 as part of the introduction of a more traditional club badge. The preferred contractors was again Ackroyd & Abbott and they were also responsible for the 1,382 seats subsequently installed in the north-west corner, taking the all-seated capacity to 35,726 by the mid-1990s. The final major development to Hillsborough was again triggered by the awarding of games in a major tournament – in this case the 1996 European Championships. The new project involved the total refurbishment and extension of the old South Stand with a colossal 500-ton single-span girder installed, which supported a new roof that reached all the way back to the River Don. This first phase of the development was completed in the summer of 1993. All the wooden seats were also replaced with plastic ones and the walkway between the covered and uncovered seats disappeared. The total cost of these initial works was £1.8 million – the Football Trust providing just over half – while the biggest expense came with Phase 2, costing £5 million to complete. This saw the construction of a new 3,000-seat grandstand section in the South Stand, along with the installation of thirty executive boxes, various hospitality suites and offices. A nod to the past was also included in the redevelopment, which virtually engulfed the whole of Leach's iconic stand, with the decorative ball restored to its prominent positon atop of the stand roof. The new structure was without doubt one the best in the country and Wednesday continued to upgrade the ground in 1997, when they ripped out the old wooden seats in the North Stand and replaced them with just under 10,000 plastic ones. Unfortunately the last major works to Hillsborough were not planned as the June 2007 flood, which devastated parts of Sheffield, hit the ground badly. Both the South and North Stands were deluged with several feet of water, mud and sewerage while the club shop, ticket office and pitch were also severely affected. The original boardroom was washed away and the total damage proved to be in excess of £1 million, thankfully paid for by the club's insurers. It would be many years before the playing surface recovered from the deluge, only the installation of a Desso Grassmaster Hybrid playing surface in 2015 rectifying that particular problem. Plans emerged in 2009 to redevelop the ground to a 45,000 all-seater stadium – again, triggered by a possible hosting of a major international championship – but the club's well-documented financial problems ensured this was a mere 'pipe dream'. The ground is now totally unrecognisable from when Wednesday FC moved in 118 years ago, but has remained a much-loved home for generations of fans and hopefully for more generations in the future.

Current capacity:
Kop 9,890**
North West Corner 0*
West Stand Upper 3,200**
West Stand Lower 1,500**
West Stand Lower (disabled enclosure) 102
North Stand 8,234
North Stand (disabled enclosure) 56
South Stand 7,303
(capacity less segregation)
Directors Box 206
Excutive Boxes 320
South Stand Upper Granstand (inc. press) 3,043

Total: 33,854

*permission of Safety Advisory Group must be obtained prior to use
**permission to increase from SAG needed

Chapter 10

Foreign Tales, Home and Away

'The Swiss are rather excitable at times. A winger once made a shot
at our goal and missed. He dropped to his knee, smacked his thighs
several times and made strange cries at his failure. I thought he was
going to lay an egg.'
Billy Marsden, May 1929, regarding the club's tour of Switzerland

It would perhaps be reasonable to suggest that for almost the first 100
years of organised football, British football was the master of what was
slowly becoming a truly planetary game, although the home nations'
insular attitude to the game did mean they were never truly tested, missing
the first few instalments of the World Cup. The first seismic shock to that
perceived order came in the 1950 World Cup finals, England losing to
the US, and that dominance was ended permanently in the early 1950s
when the magnificent Hungarian team of that era humiliated England
both home and away. In the forty years preceding that shift in world
power, Wednesday was one of countless British teams that paid almost
missionary roles to far-off destinations. Foreign sides were also faced in
Sheffield and it would seem remiss to not briefly mention many of those
tours undertaken by the Owls, in addition to some memorable friendly
games at Hillsborough, which gave Wednesday fans a brief glimpse of
how 'Johnny Foreigner' played the beautiful game.

Despite Wednesday not leaving the British Isles until 1911, the club
first met foreign opposition almost twenty years earlier when a touring
Canadian side visited Olive Grove in September 1891. On a balmy
afternoon, a healthy 5,000 crowd turned out for the unique opportunity
of seeing foreign opposition for the first time. The North American
visitors had shown they were credible opposition by arriving in Sheffield
fresh from a win over Middlesbrough Ironopolis but they were no match
for a Wednesday side who coasted to a 4-1 win, with all the goals being
scored in a frantic first half. There was also a somewhat bizarre incident

when during an altercation between visiting defender Dalton and home
man Woolhouse, the former got hold of the Wednesday man's cheek with
his teeth, before the pair were separated by players and officials! During
the 1890s Scottish visitors were a common sight at Olive Grove but as the
attraction of friendly fixtures waned they almost ceased completely, as
did non-competitive club matches in general, the twentieth century giving
way to a staple diet of preseason 'public trial' matches and the occasional
charity fixture. The first change from that new normality came at the
end of the 1910/11 season when Wednesday embarked on an ambitious
tour of Scandinavia. Fourteen players, four directors and two trainers
made the trip, departing from Sheffield train station on Wednesday
17 May 1911. They duly travelled by boat from Harwich to Esbjerg in
Denmark, although many players suffered badly from seasickness, only
five finishing one meal while the remainder found somewhere to suffer
in silence! After passing through Danish customs an eight-hour train
journey took the party through the beautiful countryside and then it
was a short stop at Copenhagen before another train journey saw them
finally alight at Gothenburg, forty-nine hours after leaving Sheffield.
They were met by the secretary of the Swedish FA and were whisked
off to watch FA Cup holders Bradford City surprisingly lose to a local
select XI before finally putting their weary feet up at the Eggers Hotel – a
late dinner was followed by much-needed sleep in a bed that was not
moving! After a day sightseeing – the party struggling to buy anything as
neither party in the transaction could understand a word – a trip to the
wonderful Trollhätten Falls showed that even back in 1911 the country
was forward-thinking, the water power being used to generate electricity
all over Sweden. The first game of the tour took place on 21 May 1911
and would be the club's first ever fixture on a Sunday, Wednesday beating
the Orgryte club 5-0, while the following morning saw a visit from a
familiar face as Fred Spiksley – who had just gained a coaching position in
Stockholm – joined the party for a few days before commencing his new
job. After some time at the local seaside resort, Wednesday completed
their short time in Sweden by beating a Swedish XI 2-1, a match refereed
by former Chesterfield resident Charles Bunyan, who famously was in
goal for Hyde when they suffered a 26-0 FA Cup defeat to Preston North
End in 1887, the biggest ever win in English football. After the game, all
were invited to a gala dinner with the travelling party presented with
silver medals, as a show of thanks from their hosts. The Sheffield group
carried on to Copenhagen where they played the highest-profile match
of the tour, facing the Danish national team under the watching gaze of
the Crown Prince of Denmark. The match also officially opened the new
municipal stadium – built by the local council – and a great crowd of
8,000 watched the proceedings. A goal from Glennon sealed a 3-2 win
before the crown prince presented the players with eleven silver scarf
pins and all parties then dined together, making several celebratory toasts

as the evening progressed. The day after, another 3-2 win was secured against a select XI team before the party enjoyed a tour around the Juborg Brewery, all of the players being made honorary members of the Juborg Society, while no doubt trying the local tipple. Another Sunday game, again won 3-2, wrapped up a hugely successful and enjoyable tour for those early pioneers and it was then time for a two-day trip back home to Sheffield.

It was not until 1929 that Wednesday again faced foreign opposition, embarking on a six-game tour of Switzerland immediately after winning the league championship – they had received various offers to tour, including invites from South America, Germany, Denmark, Sweden and France. Wednesday kicked off the tour in Zurich, beating Young Fellows 3-0 with manager Brown commenting that he had been 'agreeably surprised by the excellent football of the home side'. Around 10,000 then watched the champions beat Basle club Nordsten 2-1, and Wednesday continued to score freely, netting three versus Neuchatel side Cantonal, four against Grasshoppers Zurich and four against both Berne and Lausanne to wrap up another hugely successful tour, which had left the touring party in a whirl because they had never seen so much wonderful scenery. In 1932 it was the turn of former player Billy Marsden to feature, although it was in a more official capacity, as coach of Dutch side HBS Hague. The former England international had taken charge in December 1931 but could only watch on as his old side beat his new club 8-1 in the capital of the Netherlands. Wednesday faced a much sterner test twenty-four hours later when in Amsterdam, Austrian top-flight club Nicholson held them to a 2-2 draw to complete a whistle-stop visit to mainland Europe. Two years later the Owls emphatically showed the superior quality of English football during a six-game tour of Scandinavia, as they crashed home thirty-five goals, including nine in a June 1934 victory over a Malmo select XI in Sweden, the players again being presented to the crown prince before kick-off. In the final match of the tour, Wednesday faced what was effectively the national team of Denmark but they proved no match as 20,000 delighted fans in Copenhagen watched the powerful visitors' crash home seven goals without reply.

It was in December 1934 that the club first welcomed European opposition to Sheffield when FC Austria made the trip from central Europe. The visitors arrived in S6 unbeaten in four tour games and the fixture included a surprise debut for Sheffield University amateur goalkeeper Haydn Hill; Owls boss Walker had enquired if Hill was going to the friendly and when he said yes, Walker replied 'bring your boots, you are playing'. The Austrians showed remarkable passing ability, playing the ball almost exclusively to feet, but could not cope with Wednesday's physicality, losing 3-0 on an enjoyable occasion for all concerned. Another trip to Denmark, after the 1935 FA Cup victory, produced another plethora of wins and goals while the Owls played in France for the first time on their way home, beating Racing Club de Paris 4-0. The 1935/36 season was unique as Wednesday played foreign opponents, home and away, during the regulation season with the visit of a combined side from Prague – picked from Sparta and Slavia – to Hillsborough being first on the menu. Unfortunately poor weather, together with a 2.30 p.m. kick-off on a Monday afternoon, kept the crowd down to only 3,241 with club officials just glad that they had not offered the visitors a guaranteed income. Thirteen days later, a generous financial guarantee lured Wednesday across the English Channel to face a French League select team in Lille, just a day after facing Chelsea in the First Division. There was a spectacular build-up to kick-off as, two minutes before the allocated start time, a large plane swooped over the heads of the fans and a passenger leaned out to drop the match ball towards the centre circle. It landed just 5 yards from the centre spot and the teams duly kicked off. The Owls were not without support – it was suggested that all the English people living within a 50-mile radius must have attended – but lost 3-2 with a Polish member of the selected XI grabbing the winning goal. Owls boss Billy Walker commented that 'They deserved their win. The only excuse I have to make is that the small sized ball was a definite handicap. This is the first time I have not brought an English ball with me to the continent and demanded its use.' The players did not enjoy the flight home though due to headwinds, with many finding out for the first time that they suffered from airsickness. Another tour to Denmark in 1936 closed the book on foreign opponents in pre-war football and ten years later the Owls were back in the same country, suffering their first ever defeat to Scandinavian opposition when losing 4-2 to a Copenhagen XI in May 1946. A few months later the Owls played host to Danish opposition for the first time, losing 3-2 to a combined Copenhagen side, a healthy attendance of 7,000 (for a December Monday afternoon kick-off), watching Wednesday lose at home to a foreign side for the first time.

After another Scandinavian trip in 1950, Wednesday met Danish opposition again at Hillsborough in May 1951 under the banner of the Festival of Britain. The festival was organised by the government to promote the British contribution to science, technology, industrial design, architecture and the arts and included a multitude of static and travelling exhibitions, although the vast majority were held in London, almost 8.5 million people attending the South Bank exhibition during the summer of 1951. As part of the celebrations, numerous football matches were arranged, the vast majority against foreign opposition. Other games played included Derby County vs Borussia Dortmund, Chesterfield vs Anderlecht and Barnsley vs Rapid Vienna while at Hillsborough a penalty miss from Woodhead ensured the game against Copenhagen-based Frem finished 0-0. After winning the Second Division title in 1952, Wednesday made a return visit to Switzerland, although their opponents on this occasion included three Swiss sides, Inter Milan and a German select XI. The tour opened with a floodlight game against Bellinzona – the first time a Wednesday side had appeared under artificial light – and twenty-four hours later they lost 2-1 to a Swiss trial XI; they had expected to play a local side or a regional team before the Swiss FA decided to use the game as a shop window for players hoping to break into the team to play in the forthcoming match against England. The Swiss FA president and several of the international selection committee were in the estimated 10,000 crowd to watch a first defeat on Swiss soil. There was controversy in the 2-1 defeat to Inter, played in Berne, as left-back Curtis was sent off. The Wednesday players were kitted out with lightweight 'continental' boots for their 5-1 win against amateurs St Gallen. After travelling 1,200 miles in Switzerland alone, the Owls finished their tour with a leg-weary loss to a German select XI before players then enjoyed some rest and recuperation in Lucerne, prior to watching England beat Austria in Vienna. There was no doubt that the standard of European football had increased significantly since the Second World War and the days of English teams emphatically beating all-comers had been confined to the history books. This was not the case with non-European teams, typified by the 9-3 home win over a touring South African amateur eleven in November 1953. The tour was a steep learning curve for the Africans with team captain Dow commenting that

> We thoroughly enjoyed the match. We tried to chase shadows and found it very difficult but we have learned football lessons which we shall pass on to our youngsters when we get back home.

At the end of that 1953/54 season the Owls found out first-hand the quality of the world game as in Belgium they were thrashed 6-0 by Desportes, the Brazilians treating the spectators to 'football at its finest with every trick in the game'. If that was a sobering evening then the October 1955 Hillsborough meeting with Vasas Budapest left Wednesday fans somewhat in awe as almost 46,000 watched on as the brilliant Hungarians produced arguably the most technically perfect display of football ever seen at the ground, winning 7-1. The game was the first time that Wednesday had faced a club side under their new floodlights and virtually the whole of the crowd stayed until the final whistle to pay tribute to the visitors, who bowed to the crowd after an incredible evening, which would stay long in the memory of those fans fortunate enough to have attended. For the remainder of the 1950s and early 1960s, floodlit games against foreign opposition became highly popular and over the years that followed, Wednesday faced teams from Argentina, Romania, Croatia, Poland, Italy, Russia, Georgia, the Netherlands and Brazil. As the 1960s dawned, Wednesday also started a period of globe trekking that was unsurpassed in club history as they visited four continents to play a wide variety of exhibition games, commencing with a groundbreaking tour behind the 'Iron Curtain' in 1960. The Cold War between East and West was in full effect when Wednesday decided to tour the vast USSR at the end of the 1959/60 season, first flying to Moscow where a staggering 50,000 Russians watched CSKA score the only goal of the game. Everywhere they went in Russia, the notorious KGB was not far behind, the mammoth 1,229-mile flight to Tbilisi, where they lost 1-0 to Dynamo, failing to shake off the state secret police. While in the capital of what is now Georgia, manager Catterick almost got in hot water during a night out in the city as a local drunk was following the group around, increasingly annoying the Owls boss. There was a large roadworks hole near the team hotel and Catterick duly invited the man to look down the hole – it was only the players who stopped him when he raised his leg to boot the drunkard down it! Wednesday then flew all the way back to Moscow where they lost 3-2 to Locomotive, before the party was duly honoured with a gala dinner arranged by the Soviet Football Federation. Eric Taylor commented that 'It has been a memorable tour. We have enjoyed every minute of it.' Almost twelve months later, Taylor organised another unique tour with Wednesday flying to Africa to play four games in Nigeria. Don Megson later revealed that Taylor had a map of the world in his office with red dots where Wednesday had played and black dots where he wanted them to play. The reasons to tour a poor African country were unknown and it was certainly an experience with the streets of Ibadan, where the Owls beat a select team 11-2, actually flowed with raw sewerage! The party then travelled to the capital city of Lagos where Taylor, along with a club director, was taken on a tour in the British Consulate's Rolls-Royce. When the VIP passengers had been shown the sights, they handed the chauffeur a £5 note to show their gratitude. However, the following day the UK official was somewhat flustered and had a slight issue with Eric's generosity as he revealed the employee was only paid £5 per month! A subsequent match in Lagos was played on a pitch that contained a giant flagpole concreted into the centre circle while the dressing rooms were just a workmen's hut. The Owls played twice in Lagos and also fulfilled a fixture in Enugh, which became so bad tempered that the game had to be temporarily halted when local police and officials raced onto the pitch when the players starting throwing punches. Throughout the tour, the club's opponents played in bare feet while the fair-skinned Englishmen experienced debilitating heat, which they had never encountered before – in hindsight it was probably not the wisest trip to undertake. The club's first preseason friendly game in 1961 was against Ajax in Amsterdam while in the same calendar year Hillsborough hosted a floodlit friendly that matched the visit of Vasas in interest and prestige. This was because Pele and his Santos team visited, with a record Wednesday crowd, for a friendly game (49,058), treated to a spectacular match where Pele shone, his famous shimmy when firing a penalty past Springett being the abiding memory.

During the 1964/65 season, Wednesday experienced contrasting fortunes during visits to West Germany, Denmark and Poland with teenager Ford having an unfortunate reason to remember his Wednesday debut, against Werder Bremen in August 1964, as he suffered a broken leg as the Owls lost 1-0. New manager Brown was left fuming a few weeks later when his side unexpectedly crashed 4-1 to Danish minnows Aarhus, in a game staged as part of their country's British week celebrations. Six days later the Wednesday players got back into the new manager's good books after holding a German national XI, including several members of the side that would face England in the 1966 World Cup final, 0-0 in the Rhine Stadium, Dusseldorf. The end of the season saw the club back behind the 'Iron Curtain' with two matches played in Poland where the players had the sobering experience of touring Auschwitz. Games in Spain (Valencia) and Ireland were squeezed in on the way home while the unchartered territory of Bulgaria was next on the menu for the now travel-weary Wednesday squad – the Owls lost all three matches played during the 1965 preseason tour. The days of just staging a solitary public trial match were long gone and the 1965/66 season would be the longest on record for the senior players as from kicking off their first friendly in Bulgaria on 5 August 1965, they did not hang up their boots until losing 4-2 to Fulham on 14 June 1966, in the final match of a mammoth post-FA Cup final tour of south east Asia. That Far East trip encompassed two games in Hong Kong, three in Malaysia and one in Singapore, beginning at the former British colony when a selected XI was beaten 2-1 in a lacklustre display from the Owls. The local Hong Kong press were not impressed though, describing Wednesday's display as an 'exhibition of tomfoolery' and 'if that was the best they can produce then their brand of soccer is one import that we can well do without'. Thankfully, performances did improve, although there was a lukewarm response to a coaching clinic held by Brown at the Hong Kong Football Club with only a handful of interested parties attending.

Wednesday's professional players only had a short while back in England before they were heading for the airport again, making a return visit to Bulgaria. For the ten-day trip, the Owls were based in the beautiful Black Sea city of Varna and drew all three games, including an eight-goal thriller against Cherno More, which literally means 'Black Sea' in Bulgarian. The locals had been generous hosts and a Bulgarian select XI duly paid a reciprocal visit, just before the season started, when Wednesday finally gained a victory at the seventh attempt. The Owls' globetrotting showed no sign of slowing as at the end of the 1966/67 season they embarked on yet another trip, all the way to Mexico for a hexagonal tournament, the games being played in the famous Aztec Stadium, in the sweltering heat of Mexico City. It is believed that the English FA backed the club's trip as they wanted to see how English players would react to the heat with the 1970 World Cup having been awarded to Mexico. The answer to that question was that the games proved a real hard slog for Wednesday, the old adage of 'only mad dogs and English men go out in the midday sun' proving rather pertinent. Some of the games did actually kick-off at midday, although the Owls did win their first tie, beating local side Toluca 4-1 in front of 40,000. A trio of losses though put Wednesday out of the running for the trophy with only one more draw accrued, against America FC when Ellis was sent off. There was a considerable consolation for the Wednesday players though as Taylor and Brown decided they had suffered enough in the heat and promptly booked tickets for New York, where the players enjoyed a fun-packed few days to complete the longest tour in the history of Sheffield Wednesday. The trip to Mexico would be the club's last 'grand tour' outside of Europe for many years as the club started a decline, which advanced unabated until the mid-1970s. A few friendly games did still appear on the fixture list though, including a two-game tour of Austria in 1968, while a scheduled friendly against West Germany, due to be played at Karlsruhe in February 1969, was cancelled at the last minute as bad weather meant the Owls could not fly out of England.

The 1969/70 season featured games against Italian opposition at the beginning and end of the season, commencing with a 2-1 home success over a touring Italian U21 side. The season ended in relegation from the top flight and the players and the fans were probably not particularly enthused for the club's four scheduled games in the Anglo-Italian Competition, which started just a few days after that relegation. Without doubt the best game was the opening match when Wednesday found themselves four goals up against visitors Napoli, who were then reduced to ten men after a Bianchi late tackle on Coleman earned him an early bath. That was not the end of the story though as the Italian scored three times to leave Wednesday hanging on to claim the win. While the games in England were nothing more than glorified friendlies, the Owls drawing 0-0 versus Juventus in the other tie, it was a different story in Italy as 30,000 watched Napoli record a 5-1 win in Naples. The result was harsh on Wednesday though, with English match referee Jack Taylor (who was in charge of the 1974 World Cup final) commenting that 'it was a flattering result for Naples'. A defeat in Turin against Juventus knocked the Owls out, although the biggest story of the trip came a few days earlier when, at short notice, Wednesday arranged a friendly game in the small town of Savoia. The match was played on a pitch of black dust, watered by a cart before the game and at half-time, and after the match the whole town turned out to cheer the squad as they drove to the mayor's office for a reception and presentation of a silver cup. The biggest shock though was for 'keeper Peter Springett as after tipping the part-timer's only real effort onto the bar the match referee raced across the pitch and excitedly kissed the surprised goalie!

It has been well documented that the 1970s were the worst decade in the club's history and games against foreign opposition almost completely disappeared from the fixture lists, other than a low-key home win over Werder Bremen in November 1971 and a 1973 preseason tournament in Sweden, where the Owls finished third after two wins in their three games. By far the most high-profile fixture was a return visit from Pele and Santos in February 1972, when an astonishing crowd of almost 37,000 (the club averaged just over 17,000 for league games) flooded into Hillsborough for an afternoon kick-off; it was said that the schools and workplaces of Sheffield and its surroundings were hit with an unusually high amount of doctors and dentist appointments on that day, shown at the final whistle when the pitch was invaded by hundreds of Parka-wearing kids, in the hope of reaching the great Brazilian. The next foreign side to face Wednesday during a season did so to a much smaller audience when only 2,385 rattled around Hillsborough for the visit of Canadian side Vancouver Whitecaps in March 1981. The visitors caused a bit of a stir among the sparse crowd when they ran out wearing squad numbers – it would over a decade later before that 'Americanism' came into the British game – while their side was effectively an expat XI, with veterans such as Yorath and Lorimer (Johnny Giles was head coach), while centre-half Holton would be signed by Wednesday three months later, although he failed to make a senior appearance. Wednesday won 2-1 on the night while in the preseason of 1981 the club became reacquainted with Nigerian football. It was the national team that visited but the term friendly did not really describe the rather overzealous play of the visitors, who were on the verge of qualifying for the 1982 World Cup finals. Such was the battering that McCulloch received in the first half that he was taken off by Charlton at the break, and the simmering aggression exploded in the second period when visiting defender Ateigbu was sent off by referee Hackett, after he appeared to punch new signing Megson! In the Owls' first season back in the top flight they were invited to Sweden as part of the home FA's eightieth birthday celebrations, and on a foggy October evening in 1984 a goal from Chapman ensured parity. The remainder of the 1980s included two visits to Finland – both connected with the shirt sponsorship deal with electronics company Finlux – while in September 1986 the Owls made a midweek visit to the far warmer climes of Kuwait. The trip to the Middle East was certainly lucrative for Wednesday but for the players it meant playing in oppressing heat of over 100 degrees, although the Owls did secure a 5-2 win against the Kuwait national team, with Wilkinson commenting:

We played very well, particularly in the second half. There was a good-sized crowd and we were clapped off the field. The trip had been very worthwhile. We made a good impression. We accepted the invitation not because of the money but to nature the image of Sheffield

Wednesday abroad, particularly the Middle East, in the hope that when
invitations are being made in the future, they will think about is.

Wednesday did make a return visit, losing 4-2 in February 1988, but in
the interim toured both Canada and Germany. The four-game tour of
the latter is remembered for the only appearance in a Wednesday shirt
of a new signing, ex-England international David Armstrong, before he
had a sudden change of heart and the club agreed to tear up his newly
signed contract. With Atkinson at the helm, Wednesday played twice in
Italy during the 1990 preseason, and it was a memorable time for 'keeper
Kevin Pressman as after playing superbly in a 3-0 defeat to Genoa, he
returned to the team's hotel to discover his wife had given birth to a baby
boy at Nether Edge Hospital with the proud new father put on the next
plane home, Chris Turner taking over in goal for the next friendly against
Serie A club Cremonese.

In the summer of 1991 Wednesday made their first visit to the United
States, the League Cup win, and prominence of John Harkes, no
doubt being significant factors in receiving an invitation from 'over the
pond' to play US champions Maryland Bays and the US national XI.
For Harkes, it was a case of split loyalties when his club side faced his
national team at the Veterans Stadium in Philadelphia. He lined up in
Wednesday colours and almost 45,000 watched the home side record
a 2-0 win, the players again faced with conditions of over 100 degrees
and an AstroTurf surface. It is rare that politics and football mix but
this was the case in October 1992 when subtle pressure from the UK
government led to a whistle-stop two-match tour of South Africa. The
Owls had originally intended to undertake a six-day tour of the country,
becoming the first British side to play in Cape Town for thirty years,
as well as acting as ambassadors for the UK as sporting links were
slowly being re-established after the abolishment of apartheid in 1991.
However, just eight days before departing, the club took the decision
to cancel the trip, due to an increasing fixture pile-up after progress in
two cup competitions. Forty-eight hours later the trip was back on after
the government intervened to ensure the 'goodwill' trip went ahead as
planned. As well as running various coaching activities, Wednesday beat
Cape Town club Hellenic 2-1 before a 30,000 crowd, and the first non-
segregated seen in the Loftus Versfield Stadium watched the tourists and
home side Mamelodi Sundowns share four goals.

Usually, if Wednesday faced a club with the stature of Real Madrid, the
game would be well publicised with fans clamouring to attend the fixture
and the action being well covered in the local press, online and in social
media. However, back in March 1994, before the days of the internet,
Twitter and Facebook, Wednesday did play the Spanish giants but the
game hardly caused a ripple in the English press as they travelled to the
Andalusian town of Cordova, where Madrid had agreed to officially

open their new municipal stadium. The home side for the night included such names as Luis Enrique, Michel and Martin Vasquez but it was Sheridan who scored the goal of the night as his direct free-kick, after thirty minutes, was no doubt appreciated by the fans in the estimated 17,000 crowd. Almost thirty years after the club's tour of south-east Asia, Wednesday returned to the region in the warm-up to the 1994/95 season but their destination was the emerging football nation of Japan. The new J-League was flourishing – Lineker was a player for Nagoya Grampus Eight at the time - and the Owls went into the sweltering heat of the huge Tokyo Dome after just a week of preseason training. The first game was lost to a Brazilian-influenced Verdy Kawasaki side before almost 45,000 watched the Owls win the Summer Cup after a thrilling 4-3 win over Shimizu S-Pulse, new signing Taylor scoring a superb late goal to secure the victory. The Wednesday squad later attended a reception at the British Embassy and then set off for the 5,584-mile trip back to Sheffield.

The first foreign opposition of the twenty-first century was Dutch giants PSV Eindhoven, Wednesday sharing four goals in August 2000 at Hillsborough, while in August 2001 the club welcomed Spanish team Deportivo Alaves, who were fresh from a dramatic 5-4 UEFA Cup final defeat to Liverpool, although admittedly they were missing star man Jordi Cruyff and several summer signings. The Spanish side was actually a late replacement for Newcastle United, who were forced to pull out due to Intertoto Cup commitments, and the visitors were somewhat taken aback by the 'overenthusiastic' tackling of Alan Quinn, who was playing his first game back after a broken leg, which led to the Irishman being warned about his conduct by the match referee. However, despite those warnings Quinn did not curb his behaviour and a studs-up tackle on away player Turiel led to the referee ordering Peter Shreeves to take off Quinn, after just nineteen minutes, or he would depart accompanied with a red card! After the departure of Quinn, the preseason friendly continued at a more sedate pace, although the visitors were never comfortable with some old-fashioned English tackling, and matters flared up again in the second period, after Wednesday had taken the lead, with home man Di Piedi and away player Llorens ordered to be substituted by the referee, who steadfastly refused to issue any cards of either colour. Hundreds of Owls fans followed their club on preseason tours to Scandinavia, Netherlands and Ibiza in the early years of the naughties, although the latter preseason trip did not actually involve any foreign opposition, with Preston North End and Watford faced in a four-team tournament played at the island's capital of Sant Antonio – Wednesday fans flooding onto the island, famed for its club scene, their numbers dwarfing supporter numbers from the other English participants. The 2006 preseason tour of North America showed the devotion of many Owls fans as a good few travelled all the way to North Carolina to see the opening game of a three-match tour, which began against Wilmington Hammerheads. What they witnessed was one of the most bizarre games played by Wednesday as after thirty-seven minutes the players were forced off the pitch as a huge electrical storm rolled in off the Atlantic Ocean. Spectators and officials also dashed for cover as fork lightening lit up the sky and it looked likely that Wednesday's first game of the 2006/07 campaign would be abandoned. However, after a seventy-five-minute delay, the teams re-emerged – as did most of the fans – and the match started again at half-time with the last eight minutes of the first half scrapped. The Owls secured a draw, with Wilmington's grandly titled 'Director of Business operations' commenting that, 'We've enjoyed having the Wednesday team as well as their fans as guests in Wilmington and hope to see them or another team here next year.'

Wednesday played a second match in the state – an uneventful 0-0 against a select XI in Cary – before wrapping up their time 'over the pond' with a 2-0 win in New York State against Rochester Raging Rhinos. The preseason in Malta in 2009 was unique as all four games were forty-five minutes in duration with Wednesday facing four local sides, on the artificial surface at the Victor Tedesco Stadium, home of Maltese Premier League club Hamrum Spartans. It proved a popular trip for the travelling 'barmy army', although the heat was perhaps not so popular with the playing personnel! Over the last few years, the Owls have set up training camps in Austria (twice), Slovenia and Portugal (five times) with one or two warm-up games also played, including friendlies against Portuguese clubs Sporting Lisbon and Braga plus Russian sides FC Volga Novgorod and FC Arsenal Tula. The visit to Hillsborough of Benfica in July 2016 attracted the biggest crowd (12,207) for a visit of a foreign XI since Santos last visited and the home fans went home delighted with a Forestieri goal securing a notable victory for the Championship Wednesday and terrific fillip ahead of the new season.

Country (Excluding UK & Ireland)

	P	W	D	L	F	A
Argentina	1	1	0	0	9	0
Austria	5	2	2	1	7	4
Brazil	5	1	0	4	7	17
Bulgaria	7	1	3	3	12	16
Canada	6	3	1	2	13	7
China (Hong Kong)	1	1	0	0	2	1
Croatia	1	0	1	0	1	1
Czech Republic	1	1	0	0	4	1
Denmark	24	16	4	4	76	30

	P	W	D	L	F	A
Finland	5	3	1	1	15	9
France	4	1	0	3	7	10
Georgia	2	1	0	1	5	1
Germany	11	3	3	5	13	15
Greece	1	0	0	1	0	4
Hungary	1	0	0	1	1	7
Italy	12	4	1	7	19	22
Japan	2	1	0	1	5	5
Kuwait	2	1	0	1	7	6
Malaysia	2	1	0	1	6	3
Malta	4	2	1	1	2	1
Mexico	3	1	1	1	5	7
Netherlands	23	13	6	4	70	26
Nigeria	5	4	1	0	19	6
Poland	3	0	1	2	5	7
Portugal	10	3	3	4	6	10
Romania	1	0	1	0	3	3
Russia	5	1	1	3	5	7
Slovenia	1	0	1	0	1	1
South Africa	3	2	1	0	13	6
Spain	4	1	0	3	2	8
Sweden	16	12	3	1	59	20
Switzerland	9	7	1	1	28	7
USA	5	2	2	1	4	2

Chapter 11

Derby Days

Derby (noun): A sports match between two rival teams of the same area.

As the sport of football came to the fore in the latter part of the nineteenth century, the vast majority of England's major towns and cities could boast several senior clubs within their boundaries. Many of those teams fell by the wayside but by the dawn of the following century a distinct pattern had emerged with two major clubs in each conurbation hotly contesting 'bragging rights' and developing fierce rivalries, which continue to the present day. The oldest senior derby is, of course, played in Nottingham where the two oldest league clubs, County and Forest, lock horns. However, both of those clubs are pre-dated by teams from Sheffield as Hallam and Sheffield FC, formed before the Nottingham teams and still playing today, first played a 'derby' game in 1860, therefore rightly laying a claim to the oldest derby game in world football. In general the fiercest derby games are those played between teams of the same town or city, such as Manchester, Liverpool, London or Bristol, although matches between sides in the same local area can also be equally intense, such as Newcastle versus Sunderland. The municipal borough of Sheffield was granted city status, by royal charter, in 1893, and games between the newly formed Sheffield United and the old Wednesday club had already become the main attraction of the local sporting scene.

Before that eagerly anticipated inaugural meeting, the clubs had seemingly done nothing but publically clash on various matters, beginning in September 1889 when the sides tried to arrange a first game. As Wednesday were the older club, they claimed the right to stage the first meeting at Olive Grove while local 'upstarts' United expressed willingness to draw lots for the venue. In the end neither would move from their relevant stances and plans fell through. Three months later, Wednesday publically accused United of poaching their better amateur players and the new rivals fell out again early in 1890 when United started staging games on the same day as Wednesday. At that point it seemed a first ever meeting, in the short term, seemed unlikely but eventually the two clubs did 'bury the hatchet' and it was announced the teams would meet at Olive Grove on Monday 15 December 1890. Weeks before the game, supporters started to talk about the forthcoming derby and when it finally arrived fans were streaming though the Olive Grove turnstiles an hour before the 2.30 p.m. kick-off. Famous Sheffield match card seller Billy Whitham was seen to do a roaring trade, shouting 'all the names of each side, a penny', while the various street vendors sold pies, sandwiches and sweets to the crowd that swelled to around 10,000 (standing up to ten deep at the side of the pitch) before the teams took to the field. Betting was also prevalent as fans risked their hard-earned wages on the outcome, one enterprising bookie standing on a box and offering 5-1 against United, his offer being enthusiastically accepted! Favours – bearing the inscriptions 'Play up Wednesday' and 'Play up United' – were liberally handed out at the turnstiles and were greatly in evidence on the hats and caps of the fans. When the teams came out – Wednesday wearing a brand-new blue-and-white-striped jersey – they received a tumultuous reception and what followed was a thrilling encounter, refereed by Sheffield football legend Charles Clegg, which commenced with the home side kicking off from the Heeley end. It was United who secured the first corner in a Sheffield derby game and they also netted the first goal, Robertson putting the 'leather through' after twenty minutes. Midway through the second half Hodder or Woolhouse (depending upon which newspaper you read) levelled matters and with five minutes remaining, in the ever-increasing gloom, Winterbottom fired home the winner to trigger delight among the blue half of the town. Incidentally, United's custodian for the match, Howlett, was well known for playing in glasses and later admitted he did not even see the winning goal go in!

The return game was also played on a Monday afternoon and around 14,000 packed into Bramall Lane with every conceivable vantage point utilised, from the house windows of dwellings that overlooked the arena to the tops of telegraph poles. The home side were slight pre-match favourites – Wednesday having lost crucial defender Betts to injury – but they seemed set for a first 'derby double' when they led 2-0 late into the second half after goals from Ingram and Bob Brandon. However, United stormed back to secure a 3-2 win and fans of both clubs – thousands of whom flooded onto the pitch at full-time – were in agreeance that the real winner had been Sheffield football as a whole and the annual Sheffield vs Glasgow game would no longer be the highlight of the local football calendar. The sides did met again during that 1890/91 season, Wednesday winning 2-1 at Olive Grove in the semi-final of the Wharncliffe Charity Cup, while Wednesday's 5-0 loss at Bramall Lane in October 1891 gave rise to the publication of 'funeral cards', which were distributed around the town, lamenting the failure of the losing team:

In loving remembrance of
The
SHEFFIELD WEDNESDAY FOOTBALL TEAM

Who were safely put to rest on Monday October 26th
At Bramall Lane
Poor old Wednesday were fairly done,
When United beat them five to none;
Although they lost, they did their best;
So let them quietly take their rest
(Friends of the above club kindly accept this intimation)

Wednesday's star player, Spiksley, later revealed that the club inquest into the beating directly led to the first regular training sessions in the club's history. The extra work certainly came to fruition quickly as Wednesday won 4-1 in the return, triggering Wednesday fans to counter with their own funeral card:

In pitiful remembrance of
Our idol, the
SHEFFIELD UNITED FOOTBALL TEAM

Who departed their football life, struggling to the
End, at Olive Grove, on Monday, November 16th
1891
When United died they struggled hard
Enough to live a brighter and longer life:
Do as they would, they could not ward
Neat kicks by Wednesday; and thus the strife ended
Thus closed famous United's reign
Sheffield now mourns their death and more
Dying as they did – ne'er to rise again
And kick for fame at Wednesday's door
Yes, United have lost 4-1

Those early friendlies no doubt stoked the fire but it would be in competitive football where the inter-club rivalry would grow, commencing in the 1893/94 season when United joined Wednesday in the First Division. The big day arrived in October 1893, again on a Monday, and hosts United were firm favourites after having made an outstanding start to the new season, which meant they topped the table after eight games.

Wednesday had only just won their second game of the new season and the vast majority of the estimated 27,000 crowd fully expected two points to United. However, as is the case in almost every derby around the world, derbies are great levellers and despite the home side scoring first, the game was tied 1-1 at the break thanks to Spiksley. The match up until that point had certainly not been for the feint hearted, and just before the interval Wednesday's Davis had to be stretchered from the field, unconscious, after a particularly robust challenge from opposition defender Cain. It was at this point that the referee called the players together and they were told in no uncertain terms that they effectively had to calm down or draconian action would follow. Unfortunately for Wednesday, Davis could not return for the second half but the away side hung on valiantly to gain a much-deserved point and put a brake on their rivals run. When the return game was played just twenty-eight days later – yet again on a Monday – both sides had slipped down the league rankings, but it was Wednesday who were expected to register their third home derby win in three years. Around 15,000 were inside Olive Grove to watch, Wednesday missing half-back Jamieson who was excused due to a family bereavement. It was United who drew first blood, Drummond scoring after seven minutes, but Whittam then fouled Spiksley inside the area and it was a spot kick to the blue and whites. This was taken by Harry Brandon but, to huge cheers from the away fans and equally audible groans from the home contingent, it was straight at the 'keeper and the golden chance had passed. Wednesday were level, though, just two minutes after the restart as a shot from Miller went past several players with the away custodian, possibly unsighted, having no chance. The balance of the play had generally been in Wednesday's favour but an inability to take their chances meant that a sixty-seventh-minute goal from Hammond proved decisive as Wednesday fell to their first home loss to their new-found rivals. The sides would meet in the First Division for the next five seasons, United completing the first double in derby history in 1894/95 thanks to a 3-2 win at Olive Grove and single-goal success at Bramall Lane. On a splendid sunny Sheffield day in September 1895, Wednesday got back to winning ways, Bell firing home past United's legendary goalie 'Fatty' Foulkes, but United would certainly have the upper hand for the remainder of the 1890s, Wednesday failing to register another win in the Football League. Wednesday did register three wins in minor games, 2-1 in a Sheffield & District League fixture in April 1897, a 4-1 friendly victory at Bramall Lane in February 1898 and then a 1-0 win at Bramall Lane on Boxing Day 1899. The aforementioned 1898 fixture was actually advertised in the local press as a reserve fixture in the Yorkshire League, but was subsequently 'downgraded' to a mere friendly when both sides broke competition rules by including more than three first-team players in their respective teams. In addition, in the 1890s, the reds and blues faced each other in a competition called the United Counties League, which was effectively used as a supplementary

competition to the thirty-game-a-season Football League. The teams met
on four occasions with three games ending all square and United winning
the remaining fixture.

There was hope among Wednesday fans that a new century would
bring better fortunes and this proved the case in the first decade,
Wednesday recording two doubles and generally having the upper hand.
However, before hostilities recommenced in the Football League, the
teams met for the first time in the FA Cup when Wednesday were sent
to Bramall Lane in February 1900. That first clash in the 'English Cup'
proved controversial with the final game in a three-match tie probably
the most ill-tempered and undisciplined game ever between the rivals.
A huge crowd of 32,381 attended the first game but snow, which had
fallen slightly on the morning of the game, returned during the tie and
when it became impossible to have clear sight of the lines, the referee
took the players off after fifty-three minutes. They never returned and
all parties were set to reconvene on the following Thursday, only for a
blizzard to cause that game to be postponed. The match was eventually
played to a conclusion two days later but both sides struggled on a very
poor pitch, which was thick with mud after the inclement weather of the
previous week. After ninety minutes the teams could not be separated,
Brash netting for Wednesday only for United to level with just ten minutes
remaining, which meant a trip for United to Wednesday's new Owlerton
ground for the first time. There had been a certain amount of 'needle' in
the 1-1 draw but the roughhouse tactics of both sides reached a new level
in the third game, to such an extent that the local press commented that
'if the experience of the present season is to be repeated, it is to be hoped
that many years will elapse before another cup tie contest between them
is seen'. Wednesday started the replay missing three senior players – key
men Massey, Millar and Spiksley all being injured in the previous game –
but fought well in a goalless first half, although they suffered yet more
ill luck after thirty-seven minutes when they lost reserve centre forward
Lee to a career-ending broken leg. With the home side reduced to ten men
and full-back Layton switched to centre forward, United quickly took
advantage of the reshuffle to take the lead from the penalty spot. The
game started to take an over aggressive tone midway through the half
when Pryce was sent off after going 'over the ball' at Hedley, the away
player being forced to retire, temporarily. With five minutes remaining,
Wednesday went down to eight men when a rush down the wing by
United's Bennett was unceremoniously stopped by Langley, who was
ordered from the field by the somewhat overworked official, Mr Lewis.
A late goal from Beers, against the depleted ranks, was fairly academic
and there was no doubt that the first senior cup tie between the rivals
would not be forgotten quickly by the good people of Sheffield.

Wednesday got back to winning ways against United on the final day
of the following season, a Wilson goal enough to secure a first win over

their city rivals at Owlerton. When the fixtures for 1902/03 season were published, they pitted the Sheffield clubs together, at Bramall Lane, on the opening day of the season with Wednesday handing a debut to new signing Chapman. It was, however, the home side who took the lead early on but Wednesday stormed back to win 3-2 (Spiksley, Wilson and Davis) and record their first away win in a Sheffield league derby, at the ninth attempt. At the end of the 1901/02 campaign the two sides had met at Owlerton in a game to raise funds for victims of the Ibrox disaster, which had seen twenty-five fans killed and over 500 injured when a wall collapsed at a Scotland vs England international game. That laudable fundraising game would be the first of several charity matches played annually between the two clubs, commencing with Wednesday winning 3-1 at Bramall Lane in October 1903. The generated receipt of £238, from a crowd of 10,158, was duly donated to the Sheffield University Fund – the University College of Sheffield became a university in 1905 – while the players who played in that game, and the subsequent matches up to the start of the First World War, received handsome gold medals for participating. In later years the funds raised were donated to Sheffield medical charities, primarily the city's hospitals, and the games continued until May 1916. Back in League football, Wednesday recorded their best win so far over United: 3-0 at Owlerton in April 1904. There was another double for United in 1904/05, although the win at Bramall Lane was helped in no small measure by the absence of top-scorer Wilson and the fact that his replacement, Hemmingfield, was forced to retire after just ten minutes. Wednesday hit back though to 'double' the Blades in the following campaign – the first game, at Bramall Lane, had the extra spice of the winners receiving the gold medals usually bestowed after the charity game, which had ended in a draw just nineteen days earlier. Just under 30,000 watched goals from Chapman and Stewart secure the spoils for Wednesday while in the penultimate home match of the season, a late penalty from Davis clinched a 1-0 success. Good old Wednesday were certainly top dogs in the city during the early part of the twentieth century as doubles were also recorded in 1907/08, 1910/11, 1912/13 and 1913/14 – although the last one had to be savoured by Owls fans as it would be another ninety-five years before it happened again! The game at Owlerton in 1908 was unique as it was the only league derby ever played on Christmas Day – the teams did meet on that day during the First World War – while it needed an equaliser, with the last kick of the game, by the Blades to secure a draw at Bramall Lane in November 1911. During the years up until the First World War, crowds for Sheffield derbies had slowly risen and the first crowd in excess of 40,000 was recorded in October 1913 when 42,912 packed into Bramall Lane. Unfortunately, not all adhered to the ground rules and just after the teams had run out, hundreds raced across the cricket pitch and formed a large line along the touchline. The solitary mounted police officer tried in vain to usher them back to whence they had come and the game was held up for several minutes before the persuasive tongue of the match referee had the desired effect of restoring order. This allowed fans in the covered stands to see the action and they saw a goal from Glennon clinch two points for the away side. It should be noted that between 1910 and 1919 Wednesday were unbeaten in eleven successive league derbies, the longest spell unbeaten for either club against their rivals.

During the First World War, the teams met frequently in the Midland Section of the regional war league – a total of sixteen times – with Wednesday recording the two 'standout' wins, four goals from Glennon helping the Owls to a 5-0 Bramall Lane win in March 1918 and 20,000 watching Wednesday win 4-0 at Hillsborough on Christmas Day 1918. Over the Christmas period in the 1918/19 season the Owls and United also played a friendly at the Tankersley cricket ground, in aid of the 'Welcome Home fund', although the 2-2 draw, in front of 3,000 fans, has historically been excluded from the first-team records of both clubs due to the transient nature of the two sides on show.

Despite the first season after the war being an unmitigated disaster for Wednesday, they did have the consolation of winning their home derby, goals from Campbell and Gill securing a 2-1 win. The sides would not meet for another six seasons in league football, the next game being in the inaugural final of the Sheffield & Hallamshire County Cup, the Blades winning 2-1 at Hillsborough. Twenty-five years after those somewhat brutal FA Cup ties, the sides were pitted against each other again in today's equivalent of the fourth round, with United's name coming out of the proverbial hat first. Just over 40,000 were in attendance, the crowd being smaller than anticipated due to heavy rain that fell on the morning of the game, turning the pitch into a sea of mud. A large party of men then forked the pitch before kick-off but the home fans probably wished the match had not gone ahead as a brilliant double from Owls' legendary marksman, Jimmy Trotter, put the away side 2-0 ahead after just nine minutes. However, before twenty minutes had elapsed the tie was all square and a second-half winner ensured progress for the Blades.

The much-anticipated return of competitive derbies was shown in the 1926/27 campaign when both grounds set new official attendance records – 43,282 on the opening day at Hillsborough and 60,084 in the return game in January 1927. An aggregate of almost 200,000 fans watched the action in the season that followed, which included two league meetings and two in the FA Cup. In the league, the first game ended 1-1 while in February 1928 the great rivals met three times in just nineteen days, starting with a dramatic meeting at Hillsborough in the return fixture. Of course, that particular season is well known for the Owls' incredible escape from relegation but Wednesday had not started their revival when the Blades visited Hillsborough for the return top-flight game. What followed was one of the most dramatic derby games seen as, against all odds, Wednesday led 3-1 with just five minutes remaining, after goals from winger Wilkinson (2) and Harper. The Wednesday fans, bedecked in blue and white favours, hats and even a blue and white umbrella, were in raptures but those cheers turned to stunned silence as the visitors pulled a goal back and then grabbed a sensational last-minute equaliser from right-winger Partridge – it was breathless stuff for 41,646. Anticipation for the FA Cup fifth-round cup meeting surged even more after that six-goal encounter and another Owlerton ground record, for a derby game, was smashed when 57,076 paid for admission. The game ended 1-1 with the fans talking about an extraordinary incident after seventy-eight minutes when Wednesday captain Seed's close-range shot was knocked up into the air by visiting 'keeper Anderson. However, at this point Seed simply lost sight of the ball and was looking around for it, whereas it lay on the ground just behind him, only needing a touch to put it into the empty goal, and probably put his side into the quarter-finals. Unfortunately for Wednesday, it was the visiting goalie that reacted quickest and he cleared the ball to complete a remarkable escape for United. There was a feeling that maybe Wednesday had missed their chance and this proved the case as United proved far superior in the replay – again watched by a crowd just short of 60,000 – with a treble from Johnson taking his side to a 4-1 win.

The 1928/29 campaign was not only remembered for the Owls' third-title success but also for the only time that Wednesday has scored five times in a league game against their old foes. That memorable afternoon came in September 1928, Wednesday entering into the game on the back of a 6-0 mauling at Derby County on the previous Saturday, while United had beaten Cardiff City and had recently recruited winger Gibson, who was experiencing his first Sheffield derby. The match also saw the new Leppings Lane stand officially opened, although the terracing was not yet completed, with just fewer than 45,000 inside the ground. The game proved to be a dream for Wednesday as goals from Allen and Hooper put them up 2-0 inside eleven minutes, and with Seed outstanding, the visitors could not get a foothold in the game. Before the hour mark it was 4-0 (Hooper again and Rimmer) and although United pulled a goal back, the advantage was quickly restored by a tremendous individual goal from Allen. The Blades did have the scant consolation of scoring the games' best goal – Tunstall netting from 30 yards – but it was a day to savour for those of the blue and white persuasion. The return game ended 1-1 while in arguably the club's greatest ever season, 1929/30, both derby games also ended level – 2-2 at the lane and 1-1 back at Hillsborough. Another terrific derby day came at Hillsborough in September 1932 when the Blades led on three occasions only to be pegged back three times with goals from Ball, Rimmer and Hooper to earn Wednesday a point; the equaliser from the latter was a somewhat comical goal as Hooper's effort struck the top of the post, fell onto United goalie

Smith's back, and then defied his three or four frantic efforts to grasp it and dropped apologetically over the line! It was, however, noticeable that attendance figures had fallen sharply since the heady days of the late 1920s – there were less than 25,000 in the ground – although this was mainly attributable to the great economic downturn of the period. There was still great enthusiasm for the derby games though and United recorded their best crowd of the season when they beat the Owls 3-2 in the return match. The Blades were relegated from the top flight in 1934 but it was ironic that they completed a league double over Wednesday, the return game at Bramall Lane, in March 1934, being an afternoon to forget for Owls fans, although a third-minute goal from Burrows meant his side led 1-0 at half-time. However, a disastrous second period followed, United netting five times in the final twenty-five minutes to record their biggest ever margin of victory in a league derby game. Until competitive hostilities were resumed in 1937, meetings came in County Cup ties and benefit games, one of the latter category games being played at Hillsborough in April 1935 for the dependants of Wednesday trainer Chris Craig, who had suddenly passed away. The game, which finished 0-0, saw Owls manager Walker play as both an outfield player and then goalkeeper but a very poor crowd of around 1,500 did little to boost the funds of Craig's dependants.

When Britain's economy started to spurt back into life, over 100,000 watched the two Second Division games in the 1937/38 season, the Blades winning both in a season where Wednesday only just avoided relegation. The following campaign saw the sides meet four times – two league fixtures, one friendly and one County Cup tie – with Wednesday remaining unbeaten. The first game was actually the first ever preseason club match played by Wednesday, other than the annual 'in-house' public trial matches between stripes and whites. The occasion was to celebrate the fiftieth birthday of the Football League, with forty-four games taking place on 20 August 1938, including several London derbies plus games in Liverpool, Manchester, Bradford, Nottingham and Bristol. The Sheffield Jubilee game was emphatically won by the Owls, watched by 14,197, with a treble from Hunt in a 4-1 success. The two league meetings in the season were fiercely contested with just short of 45,000 failing to see any goals in the first game at Bramall Lane. A crowd of 48,983 was inside Hillsborough for the March return and it was a game that Wednesday desperately needed to win as they sat four points behind United in the league. Thankfully, a late goal from Fallon did clinch that much-needed victory, although in hindsight it was ultimately irrelevant, United pipping Wednesday to promotion. The teams met once more in that campaign, in the County Cup final, but that finished as the league game had, 0-0, so a replay was needed. However, the Hillsborough pitch had been dug up for relaying and Bramall Lane was about to welcome Yorkshire CCC back so at a Sheffield & Hallamshire FA meeting it was decided the trophy would be shared – each side holding it for six months – with gold medals of equal value being presented to the twenty-two players.

The teams were not due to meet in league duty in the 1939/40 season but the start of the Second World War, in September 1939, quickly changed the footballing landscape, the Football League season being abandoned and regional football hastily arranged. The two clubs would be frequent opponents in the war years that followed, meeting in the East Midlands Regional League, North Regional League and then Football League North. There were also regular derbies in the war cup competitions, County Cup ties and friendlies, the teams playing a hastily arranged VE (Victory in Europe) Day celebration match on 9 May 1945, just twenty-four hours after victory was announced. The absence of players due to the war and small crowds (especially in Sheffield, which was bombed several times during the conflict) was perhaps best shown on Christmas Day 1940 when just under 7,000 witnessed a goalless encounter – the game uniquely being a United home game but played at Hillsborough after Bramall lane had suffered severe damage. For Wednesday fans the 1942/43 season was certainly of note as it was by quite a distance the club's best during the war, the Owls finishing third and fifth in the two league competitions and memorably recording their best ever win over the Blades on 13 February 1943. A week before the game, United had won 3-1 at Bramall Lane, so the Sheffield football fraternity was shocked when Robinson (two), Melling, Thompson (two) and Reynolds all scored to put the Owls 6-1 ahead at half-time. The visitors did stem the tide somewhat in the second period, Robinson and Melling both netting again to complete a stunning 8-2 win. Wednesday completed a double in the transitional 1945/46 season but it would not be until the 1949/50 campaign that Wednesday and United met again in the Football League. In the meantime the huge post-war surge in attendances nationwide was no clearer shown than in February 1949 when an astonishing crowd of 49,980 watched the Blades progress through in the County Cup, winning 4-2 at Hillsborough. It should be noted that in the previous May, the two Sheffield teams played each other at senior level for the first time outside of the city boundaries. The occasion was a prestigious friendly encounter on the Isle of Man, the cities' sides being the first Football League clubs to play on the island. A bumper crowd of 8,000 Manx residents attended the game, played in the capital of Douglas, and it was maybe fitting the that match finished level with four goals shared.

When league battles did recommence, the teams again found themselves in direct opposition for the second promotion place to the top flight. Over 50,000 attended each game, with the teams winning their respective home matches, although this time it was Wednesday who prevailed in the league, securing runners-up spot behind Tottenham Hotspur, thanks to the smallest of goal averages (goals scored divided by goals conceded). To complete a great season, almost 32,000 watched the

Owls beat the Blades 2-1 at Hillsborough to lift the County Cup – it was admittedly a rare win over United in the competition as historically they emphatically held the upper hand. Ten months later Wednesday earned another County Cup home win (watched by another unbelievable crowd of 40,660) but our city rivals hit back in emphatic style during the 1951/52 season, winning three times and scoring thirteen goals. It is perhaps an indicator of how derby games can be great levellers as on paper Wednesday were clear favourites for both league games, lying second and first in the table, prior to both fixtures. This was also the season when Dooley set the club's seasonal scoring record and Wednesday scored 100 goals to take the Second Division title. However, that all counted for nothing on 8 September 1951 when Wednesday crumbled at Bramall Lane to lose 7-3, despite Thomas scoring after just ninety seconds, to put the away side in front. The game was actually tied at 2-2 with just over twenty minutes to play, before four goals in just eleven minutes dramatically swung the game in the Blades' direction as they recorded the highest number of goals in a derby fixture between the sides. Wednesday found little consolation in the return fixture, losing 3-1 in early January, although the crowd of 65,384 was both a record for a Sheffield derby and also for a league game at Hillsborough. The Blades completed a seasonal treble in May by winning at Hillsborough to reach the final of the County Cup, before the Owls paid back in kind two seasons later, recording their first FA Cup win over United after three defeats. The first meeting of the 1953/54 First Division season ended 2-0 to the Blades but prior to the return game at Hillsborough, the sides were drawn together in the third round of the cup. A crowd of 61,250 watched the game and it seemed to be 'advantage United' after they secured a 1-1 to take Wednesday back across the city. The Owls found themselves trailing to a Hawksworth goal at half-time in the replay (Wednesday goalie Ryalls also saved a Toner spot kick) but came back to level through Finney before the referee called both sides together, after a succession of fouls, as the game became increasingly bad tempered. Just three minutes later Kenny became the first Owls player to be sent off in post-war soccer but, against all odds, it was the ten men that progressed after late goals from Davies and Sewell secured that first FA Cup win, some fifty-four years after the first meeting. Ten days later, Wednesday rubbed salt into United's wounds by winning 3-2 in the league, but it would be the Blades who held the upper hand until the early 1960s, although relegations and promotions for both teams ensured meetings were irregular. The 1950s, though, should not be departed without mention of a remarkable event that occurred in October 1955 and had the football fans of Sheffield in full gossip mode! Wednesday had installed floodlights in the preseason of 1954 and they were used for the first time for Dooley's benefit game in the following spring. The Owls' first team though had not played a game under the lights and with a glamour friendly against Hungarian side Vasas Budapest on the horizon, it was decided to invite United to provide the opposition for a full-scale practice match. The game was played under a veil of secrecy on 5 October 1955, with only thirty individuals allowed into Hillsborough, which included the managers, directors and two gentlemen of the press. As the game was being played, a police car patrolled around the perimeter of the stadium while one fan was ordered off a stand roof as he tried to grab a glimpse of the action. Fans who were queuing for tickets for the Vasas game were met with comments of 'sorry, it's a private trial' after they inquired about the score, while the following days *Sheffield Daily Telegraph* kept its promise of not revealing the match details, commenting instead on how impressive the floodlights were, although admitting the result was a 'shock score'. Wednesday secretary-manager Taylor said 'I am satisfied that the match was worthwhile. It proved valuable match practice and we may repeat the experience.' Unfortunately his 'cloak and dagger' operation was seen to have failed as the *News Chronicle* duly printed a full report of the game, including line-ups and scorers, and the Owls won 7-2, thanks mainly to trebles from Sewell and Shiner. Taylor described the betrayal as a 'shabby trick' while the irony would not have been lost on Wednesdayites when, in early November, the Blades won 5-2 at Hillsborough in a County Cup tie.

Before league hostilities returned, there was one other meeting when in March 1960 the FA Cup draw pitted the teams together in the sixth round at Bramall Lane. Anticipation for the tie was huge with Second Division United hoping to cause a minor giant-killing against their top-division neighbours. A huge 61,180 attended the tie but although the home side had the better of the game overall, it was the clinical finishing of Owls' winger Wilkinson that proved decisive, the Wednesday man driving home after nine and thirty-four minutes to send Wednesday through. When top-flight meetings came back onto the derby menu in the 1961/62 season, the game at Hillsborough in February created a new Football league record as, with the new North Stand fully operational, a total of 16,000 fans in the 50,937 attendance were seated – the highest number so far recorded in English football. The Blades completed a double by winning 2-1 with Pace (a constant thorn for the Owls in the 1960s) adding to his winning goal in the first game by grabbing a brace in the return. The United centre forward scored in both derbies in the season that followed but Wednesday now had their own clinical attacker and it was Layne who was the thorn in the Blades side, netting twice in both games to earn a draw in the away game and then spearhead a 3-1 victory at Hillsborough, played in mid-May after Britain suffered one of its worst winters on record. The Owls recorded another win and draw in 1963/64 while, until the Blades was relegated in 1968, the teams were evenly matched with neither club gaining superiority over their neighbours. The single-goal win (Ritchie) at Bramall Lane in September 1967 remained in the record books for over forty years as the last time Wednesday took full points from their neighbour's home ground. The calendar year of 1967 also saw the teams meet in testimonial games for club legends G. Shaw and Springett, the latter game at Hillsborough watched by a 23,070 crowd, which saw the beneficiary replaced in goal by his younger brother, Peter, with Ron playing the second half as a forward. Incidentally, the derby games of the 1966/67 season were scheduled for Bramall Lane in September and the return in February but were switched when it became apparent that United's new stand would not be completed in time.

The 1970s were without doubt one of the best decades in the Blades' history while for the Owls it was an unmitigated disaster, as they tumbled down the divisions and went close to bankruptcy. It will therefore be no surprise to learn that Wednesday and United met on league duty in only two seasons: 1970/71 and 1979/80. The former campaign saw United earn promotion back to the top flight and they won 3-2 at home in the first game before a rather uninspiring 0-0 in the return game. This match in April 1971 once again showed the Sheffield public's appetite for the derby games as the attendance at Hillsborough was 47,592 – almost three times the Owls' average crowd for the season! The Boxing Day game at Hillsborough in 1979 has, of course, been well documented and even spawned a terrace chant that is still sung today by Wednesday fans. For the first time in the history of Sheffield football, both of the city's professional clubs found themselves in the proverbial backwater of the Third Division, but hopes were high among both sets of supporters that promotion was a realistic possibility. It looked more likely that the Blades were set for promotion as they sat atop the division when they made the short journey to Hillsborough for the 11 a.m. kick-off. Wednesday was fresh from a win at Reading – moving them up to sixth place – and, with seventeen-year-old full-back Williamson making his home debut, hoped to dash the hopes of United fans, who, in the build-up to the game, had been predicting a 'Boxing Day massacre'. An all-time record divisional crowd of 49,309 watched the proceedings but nobody really could have expected the final scoreline as goals from Mellor, King, Curran and a Smith penalty took Wednesday to a 4-0 win. The unexpectedly large margin of victory sent shockwaves through Sheffield football and from that point onwards the fortunes of both teams went in opposite directions as Wednesday was promoted and United dropped down to mid-table. The Easter Saturday return game ended 1-1, with *Match of the Day* highlights showcasing an outstanding individual goal from fan favourite Curran. But whereas the 1970s saw only a handful of league meetings, the 1980s did not include a single meeting between the great rivals whatsoever. There was a solitary tie in the League Cup, Wednesday winning 3-1 on aggregate at the start of the 1980/81 season, while fans had to be content with the occasional game in the soon to be defunct County Cup, plus a stable diet of friendly and testimonial games. Included in those games was a preseason encounter in 1987, staged to raise funds for the upcoming World Student Games, which Wednesday won 3-0, plus a goalless game at Bramall Lane in 1989 – held to celebrate the Blades' 100th birthday – when Palmer was controversially red-carded and forced to sit out the first three games of the new season. Sheffield United also provided the opposition for the testimonial game of Mark Smith in September 1986, when a crowd of over 10,000 contributed greatly to his benefit pot.

After almost ten years of dominance by the blue and white half of Sheffield, the tide turned again in 1990 when the city clubs swapped places, United taking the Owls' place in the top flight. Before this occurred though, the teams had rekindled competitive contests, a game in the long-since defunct Full Members Cup – a short-lived competition that was introduced after English clubs were banned from Europe following the Heysel disaster. Unfortunately, the response to the tournament was, at best, lukewarm and it would be dogged by poor crowds and general apathy among clubs and fans before it finally died a death in 1992. However, a Sheffield derby is a Sheffield derby and a crowd of over 30,000 was inside Hillsborough – creating a record for a game in the competition outside of the Wembley final – and witnessed a thrilling encounter, which saw Wednesday ahead twice only to be pegged back in the final minute to force extra-time. Without the extra thirty minutes though, Owls fans would have been denied a simply sublime winner from John Sheridan, which involved the midfielder running from inside his own half before firing home from the edge of the penalty area. After an absence of over twenty-three years, First Division league derbies restarted in the 1991/92 season. But despite the Owls finishing third in the division, they were twice undone by their city rivals, winning 2-0 at Bramall Lane (a howler from Woods greatly contributing to the defeat) and completing the double, winning 3-1 at Hillsborough on a night when Sheffield footballing legend Dooley set foot inside the ground for the first time since his sacking as Owls boss in 1973. Both games ended 1-1 in the following season but the 1992/93 campaign would be remembered for arguably the biggest Sheffield derby played: the FA Cup semi-final at Wembley. Both teams had drawn their sixth-round away games and subsequently played on consecutive nights to see if the 'dream' match-up could become a reality. Both won through but there was a huge outcry when the FA pencilled in Elland Road for Wednesday vs United but Wembley for the Tottenham vs Arsenal game. Eventually the national association backed down with often beleaguered chairman Graham Kelly commenting, 'We have listened to the strong feelings expressed by the supporters of both Sheffield clubs and of the clubs themselves and feel that their wish to play at Wembley should be granted.' The city of Sheffield was a ghost town on the day of the game and, despite derby games being notoriously unpredictable, the Owls were hot favourites to reach their second Wembley final of the season. In front of a sellout crowd of 75,364 – who had risen early to travel down the M1 for the 1 p.m., 3 April 1993 kick-off – the game burst into life in spectacular fashion as Waddle fired home a long-range effort, after just sixty-two seconds, to send the blue hordes into raptures. The teams had come out of the dressings rooms to thousands of blue, red and white balloons and the Sheffield fans provided an electric atmosphere as the game almost became a case of the Owls against inspired United 'keeper Alan Kelly. The Blades did, though, level matters just before half-time when Cork fired home and the game went into extra-time with a place in the final still in the balance. In the end a simple goal won the tie for the Owls when Bright headed home after 107 minutes from a Harkes corner. The momentous day was best summed by a 'highbrow' national newspaper, who commented

> So one set of supporters had to be disappointed but all 75,000 had made it an enjoyable day for Sheffield. The precise split along the halfway line between blue and white and red and white favours turned out to be no battle line but simply a frontier of sporting allegiance, and the match ended in the most appropriate way with embraces between the players of both sides and the men in Wednesday shirts exchanging salutes with United fans.

After the drama of the Wembley day out, the teams returned to league duty in the season that followed, although, sadly for Sheffield football, it would be the last meeting between Wednesday and United in the top flight to the present day – a span of over twenty years. Just over 30,000 watched the Premier League meeting at Bramall Lane where two early goals – Palmer equalising a Hodges goal – ensured a third straight 1-1 scoreline in the derby. The return fixture ended in a 3-1 win for Wednesday with rugged centre-half Pearce becoming somewhat of a cult hero after his header put his side 2-0 ahead during a period when Wednesday scored three times in just twelve minutes, Bright and Watson netting either side. The Hillsborough game proved to be the last competitive encounter of the twentieth century, although the sides did meet in the newly created Sheffield Challenge Cup before the dawn of the new millennia. The Owls' relegation in 2000 put derby games back on the agenda, although Sheffield fans would witness three games in the season after the draw for the League Cup Third Round pitched the sides together at Hillsborough. Wednesday's struggles, both financially and with their playing personnel, were perhaps illustrated by the fact that eight of their starting eleven were aged twenty-one or under, but it was an experienced campaigner, Efan Ekoku, who proved the difference as he scored a brace as Wednesday won 2-1 after extra-time. The first Division One encounter occurred in December 2000, a Hendon goal earning the

Owls a point before United won 2-1 in S6 on April Fool's Day, watched by 38,433, in the 100th league derby. The following season's derbies did little to enthuse fans of either side, both ending 0-0, while the home game in September 2002 will always be remembered for the contribution of Wednesday attacker Lloyd Owusu. The striker had signed in the summer from Brentford but his start at Wednesday was delayed due to injury, and when he entered the fray in the derby game, after seventy-one minutes, it was his first appearance. It would be one to remember though as with his first touch he netted from close range after Kuqi's header had rebounded back off the crossbar. His strike partner wrapped up the win in the final ten minutes, although the victory would prove only a minor consolation in a season that ended with relegation. The next two Steel City encounters were at Bramall Lane and both were won by United, 3-1 and 1-0, before Wednesday succumbed to a double in February 2006 when, despite a penalty from MacLean, the Blades triumphed 2-1. After United's brief spell back in the top flight, Wednesday would be unbeaten in the next four league encounters, coming close to an elusive double before memorably sealing two seasonal wins in 2008/09. The first game of the 2007/08 campaign ended 2-0 to Wednesday and a first double for ninety-four years seemed highly likely when a brace from loanee Bolder meant Wednesday led 2-0 at Bramall Lane at half-time. However, the home side recovered to force a draw and Wednesday returned ten months later in the hope of clinching the oft-talked-about double. The game at Hillsborough earlier in the season was certainly not without incident as United were controversially down to ten men after just twenty-seven minutes, after referee Mike Dean sent Kilgallon off for a high boot, before Watson put the Owls in front. In the second period Jermaine Johnson was also red-carded, although, uniquely, eleven Owls players stayed on the pitch as the fiery Jamaican received a second yellow card after having already left the pitch – kicking a water bottle in his temper, causing the referee to brandish a second card. The date of 7 February 2009 proved to be the day when Wednesday finally recorded a derby double as an outstanding long-range shot from Tudgay clinched a 2-1 win, to the delight of the small pocket of Wednesday fans in the ground and the 9,000 back at Hillsborough watching the game on a giant screen. United hit back to claim four points in the following season, while the 2011/12 campaign proved memorable as both sides fought 'tooth and nail' to finish above their rivals and therefore, in all probability, earn the second promotion spot behind leaders Charlton Athletic. The first meeting in October 2011 looked set to go the way of the home side as they quickly established a two-goal lead, but Megson's side dramatically rallied late in the second half with O'Grady reducing the arrears before Madine headed in a leveller with just four minutes left. Amazingly, the Owls almost won it at the death – Rob Jones headed straight into the 'keeper's arms – but it was a fine comeback, also enjoyed by 10,000-plus back at S6. When the sides met again the promotion issue was becoming crystallised with United in pole position. This time the match was beamed back to Bramall Lane while the 36,364 inside the ground witnessed a hard-fought tussle, which ended 1-0 to Wednesday thanks to O'Grady's seventy-third-minute strike. As they say, the rest is history as the Owls overtook their great rivals to gain promotion and it would not be until 2017 that the derby was back on the fixture list, after United won promotion from League One – the longest spell without an inter-club match since the meetings commenced over 127 years ago. Fans of both sides will now be able to enjoy – or perhaps the word endure would be more descriptive – a meeting between the two old rivals, in a city where modern football was born.

	P	W	D	L	F	A
League	114	36	36	42	147	157
Fa Cup	9	3	3	3	13	14
League Cup	3	2	1	0	5	2
Full Members Cup	1	1	0	0	3	2
County Cup	29	9	2	18	41	60
War Leagues	37	13	9	15	61	54
United Counties League	4	0	3	1	2	4
Wharncliffe Cup	3	1	1	1	2	2
Sheffield & District League	2	1	1	0	2	1
Friendlies	54	23	16	15	95	78
Totals	256	89	72	95	371	374

Played For Both (Competitive Games Only) (43):

Earl Barrett	Danny Batth	Carl Bradshaw
Leigh Bromby	Franz Carr	Leon Clarke
Joe Cockroft	Richard Cresswell	Terry Curran
David Ford	Derek Geary	Harry Hall
Jack Hudson	David Johnson	Tommy Johnson
Jeff King	Caolan Lavery	Jon-Paul Mcgovern
Tony Mcmahon	Chris Marsden	Brian Marwood

Joe Mattock	Billy Mellor	Owen Morrison
Billy Mosforth	Chris O'grady	Bernard Oxley
Alan Quinn	Neil Ramsbottom	Walter Rickett
Carl Robinson	Wilf Rostron	Bernard Shaw
Bernard L. Shaw	Simon Stainrod	Stanley Taylor
Keith Treacy	Oliver Tummon	Iain Turner
Imre Varadi	George Waller	Alan Warboys
Dean Windass		
Inter-club Transfers:		
Wednesday to United		*United To Wednesday*
Terry Curran		Billy Mellor
Caolan Lavery		Bernard Oxley
Leigh Bromby		
Joe Cockroft		
Jeff King		
Owen Morrison		
Alan Quinn		
Wilf Rostron		

Chapter 12

Men at the Top

'I would also like to thank the fans, whose passion and warmth gave me the inspiration to conclude the deal. I was overwhelmed with the welcome I received at my first game at Hillsborough against Bristol Rovers. It was something that I will always remember.'

Milan Mandaric, December 2010

In recent years the position of chairman has been held by the individual who actually owns Sheffield Wednesday, but in the 143 years to 2010 the position of president and then chairman was held by a greatly respected member of the Sheffield community, usually from the industrial sector. The individual was not only seen as a figurehead but took an active role in club issues after being voted into the role by his peers. The man at the top also had a great influence on club policies and the position was seen as arguably the most important role behind the scenes.

The position was created on the first day of the football club's life with local financial agent Benjamin Chatterton elected into the role of club president. Born in 1830, he started his working life as a file cutter and was aged around thirty-seven when Wednesday FC drew its first gasp of air and like all the founder members of the football section, was an active member of the cricket club. He was a well-known local cricketer – he joined Wednesday in the mid-1840s and became a committeeman in 1852 – and despite serving the football section for just one season, holds that unique place in club history as not only a founder member but the club's first president. Married to wife Harriott in 1855, Chatterton was blessed with two sons and three daughters and was a renowned bowler, being presented with a silver cup by Wednesday CC in 1863 for his outstanding season with the ball. He played in the first game staged at the newly constructed Bramall Lane in 1855, while away from the sporting scene he served four terms as a Sheffield town councillor (1868–80) and became a man of considerable stature – he was noted as living with his wife, five children and two domestic servants in 1881 in an upmarket part of town. In addition to guiding the fledgling football club through its first season, he had previously spent four years as the cricket club president before returning to the role in 1868. His brother, George, was an outstanding cricketer for Wednesday and the All England XI, while Benjamin lived to the age of seventy-two before passing away at his Nether Edge home on 16 October 1902, leaving an indelible mark on the sporting and public life of Sheffield.

He was succeeded by Sheffield-born (October 1836) Francis Smith Chambers, who had served as vice-president to Chatterton during the club's debut campaign. A keen sportsman, Chambers, known as Frank to his friends and colleagues, held a variety of jobs including cotton spinner, hardware merchant, brewery manager and brewer, but remained a bachelor throughout his life, living with his father, sister and two servants at their Ecclesall home. He would serve as Wednesday FC president for two seasons before returning to a position on the club's committee in 1870, while he was president of the cricket club between 1867 and 1870. He was a regular helper every year, despite leaving the committee in 1872, at the club's popular Athletics Days but passed away on 5 April 1892, aged fifty-five, at his Grange Crescent home.

The next incumbent was well-known businessman Henry Hawksley, who traded as a hatter from his premises on High Street. Born in the town on 3 May 1835, Hawksley served both the cricket and football sections of the Wednesday club, commencing in 1865 when he joined the committee of the summer game. He served for three further seasons before he was elected vice-president, representing both sections simultaneously. Described as being of an obliging nature and kind disposition, Hawksley would replace Chambers as president of both Wednesday sections in 1870 (he played the occasional game for the football section in the early 1870s) and remained at the helm for the following seventeen years, although his ailing health meant he played a decreasing role from the mid-1880s onwards. Throughout that period, he continued to trade from his town centre premises, although it was not without financial difficulties – a meeting of creditors applied for the liquidation of his affairs back in 1874 – but the gentlemen of Sheffield could still buy their hat of choice, even after the business changed hands following Henry's passing. Twice-married Henry had become a much-respected member of the Sheffield sporting scene, while he also served for several years on the town council. Henry passed away on 8 May 1887 while still in office as president, leaving two sons and a daughter, who lived with their mother, Sarah, and two servants in Ecclesall. As a show of respect the cricket club convened a special meeting to convey their sympathies to his family on their bereavement, with a scheduled game against Glossop postponed as a show of respect. It was perhaps fitting that all Henry's friends were invited to his wake, held at the football club's spiritual birthplace, the Adelphi Hotel.

The loss of Hawksley did, however, lead to the appointment of a man crucial to the early history of the football club, John Holmes. Born in Sheffield in 1841, Holmes' father, Adam, was a decorated war hero who served under the Duke of Wellington at the famous battle of Waterloo, losing his left leg. It's believed John was a member of the Broomhall club in the late 1860s and first became associated with Wednesday in 1872 – although he was quite possibly involved before that date – and over the ensuing years became increasingly influential behind the scenes, moving onto the committee in 1878. Holmes, who ran a successful cutlery manufacturing business in the town, employing over twenty people, was a real larger-than-life character who was said to be a genuine, thorough and candid individual, well known for his hearty ringing laugh and his stern vow to always promote local football talent; he regularly took an active role in training and regularly attended reserve fixtures in the hope of finding a jewel in the opposition ranks. Within a year of moving onto the committee, he was elected vice-president and was acknowledged as the main instigator behind the club's move to Olive Grove. The same year had seen Holmes, who married wife Clara in 1862 and unusually for the times only had one child, daughter Mary, step up into the role of president and he remained in that position until the club was restructured as a limited liability company in 1899; he was one of original seven shareholders when the club became incorporated in 1893. In addition to his role at Wednesday, Holmes was also the main instigator behind the formation of the Football Alliance League in 1889, serving as its first and only president, while he was also president of several local leagues. During the 1890s Holmes saw his beloved Wednesday gain Football League status and was overjoyed when the 'English Cup' came back to Sheffield for the first time in 1896, Holmes commenting at the time that 'I have been hunting this cup for 20 years.' He was voted onto the prestigious FA Council in 1894 and Holmes – described as a 'good old sportsman, full or reminiscences of the early days of Sheffield football, as good a judge of a joke as a footballer, or better' – was again a pivotal figure in another ground move, this time to Owlerton in 1899. When Wednesday became a company, Holmes was appointed vice-chairman to Senior and continued to provide invaluable service, although ailing health meant he became an infrequent visitor to Owlerton in his later years, passing away on 25 March 1908. He was buried in his family's plot in the Derbyshire village of Eyam, and will forever be remembered with great affection as one of the most important men in the history of Sheffield Wednesday, a man who helped the club through the often turbulent 1880s and '90s, and saw them established, through his enthusiastic endeavours, as one of England's top sides.

Whereas Chatterton was the club's first president, George Senior was Wednesday's first chairman of the board. Voted into the position at the first meeting of the new company, Senior was the archetypical self-made man who started working at the tender age of eight, helping his father manufacture nails in his Bradfield premises. Born on 17 September 1838, Senior suffered the limits of self-education – he did not receive any schooling whatsoever – but remarkably overcame his early struggles to become one of the most important and loved men in the town of Sheffield – he was affectionately known simply as 'our George' by the masses. Described as a man of 'undoubted energy, enterprise and sterling integrity', Senior had followed in the footsteps of his father and grandfather but the trade was in decline and aged thirteen he became apprenticed to a Mr George Parkin, a steel manufacturer based at Kenyon's Old Forge, Middlewood. Over the years that followed Senior rose through the hierarchy in the Sheffield steel industry and duly formed his own business in 1872, based at Pond's Forge, which would grow into the biggest importers of steel in the country by the beginning of the twentieth century – his two sons, Albert and George, later became part of George Senior & Sons Ltd. Senior was also chairman of Tinsley Rolling Mill Co., while in 1889 he was elected to Sheffield's council, becoming Lord Mayor in 1901, a considerable achievement when one considers that he was not born of inheritance and had achieved everything in his life through hard work, common sense and foresight but never forgetting his humble roots. During his tenure the club won back-to-back titles, in addition to the FA Cup, while he was said to have tears in his eyes at the club's 1908 AGM as he paid tribute to club two stalwarts, Holmes and Walter Fearnehough, who had sadly passed away. He followed in the long line of city luminaries when he was appointed Master Cutler in 1910 and passed away on 4 July 1915, aged seventy-seven, in Sheffield. His funeral was more akin to those of royal blood as his cortege was over a mile long, including around 300 work colleagues, and the streets were lined with hundreds and hundreds of mourners. It was a fitting end for a Sheffield man of substance.

If Senior was a well-respected and popular member of the Sheffield business and political scene, then his replacement, Sir John Charles Clegg, was simply one of the most important men that Sheffield has ever produced. Born in the town on 15 June 1850, J. C. Clegg would join his father's eminent law practice at an early age and, along with his brother William, was an active and high-profile member of the Sheffield sporting scene as association football grew in the town. A player for both Wednesday and Sheffield FC, Clegg first appeared for the former around 1869 and such was his impact in local football that he duly appeared in England's first ever international match – against Scotland in 1872 – although he commented that his teammates were 'snobs from the south who had no use of a lawyer from Sheffield'. He was a fine all-round sportsman, excelling at running, tennis and rugby, while he also became an eminent match referee, officiating in the 1882 and 1892 FA Cup finals. It was, however, off the field of play that Clegg would make an even greater impact, towering over the game of football for almost half a century, commencing with his appointment as president of the Sheffield & Hallamshire FA. He first started to make an impact on a national basis when appointed to the FA Council in 1886 but within three years he was vice-chairman and in 1890 was elected as the most powerful man in English football: chairman of the FA. Despite being strongly against professionalism in sport – he was often quoted as saying 'nobody ever got lost on a straight road' – Clegg had to bow to the inevitable and subsequently served as the figurehead of the domestic game for almost forty years, also becoming president (the only man to fill both roles) in 1923. At Wednesday, Clegg remained as chairman until the early 1930s and subsequently served as president until his passing in Sheffield on 26 June 1937, aged eighty-seven. In addition to his role with the FA and Wednesday, he also served as chairman of Sheffield United – often holding quick board meetings at Bramall Lane so he could 'hot foot' it over to Owlerton to deal with Wednesday's affairs – while in 1927 was knighted 'for services to the Board of Trade and the Ministry of Labour' – political speak for his huge contribution to the game of football. He counted senior politicians, and even the king, among personal friends while away from football he served as a justice of the peace. On his passing the club erected a memorial in the boardroom – sadly lost over the ensuing years – as a tribute to one of the great administrators the game of football has ever seen.

Another man of significant substance in Sheffield society, William Glasier Turner OBE, would take Clegg's position at the helm of Wednesday's board of directors. His father, also called William, had founded his rolling and smelting company back in 1887 and his son, born in 1870, would eventually take his place as both head of the family business and position on the Sheffield Wednesday board of directors. The company still trades today supplying a wide array of Sheffield made cutlery. It was the death of his father in 1906 that saw William Jr join the Wednesday hierarchy and he was awarded an OBE after the First World War for his work in munitions during the conflict; he was also president of the Sheffield branch of the British War Graves Commission and after the war led several pilgrimages to France. Like his father, William was held in great esteem in the Sheffield business community – he was an active freemason and member of the institute of metals – and he seemed the obvious choice to step into Clegg's shoes as chairman in 1931. During his time at the helm, Turner watched Wednesday win the FA Cup in 1935, although the club was also relegated in 1937, later accepting the resignation of manager Walker. Turner remained as chairman until July 1944, when he was appointed club president, before passing away, aged seventy-seven, on 21 May 1947.

While Turner could trace a family connection with Wednesday back into the late nineteenth century, his successor, William Fearnehough, could boast ancestors who were connected with the Wednesday football and cricket club back in the early 1870s and could quite possibly have been members when the football section was formed. His father, Walter, famously employed James Lang at his Sheffield knife manufacturing business and was also a player for Wednesday in the 1870s, later serving as a committeeman, and was vice-president when Wednesday achieved league status in 1892. In addition to his father, William's uncle Whiteley also served for over a decade on Wednesday's committee, so when William took over from William Turner, it was simply continuing a family tradition. He had been voted onto the board of directors in October 1910 and served thirty-four years before being handed the role of chairman, as the war in Europe came to a close. William, born 14 May 1878 in Sheffield, helped Wednesday make the transition back to peacetime football and sanctioned several high-profile, high-value forays into the transfer market. He would serve as chairman until one of the worst days in the history of Sheffield Wednesday – 14 February 1953 – when William passed away in the Sheffield Royal Infirmary, aged seventy-four, just a few hours before Dooley's career was ended at Preston. He left a widow, Margaret, and two sons, although neither became connected to the football club, therefore breaking a family connection that lasted over eighty years.

When Fearnehough was voted chairman in July 1944 it was James Longden, owner of George Longden & Sons Ltd, who took his place as vice-chairman. He had been on the club's board since October 1937, replacing the deceased Clegg, and was already a shareholder in the club. He had played amateur football in his youth – he later became president of Hallam FC and boasted a famous mother, Ann Longden, who was the first female Lord Mayor of Sheffield, serving between 1936 and 1937. Born late in 1900 in Sheffield, James eventually took over the family construction business, which actually built the Sheffield City Hall in the 1930s; the company also built the Hallamshire Hospital in the 1960s. The business had been founded by his grandfather, George, in 1850, and then handed to James' own father, William, before passing to James when his father died in 1922. Described as a 'big-hearted sportsman', James followed both of his ancestors in becoming president of the Building Trades' Employers' Association and also served on the FA Council, as well as serving for many years as a city councillor. He was appointed Wednesday supremo on 5 March 1953 but sadly his time at the helm was relatively brief as he died suddenly, aged just fifty-three, on 28 May 1954.

Sadly, the club's next chairman, Colonel Robert Luther Craig, was also only a brief incumbent, remaining at the helm for less time than his predecessor. Sheffield born in 1905, he had a strong family connection to Wednesday, his father, Donald, serving on the board of directors before the Second World War and his sibling, also called Donald, becoming a director in June 1950. Robert, who served in Italy with the Royal Army

Service Corps in the Second World War, joined the board around 1948 and became chairman in July 1954 after the sudden death of Longden. Unfortunately, he became ill not long after taking up the position and after playing a diminishing role in club affairs, resigned on 7 May 1955. A solicitor by profession, living in Hathersage, Craig failed to recover and passed away on 20 August 1955, aged just fifty.

After the relatively early passing of two consecutive chairman Wednesday needed some stability and this arrived in the form of Sir Andrew Stephen, who would follow in the sizable footsteps of Clegg by rising to also become chairman of the Football Association. Born to a family of Aberdeen tenant farmers on 20 May 1906, Andrew qualified as a doctor from Aberdeen School of Medicine in 1928 and two years later moved south to take up a position as a GP in Sheffield. His involvement with Wednesday started on New Year's Day 1937, when he was appointed medical officer, and he joined the board in March 1949, stepping up to vice-chairman in July 1954. The poor health of Craig led to his appointment as the Owls' seventh chairman on 16 May 1955 and within a few weeks faced the wrath of disgruntled supporters, at the club's Annual General Meeting, as there were calls for the directors to resign and the new chairman to hold an immediate election of directors. The club was accused of being 'dictatorial' and of running a 'closed shop' but Stephen commented 'I have been called dictatorial in trying to do my best for the club. When elected chairman I knew it was no sinecure [an office that requires little or no responsibility]. I am not prepared to take lying down any statement that this board condoned in any way sharp practice or trickery.' Thankfully for Stephen, after a disastrous 1954/55 season, Wednesday hit the ground running in his first full season and in May 1956 the club was back in the First Division. He would subsequently work in hand with Taylor to develop Hillsborough while the club became a permanent resident in the upper echelons of the English league during the 1960s. Sadly, the decade also included the infamous bribes scandal with Stephen quoted in the local press: 'I would rather see Sheffield Wednesday relegated to Division Four than be involved in anything shady.' The scandal was a huge blow to the club but Stephen's stock continued to rise and in January 1967 he became the first Scot to be appointed chairman of the FA. He was knighted for his services to medicine and football in June 1972, but was given the unviable task a year later of informing World Cup-winning manager Alf Ramsey that his services were no longer required. The Owls' chairman remained at the helm of the FA until 1976 but stepped down at club level in December 1973, accepting a vice-president role a month later. Stephen, who also served on FIFA's medical committee, remained a supporter of the Owls before passing away in Wisewood, Sheffield, aged seventy-three, on 25 February 1980.

It was perhaps unfortunate for the club's next chairman, Matt Sheppard, as he was appointed to the position at arguably the worst time in Wednesday's history with the club on a downward spiral, both on and off the pitch. It was also unfortunate for the new incumbent that one of his first tasks was the ill-timed dismissal of Dooley as team manager. Sheppard, born in the city in 1925, had only been chairman for eighteen days when the axe fell and Sheppard would, rightly or wrongly, be remembered almost solely for that one moment during his tenure. In fact, Sheppard's time on the Owls' board was somewhat troublesome from the start as he was initially appointed at a stormy AGM in April 1971, when a rebel shareholders group was angry that none of their members had been considered. Brought up in the Sheffield district of Firth Park, Sheppard was a Wednesday fan and first came into contact with the club, on a professional basis, when he started working for their auditors. The one-time president of the Sheffield Chamber of Commerce subsequently became club advisor and then company accountant. He also acted as advisor for a wide array of businesses, often serving as a director or chairman, while also serving as a magistrate. His appointment as chairman occurred in a season when Wednesday just avoided relegation to the Third Division, but there was no escaping the drop twelve months later and with the club struggling near the foot of the old Third Division (League One), he resigned his chair on 26 September 1975, reverting back to vice-chairman. Within a few weeks he left the club altogether, citing 'pressure of business'. He continued to support Wednesday and lived in the city until 2007 before moving to Gloucestershire. He passed away, aged ninety, on 2 April 2015 in Tetbury, leaving three children, eight grandchildren and one great-grandchild.

It was new chairman Bert McGee who would stop the haemorrhage of money and turn around the club's fortunes by the end of the decade. Born in Hillsborough on 11 August 1917, Herbert Edward McGee's first memory of watching the Owls came back in 1926 when he watched Newcastle legend Hughie Gallagher score past Wednesday custodian Brown at Hillsborough. His passion for the club was passed down from his father, who sadly suffered a heart attack while attending a Wednesday game and passed away a few months later. The early death of his father meant McGee abandoned his dream of becoming a doctor and left school to secure employment to help support his family. He became an apprentice engineer and from these humble beginnings rose to become managing director at Penistone Road-based tooling company Presto Tools, turning the business into one of Sheffield's most successful manufacturing concerns. His rise in business circles meant that in 1980 he emulated the club's first chairman, George Senior, by becoming Master Cutler, an honour which has been bestowed, usually yearly, since 1624. He'd initially joined the board of directors in December 1973, following the resignation of Stephen, and he found Wednesday in deep financial trouble. His influence quickly became apparent as several cost-cutting measures took place and after replacing Sheppard as chairman the club's financial crisis slowly started to abate – McGee had moved up to vice-chairman in March 1975 before ascending to the head of the table a few months later. McGee, who had strong links with the Sheffield Chamber of Commerce and Sheffield University, was instrumental in appointing Charlton as manager in 1977 and his shrewd management of the club's finances ensured that by 1978 Wednesday were back in profit, recording a considerable surplus on the 1977/78 campaign – the first profit since relegation from the top fight in 1970. The Owls' subsequent promotions from the Third Division in 1980 and from the Second Division in 1984 also greatly helped the finances, while also restoring the club to the top flight. However, his later years as club chairman saw criticism that Wednesday was unwilling to loosen the Hillsborough purse strings. The Hillsborough Disaster in the following year was a definite low point of his reign and in March 1990 he resigned to concentrate on his other sporting passion – golf. Sadly, just over five years later he passed away in Sheffield, aged seventy-seven, on 29 April 1995.

His replacement, Sir Dave Richards, would prove a controversial appointment, although the club experienced great success during his early years as chairman. Born in the Sheffield district of Walkley in October 1943, Richards was the son of a steelworker and started his working life as an engineering apprentice after leaving Burgoyne School in 1958. One of seven children, Richards moved to Chesterfield-based Three Star Engineering in 1970 as general manager, quickly progressed through the ranks to become managing director, and was instrumental in a move of premises to Sheffield. His association with the Owls began in October 1989 when he joined the club's board of directors and there was general surprise when he was voted chairman in March 1990. Arguably it was Richards himself who was most surprised by the decision, commenting at the time 'when my colleagues on the board invited me to succeed Bert McGee I was absolutely flabbergasted'. His reign started badly as Wednesday were relegated but the diminutive Richards would then preside over several seasons of success. He was also a driving figure behind the club becoming more competitive in the transfer market, in terms of both fees and wages, with Wednesday's transfer record broken on several occasions. When much-loved manager Atkinson resigned from his position in the summer of 1991, Richards seemingly persuaded him to stay, only for 'Big Ron' to walk out a few days later. Despite his departure, Wednesday enjoyed many happy days under the tutelage of Francis, while off the field the ground was significantly upgraded. Unfortunately, from the mid-1990s the Owls struggled to compete, financially and on the field, in the Premier League and an ill-advised partnership with London-based finance house Charterhouse did nothing to stem the downward spiral. In fact, the £17 million pumped into the club to secure 20 per cent of the shareholding was partly to settle accumulated debts while the buying of additional shares by the majority of the club's directors, pre-sale, received criticism. Some of the new finance was certainly used to sign Di Canio but in the final five seasons in the Premier League the Owls lost almost £30 million, a large financial headache that accompanied the club as they tumbled out of the top flight in 2000. Criticism was also aimed at Richards and this increased when he was appointed temporary chairman of the FA Premier League in April 1999 – fans perhaps understandably questioning his commitment. Richards had also been appointed to the FA Council in 1994 and he subsequently cut all ties with Wednesday on 12 February 2000, with the club struggling against relegation from the Premier League and in serious financial trouble. He was immediately appointed full-time chairman of the Premier League. His misfortunes at the helm of Wednesday were somewhat mirrored in his business life as Three Star Engineering closed down while Richards was then a director of a wide range of companies, several of which entered receivership or were dissolved. Now ensconced full time in London, Richards was knighted for his services to football in 2006 and also spent five years as chairman of the Football Foundation (2003–08). In addition to his appointment at the head of the Premier League he also serves on the FA Council and is vice-chairman of the governing body, although a conflict of interest had always been denied by Richards. Labelled with the rather unfortunate nickname of 'Gunner' (due to his propensity to talk about what he's 'gunna do'), he remains one of the most powerful men in English football. His time at Hillsborough will forever be remembered for the financial millstone that hung around the club's neck until the arrival of Mandaric over a decade later.

With the club on the brink of relegation, and with finances deteriorating fast, it was a rather unenviable job for new chairman Howard Culley, a prominent local solicitor. A lifelong Wednesdayite, Culley was born in Sheffield in October 1943 and after graduating from Sheffield Hallam University joined criminal law solicitors Irwin Mitchell as a trainee in 1977, when the business was just a six-partner firm. He remained employed there until 2009, having held the position of national managing partner for twenty-one years, during which time the business had grown into one of the top-ten legal firms in the UK. It was in July 1995 that Culley first joined the board, replacing Ernest Barron, but his tenure as chairman would be short-lived as in the summer of 2000 he chaired an extraordinary, hostile general meeting where fans called for his resignation, and that of accountant Bob Grierson. There were again calls for the board to resign at the AGM in October 2000 and eventually, on the same day Jewell was dismissed, Culley tendered his resignation. He did remain on the board of directors for a few more months before cutting ties in August 2001 to concentrate on his various business interests. He continues to play a prominent role in Sheffield society, chairing various Irwin Mitchell-based companies, while working as a consultant for the company. He also has several voluntary roles with the likes of Sheffield Hallam University (governor), the Sheffield City Trust (the body that is responsible for running Sheffield recreational facilities such as Ponds Forge and Sheffield Arena) and is also a trustee of the Sheffield Museums and Galleries.

The successor to Culley was lifelong Wednesday fan Geoff Hulley, who was born in Sheffield on 19 June 1930. Hulley had first started to watch Wednesday at the age of just five and was co-opted onto the board back in September 1980. When he stepped up to chairman he became the oldest man to be appointed to the role, although, like his predecessor, the position was somewhat of a poisoned chalice, Wednesday still reeling from relegation and the financial fallout therefrom. After being handed the reins at Hillsborough he officially retired from his family's ice-cream and frozen foods business, which began in 1967. One of his first acts as chairman, along with fellow directors Allen and Addy, was to purchase the 36.7 per cent shareholding held by finance company Charterhouse, ending their connection to the club, which was certainly a failure for all parties concerned. As company law dictates that any shareholding over 29.9 percent triggers a mandatory bid for the remaining shares, it was agreed to gift 9.46 per cent of the shares to newly formed fans group The Owls Trust. While at the helm he saw the departure of both Shreeves and Yorath from the manager's chair while Wednesday suffered relegation to England's third tier. However, financial problems almost overshadowed woes on the pitch and after trying to stem the proverbial tide, with little success, he handed the role over to Dave Allen in June 2003. He did remain on the board – he was central in the failed takeover bid by businessman Geoff Sheard in 2008 – and had completed thirty years of service when he sold his shareholding to new owner Mandaric in December 2010, and severed direct links with Wednesday.

It would perhaps be fair to say that the rein of the next chairman, Dave Allen, was the most colourful of any incumbent of the chair, ranging from helping the club financially – his company A & S Leisure group were shirt sponsors for two seasons – to falling out with fans, fighting off an unwelcome takeover bid from Ken Bates and seeing the club regain their place in the Championship. At the time, Allen was unique as he became the first chairman to be appointed who had no allegiance to the club; he was better known for his keen interest in pigeon racing, writing a book on the subject entitled *The Widowhood Year*. He was initially invited by former chairman Howard Culley to inject some much-needed business acumen, and became a non-executive director on both the football and PLC board on 2 June 2000. Born in Sheffield in 1942 and brought up in Stannington, Allen came from a musical background with his father a professional musician and his mother a dance teacher. A teenage Allen learned to play the trumpet and after leaving Firth Park Grammar School, formed a dance band (the Dave Allen Sound) before starting to work with Eric Morley (a man who later became synonymous with the Miss World pageants) and touring with his expanded band for around five years. He's credited with starting the first mobile disco and in 1968 bought a struggling jazz club in Rotherham, which was turned into a nightclub called The Charade. A string of nightclubs followed, including the Roxy in Sheffield, and he then opened his first casino, Napoleon's on Ecclesall Road. The much-loved Josephine's nightclub in Sheffield was also added to his business empire before he took over and greatly revived the ailing fortunes of Owlerton greyhound stadium. After joining the Owls' board of directors the blunt-speaking, determined and single-minded Allen became an increasingly influential figure behind the scenes. He was instrumental in appointing Turner as manager and eventually took over as chairman in June 2003 before being faced with the rather unwelcome attentions of former Chelsea supremo Ken Bates, who attempted to seize control of Wednesday. The backing of former chairman Dave Richards, ex-director Joe Ashton and fans groups made for a somewhat lively, and very public, debate, which only succeeded in having a destabilising effect on Wednesday. When Bates finally gave up the ghost, Allen could concentre on getting Wednesday back into the Championship, a feat achieved after Sturrock took over from Turner. The Owls stabilised in the Championship but it was not plain sailing for Allen, who was cast in the no-nonsense mould of his predecessors of pre-war years, and he had several publicised disagreements with supporters with the threat of court action against one making him *persona-non grata* with many supporters. He was later cleared by the FA of bringing the game into disrepute after referring to some fans as 'scum' and 'cretins' and eventually, on 23 November 2007, Allen resigned from his position. He subsequently dropped his legal action against a fan two months later and cut all ties in December 2010 when he sold his shareholding to Mandaric. While still a shareholder at the Owls, it was reported that Allen, known for his sharp sense of humour, invested £4 million to become the majority shareholder at neighbours Chesterfield. His greatest achievement was undoubtedly the move to the new stadium at Whittingham Moor in 2010, while the Spireites also won the League Two title twice and the Johnstone's Paint Trophy in 2012. He resigned as Chesterfield chairman in November 2016 but remains the majority shareholder.

After Allen's departure the club was faced, for the first time in their history, with no figurehead as it was not until 7 January 2009 that a new chairman was named. During this hiatus Lee Strafford joined the board, in December 2008, and it would be Strafford who was next in the 'hot seat'. The Wednesdayite from Parson Cross had first become directly involved when the company he co-founded, PlusNet, was named as shirt sponsors in 2005 and the income from that deal, which lasted four years, greatly helped Wednesday's flagging finances. Along with new chief executive Nick Parker, the pair worked for many months behind the scenes, attempting to restructure the club's ever-growing debt and secure much-needed investment. One of his first tasks after being co-opted onto the board, the day after the AGM, was to dismiss chief executive Kaven Walker and when he stepped up to the chairmanship he became the youngest in the Owls' history, aged just thirty-six years old. The duo was effectively working to a self-imposed 31 March 2010 deadline to secure investment with Strafford acting as a figurehead, while Parker restructured all aspects of the club's finances. However, relegation from the Championship, coupled with boardroom disharmony, meant finances deteriorated dramatically and Strafford tendered his resignation on 17 May 2010, after failing in his task of securing investment. After leaving the Owls, Strafford has continued to be closely connected to the Sheffield business community, working for the city council and the two universities to help create more technology start-up businesses. He was also a board member of the Sheffield City Region Enterprise Partnership while he has founded and mentored several entities in the technology sector, but still watches Wednesday.

After being appointed to the board by Strafford as an unpaid technical advisor, former player and manager Howard Wilkinson agreed to act as temporary chairman after his resignation. He was still at the helm when the Owls were issued with a winding-up order in November 2010, before relinquishing the role to Mandaric a month later. He remained on the board for a few more weeks before departing, with the thanks of the new owner, in January 2011.

Since their formation in 1867, the Owls had always been run either by a committee or board of directors but the arrival of Milan Mandaric in December 2010 saw the Serbian-born businessman become owner-chairman after paying off all of the club's debts and effectively saving them from administration or even worse. Not unlike the self-made men of his predecessors, Mandaric had started his working life in his father's machine shop, aged twenty-one, and would rise to become a major figure in the production of computer circuit boards in what became known as Silicon Valley in the US. Born on 5 September 1938 in modern-day Croatia, Mandaric experienced a traumatic early childhood as his family, living in the former socialist state of Yugoslavia, had to hide in the mountains from their enemies and his father was even taken to a concentration camp. In the mid-1940s the family managed to flee to the town of Novi Sad and it was here that Mandaric qualified as a mechanical engineer. In a few short years he would turn his father's business into one of the most successful in Yugoslavia, but this led him on a collision course with authoritarian leader General Tito and he was denounced as a 'capitalist traitor' when the flourishing entrepreneur moved his family to Switzerland in 1969. He stayed for a year as he tried to extract some of his wealth from Yugoslavia, but in 1970 settled in California, working for a computer component manufacturer. By the mid-1970s the company he formed, Lika Corp, was the biggest manufacturer of computer components in the US – one of his first orders was from Steve Jobs, the mastermind behind Apple – and in 1976 he became a US citizen. After selling his business to the Tandy Corporation in 1980, Mandaric set up a new company and continued to enjoy success, amassing a considerable personal fortune. It was back in the 1970s that he first became involved in football as from a young age he had been an enthusiastic competitor, and the passion came to fruition when he formed FC Lika and then San Jose Earthquakes. The Earthquakes played in the fledgling North American Soccer League (NASL) and Mandaric played a role in bringing the likes of Best, Moore and Pele to the razzamatazz of the NASL. He duly purchased another franchise, the Connecticut Bicentennials, which then moved to California to become the Stompers and eventually metamorphosed into the Edmonton Drillers. However, when the NASL collapsed, the game in the US moved indoors and Mandaric briefly owned St Louis Storm before the league ceased in the early 1990s. By this time Mandaric was sceptical as to the future of the sport in the US and looked to Europe, initially taking shares in Belgium Club Standard Liege before buying Sporting de Charleroi outright. Ownership of French club OCG Nice followed, with a French Cup win in 1997, before buying his first English team, Portsmouth, in 1999. He bought Pompey out of administration and the appointment of Harry Redknapp proved a masterstroke as the Fratton Park club was promoted into the Premier League in 2003. After seven years on the south coast he resigned as chairman in September 2006, having sold all his shares, but was quickly back in football, buying Leicester City for a reputed £6 million. He earned a reputation of hiring and firing managers while at the Walkers Stadium but City won League One in 2009 and he left them on a firm footing for a Thai consortium to continue their rise, selling for a reputed £40 million. He had certainly been bitten by the English football bug as later in 2010 he proved the saviour Wednesday fans had hoped for as he completed a takeover for a nominal £1, clearing a HMRC debt and wiping off the club's long-term liabilities. His reign was rubber-stamped when 99.7 per cent of shareholders voted to sell the company to Mandaric's UK Investments. Within a few weeks of taking over, Wednesday had slid dramatically down the league, costing manager Irvine his job, but happier times soon followed with promotion to the Championship and the club consolidating in the higher league. However, Mandaric knew that further significant investment was needed and looked to have secured this when it was announced in the summer of 2014 that Azerbaijani businessman Hafiz Mammadov had completed a takeover. Sadly, the deal fell through but a few months later an agreement was reached with a Thai consortium, led by Dejphon Chansiri, paying a reputed £37.5 million to take control. Mandaric duly said an emotional goodbye to fans prior to the home game with Cardiff City, commenting 'I ask you to give support to Mr Chansiri, the same that you gave to me. He convinced me he is going to take the programme forward to get us into the Premier League. In a few days time I will step down as your chairman but I will never step down as your friend and a supporter of your wonderful club.' He looked set to enjoy his retirement and spend more time with his family but his love for the game meant that within months he had returned to his roots, taking over Slovenian club Olimpija Ljubljana in the summer of 2015. The workaholic continues to be involved with countless business interests around the globe.

Current chairman Dejphon Chansiri officially took over from Mandaric on 26 February 2015 and vowed to secure Premier League status before the club's 150th birthday in 2017. The new owner arrived in Sheffield with literally no experience, or real interest, in the game of football, his son, Att, being one of the main reasons why he decided to invest his considerable personal fortune in Wednesday. The football-mad youngster was club mascot on Boxing Day 2014 before the takeover news broke, and was without doubt a deciding factor in the Thai-born Chansiri following his childhood friend Narin – co-owner of Reading – into English football. It was the fathers of the two, Kraisron Chansiri and Cheng Niruttinanon, who bought a small cannery in Samut Sakhon, south-east Bangkok, back in 1977 and built their business into the world's biggest supplier of canned tuna, worth billions. Their company, Thai Union Frozen (TUF), expanded worldwide, buying English brand John West, and ensured Dejphon and Narin could benefit from the entrepreneurial skills of their respective fathers. Despite being an heir to the TUF empire, Chansiri has also built his own business portfolio, mainly through property, and amassed a not inconsiderable personal fortune. As the head of the consortium, Chansiri has become the public face of the new owners and his unassuming persona quickly endeared him to Owls fans, no doubt helped by promises of a new £1-million pitch, new big screen and forays into the transfer market. Chansiri, who quickly learnt English, delivered on all of his early promises, while Wednesday enjoyed a tremendous first season under his ownership. Several more moves into the transfer market saw the club transfer record broken twice – Reach and then Rhodes – while Chansiri vowed he would do everything in his power to get the club back into the top flight of the English game.

Chapter 13

Curios, Tall Stories and Strange Tales

Over the past 150 years, a multitude of events have occurred in relation to Wednesday which cannot really be classified under one heading. Below is a few of those happenings – some strange, some funny and some bizarre – which have helped make the club's history one of the most interesting and rich in the English game.

*

Deep into extra-time in the FA Cup tie against Aston Villa at Olive Grove in February 1894, Wednesday scored to lead 3-2 and from the kick-off Ambrose Langley kicked the ball directly into nearby allotments. When another ball came onto the field he kicked it onto the railway line – the next ball went even further and at a time when referees did not extend play for time-wasting, his actions ensured his side hung on to progress into the next round.

*

Wednesday have been involved in a case of mistaken identity on at least three occasions in their history, the first instance being recorded back in March 1888 when, during a friendly at Lincoln, Tom Cawley was sent off after fouling a home player. However, when it was pointed out that home player Slater had actually injured himself in fouling Cawley, the match official reversed his decision, although Cawley refused to return as a matter of principle. Almost a hundred years later, Wednesday were at Everton in a League Cup tie and there was general surprise when the referee managed to book Lawrie Madden despite the fact that Paul Hart had committed the offence. This would not have mattered but later in the game Madden received a legitimate booking and was red-carded, leaving his side down to ten men, the dismissal certainly having a significant bearing on the eventual defeat. In a reversal of that incident, the game at Huddersfield Town in December 2012 saw Jeremy Helan commit a first-half foul but, although the referee waved a yellow card at the Frenchman, he actually wrote the name of Antonio in his little black book. Hence, when Helan was handed a second yellow card, a red did not follow, much to the amusement of Wednesday fans and ire of the home supporters!

*

The date of 21 April 1991 will forever be treasured by Wednesday fans, who watched the Owls beat Manchester United to lift the League Cup. However, it was the events immediately after the final that caused controversy, as after Wednesday had won the trophy all the supporters who had witnessed the triumph on TV sat back to lap up all the post-match coverage (not forgetting the thousands at Wembley who had set their VCR to tape, just in case the impossible did happen). However, Owls fans were speechless when Yorkshire TV, in their infinite wisdom, decided there would be no demand for further coverage, infamously broadcasting *War of the Monster Trucks* instead. The cries of derision and accusations of Leeds bias rained down on the station, especially as it was revealed that every ITV region in the country showed the post-match festivities except the county of the winning side!

*

Attacker Harry Millar scored sixteen times in thirty-four games for Wednesday, around the dawn of the twentieth century, and was known as a prankster – he once turned up in Sheffield's Empire Theatre and started to conduct the orchestra before being chased out by the manager!

*

When Wednesday were relegated to the Third Division in 1975, it was hard to take for many fans, although it did hit one particularly badly with Ken Wood so unable to face the prospect that he tore up his rosette, burnt his scarf, gave away his rattle and announced his decision to emigrate! A few years later, another disgruntled fan, Bob Montgomery, attempted to the take the club to court under the Trade Descriptions Act after an uninspiring performance in an FA Cup replay against Southend United, claiming Wednesday had played so badly that it was not football at all and therefore an offence under the legislation. He failed to take the case to court and his demand of being repaid his admission money was not fulfilled.

*

During the 2006/07 preseason Wednesday lost forward Marcus Tudgay after a freak accident at a family barbeque. He severed tendons in his foot after standing on broken glass and was out of action for several weeks.

*

One of the greatest players in the club's history, goalie Jack Brown, almost left before his career had really started as he was not offered a new contract at the end of the 1923/24 season. However, with first-choice 'keeper Davison sidelined with a broken arm, the club found themselves without a custodian for the final of the Sheffield County Cup against Sheffield United. Wednesday were poised to sign Carr from Newport County but when the move hit a snag they had no choice but to re-sign Brown for another season. Carr did eventually sign but never played a first team game as Brown was virtually ever-present for over a decade. Over eighty-one years later almost the same situation arose as 'keeper Chris Adamson was released on 30 June 2005, only to be re-signed by Paul Sturrock just eleven days later – unfortunately his impact was considerably less than Brown's.

*

Future Sheffield United player Arthur Bottom was a thirteen-year-old ball boy at Bramall Lane during the Second World War but was a staunch Wednesday fan. During a game versus Wednesday he celebrated a goal from Charlie Tomlinson a little too enthusiastically and was subsequently informed by the Blades that in the future his services would no longer be required.

*

On Christmas Day 1936 the Football League fixture list kindly sent Wednesday down to Brentford for an 11.15 a.m. kick-off. The day after they had to face Sunderland on Wearside for a 2 p.m. kick-off, with tiredness probably a factor in losing both games 2-1.

*

In 1922 the eight-year-old daughter of Wednesday trainer Jerry Jackson was sent out by her mother for a Green 'Un. She returned and said 'they're two for three-ha'pence, mother, handing her two Green 'Un apples'.

*

In June 2012 former Owls winger Michael Gray underwent the first hair transplant to be streamed live on the internet in the UK. He tweeted through his surgery.

*

Travelling reserve Charlie Petrie was taken ill, with what proved to be appendicitis, during a match at Hull in November 1922 and a Wednesday director looked after him on the journey home. However, the train kept stopping at various stations and passengers insisted on trying to get into the compartment where the stricken Petrie was lying in obvious agony. The only way the director could persuade them to leave was to comment, in a sympathetic tone, 'I'm sorry gentleman, but this poor lad is suffering from scarlet fever!' Suffice to say Petrie reached Sheffield with just the club official for company.

*

During one of Howard Wilkinson's notorious cross-country runs in the 1983/84 season, an unnamed player (to protect his embarrassment) got hopelessly lost and was eventually found by a farmer, wet, miserable and somewhat confused.

*

The old adage of 'it's not what you know, but who you know' certainly applied in the case of 1935 FA Cup-winner Jack Surtees, due to his brother, Albert, being a former Aston Villa teammate of Wednesday boss Billy Walker. His sibling Jack was without a club in the summer of 1934 and his brother duly wrote to Walker saying that 'You used to say I was a good player. Well he is a better player than I was.' Probably just as a favour to an old playing compatriot, Walker said he would give twenty-three-year-old Surtess a trial but in the interim he had signed for Northampton Town. He was not with the Cobblers very long though and after becoming disillusioned with the game, obtained his passport and booked a passage to America. It was at this point that his sibling intervened again, getting Jack to promise that he would not do anything until he had spoken to Walker. Eventually, in late November 1934, the two brothers arrived at Hillsborough and Wednesday were so impressed that Jack was offered, and signed, a contract, making his debut on Christmas Day. It would be a real-life fairy tale for Surtees as he remained in the side and less than six months after arriving was the club's inside right at Wembley.

*

For the first eighty years of the club's history it was believed that Wednesday had been formed in 1866, the decorative ball on the top of the South Stand a testament to that date. However, during the 1947/48 season the date on the ball – which now sits atop the revamped South Stand – was adjusted to 1867.

*

The 1974/75 season was a grim campaign for Wednesday fans, although there was a light-hearted moment during a rare win at home to York City in November 1974, when play was interrupted when a man streaked across the pitch wearing only his socks, shoes and a pair of spectacles. He was described as 'prancing down the pitch' before being ushered off so the game could continue.

*

During the First World War, Wednesday player George Shelton was serving in Italy with the 8th Battalion Yorkshire and Lancaster Regiment when he and his comrades came across a large amount of Austrian currency. They were told it was worthless so lit their cigarettes with the notes, only to be told later, when they were reposted, that it was legal tender and they had burnt a small fortune!

*

The referee for the Wednesday vs Small Heath FA Cup tie at Olive Grove in January 1892 was a gentlemen called Sam Widdowson, who several years earlier had famously visited Sheffield in an attempt to find proof of Wednesday having fielded an ineligible player against his side, Nottingham Forest. He failed to find any wrongdoing and seemingly had not forgotten his wasted journey as he proceeded to send off two home players. Wednesday captain Billy Betts duly confronted the referee and asked 'As ta finished sending 'em off?', to which Widdowson replied 'Aye, I think so.' Good, nah we'll set abaht 'em' retorted Betts. Wednesday won 2-0.

*

Scotsman Bill Collier played for Wednesday in the early 1920s but during the First World War he was serving in the 14th Battalion Black Watch during the latter stages of the Battle of the Somme. His unit suffered terrible casualties with every officer either wounded or killed. It was Sargent Collier who duly took command of the remnants of battle and he was in charge for two days before being relieved. He was awarded the Distinguished Service Medal (DCM) for his actions. He later played for Raith Rovers, who in 1923 undertook an adventurous tour of the Canary Islands. However, their journey was not exactly without incident as their ship, bound for Argentina, ran aground on a sandbank off the coast of northern Spain after being caught in a violent storm. It literally was 'abandon ship' but luckily for all concerned, a fishing boat was passing by and managed to rescue all of the passengers. Undeterred, Rovers stayed in emergency accommodation and hitched a lift on a passing cruise liner to complete their journey.

*

In November 1927 new signing Ted Harper became the first, and only, Owls player to score a hat-trick on his league debut. For many years it was thought he scored three in a 6-4 win at Derby County, but it is now known the club, via their matchday programme, credited Harper with four goals, Collin's own goal being reallocated. However, the mystery does not end there as a journalist from a Sheffield newspaper revealed that he had asked Collin about the goal with the defender admitting that it was he who had the final touch. It is clearly an issue that will never be settled, conflicting reports meaning that Harper remains in the record books with three goals.

*

The club was not blessed with much luck during the 1921/22 season as not only did nine of the playing personnel have minor operations but the vast majority were also struck down with a particularly virulent strain of influenza.

*

Over twenty years after the record was set, David Hirst stills holds the title of fastest shot in the Premier League, his effort at Highbury in September 1996 being recorded by Sky TV as travelling at 114 mph when it struck the Gunners' crossbar.

*

Nineteenth-century Wednesday player Jack Darroch earned the reputation as the cleanest 'dirty' player as he had the knack of running alongside an opponent before sending him tumbling, head over heels, with the referee unable so see how he had fouled his adversary.

*

In December 1936, Owls manager Billy Walker revealed that several players in his side had started to wear lightweight 'Hungarian' boots and lighter shirts and stockings. It made a considerable difference in weight but sadly did not make any difference to the results as Wednesday were relegated at the end of the season.

*

In a February 1915 away game at Manchester United, Wednesday left-back Jimmy Blair was kicked so hard in the face that he was knocked out cold and departed the game on a stretcher with, what proved to be, a broken jaw. In the same match Owls player Patrick O'Connell accidently kicked the referee and the official was forced to hobble his way around the pitch for the rest of the game.

*

1940s defender Norman Jackson had the misfortune to have his debut for Wednesday wiped out after his first appearance, at Coventry City in November 1949, was cut short due to thick fog after sixty-three minutes. He was not the only Wednesday man to experience trouble on his debut as 1930s inside forward Bob Curry made his debut at Aston Villa in October 1937, only to find that he had been incorrectly registered by the Owls and therefore his appearance – his only senior game for Wednesday – was actually illegal!

*

In the twenty-fourth minute of Wednesday's game at Aston Villa in November 1973, a message was relayed over the public address system telling supporters that an anonymous caller had claimed that a bomb had been left in the ground. The announcement continued to say 'Anyone wishing to leave the ground may do so and you are asked to look around you for any suspicious-looking parcels. We are pretty sure this is a hoax and the game will continue.' Today's treatment of the incident would have been totally different, illustrated by the Manchester United vs Bournemouth game of May 2016, although just over a year later, ten people were killed when an IRA bomb exploded in the city – Villa Park was perhaps a close call for all involved.

*

During Harry Catterick's time in charge at Wednesday he decided that one of his players, who was a smoker, needed a scare so he arranged for a doctor to check him over and look suitably concerned when he scanned his chest, suggesting he went for an x-ray. It is not known if the unnamed individual stopped smoking immediately!

*

When Sheffield Wednesday were returning from a game at West Bromwich Albion in September 1965, they spotted the Sheffield United team bus broken down, which was carrying the Blades' reserve team from a game at Wolves. Wednesday kindly gave the stranded Blades players a lift home.

*

During Wednesday's February 1898 FA Cup tie at West Bromwich Albion's old Stoney Lane ground, full-back Ambrose Langley knocked the ball out for a throw-in and caught the ball as it rebounded back off pitch hoardings. However, the linesman promptly awarded Albion a free-kick for handball, from which the Baggies scored to win the match!

*

Sheffield Wednesday was the first Football League club to join Twitter, registering an account in 2007, a year after the social media phenomenon started.

*

Sports store Suggs Sports was a much-loved city centre business, initially situated on Snig Hill before moving down the Moor. The Owls bought their 1935 FA Cup final strip from the shop, which was first opened in Liverpool in the 1890s by brothers Walter and Frank Sugg. The siblings were fine sportsmen, Frank playing twice for England in the summer game, as well as appearing for Hull Town, Yorkshire, Derbyshire and Lancashire in first-class matches – he also represented Wednesday Cricket Club in the 1880s. His football career started at Pyebank – he was in the side that lost to Wednesday in the 1882 Wharncliffe Final – and played for Derby County and Burnley during the decade. A fine all-round sportsman, Frank excelled at shooting, weightlifting, billiards and long-distance swimming. He passed away in 1933, while his store remained in business until January 2001 when all eleven branches were closed.

*

When Derek Dooley was in charge of the Owls' youth team he was asked by manager Vic Buckingham to go on a scouting mission to watch Doncaster & Dearne vs Barnsley. The Barnsley right-winger caught his eye by scoring a hat-trick and with his ability to take excellent corner kicks. Although Dooley expressed concerns about the youngster's reluctance to get involved in the physical side of the game, the teenager was still invited to Hillsborough for a trial. However, this never took place as the player – Alan Woodward – signed for Sheffield United in the following week, playing over 500 league games and becoming their post-war top goalscorer.

*

It was not until 10 February 1974 that Wednesday first played on a Sunday in an English domestic fixture, beating Bristol City 3-1 at Hillsborough. The reason behind the trial on the Sabbath was that a nationwide power crisis, caused by a series of countrywide strikes by coal miners, meant that football was allowed to be played on a Sunday for the first time. The strikes led to acute electricity shortages, which of course meant floodlights could not be used, and earlier in the season the Owls played a FA Cup replay at Coventry City on a Tuesday afternoon at 1.30 p.m. Many Saturday games kicked off at 2.30 p.m. or earlier while clubs got around the Lords Day Observance Act, which prohibited payment to enter sporting activities, by giving fans a small team sheet, which they had 'paid' for. Teams were also compelled to have at least one free turnstile open, although no one could ever find the one at Hillsborough on that particular day!

*

Outstanding pre-First World War inside forward Harry Chapman had a recurring problem with his cartilage as it was prone to 'popping out' during games. He would simply push it back into place, without leaving the field, and carry on playing.

*

In the February 1974 Second Division game at Bolton Wanderers, the Wednesday side emerged from the half-time dressing room with two players wearing the No. 3 shirt – Bernard Shaw and Ken Knighton. After a few minutes the referee noticed and promptly sent Shaw off the pitch to change his shirt. He returned a few minutes later but was then booked by the match official after running onto the pitch without permission!

*

There was a quite remarkable coincidence in July 1897 when Wednesday captain Tommy Crawshaw got into difficulties while swimming off the east coast when his feet became entangled in weeds. He was saved by Boston Town secretary Harry Smith, who just happened to be passing in a boat.

*

Wednesday played at Burnley in December 1937 on a pitch that was covered in 2 inches of snow with a thin layer of ice on top. The referee tested the pitch by taking a hammer to it and when the match started the players were sliding in every direction and most were unable to keep on their feet. The match was completed though, with the Owls securing a 1-1 result in their own version of *Dancing on Ice*.

*

The club minutes in December 1947 revealed that Wednesday had a major off the field problem, which had shaken the club to its very core. The problem concerned the secretary-manager's office where supplies of whisky seemed to be running out too quickly on matchdays. A solution was therefore agreed that only home and visiting directors, plus their guests, would be allowed to take a 'wee dram' before games.

*

During the club's twelve years at Olive Grove, a fan was given the task, for a small remuneration, of retrieving the ball when it was kicked over the perimeter fence onto the Midland Railway line. It was later claimed by mischievous Sheffield United fans that the 'ball boy' had two speeds: 'go slow' if Wednesday were holding onto a single-goal lead and 'at the double' if they were trying to force a late equaliser or winner.

*

The final game of the 1981/82 season at home to Norwich City had looked destined for weeks that it would be a promotion decider with both sides involved in the battle to get out of the Second Division. Unhappily for Wednesday, they stumbled at the last minute, which meant it was only the Canaries who needed a result. In the end, despite Wednesday winning 2-1, they were still promoted, the enduring image from the game coming in the final minute when a fan ran onto the pitch, from the Kop, as Sterland crossed the ball into the area. As Bannister fired home the winning goal the unidentified spectator belly flopped onto the pitch before a full pitch invasion delayed the finish of the game by four minutes.

*

At the start of the First World War, Wednesday goalkeeper Arnold Birch joined the 1st Royal Naval Brigade but within five weeks of joining up he was captured in Belgium and spent the remainder of the hostilities in an internment camp in the Netherlands. During that time, he would regularly play in inter-battalion matches inside the camp, but later received special permission to play twelve times for local side Go Quick, based in Groningen. He made such an impact that he was later picked to represent a north Netherlands select side and played against his own camp on one occasion. He made such a splash in Dutch soccer that decades later a local football fan produced a book about the Grenoside custodian's time in the country.

*

When Wednesday signed Scottish international Neil Dewar from Manchester United in January 1934, the transfer affected matters of the heart for Dewar as the move meant he would be parted from his girlfriend, who he had been secretly courting for ten months – the girl in question was the daughter of a Manchester United director, which probably explained the subterfuge! The solution to the problem was for the couple to elope to the romantic destination of Manchester registry office where the love-struck couple were married before Dewar raced back to Sheffield to make his debut. His new wife went back to her parents' home and they were unaware of the secret marriage until she crept out on the following Monday to join her husband in Sheffield. They then made a joint phone call to break the news to her shocked parents!

*

One of the most popular Owls players of modern times, Jose Semedo, will certainly always remember a November 2012 day at Nottingham Forest, which Wednesday fans dedicated as 'Semedo Day' in honour of the midfielder. The idea, a brainchild of Kop season ticket holder Matthew Gornall, saw thousands of Semedo masks distributed among the 4,405-strong travelling support and the away end was awash with Portuguese flags, balloons, inflatables, scarves and shirts in a unique and memorable tribute to the man who led Wednesday to promotion a few months earlier. Wednesday lost 1-0 but it was events off the field that will always be remembered with affection by all concerned.

*

During the latter part of Eddie Gannon's career, he actually lived in Dublin and flew over for the games. In fact, before moving back to Ireland permanently, Wednesday had to send an official to Dublin every summer to bring Eddie back. He was considered one of the game's real gentleman and his generous nature was typified during one of those summers back in Ireland when he donated all eleven – at that point – of his precious international jerseys to a newly formed youth team that could not raise the money to buy themselves a strip.

*

Nineteenth-century player Billy Ingram, who appeared for Wednesday in the 1890 FA Cup final, was a staunch Owls fan throughout his life and after his playing days ended he continued to attend home games. He attended a reunion of that cup team in October 1941 and duly met his captain on that day, Haydn Morley, for the first time in forty-eight years. His devotion to the club remained until his very last breath as on his deathbed he asked 'How have Wednesday got on?' After being told they had won (beating Nottingham Forest 2-1 at Hillsborough in March 1949) he said 'That's good' and passed away.

*

Pre-First World War Owls player Andy Hunter had a rather bizarre way of keeping fit outside of the season. When asked by one of his teammates 'How do you manage to get over the close period, my boy?', he replied, laughing, 'Oh, I just take a course of bullet throwing.' He duly explained that the hobby was quite popular back in his Irish homeland with those who indulged in the pastime walking quickly along a country road and throwing, or rather spinning, a bullet of around 2lbs pounds in weight as far as you could, usually competing with another fellow. The Wednesday attacker reckoned you could not beat the 'sport' for developing the muscles while it was not known if any countryside animals had any nasty surprises while they were going about their daily business!

*

1930s Wednesday winger Bill Fallon was a highly popular member of the playing staff and a real character. While on the books of Notts County he was often in 'hot water' with his club, especially during cross-country runs when he would often catch the bus and wave to his teammates as he went past them. He once rode past them on a kid's bike, with the youngster sat on the handlebars. During later life, while coaching non-league clubs in the Nottingham area, he would occasionally get his players to run around the pitch during evening training sessions. However, sometimes his players would still be running around only to notice that Bill had slipped away to the local public house!

*

When 1980s Owls midfielder Pat Heard retired from the game he used PFA funding to retrain as a hypnotist. He used the stage name of Patrick Stewart – a name later associated with the Huddersfield-born *Star Trek* actor – and toured the northern club circuits, after making his stage debut in 1997, the extra income supplementing his earnings from running a public house in Derbyshire.

*

Outstanding inside forward Jackie Robinson was sold to First Division Sunderland in October 1946 for £7,500, but it was later discovered that he'd lied about his age when originally signing for Wednesday. It transpired that he was actually two years older than everyone had thought and Sunderland had £700 knocked off his fee.

*

It was only in the 1893/94 season that Wednesday players stopped taking their own sandwiches to away games, the club providing them plus a bottle of ginger beer for the train journey. Early in the twentieth century Wednesday started paying the railway company to serve hot lunches to the players and club officials.

*

The name of Ron Eyre will be a complete unknown to Wednesday fans as he spent less than a year at Hillsborough in the mid-1920s. He played only once in the first team but after joining Bournemouth he emerged as arguably their greatest ever player, scoring a club record 259 goals in only 367 competitive games. His feat of scoring in seven consecutive games was only bettered early in the twenty-first century when loan attacker Jermaine Defoe netted in ten.

*

After starting exactly 100 games for Wednesday, Frenchman Jeremy Helan shocked the football world in September 2016 when he announced his disillusionment with the game and that he intended to quit the sport to concentrate on his religious studies. A few days later, Wednesday agreed to cancel his contract and his career ended somewhat abruptly, aged just twenty-four years old.

*

When Wednesday signed England U21 goalkeeper Iain Hesford from Blackpool in the summer of 1983, he seemed the ideal replacement for the departed Bob Bolder, who had joined European Champions Liverpool. He looked set be the club's No. 1 for the start of the season but the arrival of loan player Martin Hodge meant that Howard Wilkinson's first Owls XI included his new rival. The newcomer remained in goal for a club record 214 consecutive games and Hesford never played a senior game for Wednesday.

*

In the early 1980s, Queens Park Rangers were the first club to install what commonly became known as a 'plastic pitch,' made from synthetic fibres, Wednesday first visiting for a Second Division fixture in March 1982. The Owls won 2-0 on that occasion and, just over six years later, were the last away side to play on the controversial pitch, drawing 1-1 on 23 April 1988.

*

Trainer William Johnson was employed by the club in the 1890s and was in charge of the team that lifted the FA Cup in 1896. The Stockton-born Johnson first came to fame as an outstanding sprinter and was highly respected by the club's playing personnel. He sent his players out of the dressing room with the words 'go on my beauties, you are sure to win' and the air was blue when they returned if they had not.

*

Early nineteenth-century goalie Frank Stubbs holds the unique record of transferring from one Wednesday to another as after leaving Owlerton he signed for non-league club Loughborough Wednesday. The goalie was also involved in one of the strangest stories in the club's history, which revolved around a First Division game at Notts County in September 1901. During the first half he received a heavy knock to his head, which seemingly caused the 'keeper to be concussed as he had to ask his teammates at half-time what the score was. It then became somewhat of an urban myth that early in the second half, Stubbs proceeded to catch the ball, turn around and place it over the goal line to gift the hosts a goal. He duly conceded another five times in the match – various stories emerging about his culpability – although a contemporary journalist did describe Stubbs as 'suffering from an attack of nervous excitement'.

*

It has long since been forgotten that Frenchmen Mickael Antoine-Curier appeared in just one game for Wednesday as a very, very late substitute in the home match against Luton Town in November 2003. He did create a remarkable record though as during that season he made appearances for six different Football League clubs: Oldham Athletic, Kidderminster Harriers, Rochdale, Wednesday, Notts County & Grimsby Town – which is a feat that will surely never be surpassed.

*

If an FA Cup tie against Glossop North End at Owlerton in February 1909 had not been surprisingly lost then Wednesday's nickname could quite easily have not been the Owls but the monkeys. The reason being that before the game a supporter of the club, just back from India, had presented the animal, christened 'Jacko', to player James McConnell and he duly led the teams out, regaled fully in blue and white. It must have been a strange sight for the 35,000-plus crowd inside the ground but it would be the monkey's only appearance after Wednesday crashed out of the competition to their lower-ranked Derbyshire opponents. From that match onwards McConnell could not shake of the nickname of 'Monkey' while there is no record of what happened to the club's short-lived unlucky mascot.

*

Defender Brian Linighan experienced a Wednesday career that was totally unique as although he registered only three senior games in January 1994, all were in different competitions, namely the Football League Cup, Premier League and FA Cup. The first two were against Wimbledon at Selhurst Park, his last start being in a 2-0 win at Nottingham Forest to complete a flurry of appearances over a nine-day period, all away from home.

*

The incredible story of pre-First World War player James Monaghan has only recently came to light with a remarkable series of coincidences leading his family and Wednesday to believe he was one of the estimated 20 million people killed in the bloodiest war the world has seen. When the news came through that Monaghan had joined the 'great majority', a collection was held at a wartime Hillsborough game and there was sadness that another pre-war player had lost his life. However, that was not the end of the story as it later emerged that there was in fact two men named James Monaghan, both of whom were from the same area and served in the same regiment. The individual who played for Wednesday was actually injured in the infamous Battle of the Somme, suffering temporary blindness after a bullet penetrated his temple and exited through his eye, and lay delirious in no man's land before being rescued. He was subsequently taken to another regiment's medical station, which it's believed led to his own regiment recording that he had been killed in battle. Incredibly, on the same day, the other James Monaghan was killed in action and this led to the Ministry of Defence giving the wrong news to the relative sets of families. Back home in England, the family of the ex-Wednesday man visited the local Co-op to buy their black mourning clothes and his sister Margaret remembered a stranger visiting their house, just after James' death had been confirmed. It transpired that the two men had vowed that if one perished, the family of the other would personally pay their condolences to the family of the deceased. It was not long though before the heart-wrenching news, for the other Monaghan family, came through with regard to the mistaken identity, the Wednesday man having being invalided back to London and discharged in April 1917. He returned home to the north-east and worked as a telephonist after being trained by a charity that helped blind and visually impaired servicemen, and later in a bank. He lived a long life before passing away in Newcastle, aged ninety-six, in December 1989.

*

A piece of turf has entered Rotherham United folklore after helping them to a 1-0 victory at Hillsborough in December 1982. The Second Division game was tied at 0-0 when a harmless kick upfield by Gerry Gow looked set to be comfortably caught by Bob Bolder in the Owls net. However, the divot had other ideas and managed somehow to deflect the ball away from Bolder and straight to the surprised Joe McBride, who scored into an empty net.

*

The Owls' success in the 1980s and early 1990s spawned a rash of 7-inch records but two moments in the club's history have also been recorded on good old-fashioned long-playing vinyl, which is currently in the middle of a revival. The most common disc is the one produced in the aftermath of the 1966 FA Cup final, containing full match commentary, while in 1985 the club produced a homespun effort entitled 'Alive and Well', which was effectively a review of the club's first season back in the top flight and attempted to offer a positive note after a season that saw Heysel and the Bradford fire. The fascinating disc contains snippets of goal commentary, player interviews, terrace songs and includes the title track of the album sung by local vocalist Lynn Carter.

*

Wednesday left-back Walter Holbem appeared in eighty-nine games for the club before the First World War but met a grisly end at Ascot Races in June 1930, when Walter's metal-framed umbrella was struck directly by a bolt of lightning. The strike not only ripped his umbrella into pieces but it struck poor old Walter in the throat, causing him to collapse to the floor, unconscious. He was rushed to hospital but did not survive, passing away later the same day.

*

The ultimate suspension for any player is to be banned 'sine die', which effectively means you are banned for life. This punishment has been meted out to three Owls players over the years, with one actually being banned twice! The two-time offender was Scottish international attacker Charlie Napier, who was banned in 1941 while appearing as a guest player for Falkirk. This punishment was subsequently lifted in 1943 only for Napier to be banned for life again in January 1944, following a referee's report on a Wednesday wartime game against Grimsby Town in October 1943. Incredibly, Napier was reinstated for a second time in 1945, when as part of the celebrations surrounding VE day all players serving suspensions were pardoned.

*

In 1983 the Owls reached the FA Cup semi-final and were drawn to face Brighton & Hove Albion at Highbury. Wednesday were staying at a local hotel and when the bus carrying the team arrived at the ground, it was suddenly realised that both Pat Heard and David Mills had literally missed the bus; the departure time had been brought forward on police advice and obviously the duo had missed the memo!

*

During the late 2000s, Wednesday were becoming increasingly reliant on loan players as club finances continued to be perilous, and they found themselves in hot water in March 2008 when six players were named in the matchday squad for the home fixture against Stoke City. The six men in question were Graham Kavanagh, Franck Songo'o, Ben Sahar, Enoch Showumni, Adam Bolder and Bartosz Slusarski and although only four took the field of play, Wednesday found themselves in trouble as they had breached the allowed maximum of five loan men. With Wednesday immersed in a relegation battle, the possibility of a points deduction loomed large on the horizon but thankfully the punishment was relatively light with just a £2,000 fine. Just over eight years later, the club almost erred again when six loanees were named on their team sheet before the Championship game at Bristol City in April 2016. It was thanks to the eagle eye of a supporter this time who noticed that Michael Turner, Daniel Pudil, Alex Lopez, Aiden McGeady, Vincent Sasso and Joe Bennett were all in the matchday eighteen. To rectify the situation, the Owls drafted in Jack Hunt for Bennett with Carlos Carvalhal commenting, 'The person who did the team sheet made a mistake and we corrected it.'

*

Since the advent of the internet, Google and Wikipedia, information about virtually any subject can be gleaned immediately, at any time of the day. However, the internet is fallible and is often prone to error and to mischievous individuals who can alter information at a whim. For a historian, it is always advisable to check your sources but I failed to follow this cardinal rule when a story emerged about former winger Michael Reddy. The tale stated that he had moved to Greenland after signing for Malamuk in 2007, and while living there attended the Greenland Fishing Festival, meeting his future wife. He then moved to the British territory of the Falklands Islands and while playing amateur football for Port Stanley Albion, became the first student to enrol for the Football Association's new 'remote teaching programme'. His story made fabulous reading but sadly there was only one problem – it was totally fabricated! The former Barnsley and Grimsby Town player was forced to retire early in 2006 and subsequently began studying business at Manchester University before taking his UEFA 'B' coaching badge in

2015. He certainly never set foot on either of the two islands and did not marry a Greenland woman!

*

As health and social conditions have improved over the last century, humans have started to literally grow taller with football teams now full of players over 6 feet tall. This was not always the case though and when trialist 'keeper Percy Kite made his solitary appearance for the Owls, on 1 May 1920, he must have been a rare sight as he stood 6 feet 6 inches tall, towering over everybody on the field. He was such a rarity for his era that it was not until 2011 that Wednesday fielded a player taller, centre half Rob Jones, who stood 1 inch taller at 6 feet 7 inches.

*

During the club's early years, a gentleman called Jack Housley appeared for Wednesday, as well as several other clubs including Hallam and Sheffield United. Such was his popularity in local football circles that he was even given a benefit game in 1885, but his story had a sad ending as in September 1908 Jack alighted from a tram and went head over heels after slipping on a discarded banana skin; he suffered broken ribs and internal injuries in the fall and passed away hours later in the Sheffield Royal Hospital.

*

Question: Which Wednesday player scored three times on the same day against the same opponents but did not score a hat-trick?

Answer: Fred Richards in March 1899 when he scored the Owls' fourth goal – in the final ten and a half minutes of the league game versus Aston Villa, abandoned in November 1898 – and then twice in the friendly game played after the abridged league fixture was completed.

*

Paul Frith, the club's trainer during their FA Cup-winning campaign of 1907, was a well-known local sprinter who in 1883 caused a near riot when he won his handicapped semi-final race only for the referee to controversially decide in favour of his opponent. The spectators were so incensed (there was big money staked on such races) that they pulled up the track stakes and did not allow the final to be run. There was such indignation that when the organiser tried to rerun the final a few days later, the crowd encroached onto the track and the only solution possible was for the monies to be split between the four semi-finalists. In the early 1890s he worked as a gamekeeper at Hassop Hall, near Bakewell, before enjoying a successful career at Owlerton, helping the club to numerous honours in the first decade of the twentieth century.

*

When Eric Nixon arrived at Hillsborough in 2003 as part-time goalkeeping coach, he probably never imaged that a few months later a goalie crisis would mean the Owls had no choice but to register the vastly experienced custodian, so he was able to warm the substitutes' bench, with both Tidman and Stringer out injured. He had first arrived in Sheffield as a replacement coach for Pressman – who had decided to relinquish his coaching positon to concentrate on just playing – and it would be Pressman who was forced to the leave the field in the 27 September 2003 home League One game against Grimsby Town. This meant Nixon entered the fray, becoming the club's oldest post-war player at just a week short of forty-one years old. He kept a clean sheet in his surprise cameo appearance and remained on the Wednesday staff until July 2004.

*

During the late nineteenth century, Harry 'Toddles' Woolhouse was a popular member of the Wednesday playing staff, scoring five times in the club's biggest ever victory, 12-0 against Halliwell in 1891. A real home boy – he never moved from Ecclesfield – Woolhouse met an untimely end on his home turf when in December 1911 he became involved in an argument with a fellow drinker in the Greyhound Inn. The disagreement eventually escalated to the two men fighting, both being considerably worse for wear. File cutter Woolhouse received a bad head injury, which needed treatment. Sadly, he never recovered and died of lockjaw a few days later, giving a statement to the police on his deathbed that Percy Walker, of Thorpe Hesley, had called him a traitor and the pair had quarrelled and come to blows. At a later inquest, his death was ruled as accidental due to the fact that forty-three-year-old Woolhouse was inebriated.

*

Several players in Wednesday's history have returned for two, or even three, spells, the likes of Carlton Palmer and Luke Varney spending three different spells at S6 and Peter Shirtliff, Peter Eustace, Chris Turner, Vincent Sasso and Gary Megson examples of men who returned for a second time. Both David Layne and Peter Swan were re-signed by Wednesday in 1972, eight years after they were banned due to their involvement in the bribes scandal of 1964, but the prize for the longest time between appearances for Wednesday is won emphatically by John Pearson. His playing career at S6 seemingly ended in 1985 when he left for Charlton Athletic but ten years, one month and eighteen days after his last appearance he was on the team sheet again for a UEFA Intertoto Cup game in Switzerland in June 1995. Due to the game being played in late June, the club had to sign several players on one-game contracts and also drafted in several youngsters with Pearson, who had just been released by Cardiff City, making a surprise reappearance.

*

On Boxing Day 1923 against Coventry City at Hillsborough, the goalposts were painted blue by the groundsman to make them more visible on a snowbound pitch. Blue paint was again used in November 2010 when the Associate Members Cup tie at Carlisle United was played on a frost-bound pitch with all the lines painted blue.

*

The December 2016 home game against Preston North End uniquely saw two players from the same side red-carded, Jermaine Beckford and Eoin Doyle being dismissed for fighting. It was not, however, the first time that Wednesday had been involved in a game where one team had been reduced to nine players, Wednesday themselves twice having two players dismissed in early FA Cup football, versus Small Heath in 1892 and Sheffield United in 1900. Wednesday have only been reduced to nine men in a league fixture on two occasions – a 3-1 defeat at Coventry City in November 2006 and in an eventful match at Brighton & Hove Albion in January 2017, when Steven Fletcher and Sam Hutchinson saw red. It was also relatively recent (January 2011) that the Owls faced a Yeovil Town side at Hillsborough that was reduced to nine men – Luke Ayling and Adam Virgo being sent off – although Wednesday still needed a last-gasp equaliser to earn a point.

*

Two Owls fans enjoyed a slice of cup luck when they travelled ticketless to Wembley on cup final day in 1966. Hackenthorpe couple Jean Strafford, nineteen, and Graham Booth, eighteen, could not afford the exorbitant amounts asked by the touts and so were resigned to missing the big match before non-playing centre-half Vic Mobley spotted the couple near the players' entrance. 'Vic asked me if we had tickets and we said we hadn't. He then told us that captain Don Megson had sent two out and that we could have them. We could hardly believe it' explained Jean, who promptly wrote thank you letters to the two Wednesday players after being in the right place at the right time.

*

On the eve of the Rumbelows League Cup final in 1991 the players went out and most were worse for wear on their return, Phil King getting back in his bed around 4.30 a.m. Manager Ron Atkinson had said to the players 'drink as much as you want and stay out as late as you want, as long as you don't get in before me'. The Manchester United chairman, Martin Edwards, was totally bemused at the events and there is no doubt that it would never happen these days, as Wayne Rooney found out to his cost in 2016.

Bibliography

General Register Office birth records, 1837–present

Jason Dickinson and John Brodie, *Sheffield Wednesday: The Complete Record* (2011)

Jason Dickinson and John Brodie, *The Wednesday Boys: A Definitive Who's Who of Sheffield Wednesday Football Club 1880–2005* (2005)

Jason Dickinson, *100 Years At Hillsborough* (1999)

Jason Dickinson, *Sheffield Wednesday Miscellany* (2010)

Jason Dickinson, *The Origins of Sheffield Wednesday* (2016)

Richard A. Sparling, *The Romance of the Wednesday: 1867–1926* (1926)

Sheffield & Rotherham Independent (1819–1938)

Sheffield Daily Telegraph (1855–1986)

Sheffield Iris (1794–1848)

Sheffield Star (1970–present)

The Sheffield Mercury (1807–48)

UK Census Records 1841–1911

www.findmypast.co.uk

www.sheffield.gov.uk/libraries/archives-and-local-studies/collections/obituaries.html

www.thewednesdaycc.co.uk